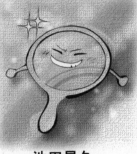

池田晃久
**AKIHISA IKEDA**

**I have a different managing editor starting with this volume. This is my first personnel change…and it's a shock. A managing editor is a really important presence in a mangaka's life—someone who helps to create the story and acts as a sort of objective mirror. It's especially shocking considering that I've known my previous editor since I was 16! I was really lucky to have someone I could lean on for so long… From here on, I'm going to have to work extra hard to return the favor! Although I feel like I'm going to be leaning on my new editor soon enough…**

Akihisa Ikeda was born in 1977 in Miyazaki. He debuted as a mangaka with the four-volume magical warrior fantasy series *Kiruto* in 1999, which was serialized in *Monthly Shonen Jump*. *Rosario+Vampire* debuted in *Monthly Shonen Jump* in March of 2002, and is continuing in the new magazine *Jump Square* (Jump SQ). In Japan, *Rosario+Vampire* is also available as a drama CD. In 2008, the story was released as an anime.

Ikeda has been a huge fan of vampires and monsters since he was a little kid.

He says one of the perks of being a manga artist is being able to go for walks during the day when everybody else is stuck in the office.

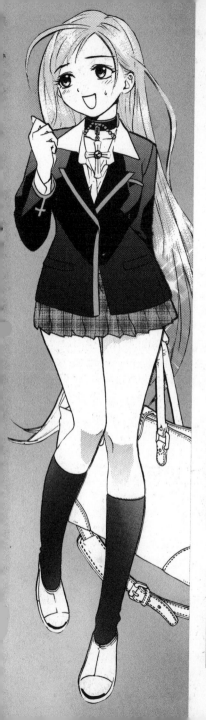

# ROSARIO+VAMPIRE 7
### SHONEN JUMP ADVANCED Manga Edition

**STORY & ART BY AKIHISA IKEDA**

Translation/Kaori Inoue
English Adaptation/Gerard Jones
Touch-up Art & Lettering/Stephen Dutro
Design/Ronnie Casson
Editor/Annette Roman

VP, Production/Alvin Lu
VP, Publishing Licensing/Rika Inouye
VP, Sales & Product Marketing/Gonzalo Ferreyra
VP, Creative/Linda Espinosa
Publisher/Hyoe Narita

ROSARIO TO VAMPIRE © 2006 by Akihisa Ikeda
All rights reserved. First published in Japan in 2006 by SHUEISHA Inc.,
Tokyo. English translation rights arranged by SHUEISHA Inc.

The rights of the author(s) of the work(s) in this publication to be so
identified have been asserted in accordance with the Copyright, Designs
and Patents Act 1988. A CIP catalogue record of this book is available
from the British Library.

The stories, characters and incidents mentioned in this publication
are entirely fictional.

No portion of this book may be reproduced or transmitted in any form or
by any means without written permission from the copyright holders.

Printed in the U.S.A.

Published by VIZ Media, LLC
P.O. Box 77010
San Francisco, CA 94107

10 9 8 7 6 5 4 3 2
First printing, June 2009
Second printing, June 2009

www.viz.com    www.shonenjump.com

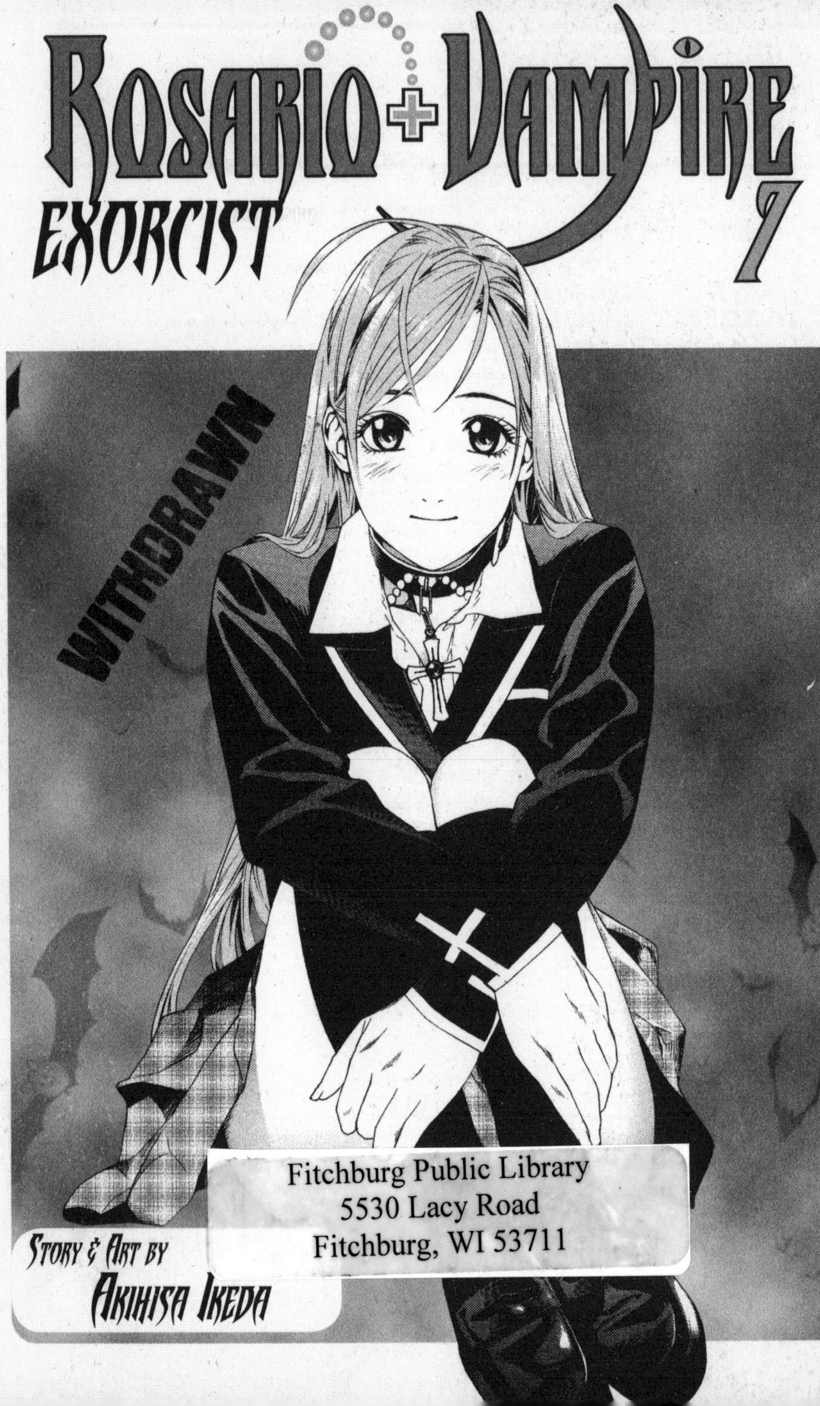
ROSARIO+VAMPIRE
EXORCIST
7
STORY & ART BY
AKIHISA IKEDA

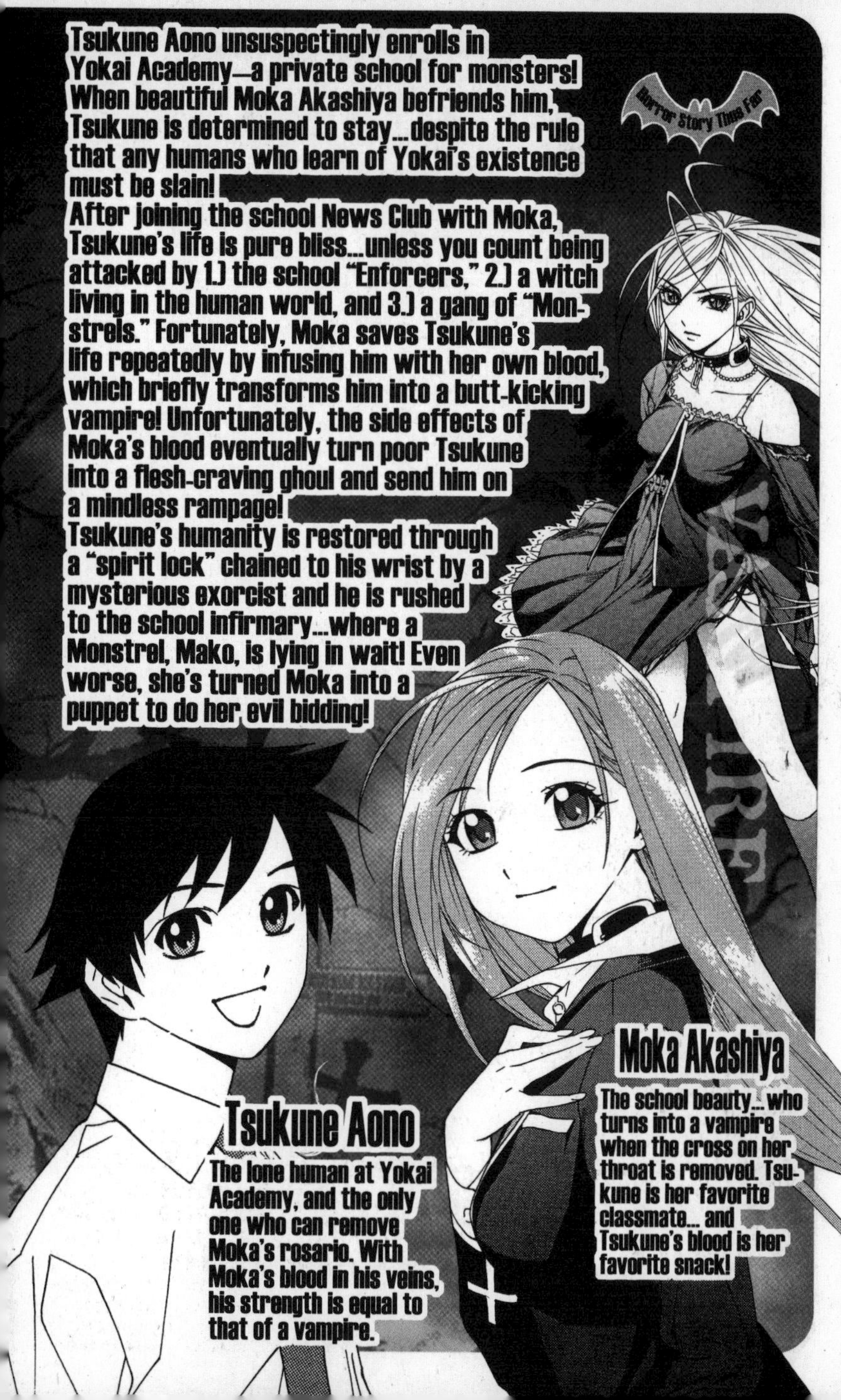

Horror Story Thus Far

Tsukune Aono unsuspectingly enrolls in Yokai Academy—a private school for monsters! When beautiful Moka Akashiya befriends him, Tsukune is determined to stay...despite the rule that any humans who learn of Yokai's existence must be slain!

After joining the school News Club with Moka, Tsukune's life is pure bliss...unless you count being attacked by 1.) the school "Enforcers," 2.) a witch living in the human world, and 3.) a gang of "Monstrels." Fortunately, Moka saves Tsukune's life repeatedly by infusing him with her own blood, which briefly transforms him into a butt-kicking vampire! Unfortunately, the side effects of Moka's blood eventually turn poor Tsukune into a flesh-craving ghoul and send him on a mindless rampage!

Tsukune's humanity is restored through a "spirit lock" chained to his wrist by a mysterious exorcist and he is rushed to the school infirmary...where a Monstrel, Mako, is lying in wait! Even worse, she's turned Moka into a puppet to do her evil bidding!

## Moka Akashiya

The school beauty... who turns into a vampire when the cross on her throat is removed. Tsukune is her favorite classmate... and Tsukune's blood is her favorite snack!

## Tsukune Aono

The lone human at Yokai Academy, and the only one who can remove Moka's rosario. With Moka's blood in his veins, his strength is equal to that of a vampire.

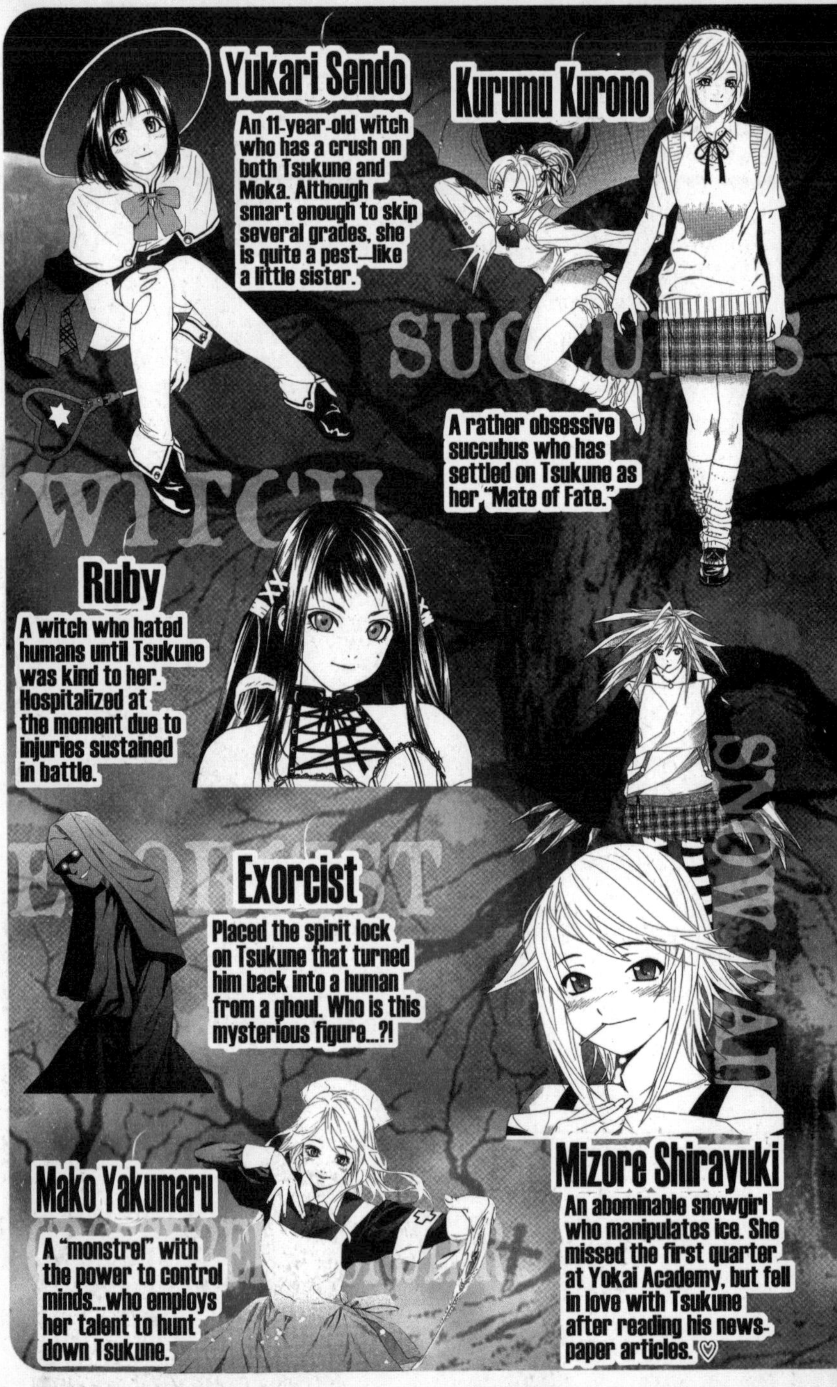
Yukari Sendo
An 11-year-old witch who has a crush on both Tsukune and Moka. Although smart enough to skip several grades, she is quite a pest—like a little sister.
Kurumu Kurono
A rather obsessive succubus who has settled on Tsukune as her "Mate of Fate."
Ruby
A witch who hated humans until Tsukune was kind to her. Hospitalized at the moment due to injuries sustained in battle.
Exorcist
Placed the spirit lock on Tsukune that turned him back into a human from a ghoul. Who is this mysterious figure...?!
Mako Yakumaru
A "monstrel" with the power to control minds...who employs her talent to hunt down Tsukune.
Mizore Shirayuki
An abominable snowgirl who manipulates ice. She missed the first quarter at Yokai Academy, but fell in love with Tsukune after reading his newspaper articles. ♡

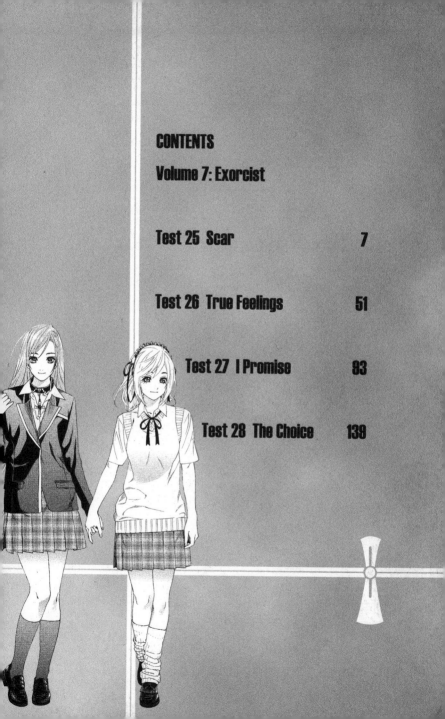

# CONTENTS

## Volume 7: Exorcist

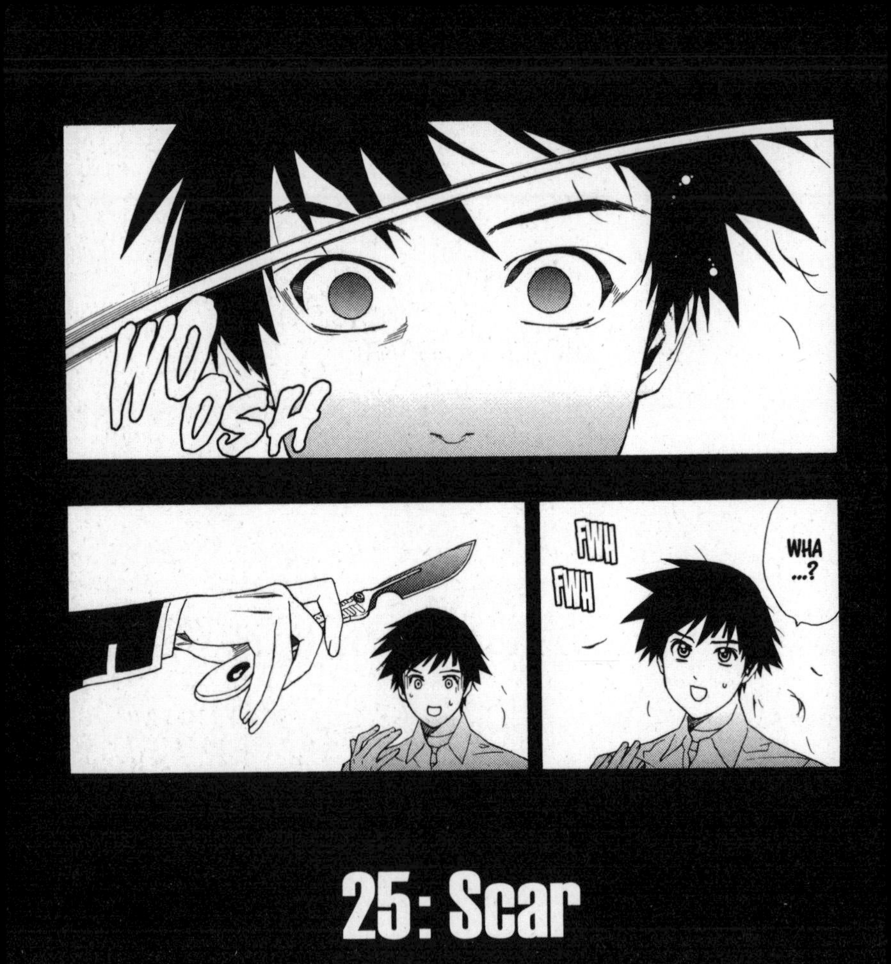
WOOSH
FWH
FWH
WHA ...?

# 25: Scar

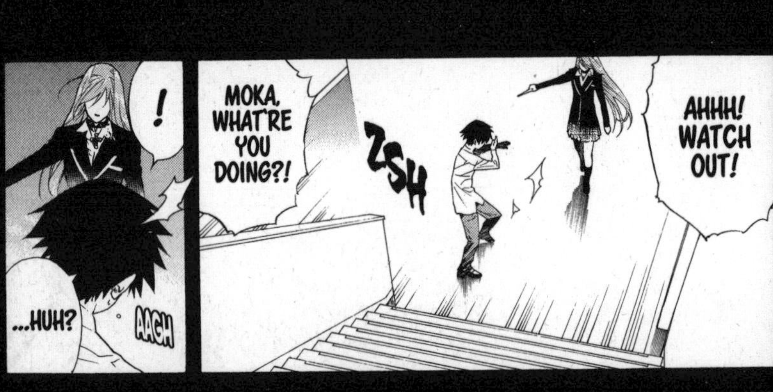
AHHH! WATCH OUT!
ZSH
MOKA, WHAT'RE YOU DOING?!
!
AAGH
...HUH?

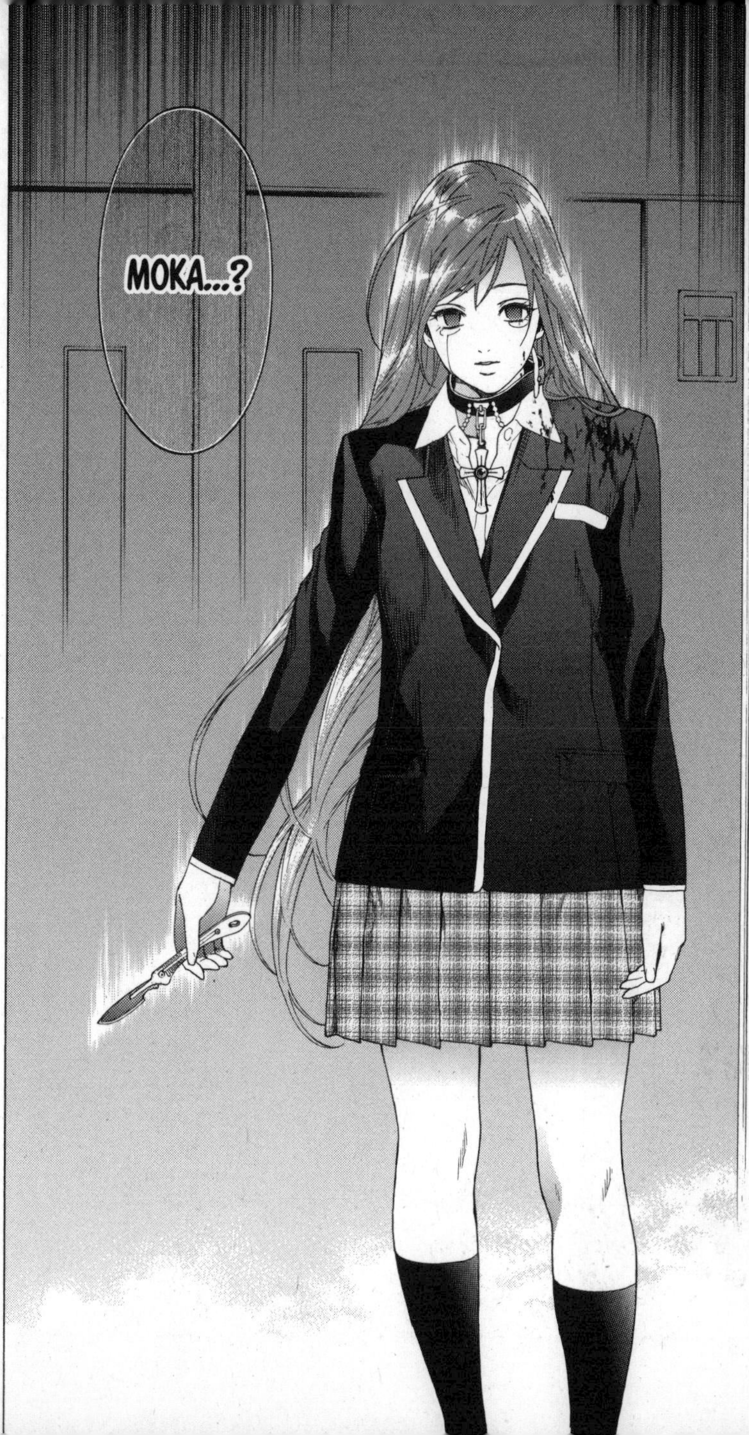
MOKA...?

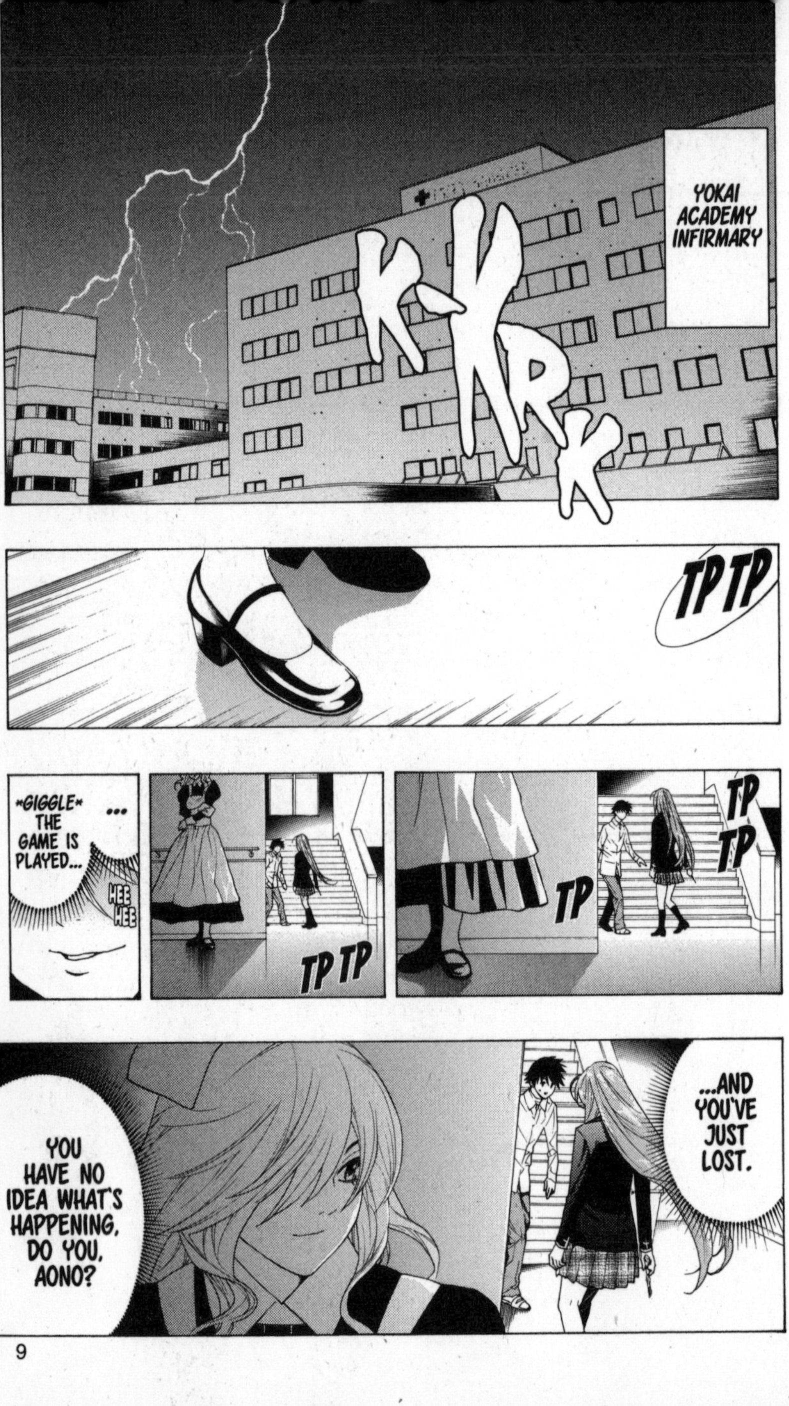
YOKAI ACADEMY INFIRMARY
K-KRK
TP TP
TP TP
TP
TP TP
*GIGGLE* THE GAME IS PLAYED...
...
HEE HEE
...AND YOU'VE JUST LOST.
YOU HAVE NO IDEA WHAT'S HAPPENING, DO YOU, AONO?

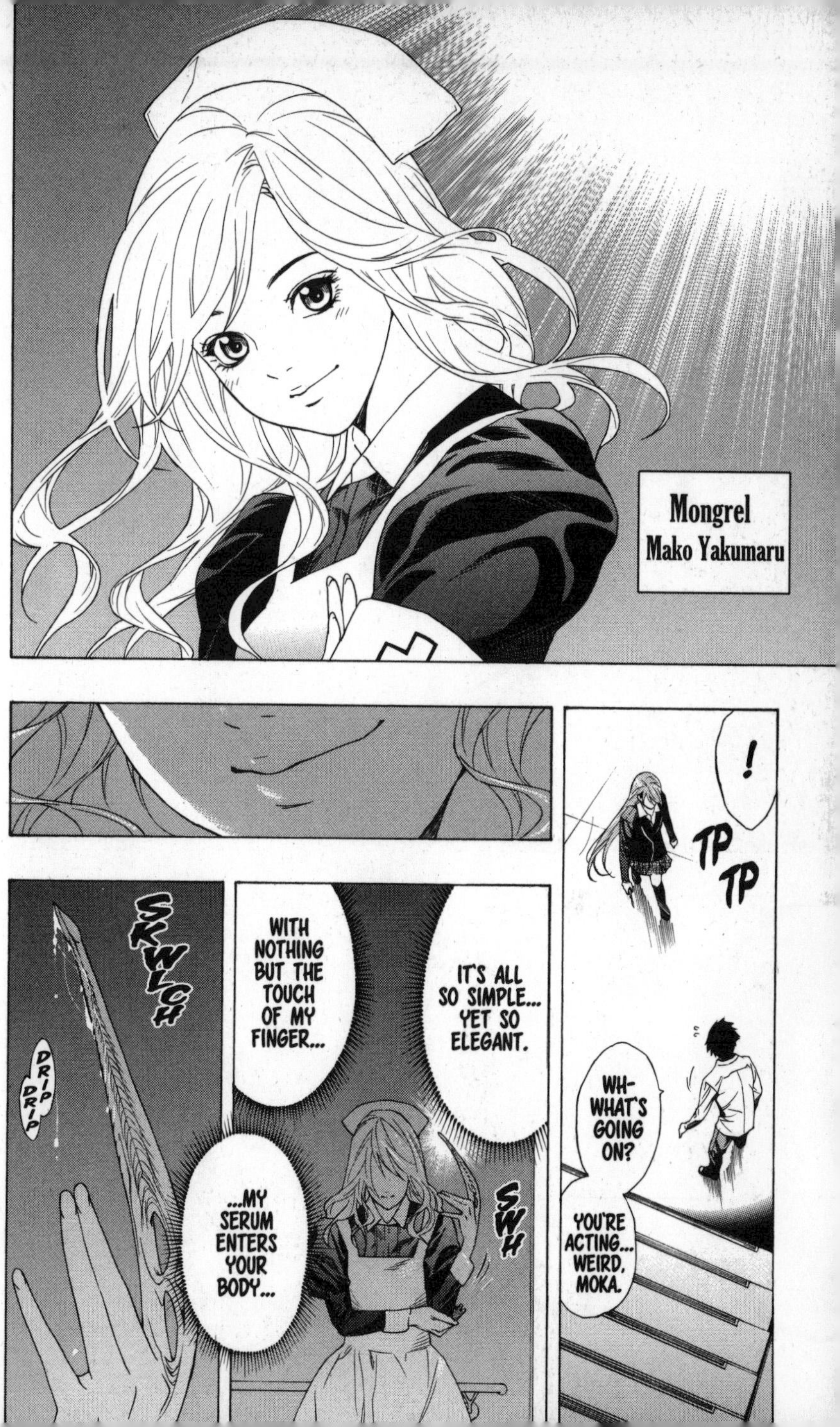
Mongrel
Mako Yakumaru
!
TP
TP
WH-WHAT'S GOING ON?
YOU'RE ACTING... WEIRD, MOKA.
IT'S ALL SO SIMPLE... YET SO ELEGANT.
WITH NOTHING BUT THE TOUCH OF MY FINGER...
SWH
...MY SERUM ENTERS YOUR BODY...
SKWLCH
DRIP DRIP

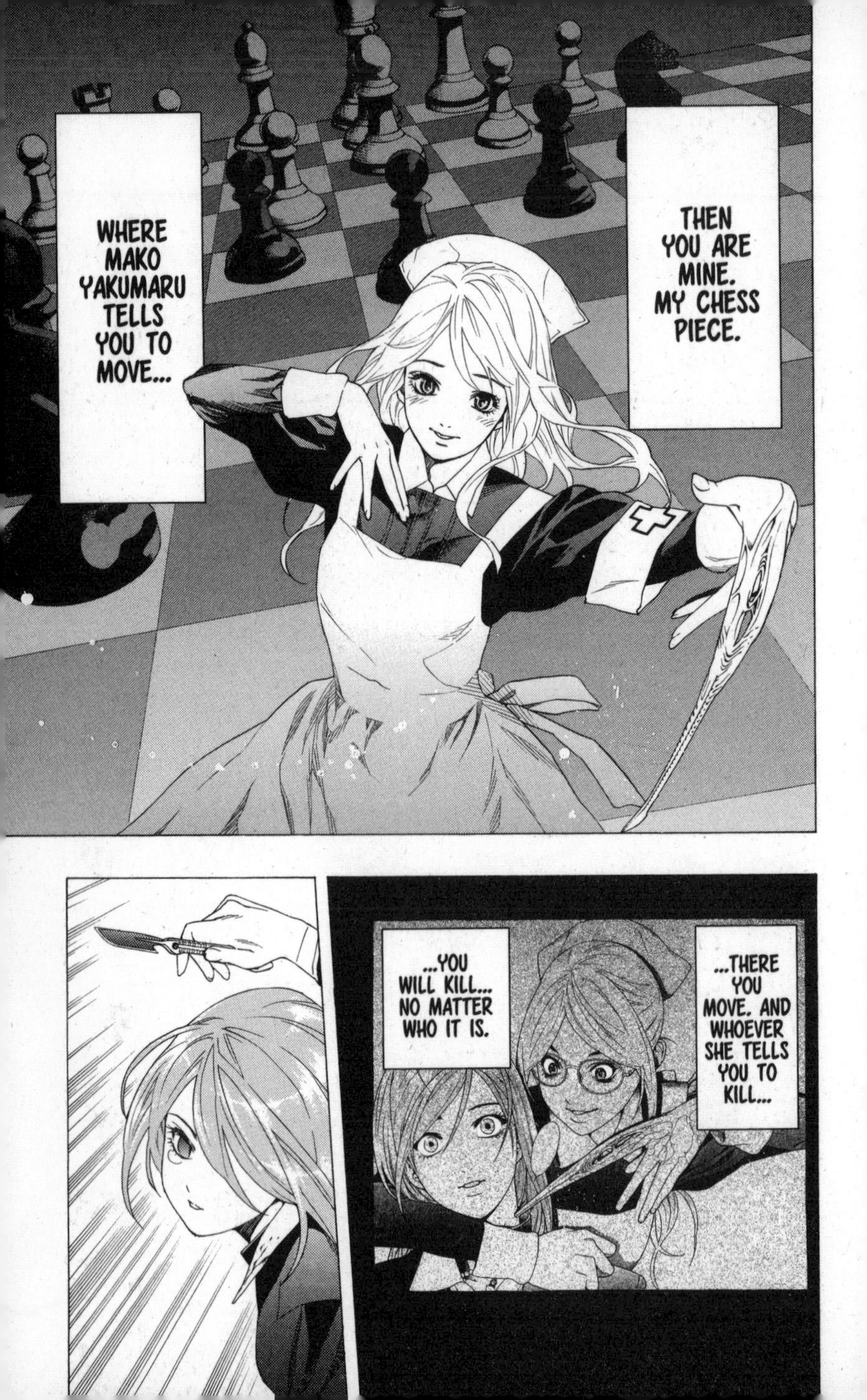
THEN YOU ARE MINE. MY CHESS PIECE.
WHERE MAKO YAKUMARU TELLS YOU TO MOVE...
...THERE YOU MOVE. AND WHOEVER SHE TELLS YOU TO KILL...
...YOU WILL KILL... NO MATTER WHO IT IS.

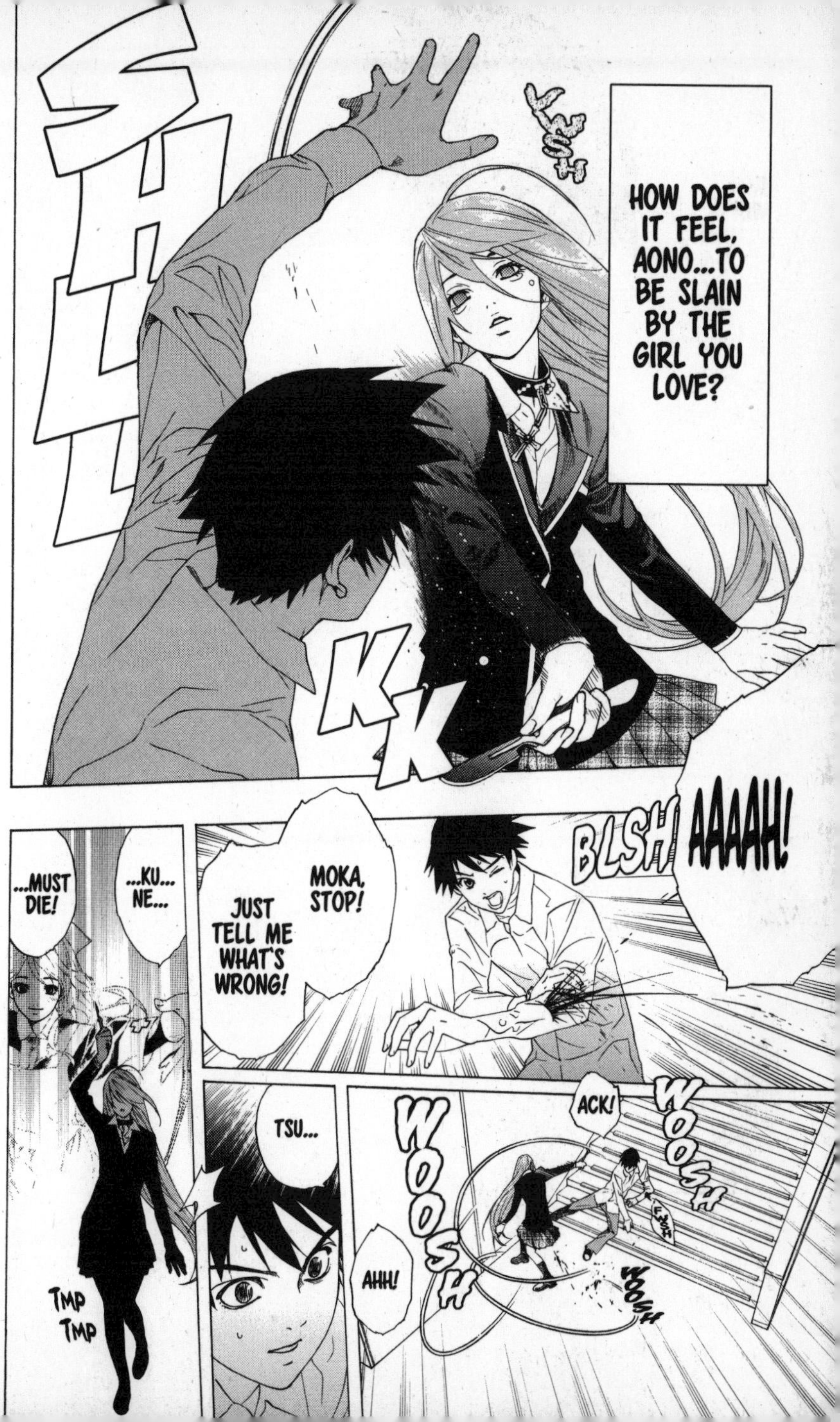
YWSH
HOW DOES IT FEEL, AONO...TO BE SLAIN BY THE GIRL YOU LOVE?
SHLL
KK
BLSH
AAAAH!
MOKA, STOP!
JUST TELL ME WHAT'S WRONG!
WOOSH
ACK!
FWSH
WOOSH
WOOSH
TSU...
AHH!
...KU... NE...
...MUST DIE!
TMP TMP

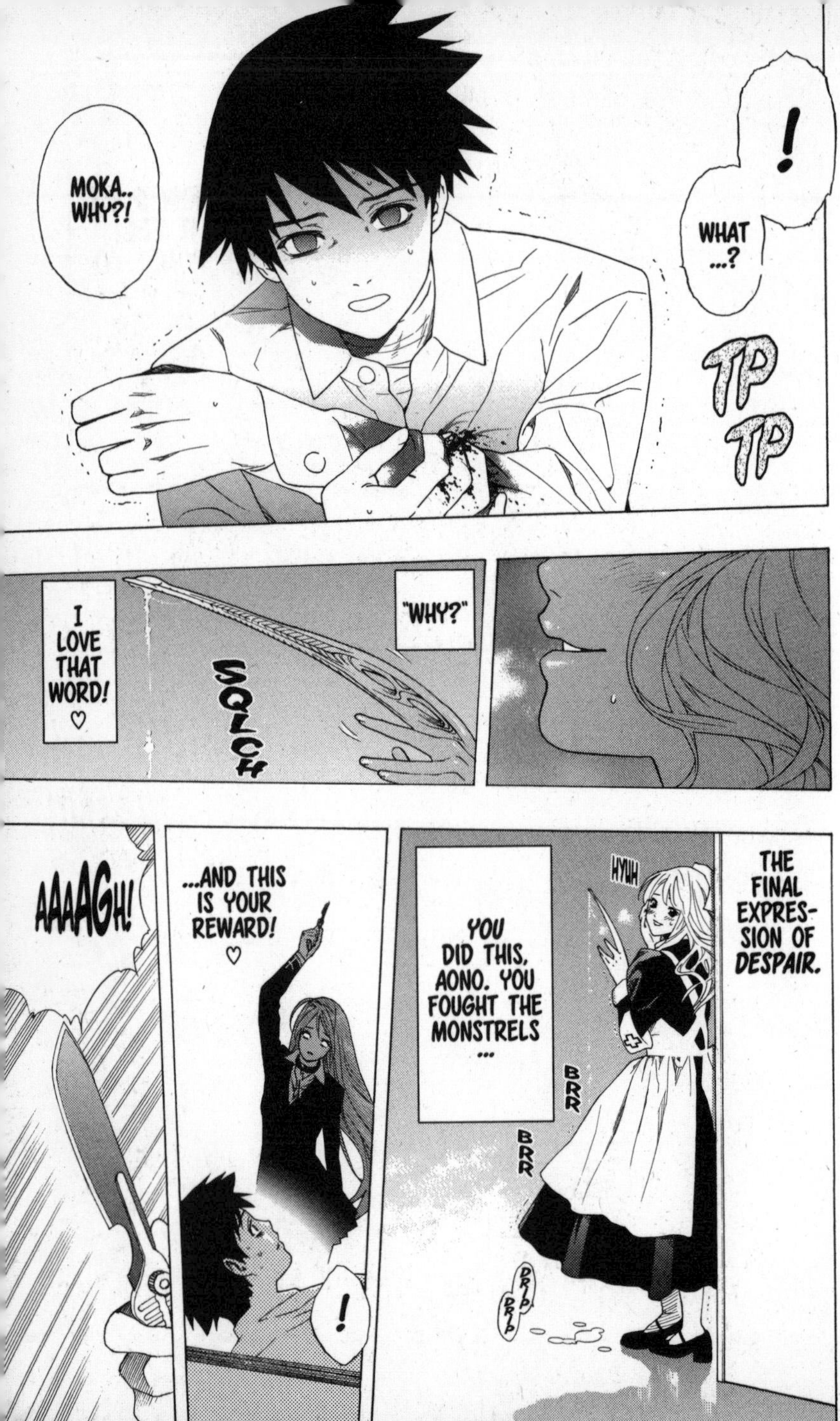
!
WHAT ...?
TP TP
MOKA.. WHY?!
"WHY?"
I LOVE THAT WORD! ♡
SQLCH
THE FINAL EXPRES-SION OF DESPAIR.
HYUH
YOU DID THIS, AONO. YOU FOUGHT THE MONSTRELS ...
BRR
BRR
DRIP DRIP
...AND THIS IS YOUR REWARD! ♡
!
AAAAGH!

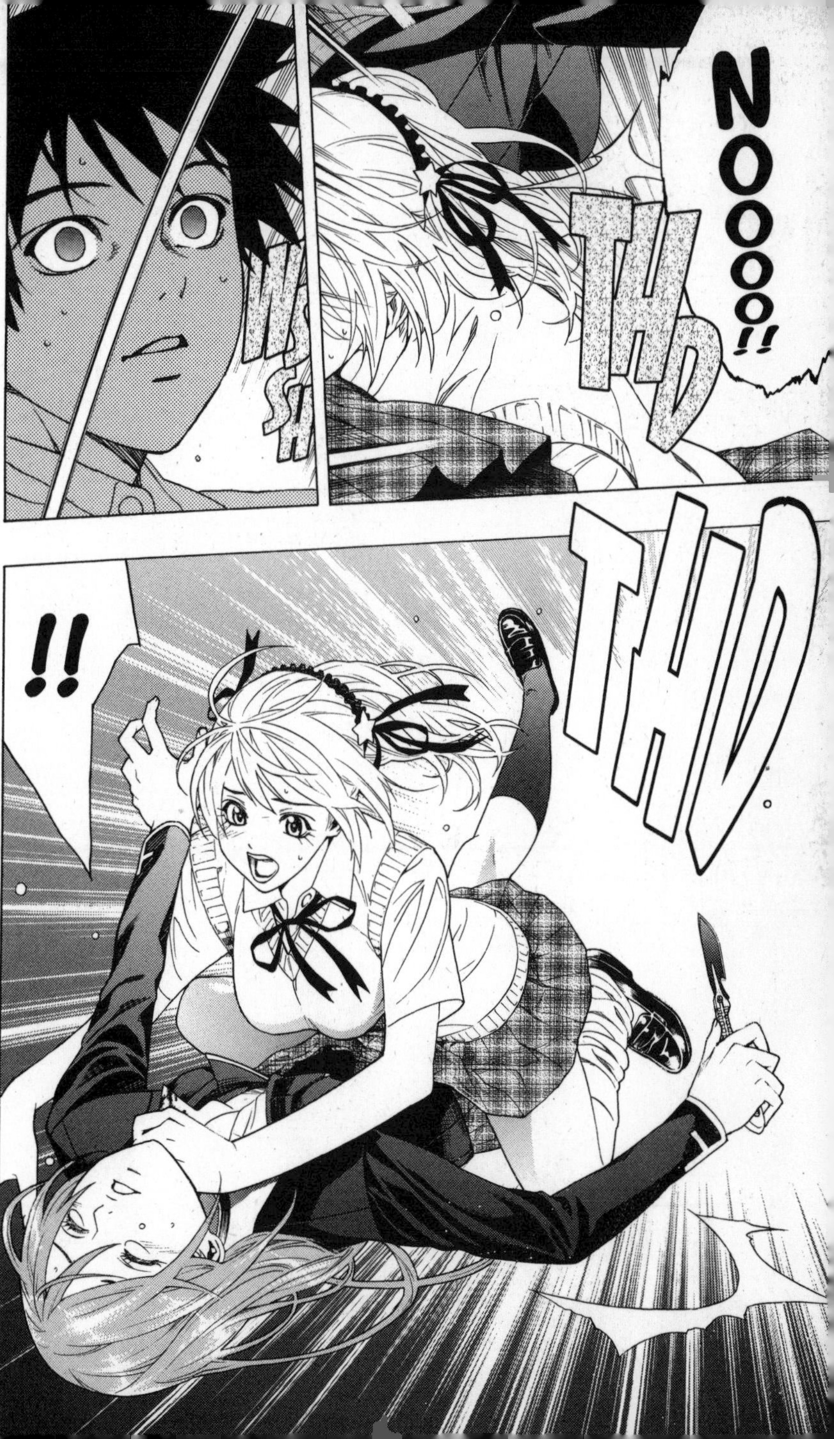
NOOOO!!
THD
THD
!!

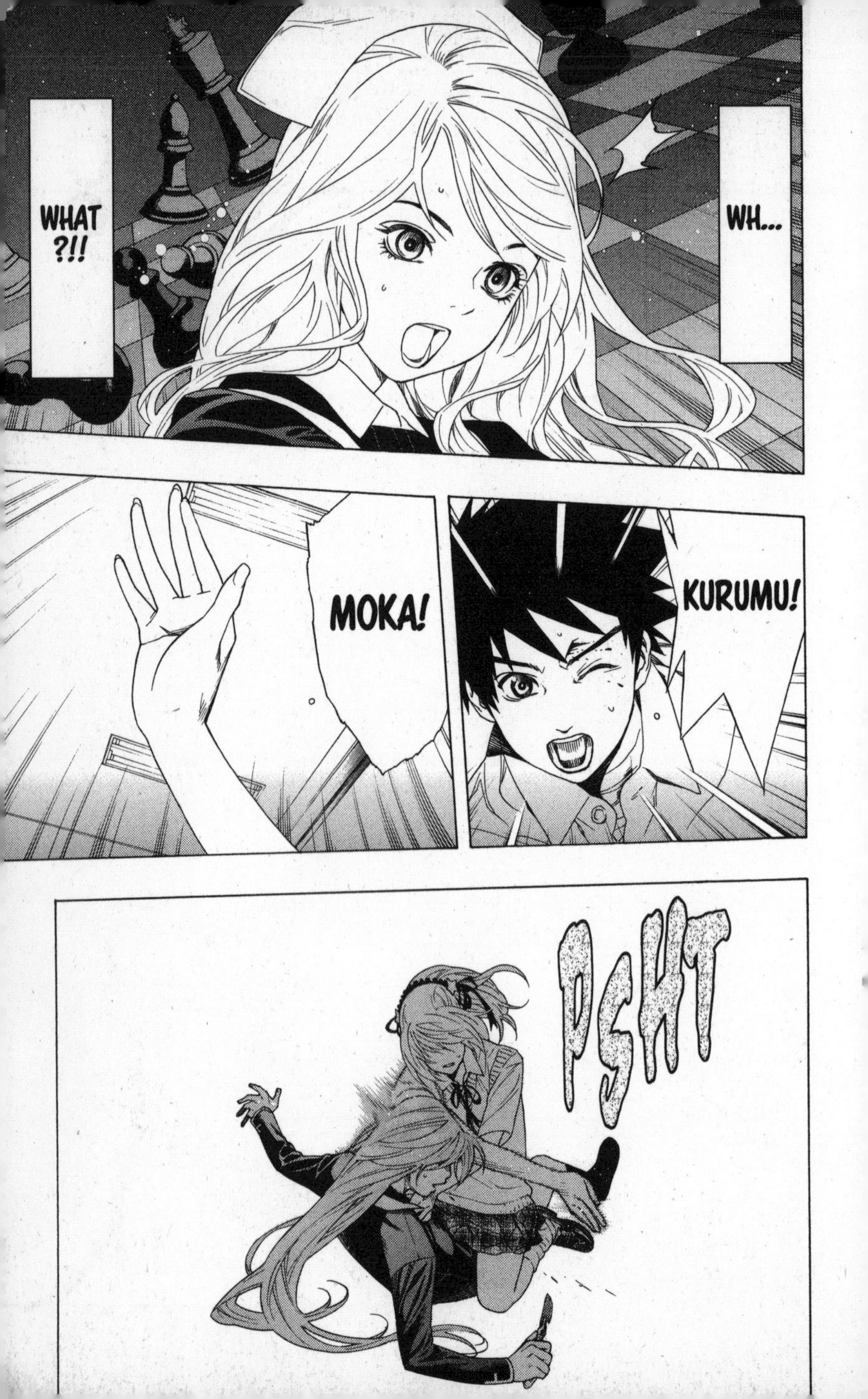
WH...
WHAT ?!!
KURUMU!
MOKA!
PSHT

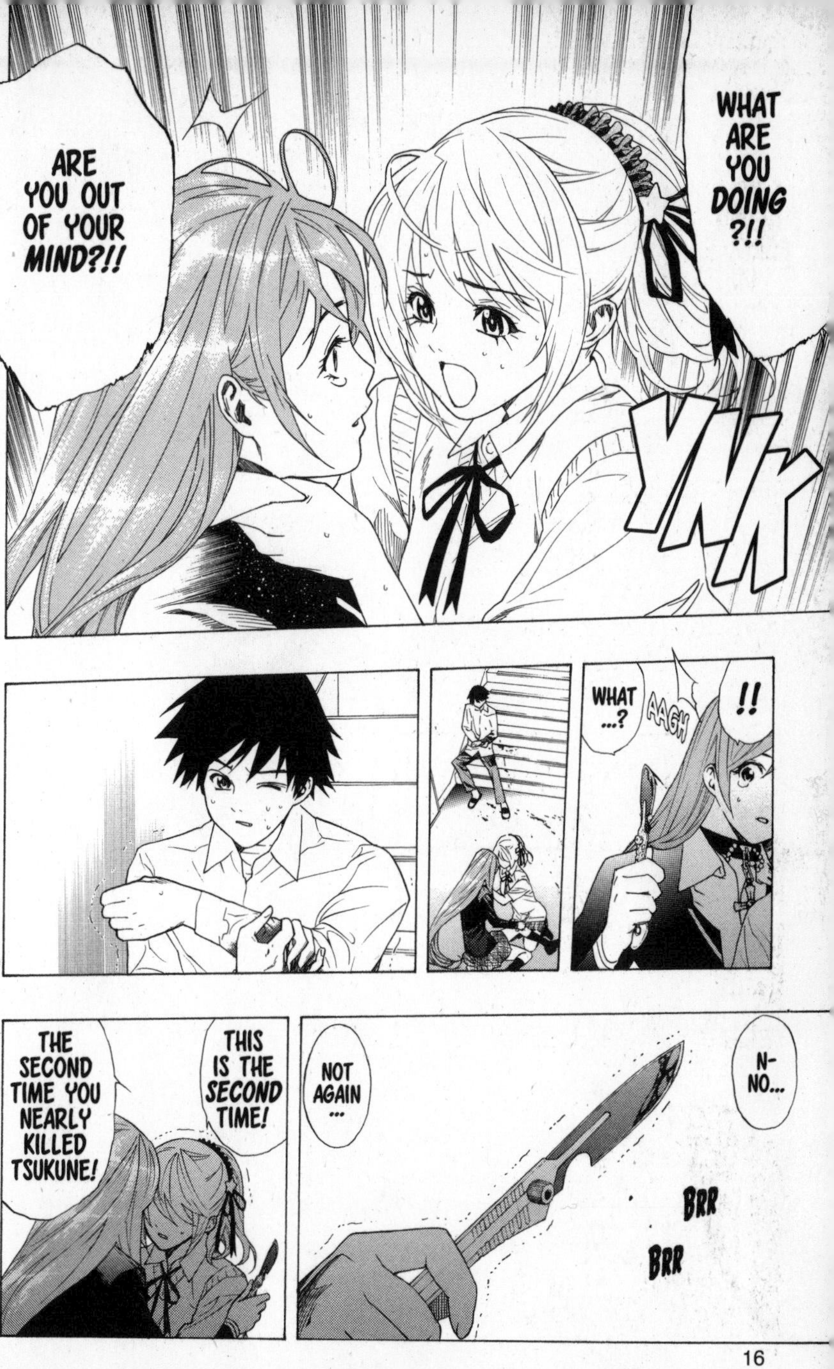
WHAT ARE YOU DOING?!!
YNK
ARE YOU OUT OF YOUR MIND?!!
!!
AAGH
WHAT ...?
N-NO...
BRR
BRR
NOT AGAIN ...
THIS IS THE SECOND TIME!
THE SECOND TIME YOU NEARLY KILLED TSUKUNE!

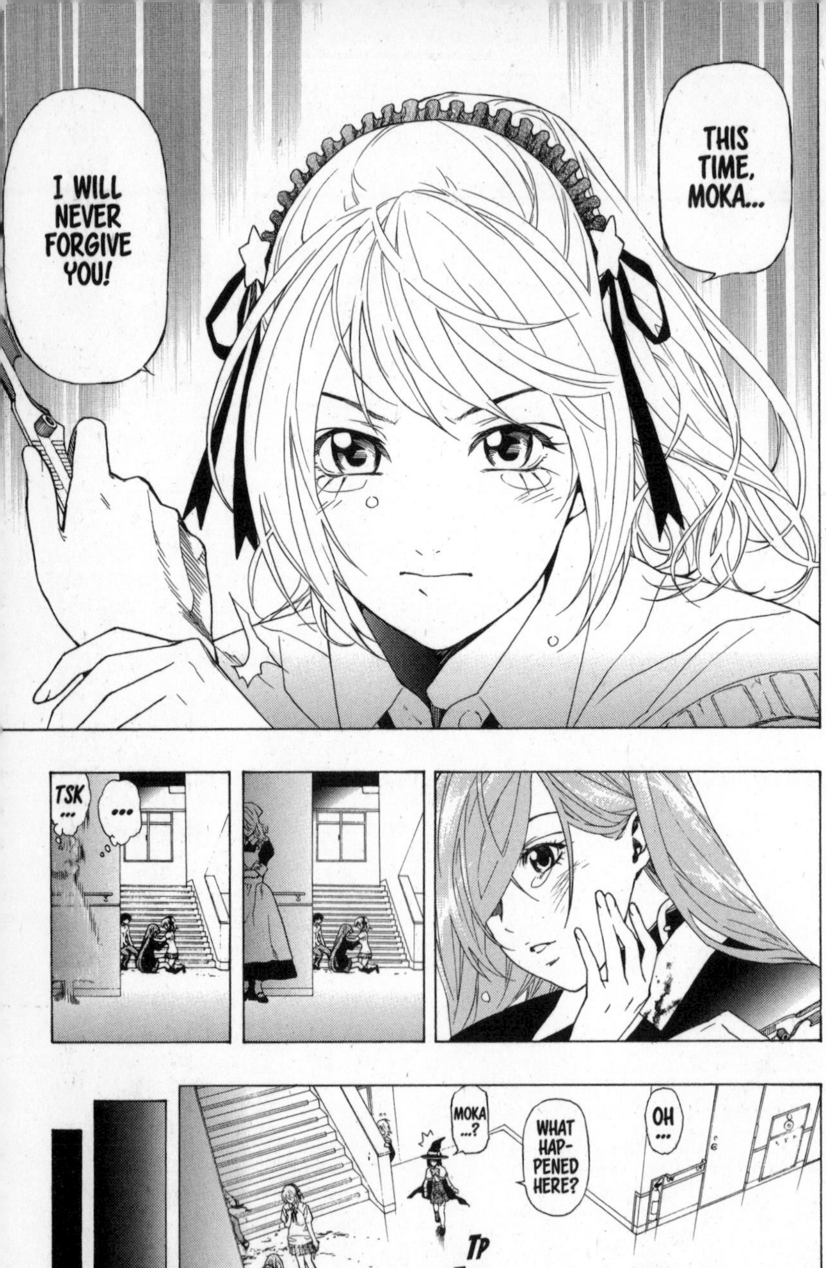
THIS TIME, MOKA...
I WILL NEVER FORGIVE YOU!
...
TSK ...
OH ...
WHAT HAP-PENED HERE?
MOKA ...?
TP TP TP

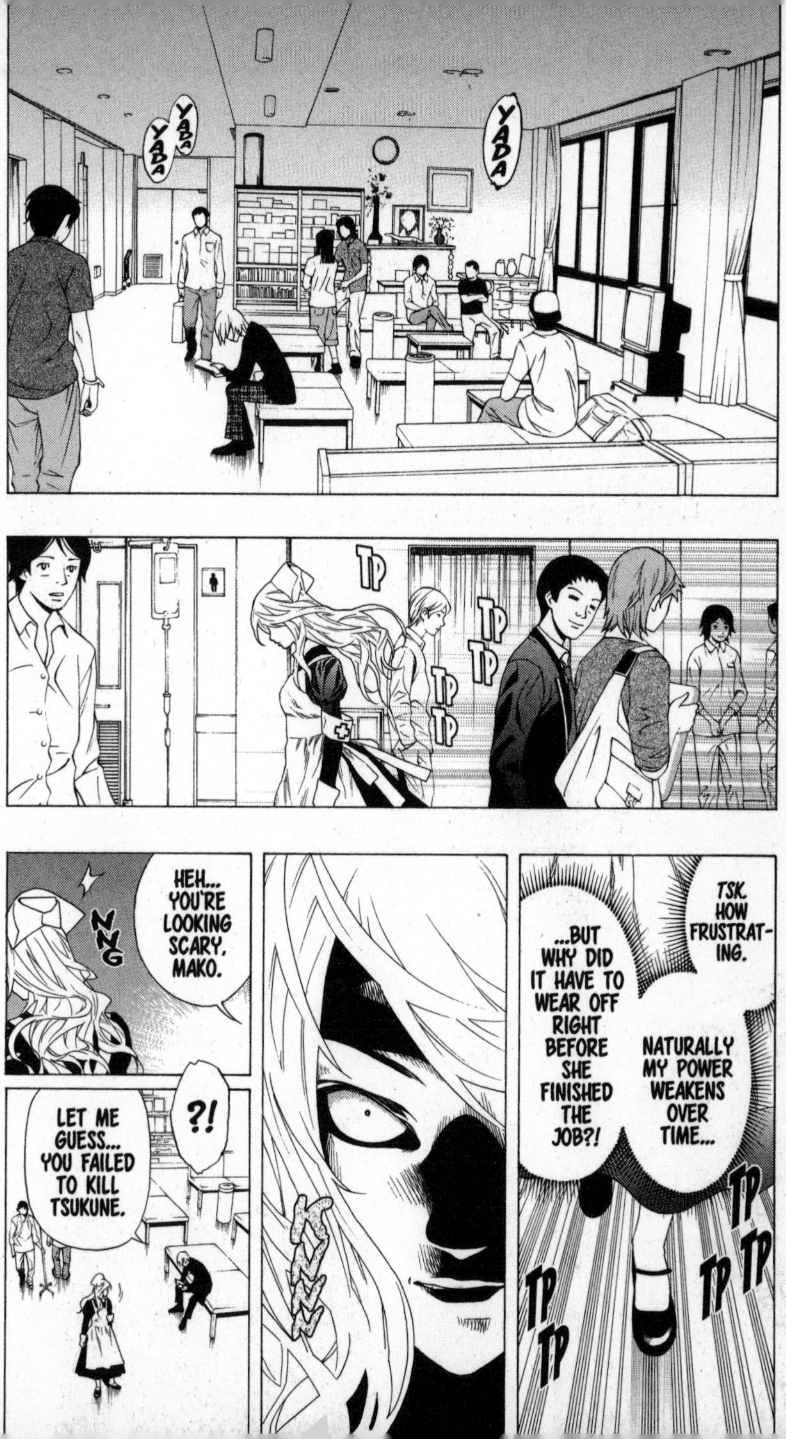
YADA
YADA YADA
TP
TP
TP
TP
TP
TSK. HOW FRUSTRAT-ING.
NATURALLY MY POWER WEAKENS OVER TIME...
...BUT WHY DID IT HAVE TO WEAR OFF RIGHT BEFORE SHE FINISHED THE JOB?!
TP TP
TP
TP TP
HEH... YOU'RE LOOKING SCARY, MAKO.
NNG
?!
LET ME GUESS... YOU FAILED TO KILL TSUKUNE.

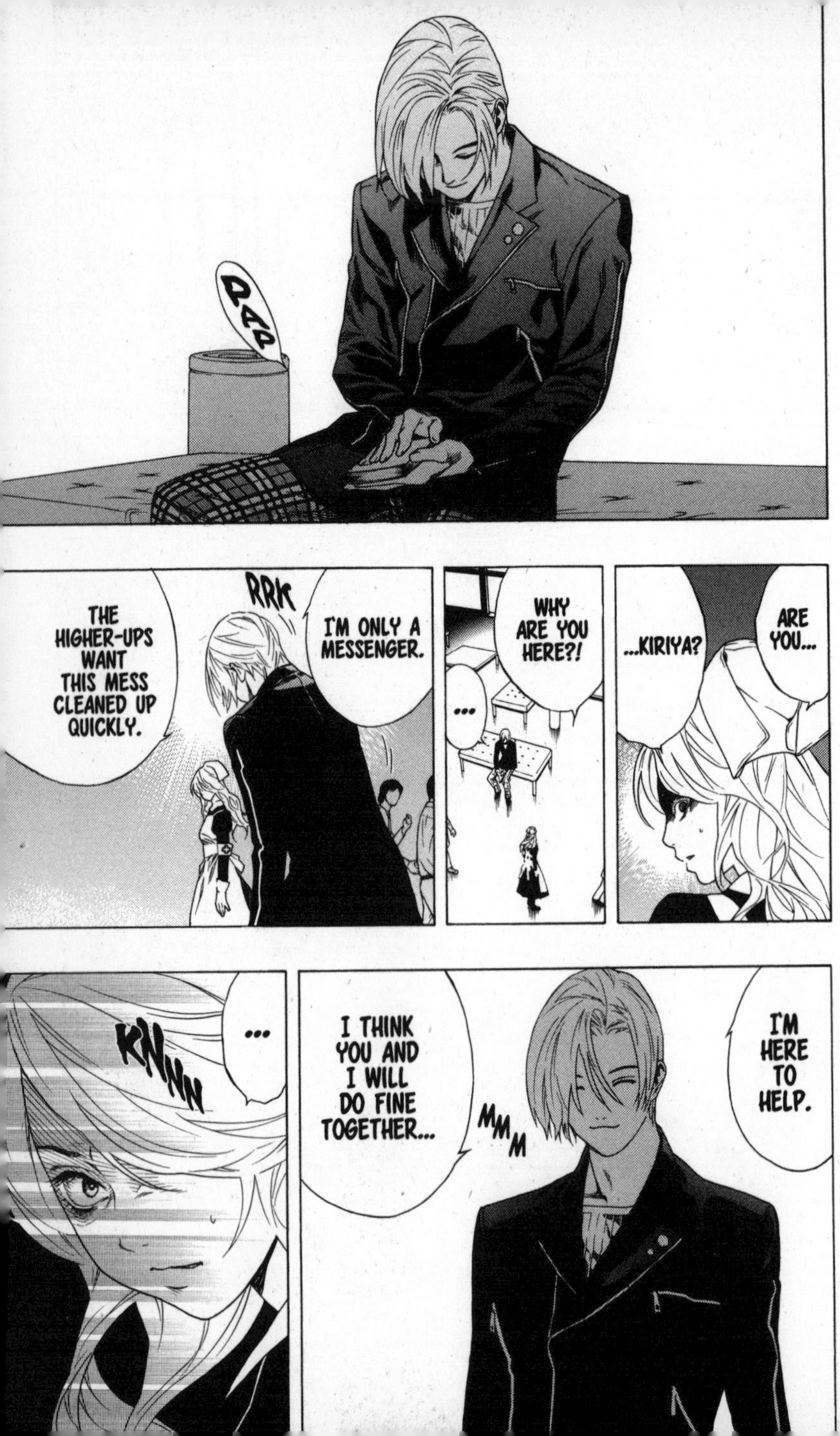
RAP
ARE YOU...
...KIRIYA?
WHY ARE YOU HERE?!
...
I'M ONLY A MESSENGER.
RRK
THE HIGHER-UPS WANT THIS MESS CLEANED UP QUICKLY.
I'M HERE TO HELP.
MMM
I THINK YOU AND I WILL DO FINE TOGETHER...
...
KNNNN

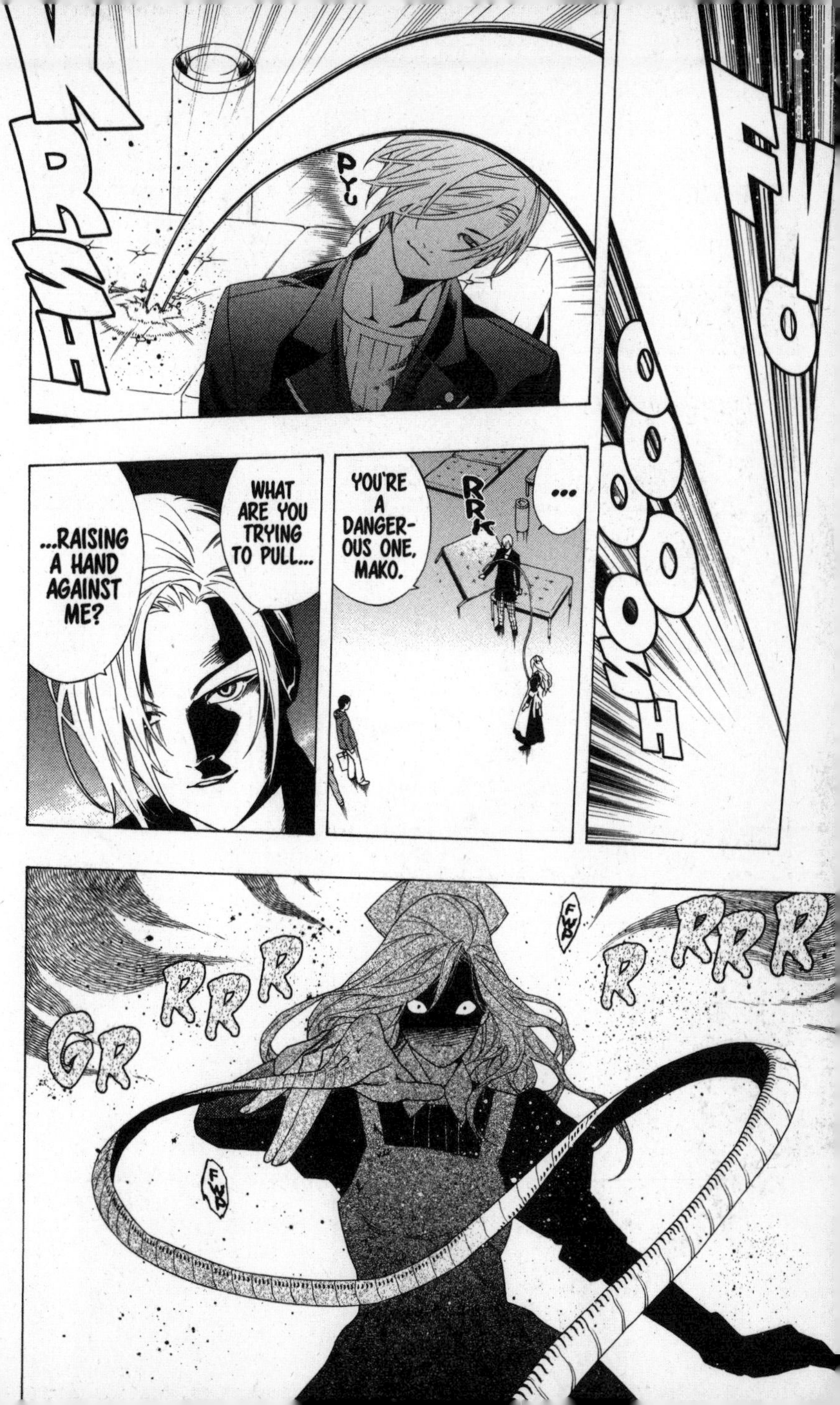
FWOOOOOOOOOOSH
PYU
KRSH
...
RRK
YOU'RE A DANGEROUS ONE, MAKO.
WHAT ARE YOU TRYING TO PULL...
...RAISING A HAND AGAINST ME?
FWP
RRRR
GRRRR
FWP

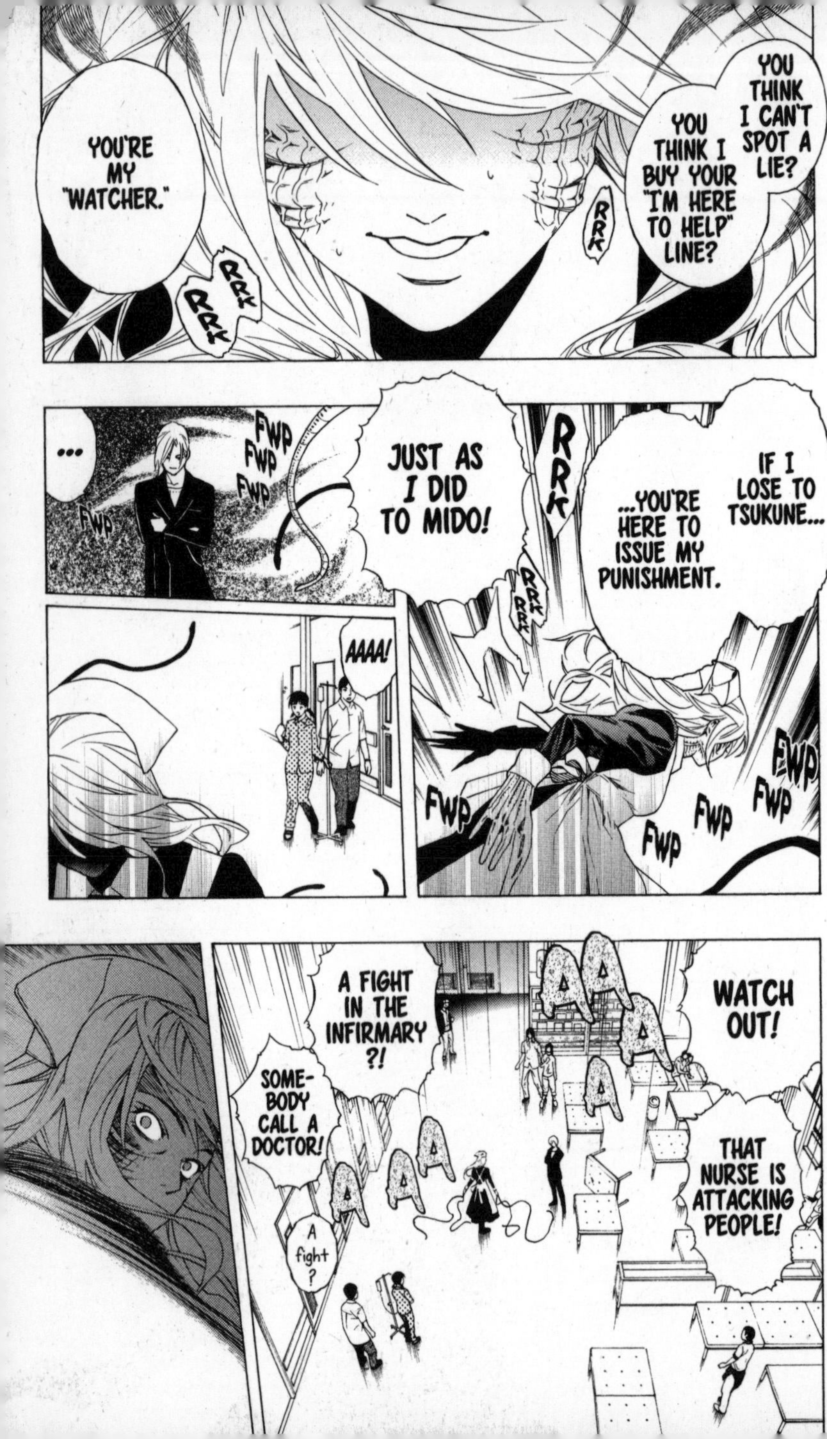
YOU THINK I CAN'T SPOT A LIE?
YOU THINK I BUY YOUR "I'M HERE TO HELP" LINE?
RRK
YOU'RE MY "WATCHER."
RRK RRK
IF I LOSE TO TSUKUNE...
...YOU'RE HERE TO ISSUE MY PUNISHMENT.
RRK
JUST AS I DID TO MIDO!
RRK RRK RRK
FWP FWP FWP FWP FWP
...
FWP FWP FWP FWP
AAAA!
WATCH OUT!
A FIGHT IN THE INFIRMARY?!
THAT NURSE IS ATTACKING PEOPLE!
SOME-BODY CALL A DOCTOR!
A fight?

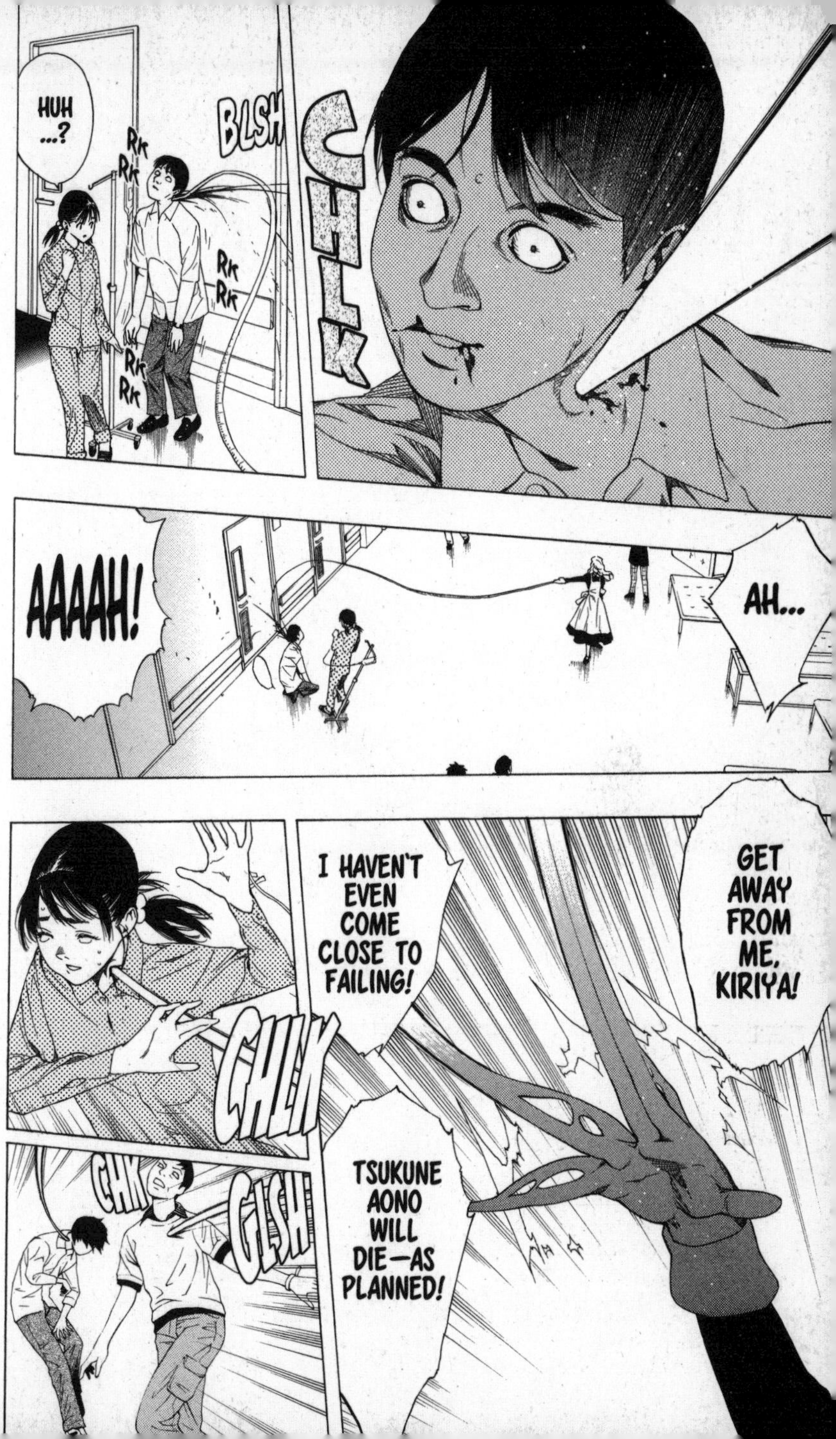
CHLLK
BLSH
HUH ...?
RK RK
RK RK
RK RK
AH...
AAAAH!
GET AWAY FROM ME, KIRIYA!
I HAVEN'T EVEN COME CLOSE TO FAILING!
TSUKUNE AONO WILL DIE—AS PLANNED!
CHLNK
CHK
GLSH

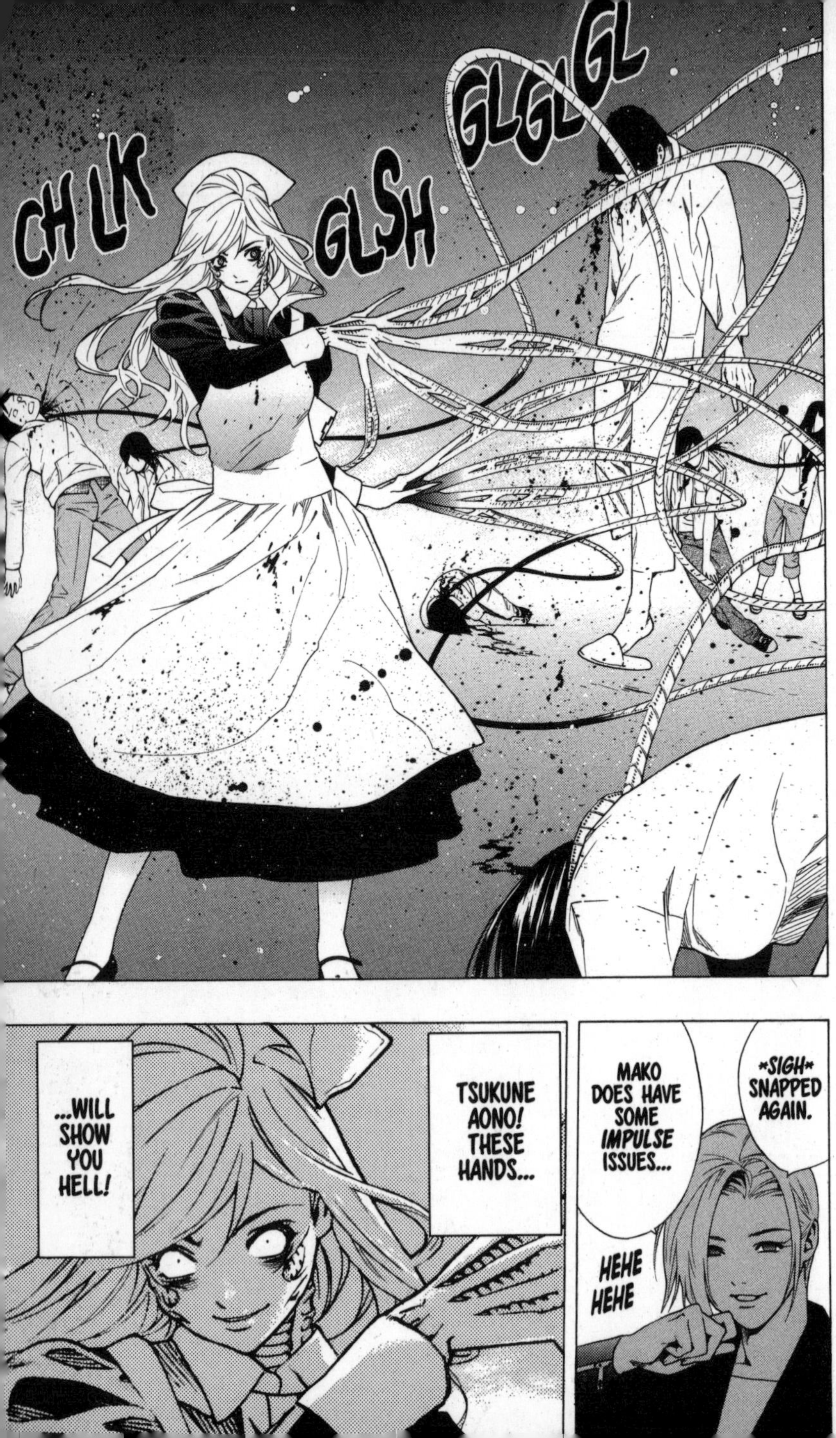
GLGLGL
GLSH
CHLK
*SIGH* SNAPPED AGAIN.
MAKO DOES HAVE SOME IMPULSE ISSUES...
HEHE HEHE
TSUKUNE AONO! THESE HANDS...
...WILL SHOW YOU HELL!

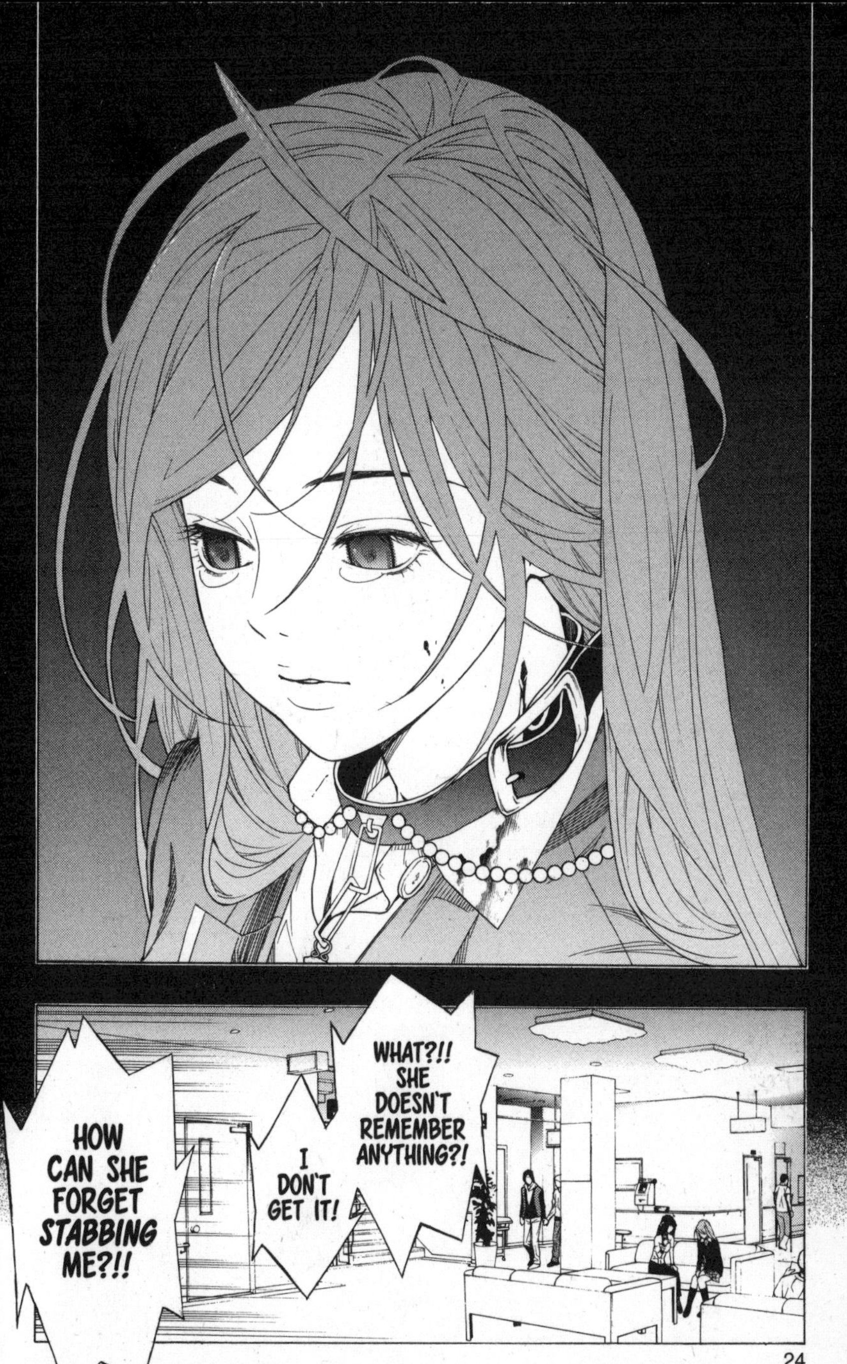
WHAT?!! SHE DOESN'T REMEMBER ANYTHING?!
I DON'T GET IT!
HOW CAN SHE FORGET STABBING ME?!!

READ THIS WAY

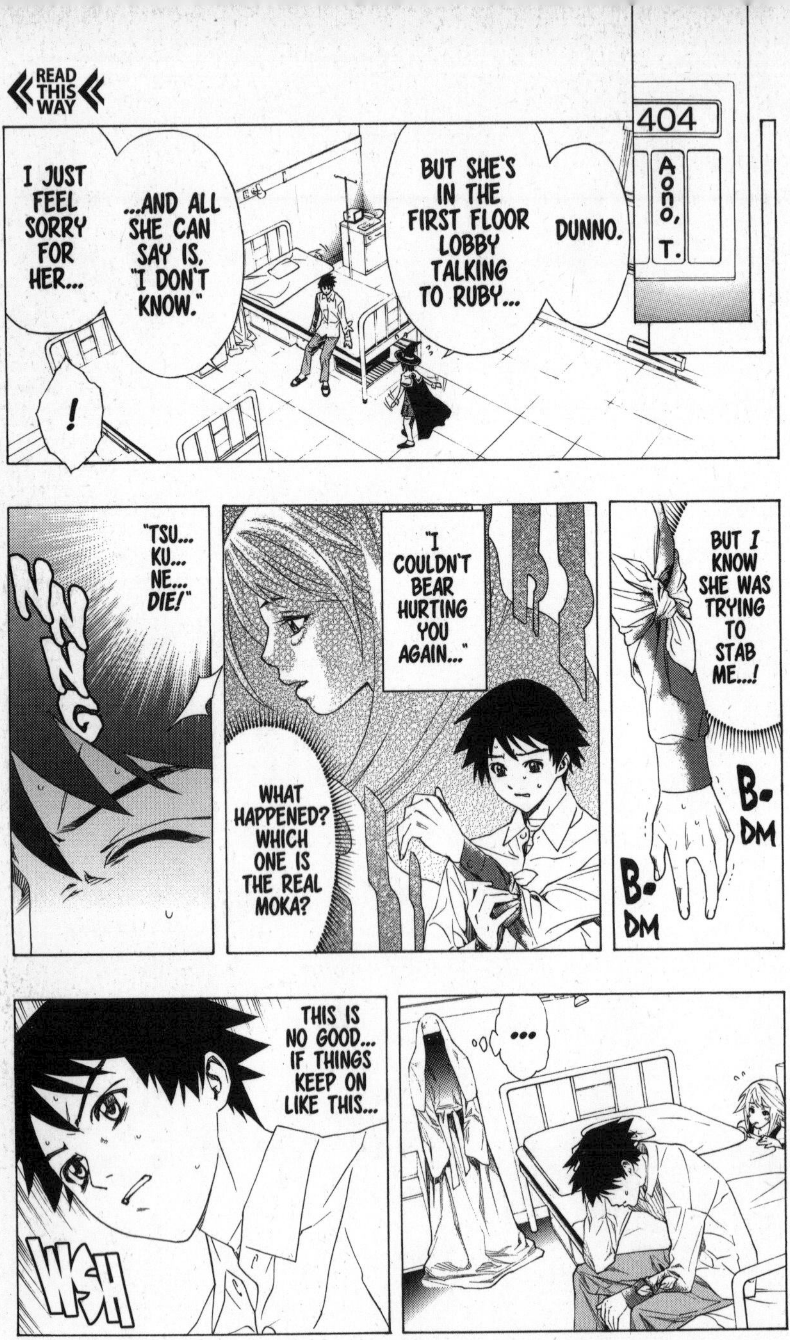

404
Aono, T.
DUNNO.
BUT SHE'S IN THE FIRST FLOOR LOBBY TALKING TO RUBY...
...AND ALL SHE CAN SAY IS, "I DON'T KNOW."
I JUST FEEL SORRY FOR HER...
!
BUT *I* KNOW SHE WAS TRYING TO STAB ME...!
B-DM
B-DM
"I COULDN'T BEAR HURTING YOU AGAIN..."
WHAT HAPPENED? WHICH ONE IS THE REAL MOKA?
"TSU... KU... NE... *DIE!*"
NNNG
...
THIS IS NO GOOD... IF THINGS KEEP ON LIKE THIS...
WSH

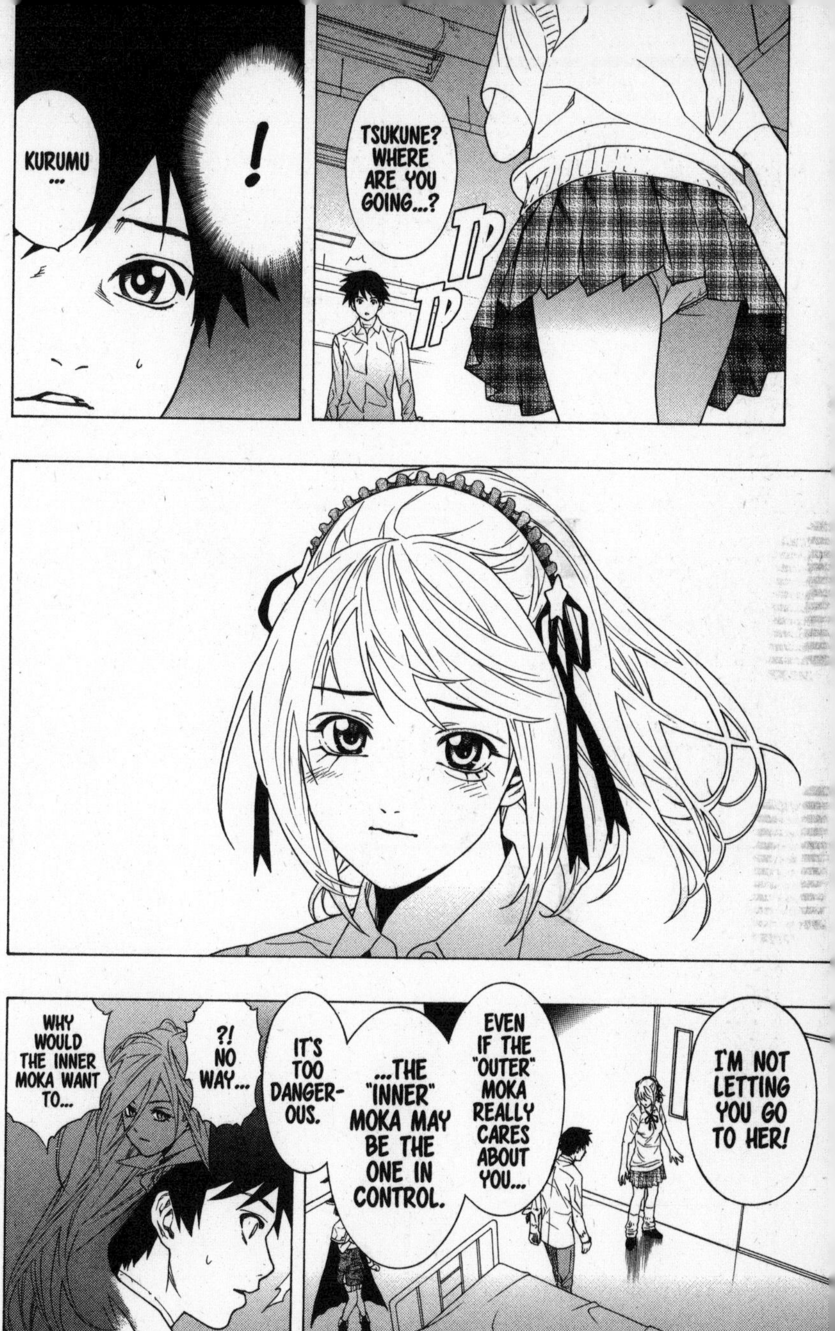
TSUKUNE? WHERE ARE YOU GOING...?
TP
TP
!
KURUMU ...
I'M NOT LETTING YOU GO TO HER!
EVEN IF THE "OUTER" MOKA REALLY CARES ABOUT YOU...
...THE "INNER" MOKA MAY BE THE ONE IN CONTROL.
IT'S TOO DANGER-OUS.
?! NO WAY...
WHY WOULD THE INNER MOKA WANT TO...

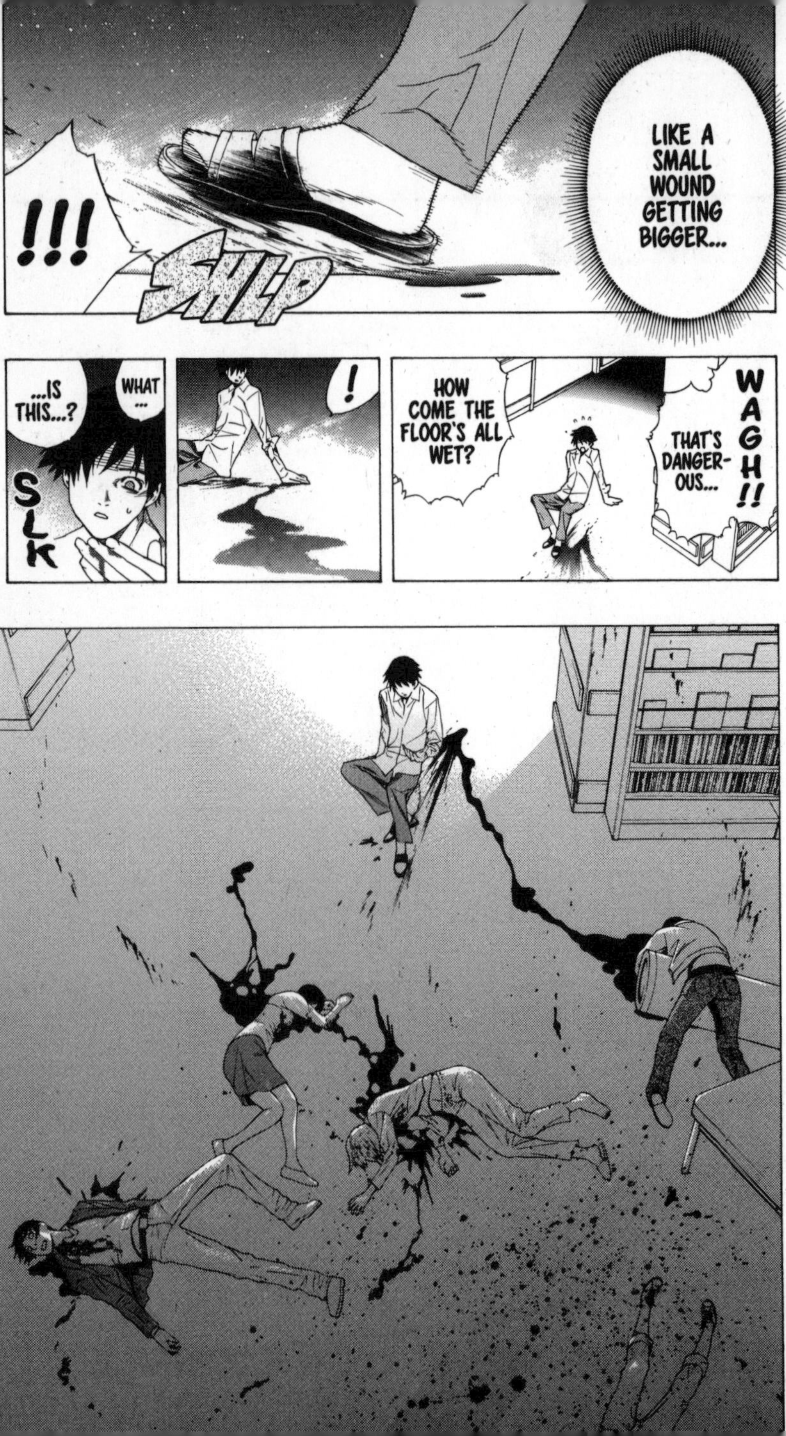
LIKE A SMALL WOUND GETTING BIGGER...
SHLIP
!!!
WAGH!!
THAT'S DANGER-OUS...
HOW COME THE FLOOR'S ALL WET?
!
WHAT...
...IS THIS...?
SLK

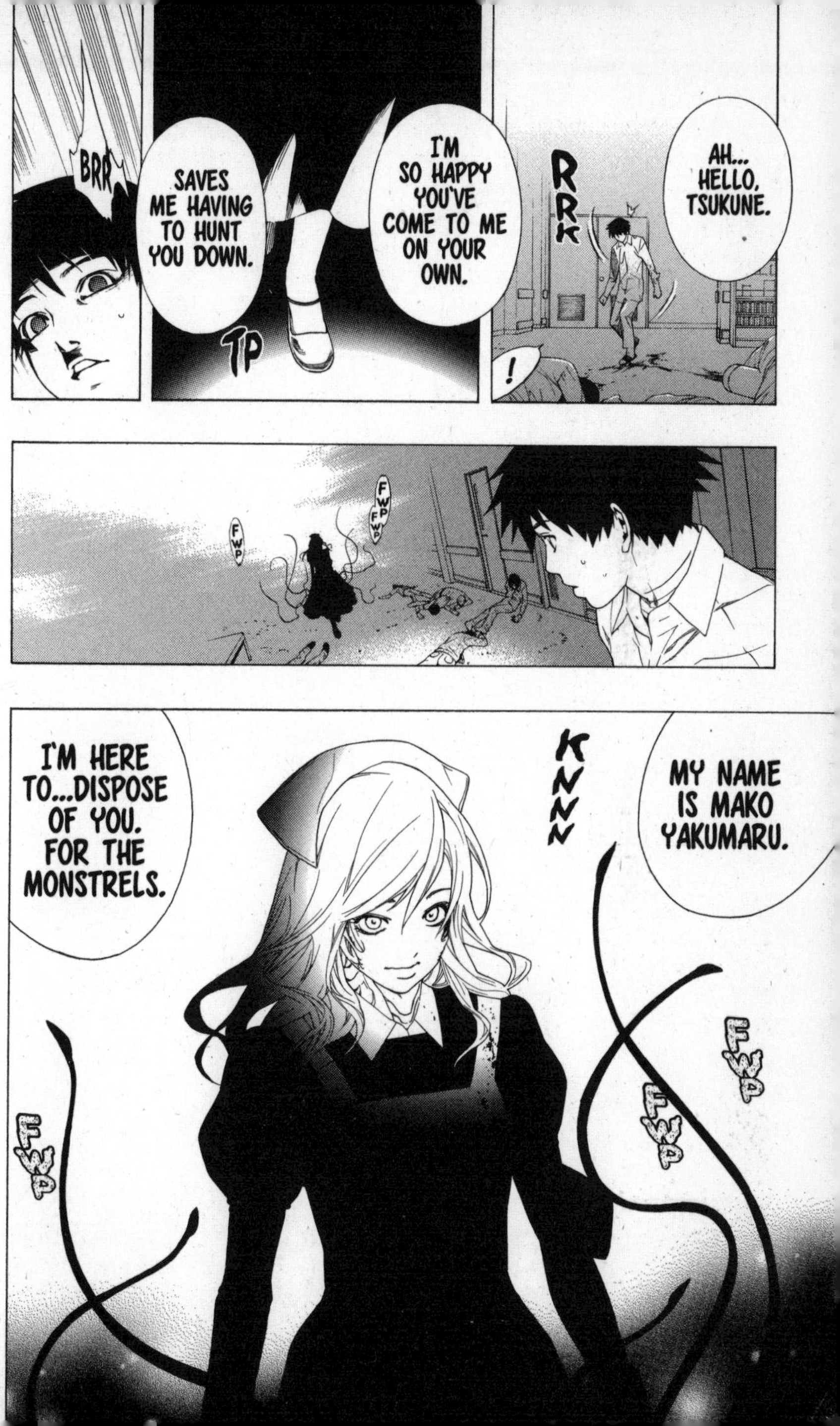
AH... HELLO, TSUKUNE.
RRK
!
I'M SO HAPPY YOU'VE COME TO ME ON YOUR OWN.
TP
SAVES ME HAVING TO HUNT YOU DOWN.
BRR
FWP FWP
FWP
FWP
MY NAME IS MAKO YAKUMARU.
KNNN
I'M HERE TO...DISPOSE OF YOU. FOR THE MONSTRELS.
FWP
FWP
FWP

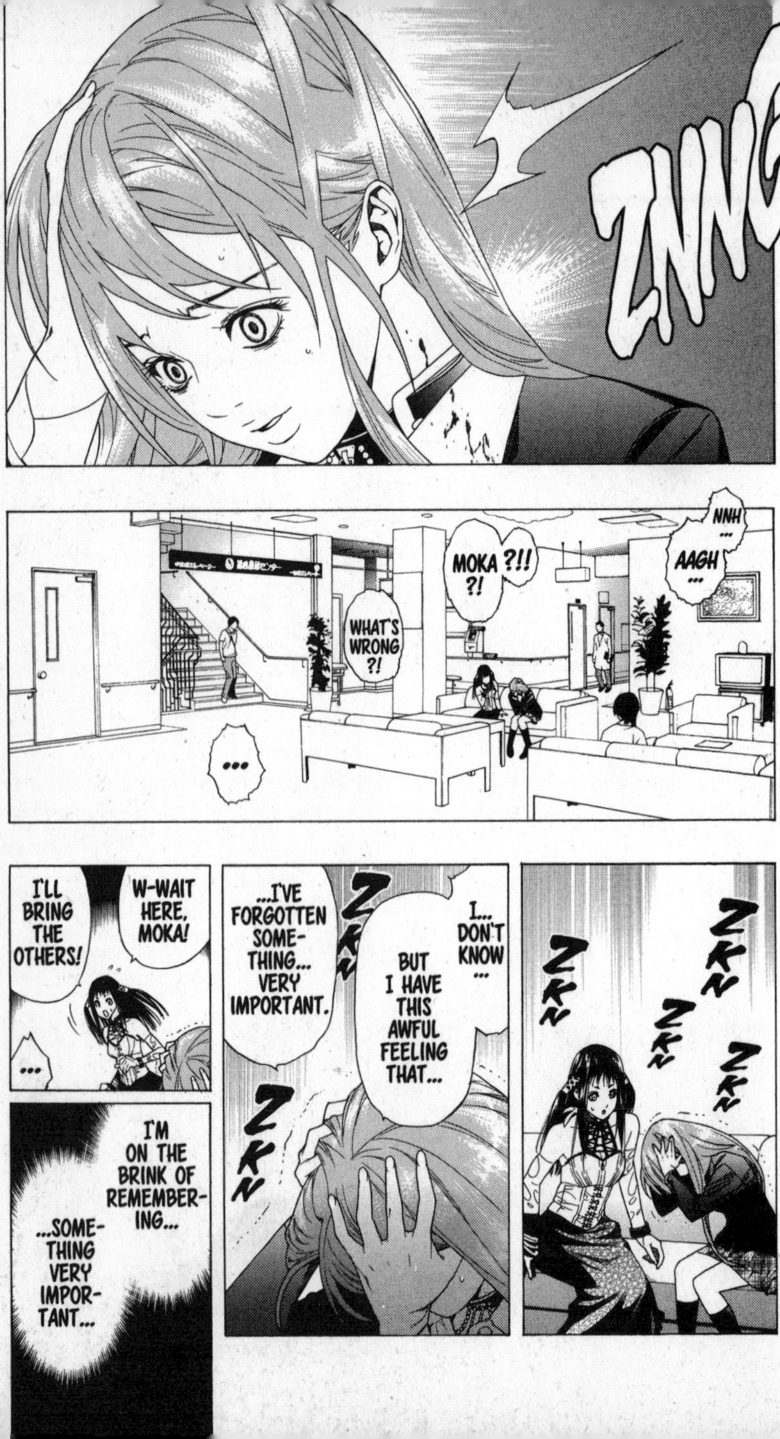
ZNNG
NNH... AAGH...
MOKA ?!
?!!
WHAT'S WRONG ?!
...
ZKN
ZKN
ZKN
ZKN
I... DON'T KNOW...
BUT I HAVE THIS AWFUL FEELING THAT...
...I'VE FORGOTTEN SOMETHING... VERY IMPORTANT.
ZKN
ZKN
W-WAIT HERE, MOKA!
I'LL BRING THE OTHERS!
...
I'M ON THE BRINK OF REMEMBERING...
...SOMETHING VERY IMPORTANT...

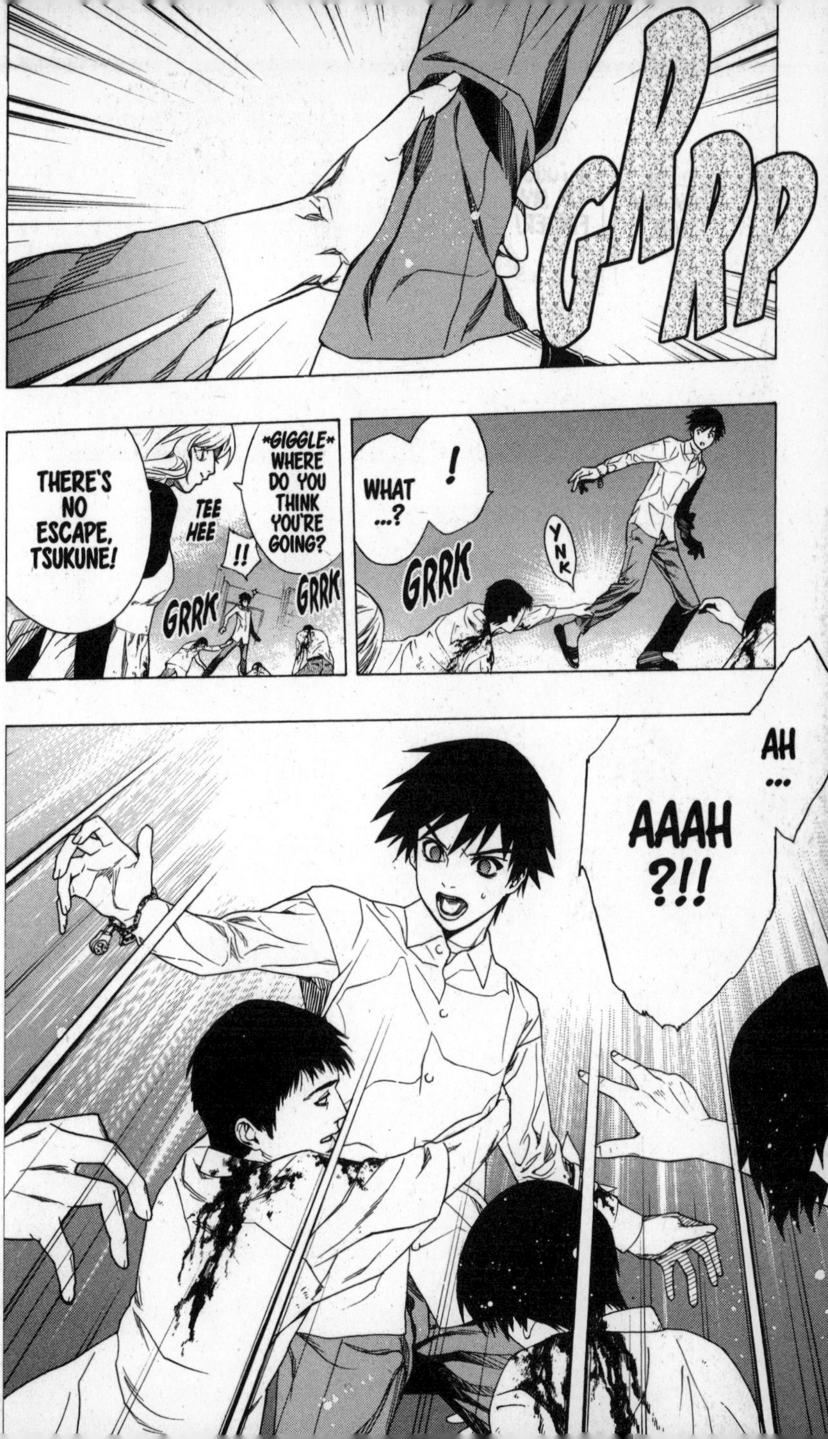
GRRP
!
WHAT ...?
YNK
GRRK
*GIGGLE* WHERE DO YOU THINK YOU'RE GOING?
GRRK
TEE HEE
!!
THERE'S NO ESCAPE, TSUKUNE!
GRRK
AH ... AAAH ?!!

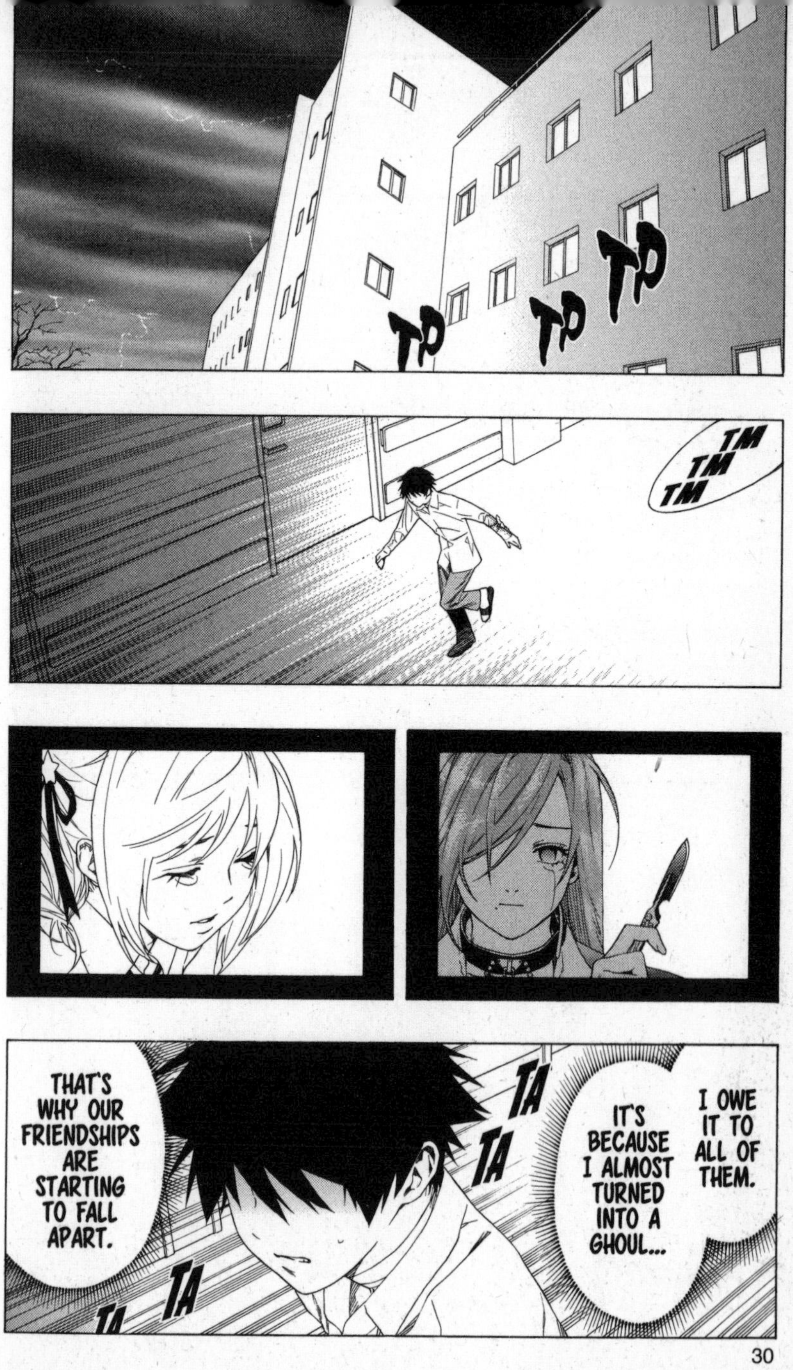
TP
TP
TP
TP
TM
TM
TM
I OWE IT TO ALL OF THEM.
IT'S BECAUSE I ALMOST TURNED INTO A GHOUL...
TA
TA
THAT'S WHY OUR FRIENDSHIPS ARE STARTING TO FALL APART.
TA
TA

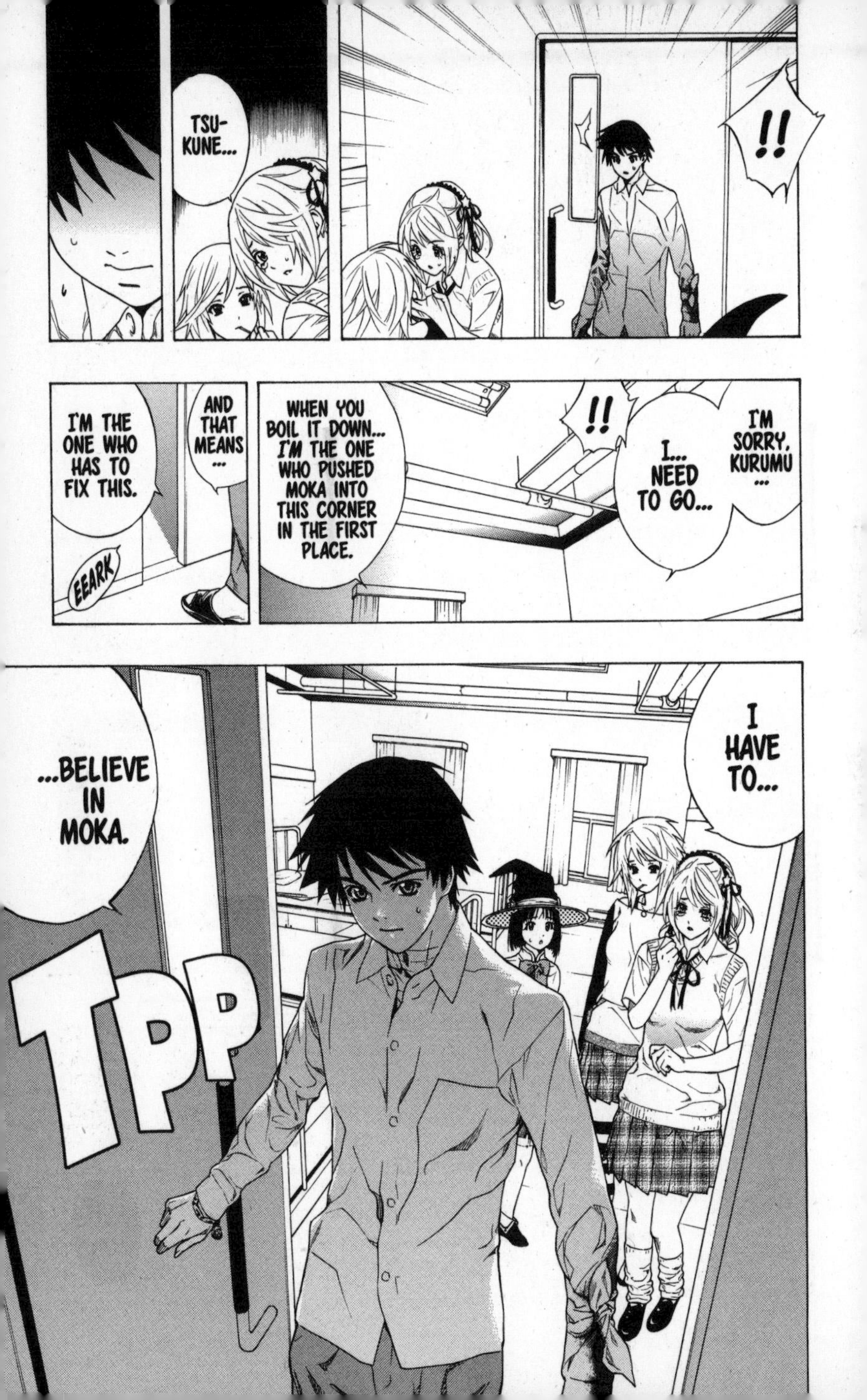
!!
TSU-KUNE...
I'M SORRY, KURUMU...
I... NEED TO GO...
!!
WHEN YOU BOIL IT DOWN... *I'M* THE ONE WHO PUSHED MOKA INTO THIS CORNER IN THE FIRST PLACE.
AND THAT MEANS...
I'M THE ONE WHO HAS TO FIX THIS.
EEARK
I HAVE TO...
...BELIEVE IN MOKA.
TPP

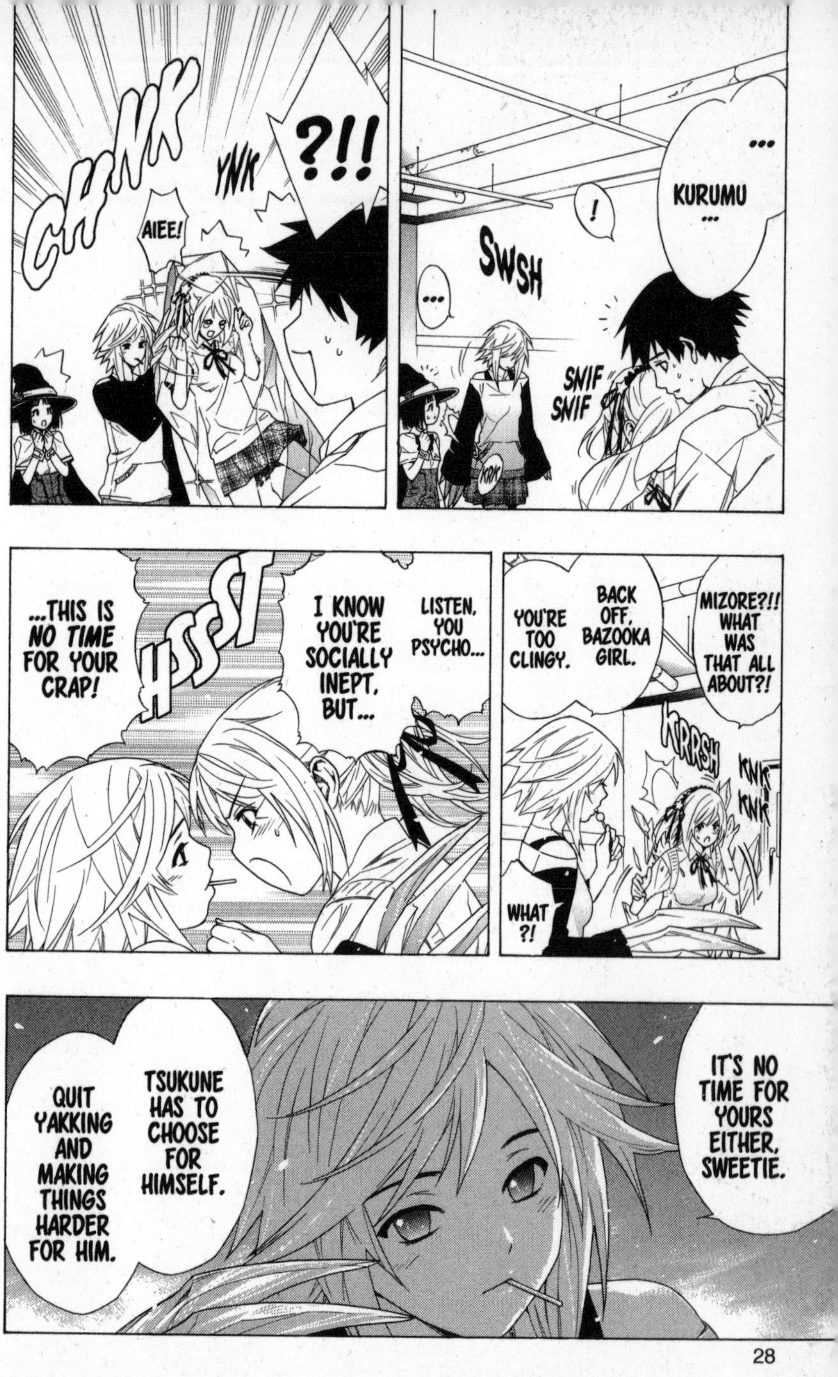
... KURUMU ...
!
SWSH
...
SNIF SNIF
KRK
?!!
YNK
CHINK
AIEE!
MIZORE?!! WHAT WAS THAT ALL ABOUT?!
BACK OFF, BAZOOKA GIRL.
YOU'RE TOO CLINGY.
KRRSH
KNK KNK
WHAT?!
LISTEN, YOU PSYCHO...
I KNOW YOU'RE SOCIALLY INEPT, BUT...
HSSST
...THIS IS NO TIME FOR YOUR CRAP!
IT'S NO TIME FOR YOURS EITHER, SWEETIE.
TSUKUNE HAS TO CHOOSE FOR HIMSELF.
QUIT YAKKING AND MAKING THINGS HARDER FOR HIM.

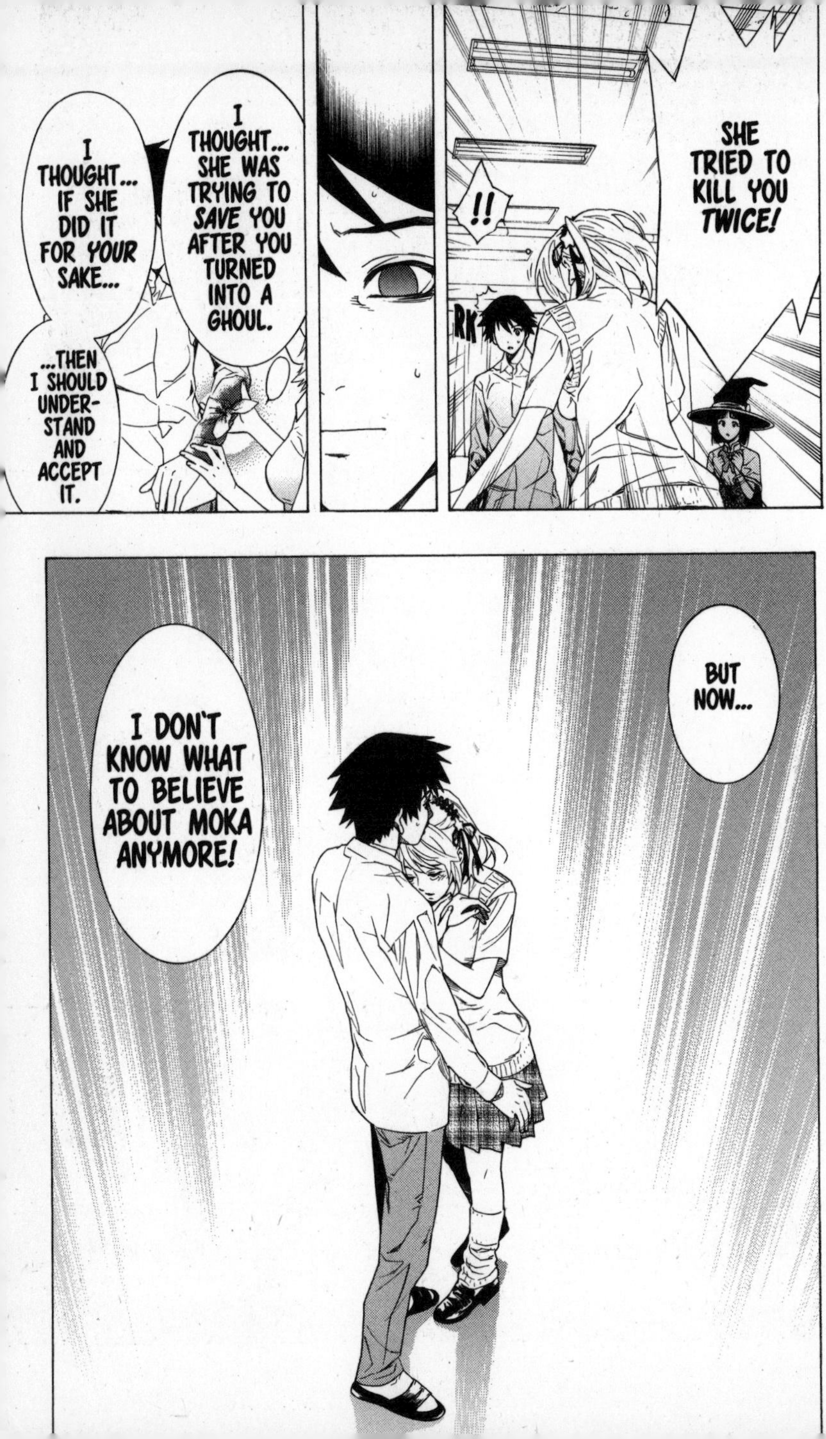
SHE TRIED TO KILL YOU *TWICE!*
!!
RK
I THOUGHT... SHE WAS TRYING TO *SAVE* YOU AFTER YOU TURNED INTO A GHOUL.
I THOUGHT... IF SHE DID IT FOR *YOUR* SAKE...
...THEN I SHOULD UNDERSTAND AND ACCEPT IT.
BUT NOW...
I DON'T KNOW WHAT TO BELIEVE ABOUT MOKA ANYMORE!

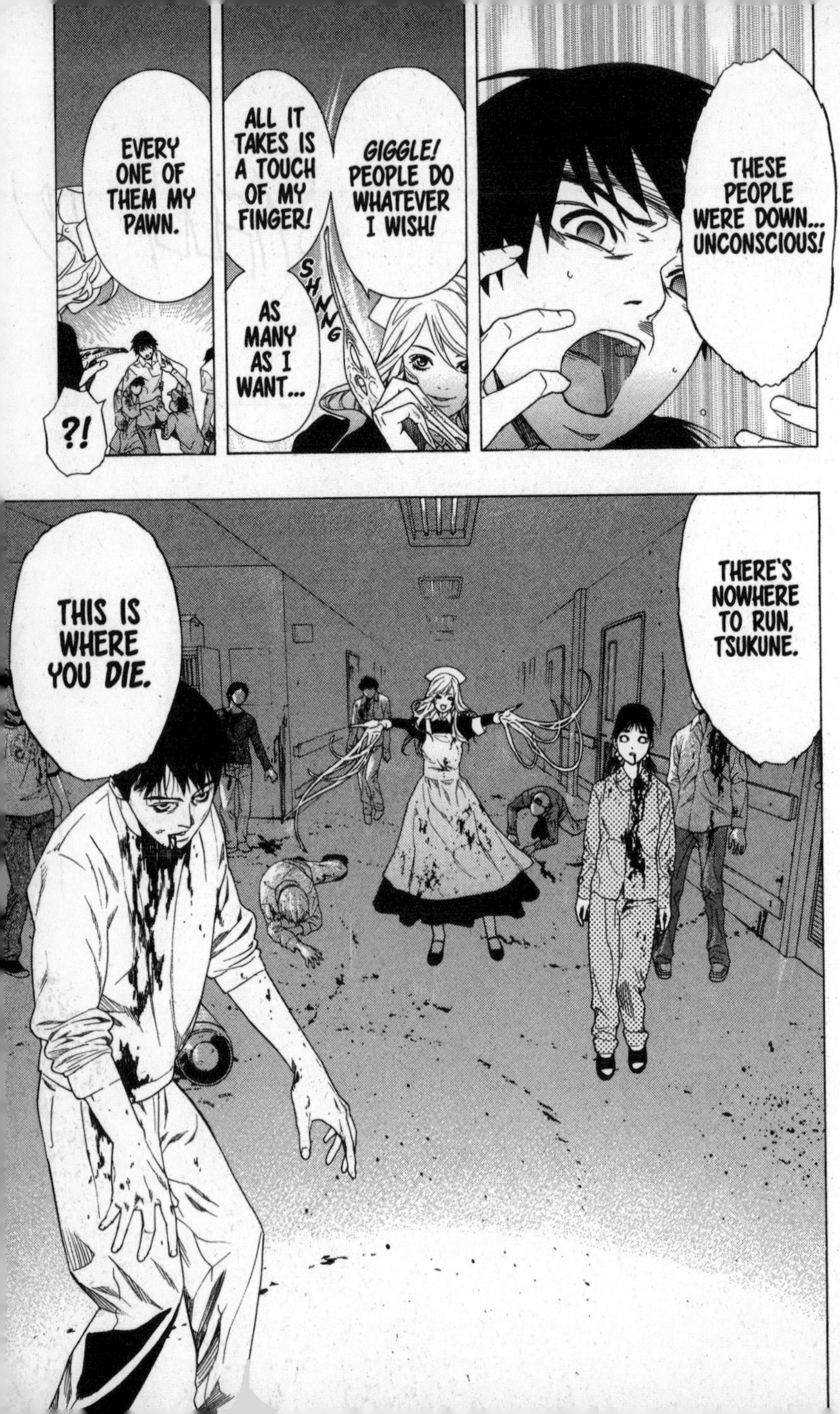
THESE PEOPLE WERE DOWN... UNCONSCIOUS!
GIGGLE! PEOPLE DO WHATEVER I WISH!
ALL IT TAKES IS A TOUCH OF MY FINGER!
SHHNG
AS MANY AS I WANT...
EVERY ONE OF THEM MY PAWN.
?!
THERE'S NOWHERE TO RUN, TSUKUNE.
THIS IS WHERE YOU *DIE.*

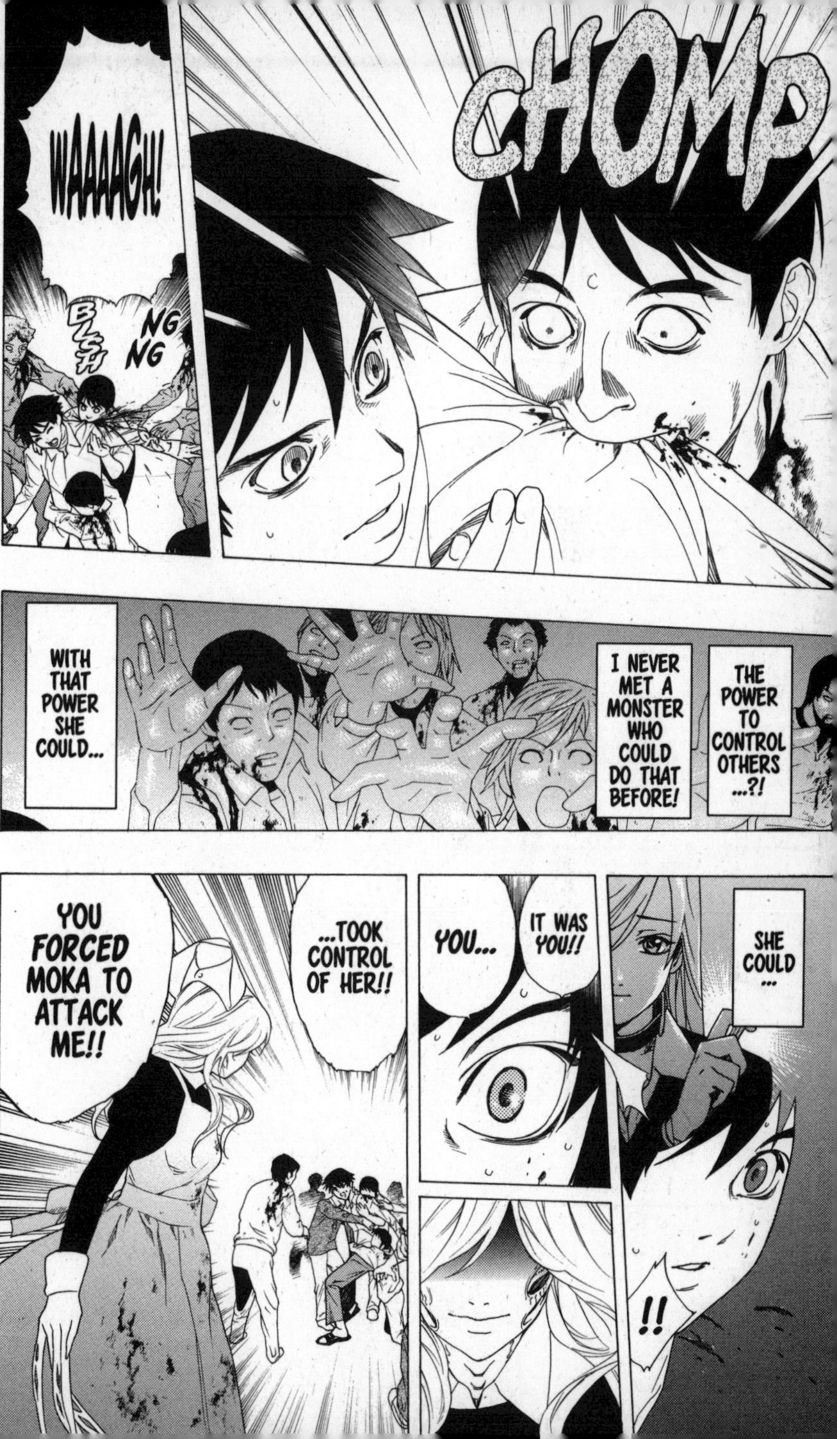
CHOMP
WAAAAGH!
BLSH
NG NG
THE POWER TO CONTROL OTHERS ...?!
I NEVER MET A MONSTER WHO COULD DO THAT BEFORE!
WITH THAT POWER SHE COULD...
SHE COULD ...
!!
IT WAS YOU!!
YOU...
...TOOK CONTROL OF HER!!
YOU FORCED MOKA TO ATTACK ME!!

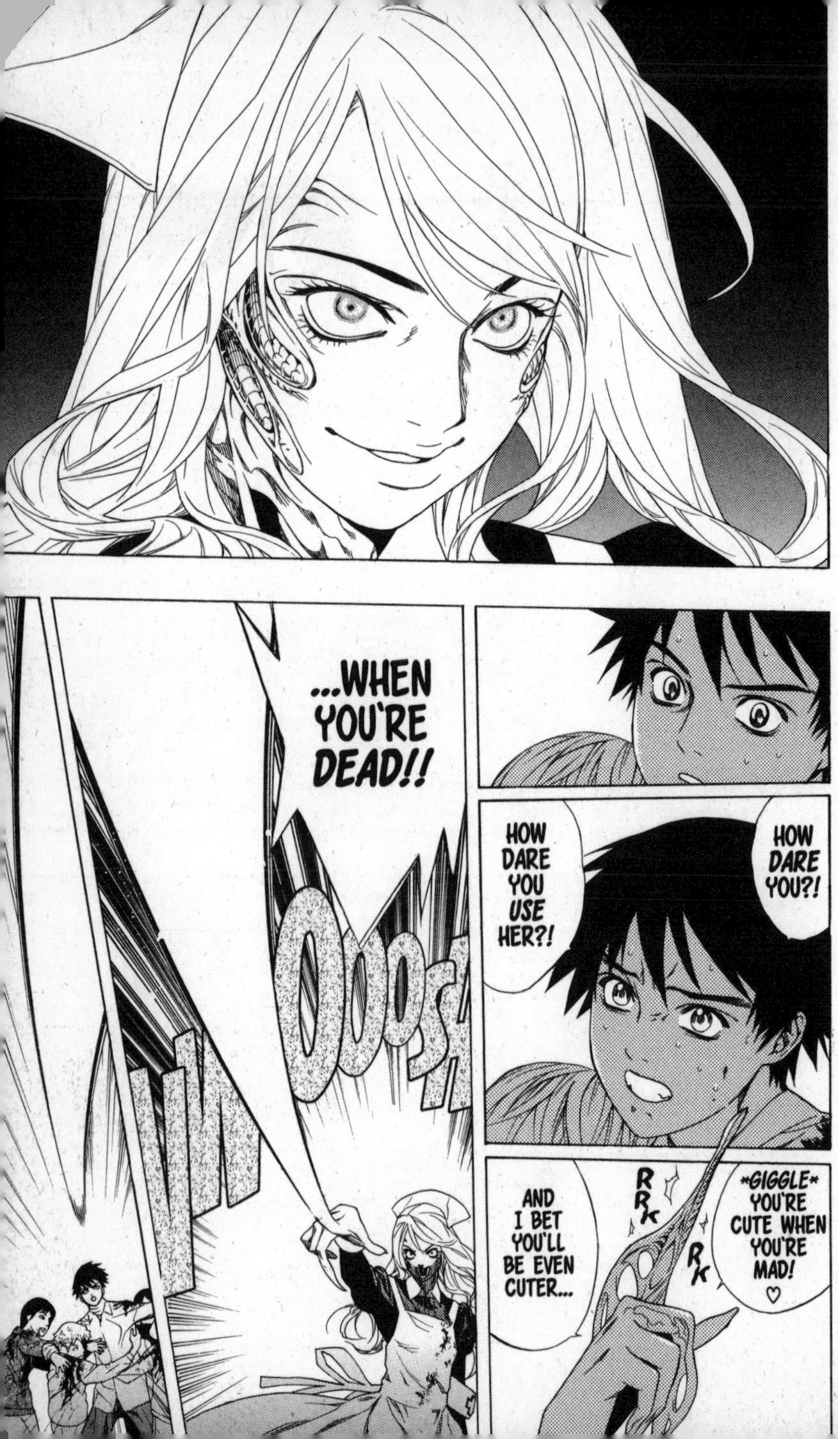
HOW DARE YOU?!
HOW DARE YOU USE HER?!
*GIGGLE* YOU'RE CUTE WHEN YOU'RE MAD! ♡
RRK
RK
AND I BET YOU'LL BE EVEN CUTER...
...WHEN YOU'RE DEAD!!
WHOOOSH

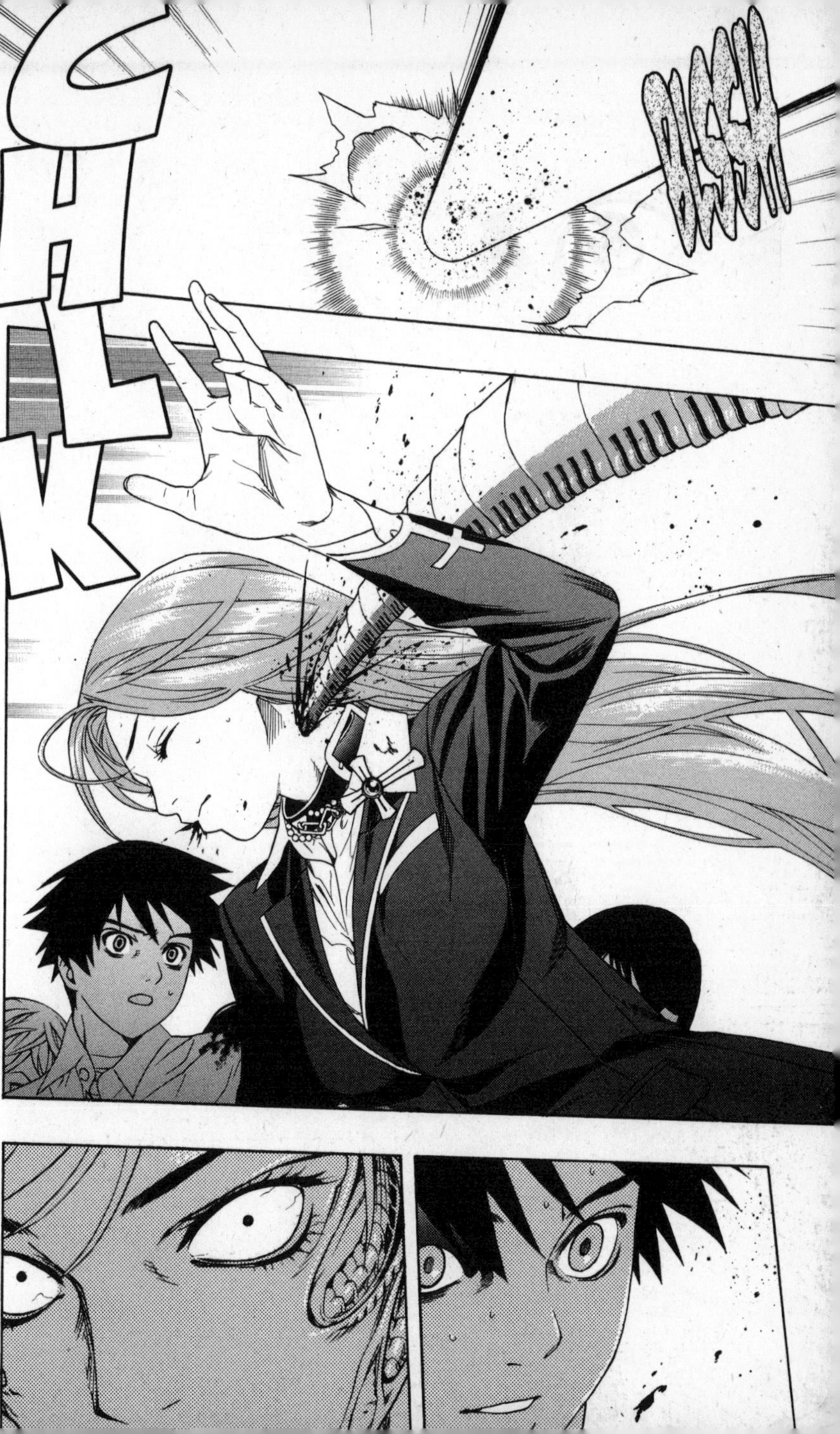
BLSCH
CHALK

READ THIS WAY

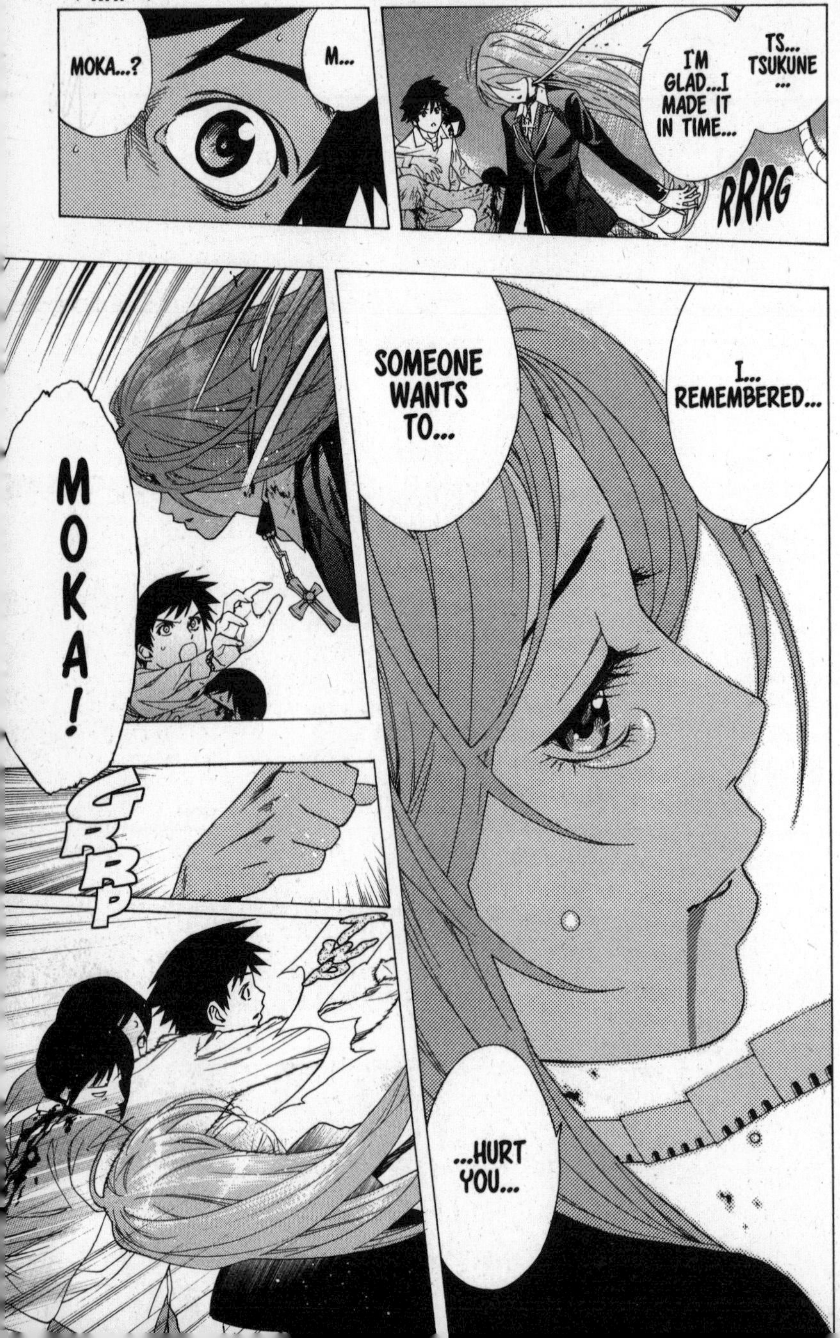
TS... TSUKUNE ...
I'M GLAD...I MADE IT IN TIME...
RRRG
M...
MOKA...?
I... REMEMBERED...
SOMEONE WANTS TO...
...HURT YOU...
MOKA!
GRRP

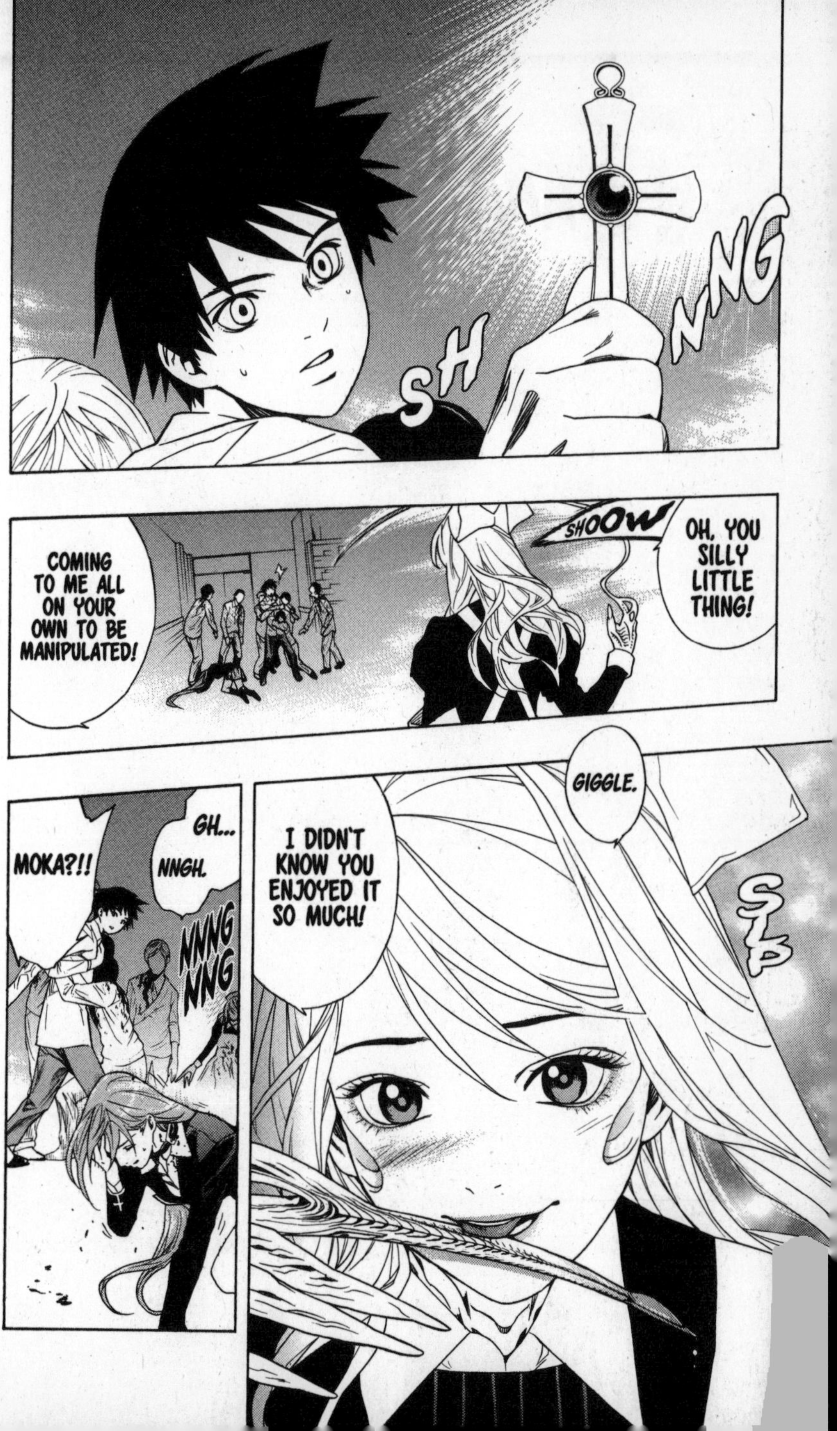
SH
NNG
SHOOW
OH, YOU SILLY LITTLE THING!
COMING TO ME ALL ON YOUR OWN TO BE MANIPULATED!
GIGGLE.
I DIDN'T KNOW YOU ENJOYED IT SO MUCH!
GH... NNGH.
MOKA?!!
NNNG NNG

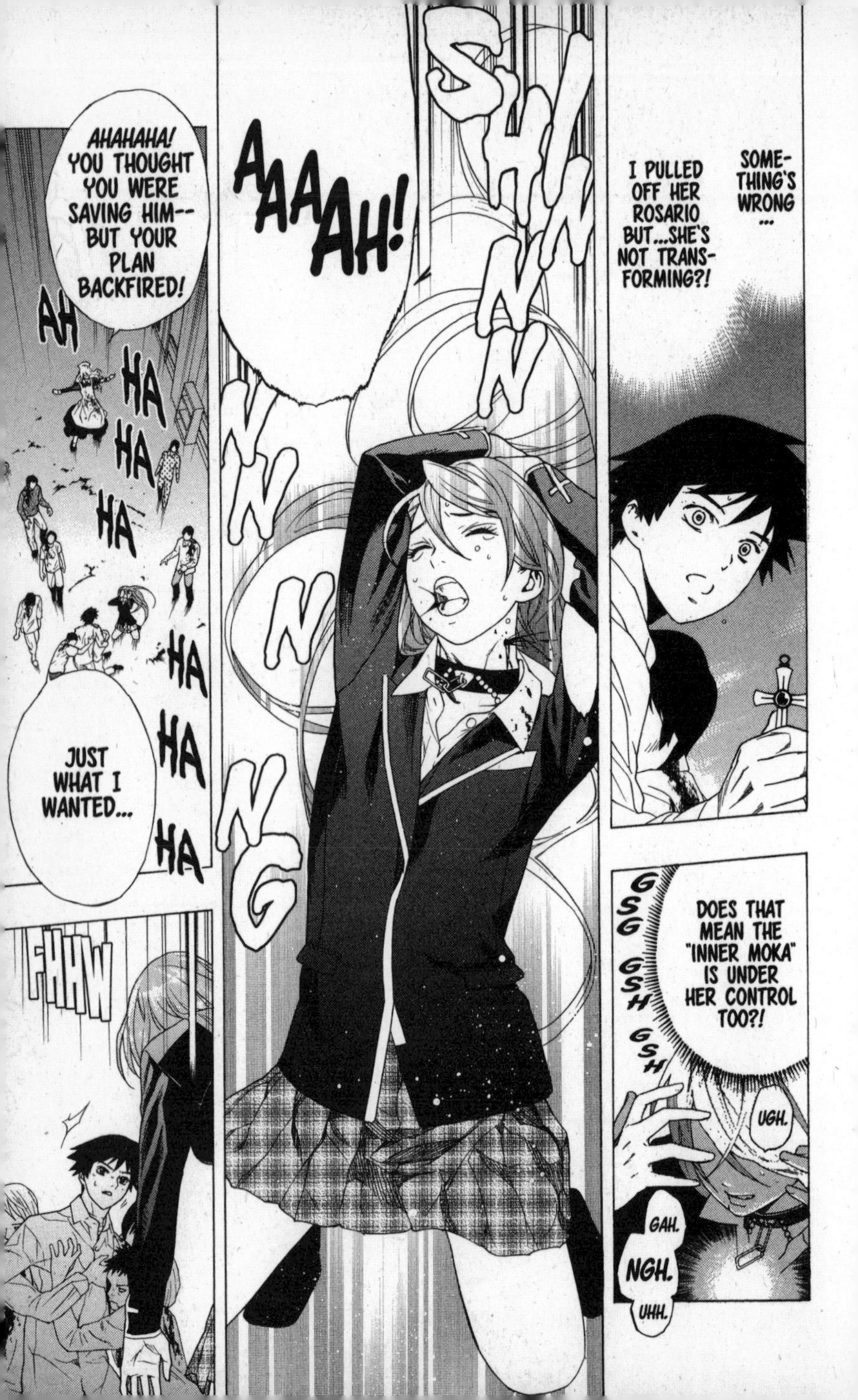
SOME-THING'S WRONG...
I PULLED OFF HER ROSARIO BUT...SHE'S NOT TRANS-FORMING?!
GSG GSG GSH GSH GSH
DOES THAT MEAN THE "INNER MOKA" IS UNDER HER CONTROL TOO?!
UGH.
GAH.
NGH.
UHH.
SHNNNNNNNNNG
AAAAAH!
AHAHAHA! YOU THOUGHT YOU WERE SAVING HIM-- BUT YOUR PLAN BACKFIRED!
AH HA HA HA HA HA HA
JUST WHAT I WANTED...
FHHW

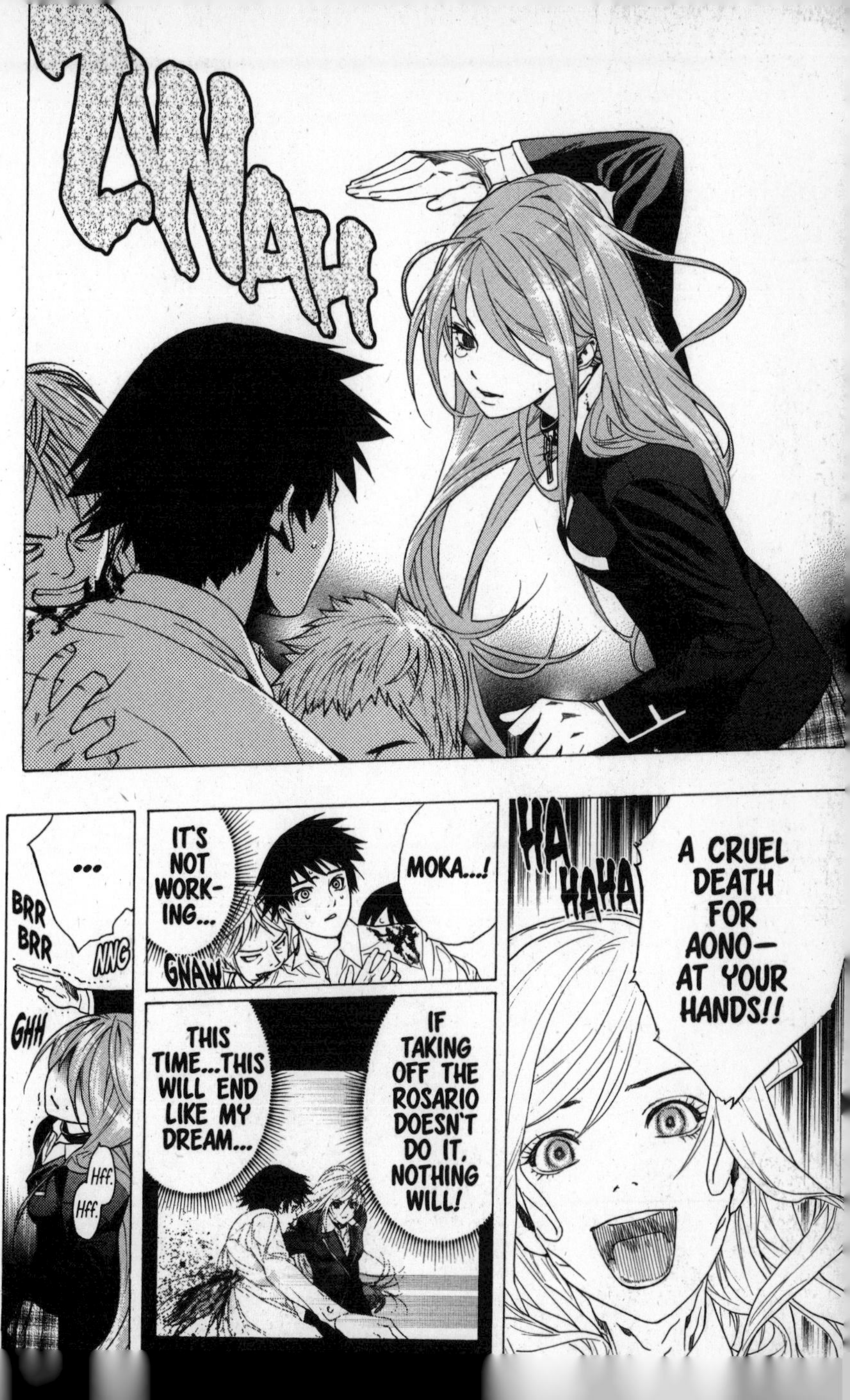
ZWAH
HA HAHA
A CRUEL DEATH FOR AONO— AT YOUR HANDS!!
MOKA...!
IT'S NOT WORKING...
GNAW
IF TAKING OFF THE ROSARIO DOESN'T DO IT, NOTHING WILL!
THIS TIME...THIS WILL END LIKE MY DREAM...
...
BRR BRR
NNG
GHH
Hff.
Hff.

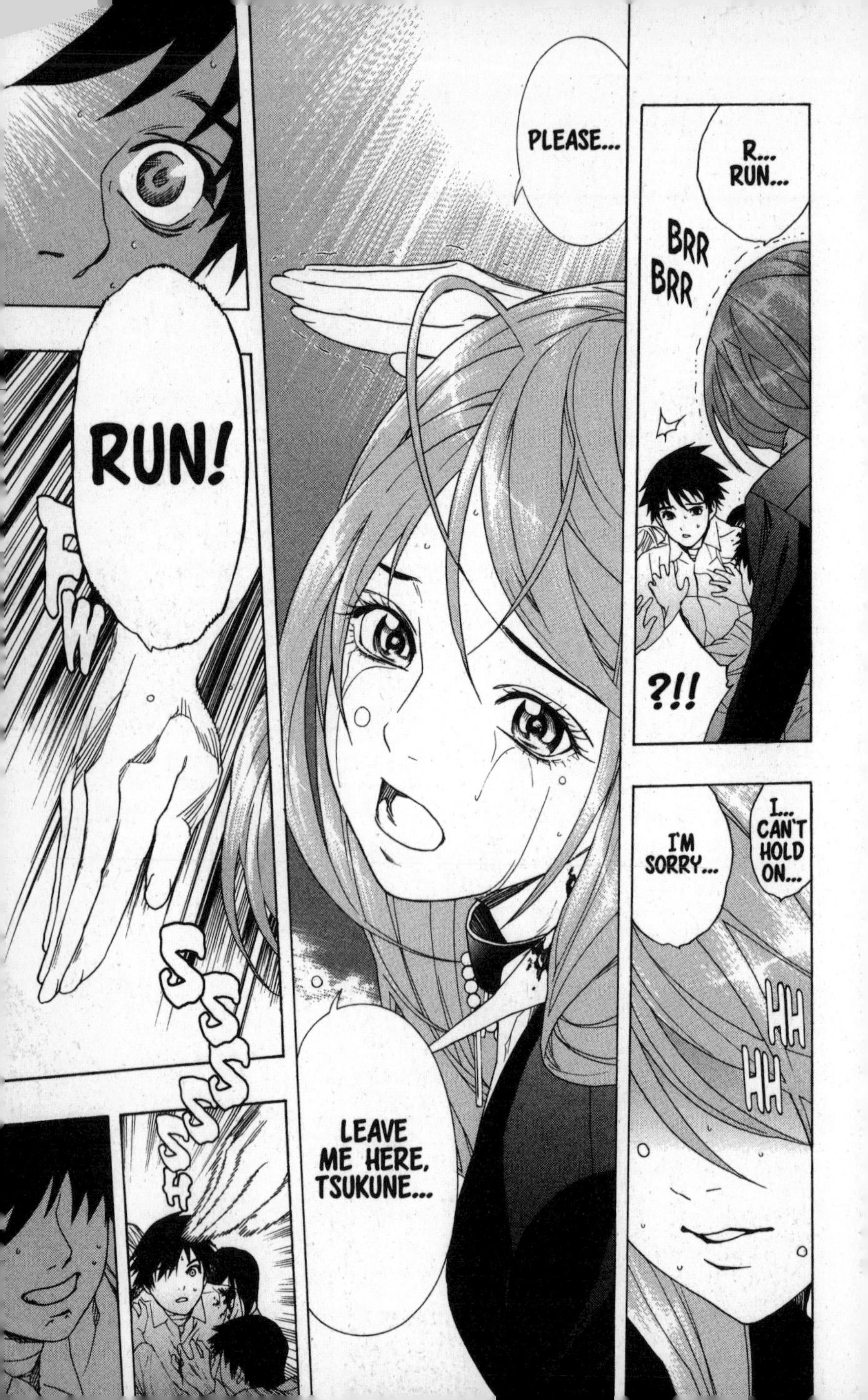
R...
RUN...
BRR
BRR
?!!
I... CAN'T HOLD ON...
I'M SORRY...
HH
HH
PLEASE...
LEAVE ME HERE, TSUKUNE...
RUN!

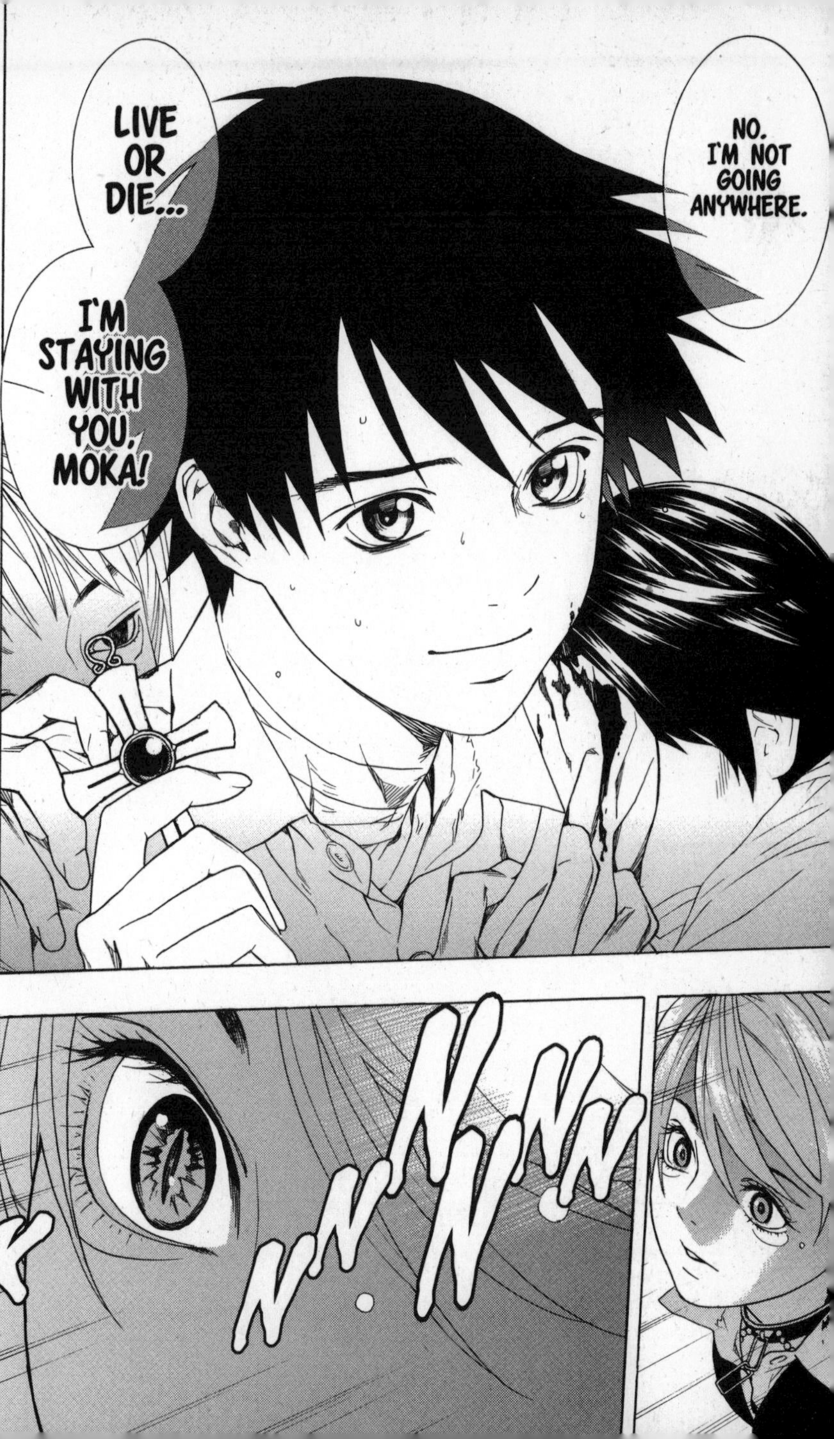
NO. I'M NOT GOING ANYWHERE.
LIVE OR DIE...
I'M STAYING WITH YOU, MOKA!
NNNNNNNNN

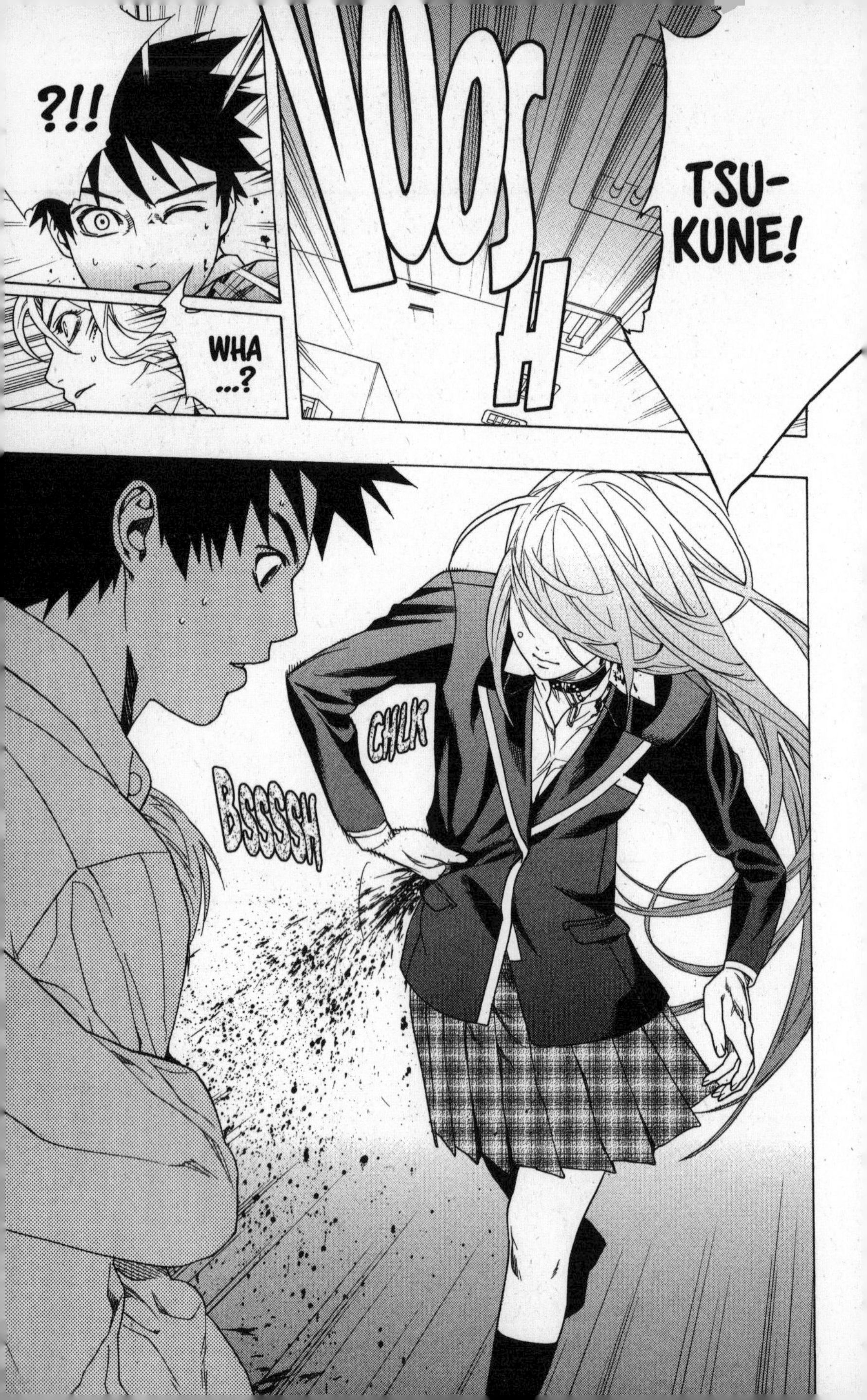
VOOSH
TSU-KUNE!
?!!
WHA ...?
CHLK
BSSSSH

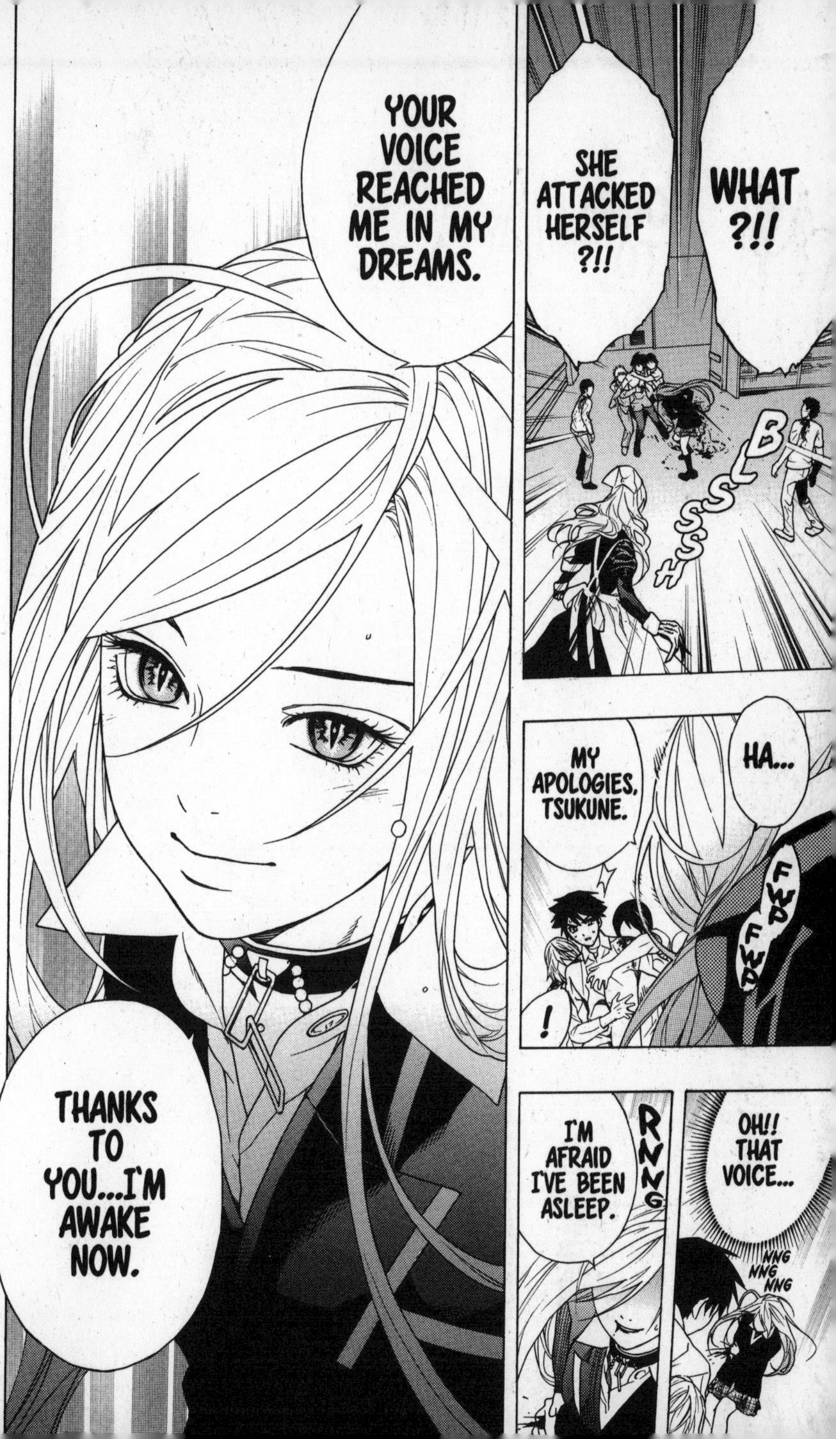
WHAT ?!!
SHE ATTACKED HERSELF ?!!
BLSSSSH
HA...
MY APOLOGIES, TSUKUNE.
FWP FWP
!
OH!! THAT VOICE...
NNG NNG NNG
RNNG
I'M AFRAID I'VE BEEN ASLEEP.
YOUR VOICE REACHED ME IN MY DREAMS.
THANKS TO YOU...I'M AWAKE NOW.

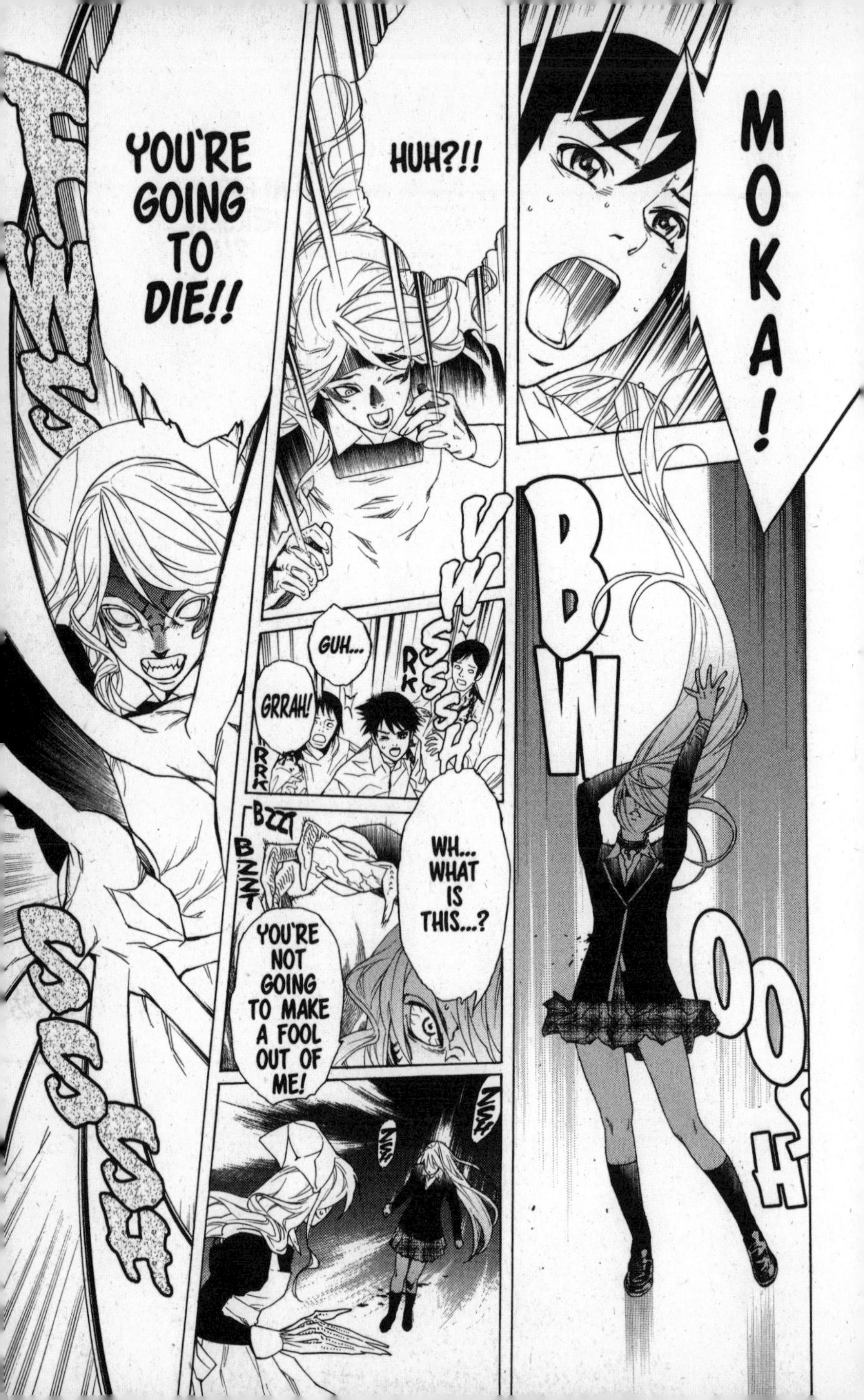
MOKA!
BWOOOSH
HUH?!!
VWSSSH
GUH...
RRK
GRRAH!
RRK
BZZT
BZZT
WH... WHAT IS THIS...?
YOU'RE NOT GOING TO MAKE A FOOL OUT OF ME!
YOU'RE GOING TO DIE!!
FWSSSSH

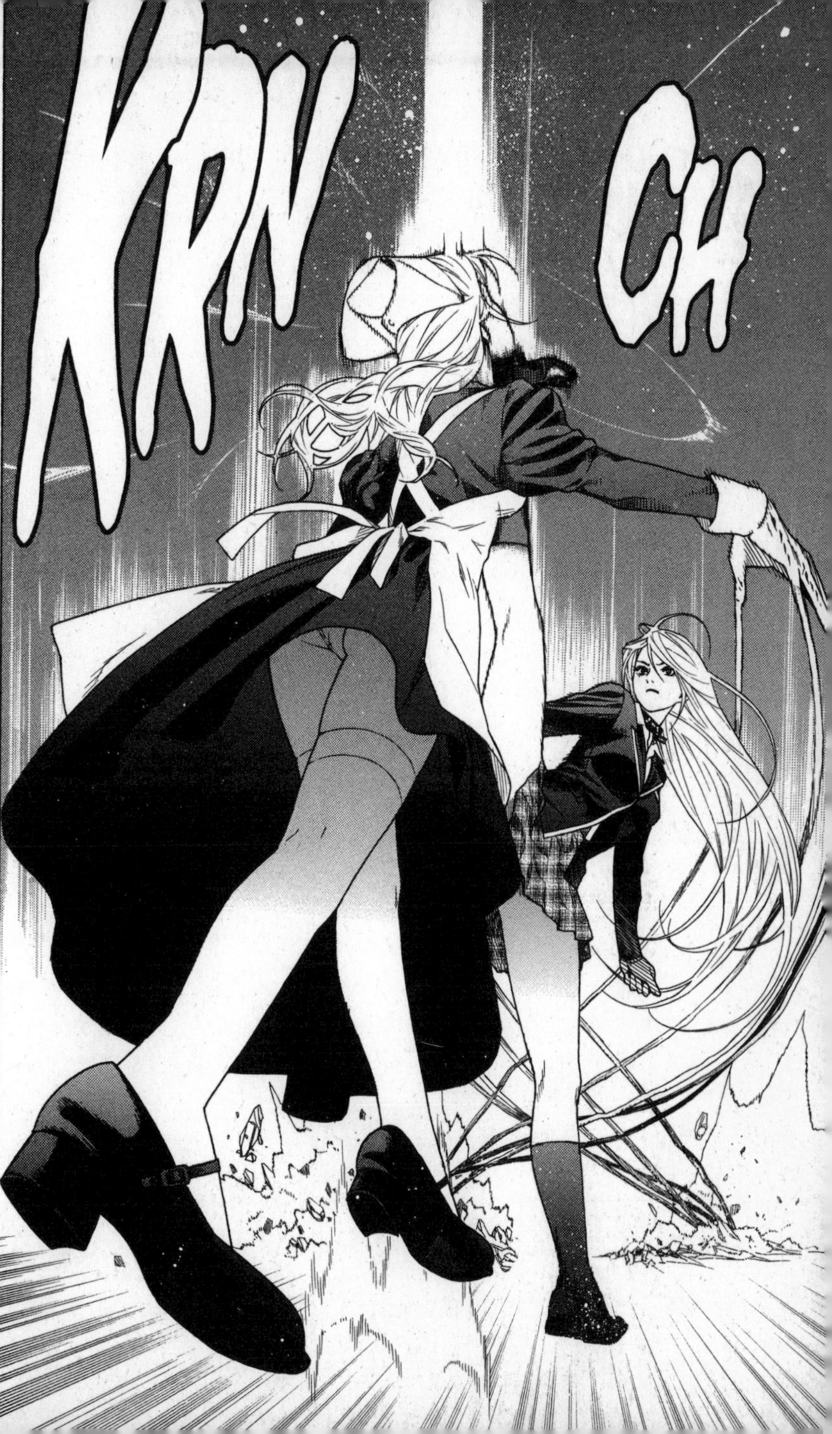
KRN
CH

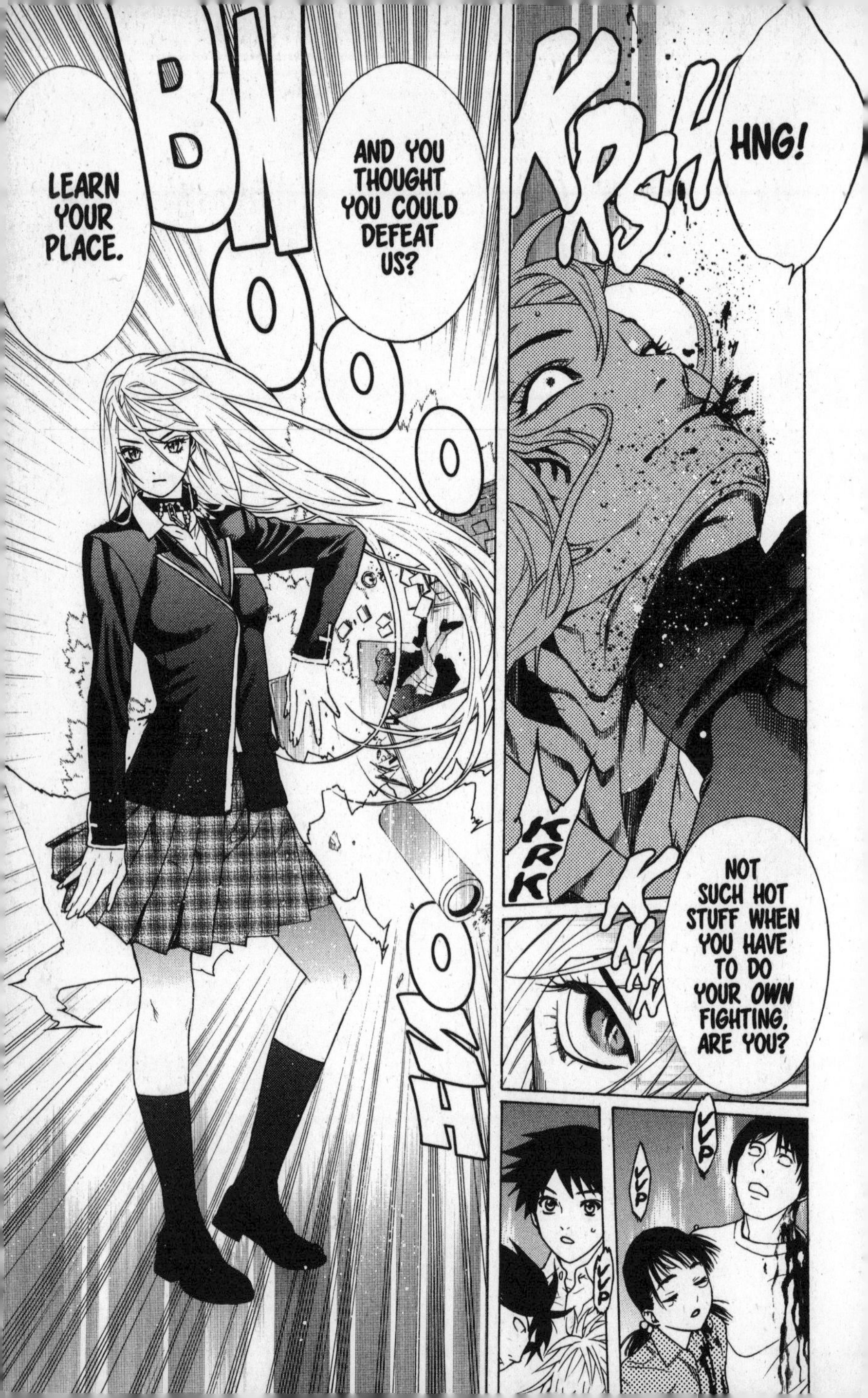
KRSH
HNG!
KRK
NNN
NOT SUCH HOT STUFF WHEN YOU HAVE TO DO YOUR OWN FIGHTING, ARE YOU?
VVP
VVP
VVP
BWOOOOOOSH
AND YOU THOUGHT YOU COULD DEFEAT US?
LEARN YOUR PLACE.

ROSARIO+VAMPIRE

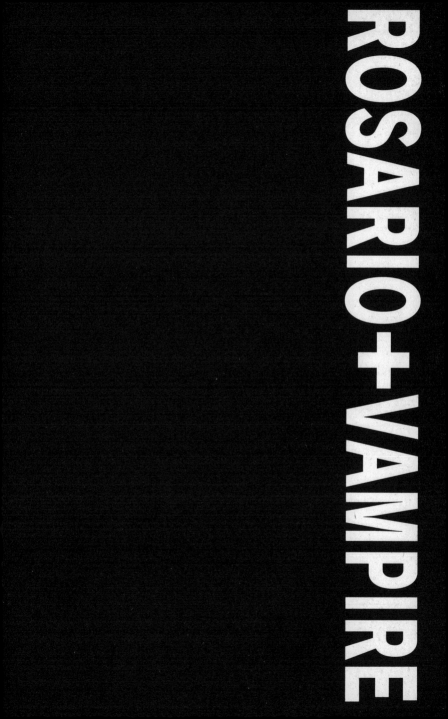

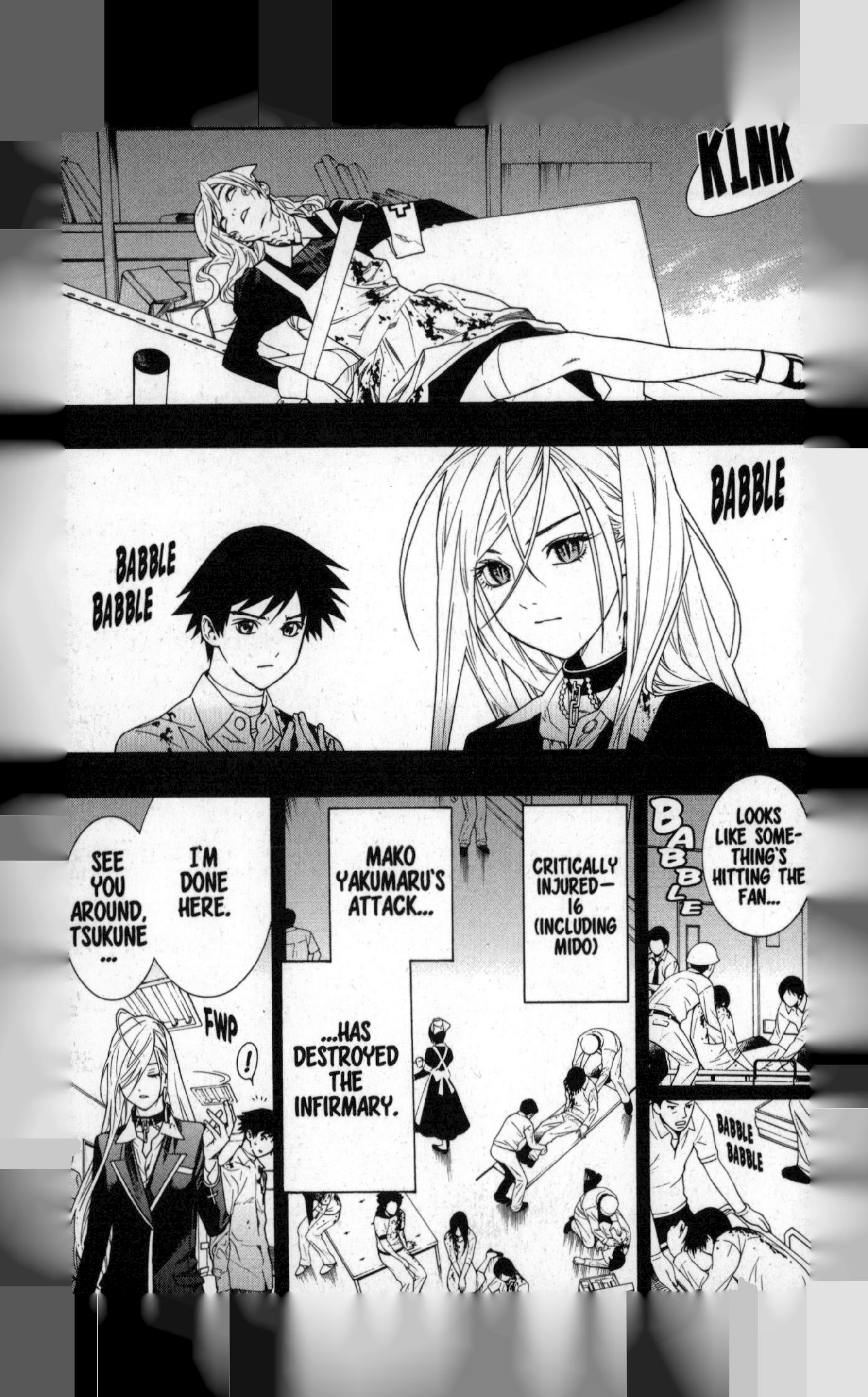
KLNK
BABBLE
BABBLE BABBLE
LOOKS LIKE SOME-THING'S HITTING THE FAN...
BABBLE
BABBLE BABBLE
CRITICALLY INJURED—16 (INCLUDING MIDO)
MAKO YAKUMARU'S ATTACK...
...HAS DESTROYED THE INFIRMARY.
I'M DONE HERE.
SEE YOU AROUND, TSUKUNE...
FWP
!

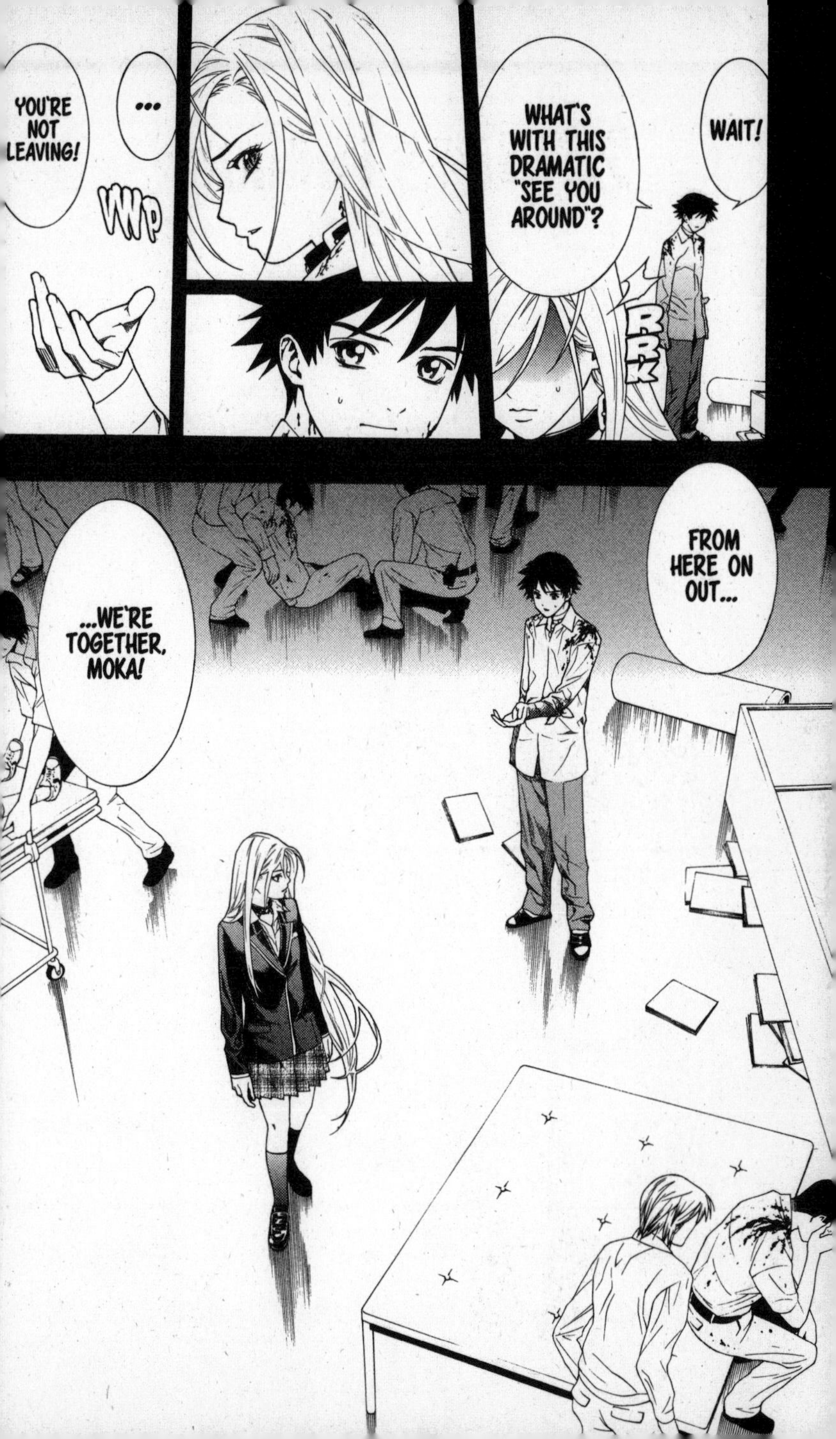
WAIT!
RRK
WHAT'S WITH THIS DRAMATIC "SEE YOU AROUND"?
...
YOU'RE NOT LEAVING!
VWP
FROM HERE ON OUT...
...WE'RE TOGETHER, MOKA!

# 26: True Feelings

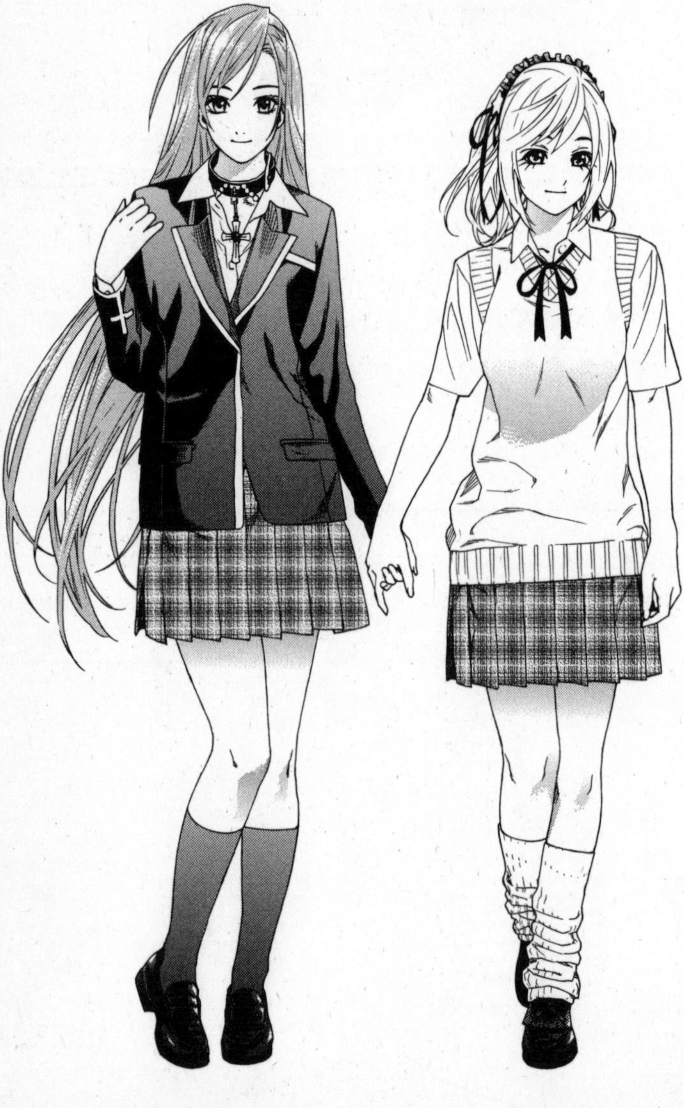

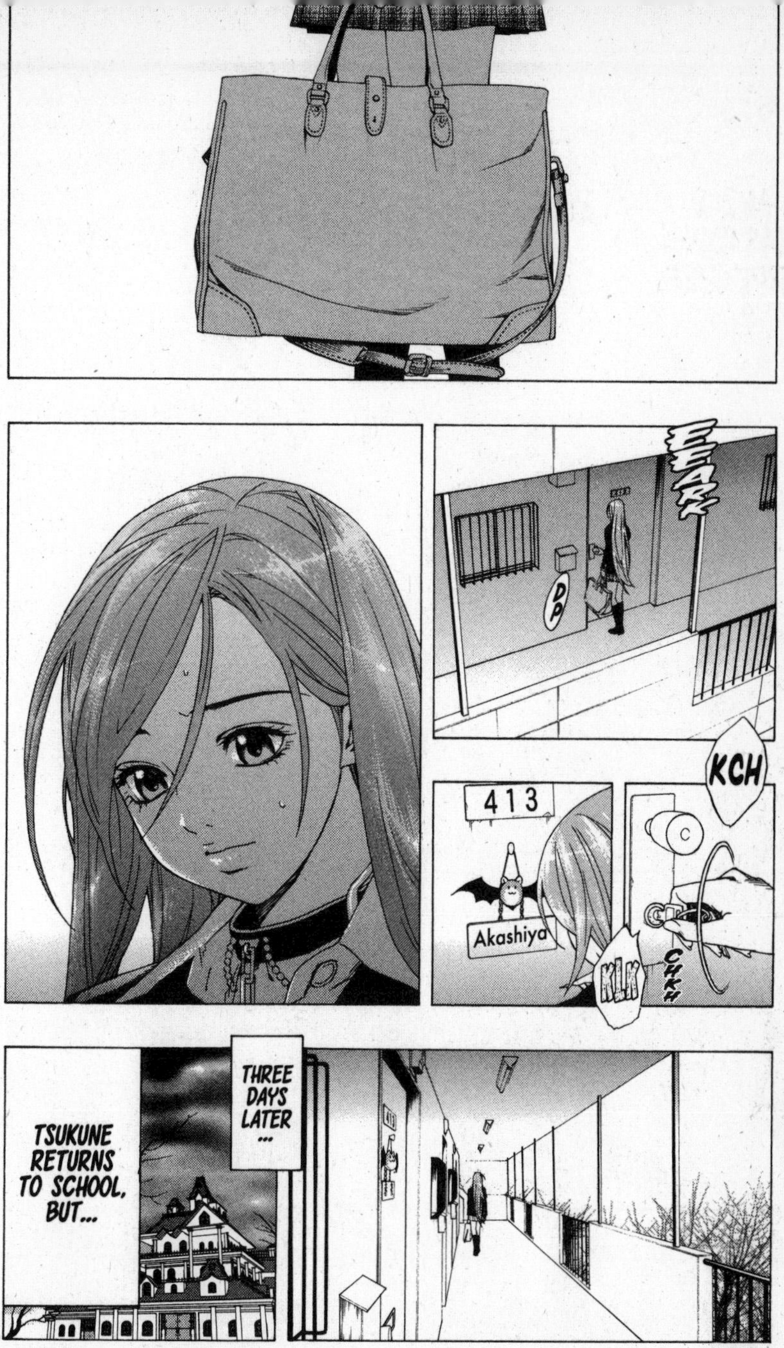
EEARK
DP
KCH
KLIK
CHKH
413
Akashiya
THREE DAYS LATER...
TSUKUNE RETURNS TO SCHOOL, BUT...

READ THIS WAY

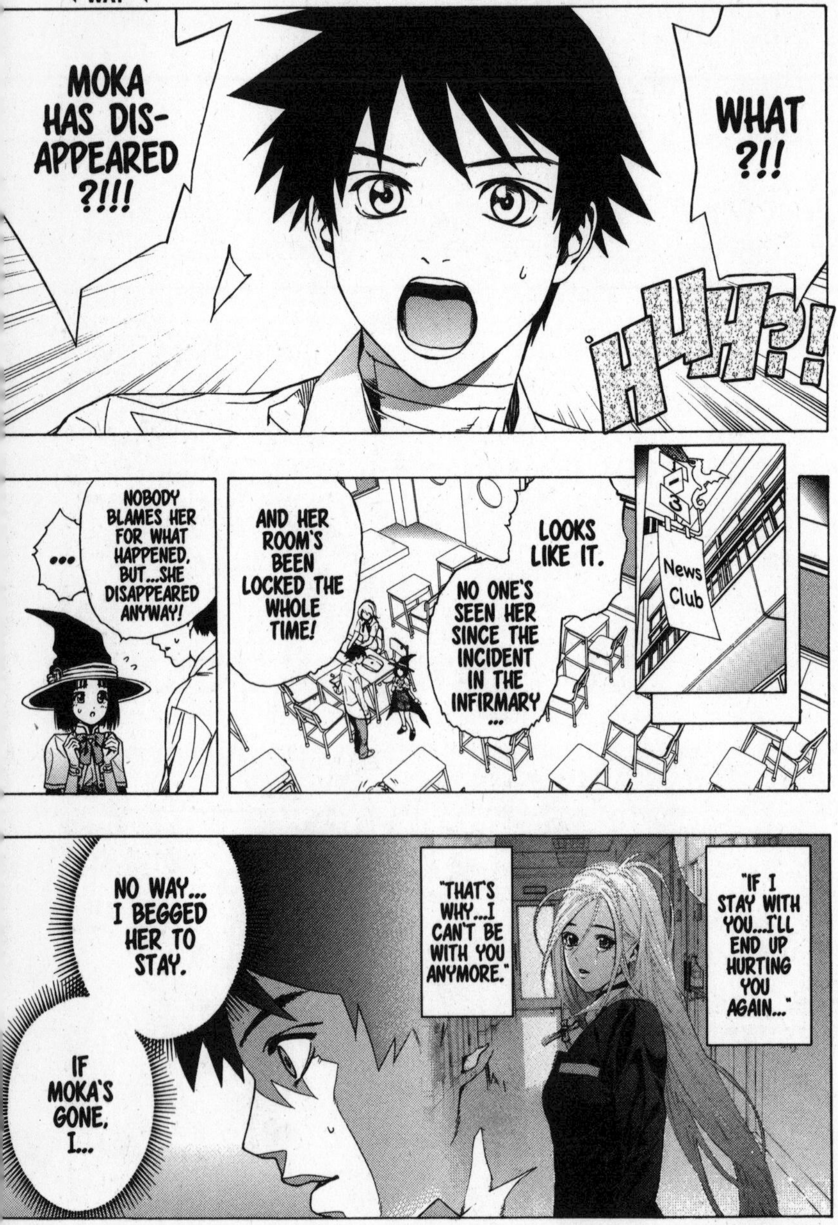

WHAT ?!!
MOKA HAS DIS-APPEARED ?!!!
HUH?!
1-3
News Club
LOOKS LIKE IT.
NO ONE'S SEEN HER SINCE THE INCIDENT IN THE INFIRMARY...
AND HER ROOM'S BEEN LOCKED THE WHOLE TIME!
NOBODY BLAMES HER FOR WHAT HAPPENED, BUT...SHE DISAPPEARED ANYWAY!
...
"IF I STAY WITH YOU...I'LL END UP HURTING YOU AGAIN..."
"THAT'S WHY...I CAN'T BE WITH YOU ANYMORE."
NO WAY... I BEGGED HER TO STAY.
IF MOKA'S GONE, I...

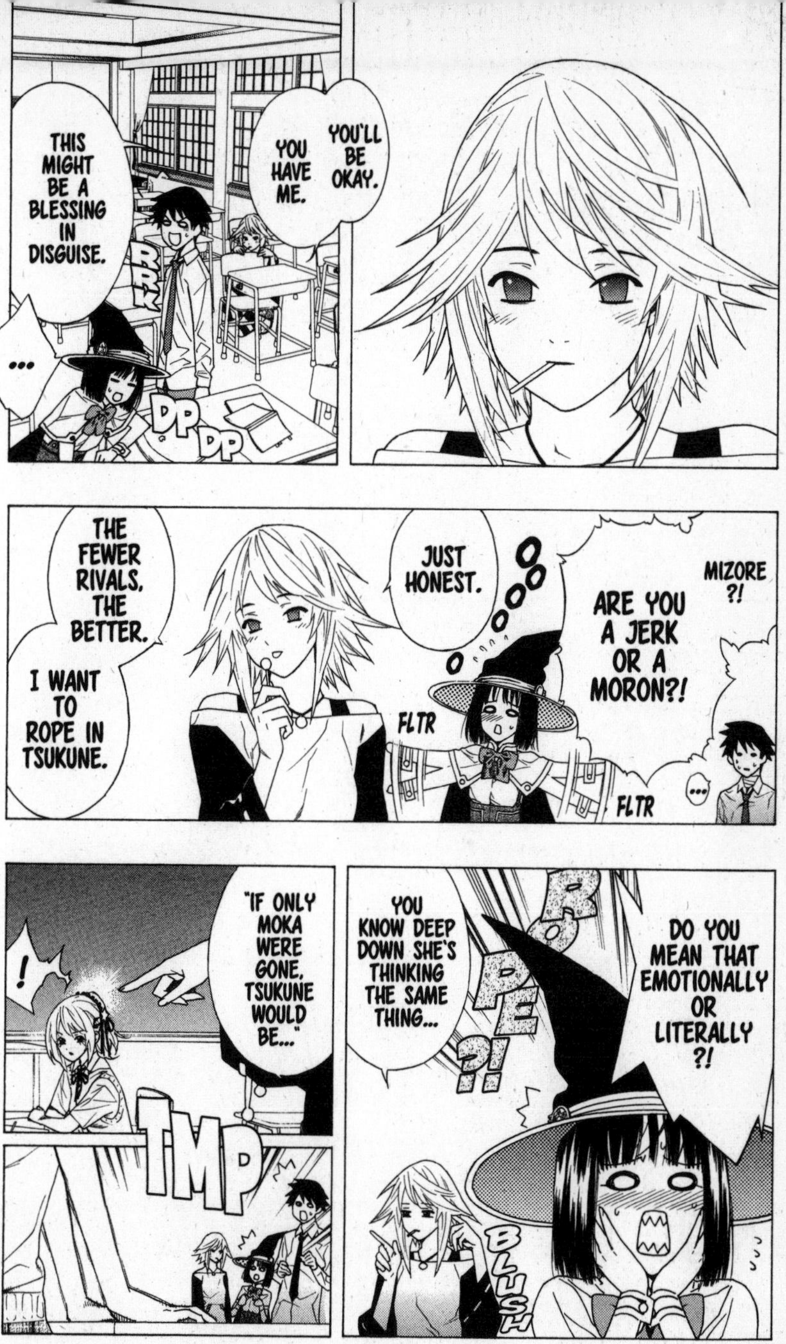
YOU'LL BE OKAY.
YOU HAVE ME.
THIS MIGHT BE A BLESSING IN DISGUISE.
RRK
...
DP DP
MIZORE?!
ARE YOU A JERK OR A MORON?!
...
FLTR FLTR
JUST HONEST.
THE FEWER RIVALS, THE BETTER.
I WANT TO ROPE IN TSUKUNE.
DO YOU MEAN THAT EMOTIONALLY OR LITERALLY?!
ROPE?!
YOU KNOW DEEP DOWN SHE'S THINKING THE SAME THING...
BLUSH
"IF ONLY MOKA WERE GONE, TSUKUNE WOULD BE..."
!
TMP

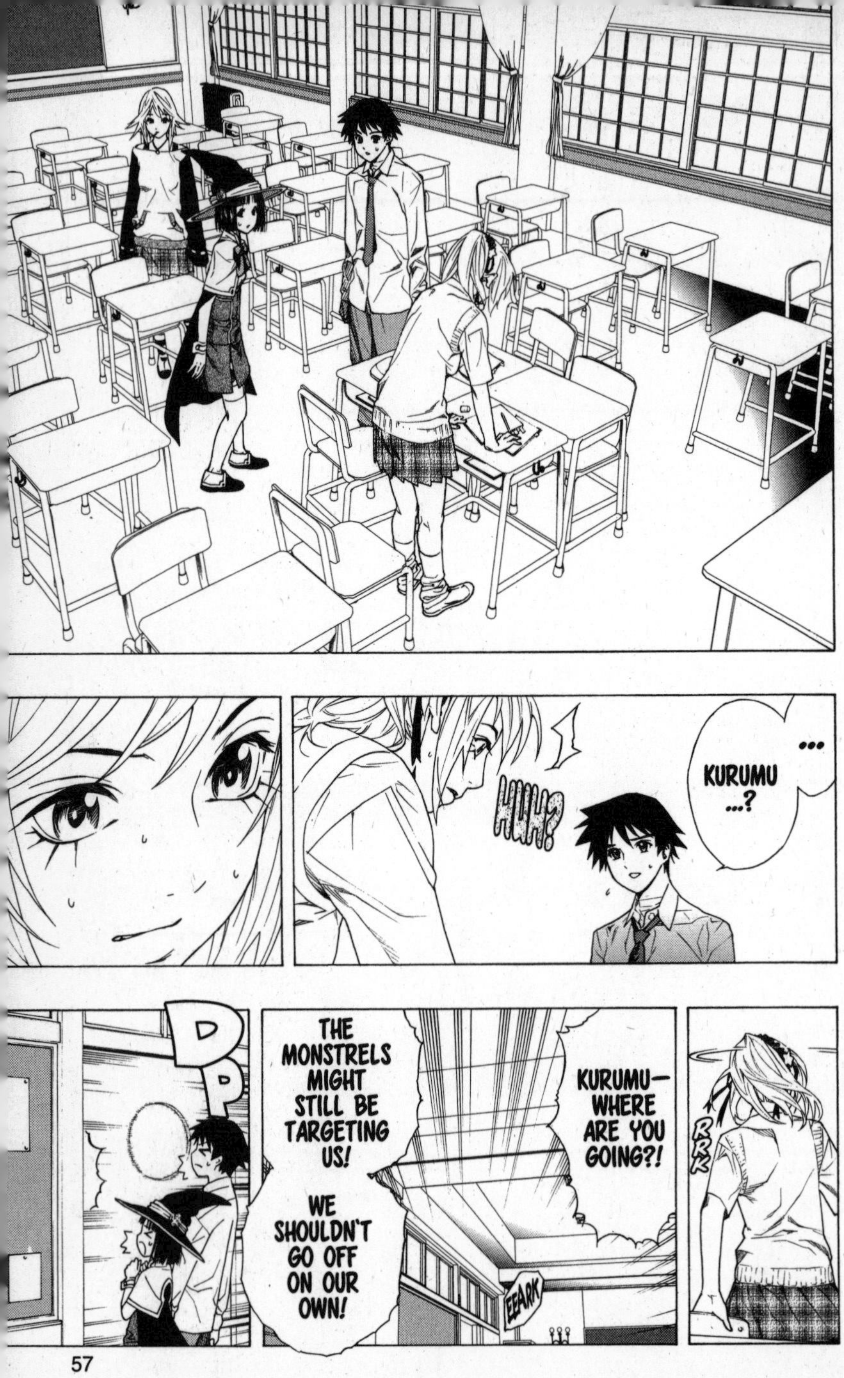
... KURUMU ...?
HUH?
RRK
KURUMU— WHERE ARE YOU GOING?!
EEARK
THE MONSTRELS MIGHT STILL BE TARGETING US!
WE SHOULDN'T GO OFF ON OUR OWN!
DP

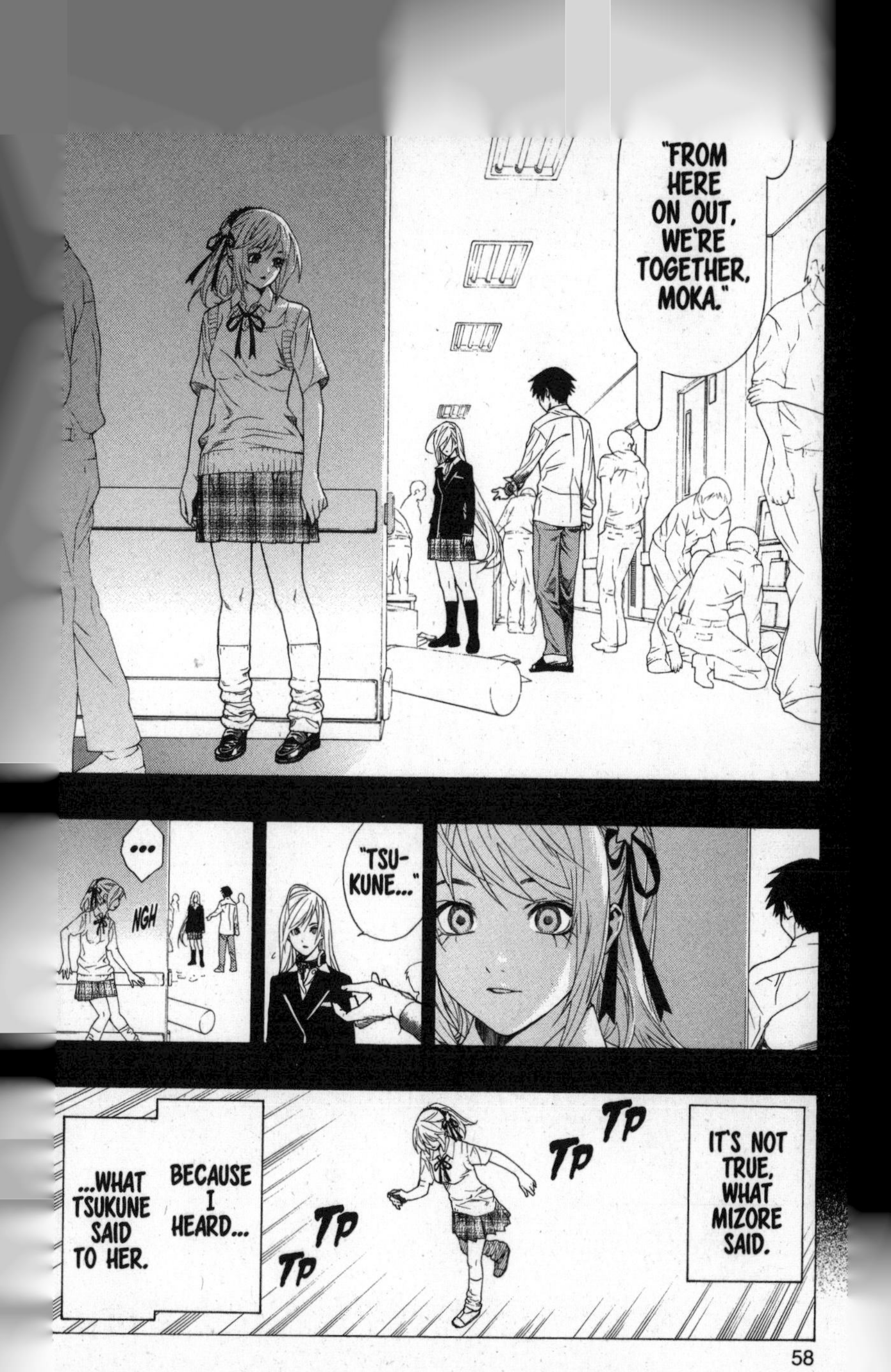
"FROM HERE ON OUT, WE'RE TOGETHER, MOKA."
"TSU-KUNE..."
...
NGH
IT'S NOT TRUE, WHAT MIZORE SAID.
Tp Tp
BECAUSE I HEARD...
...WHAT TSUKUNE SAID TO HER.
Tp Tp

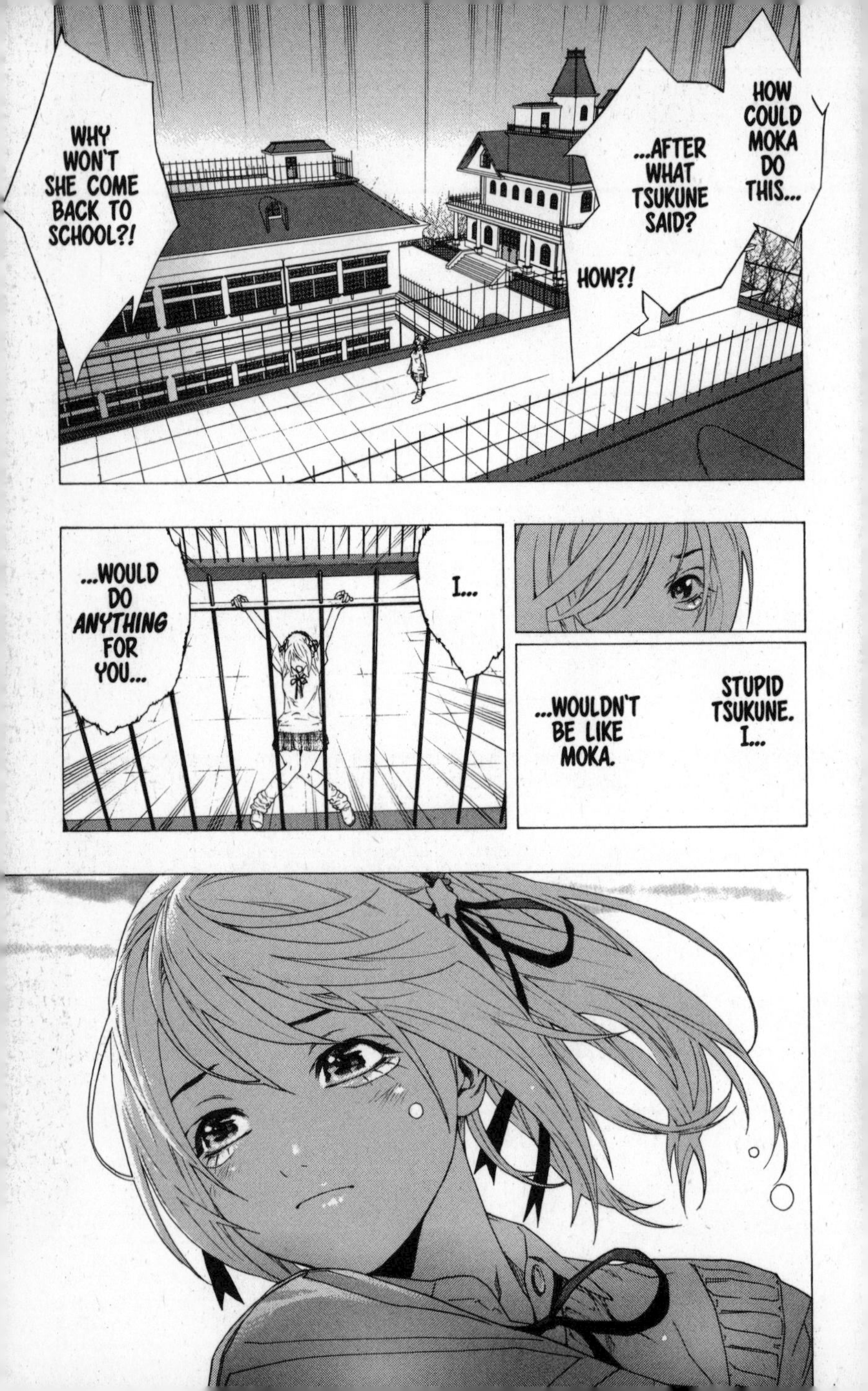
HOW COULD MOKA DO THIS...
...AFTER WHAT TSUKUNE SAID?
HOW?!
WHY WON'T SHE COME BACK TO SCHOOL?!
STUPID TSUKUNE. I...
...WOULDN'T BE LIKE MOKA.
I...
...WOULD DO *ANYTHING* FOR YOU...

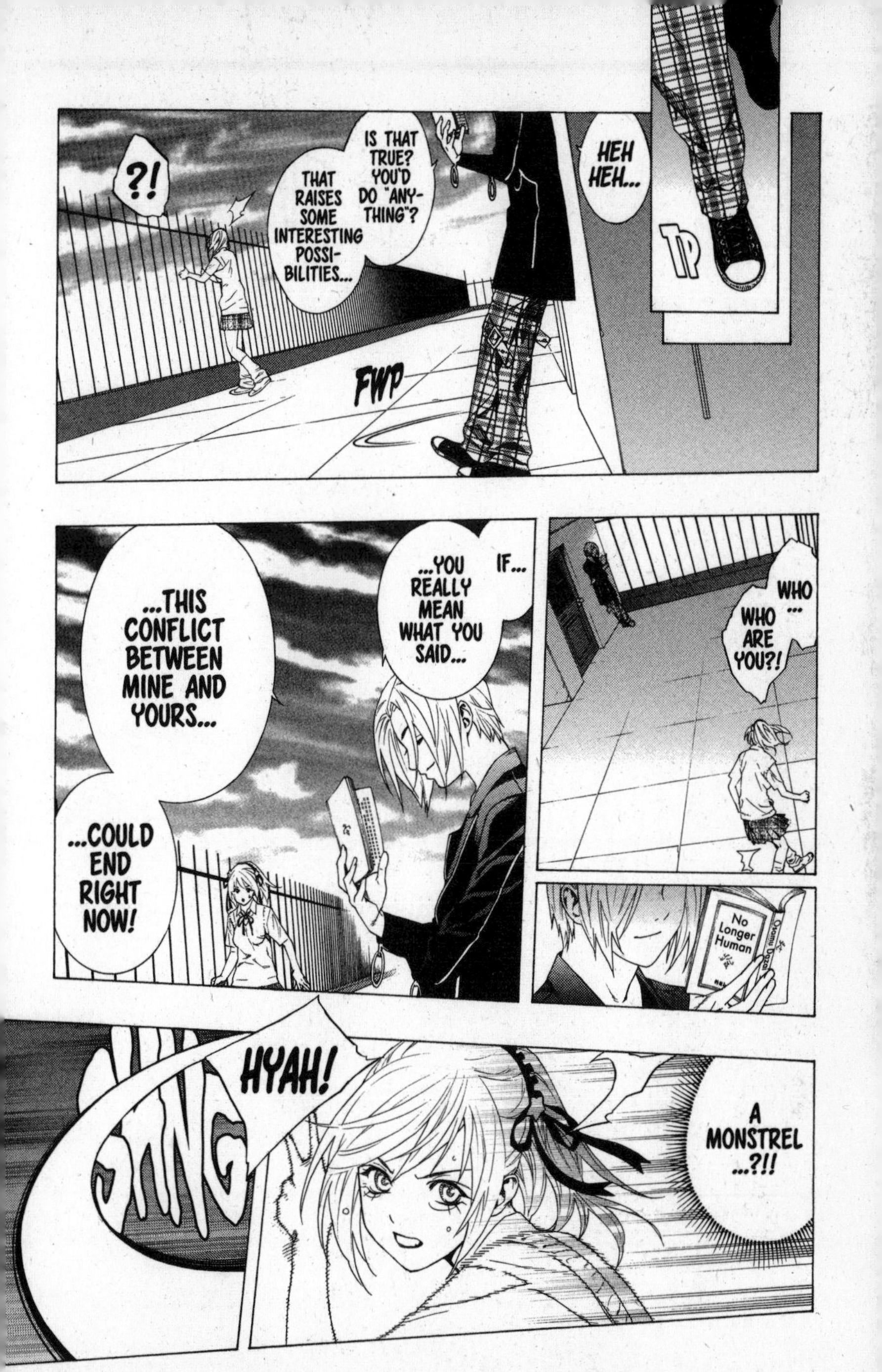
TP
HEH HEH...
IS THAT TRUE? YOU'D DO "ANY-THING"?
THAT RAISES SOME INTERESTING POSSI-BILITIES...
?!
FWP
WHO... WHO ARE YOU?!
No Longer Human
Osamu Dazai
IF...
...YOU REALLY MEAN WHAT YOU SAID...
...THIS CONFLICT BETWEEN MINE AND YOURS...
...COULD END RIGHT NOW!
A MONSTREL ...?!!
HYAH!

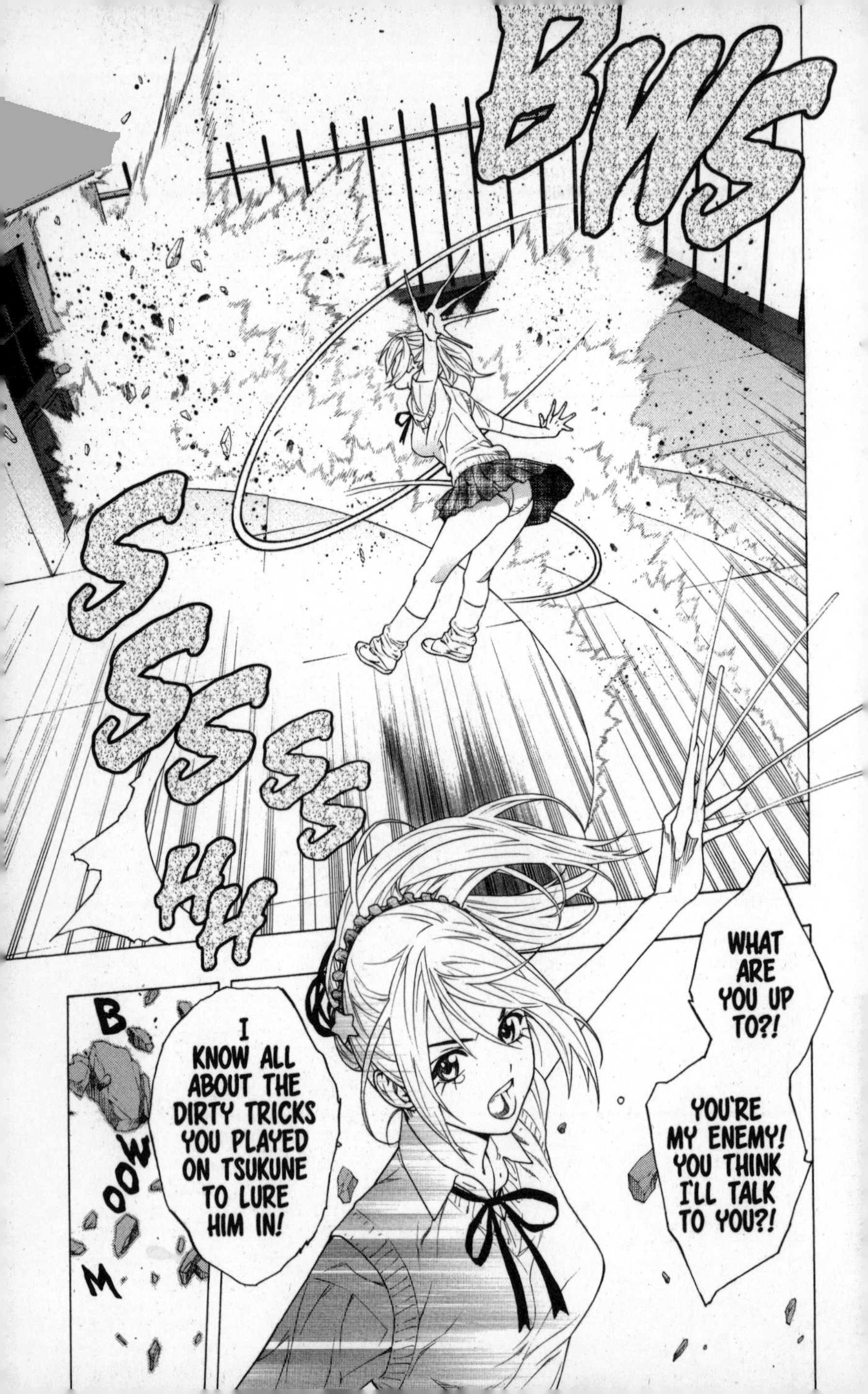
BWS
SSSSSHH
WHAT ARE YOU UP TO?!
YOU'RE MY ENEMY! YOU THINK I'LL TALK TO YOU?!
I KNOW ALL ABOUT THE DIRTY TRICKS YOU PLAYED ON TSUKUNE TO LURE HIM IN!
BWOOM

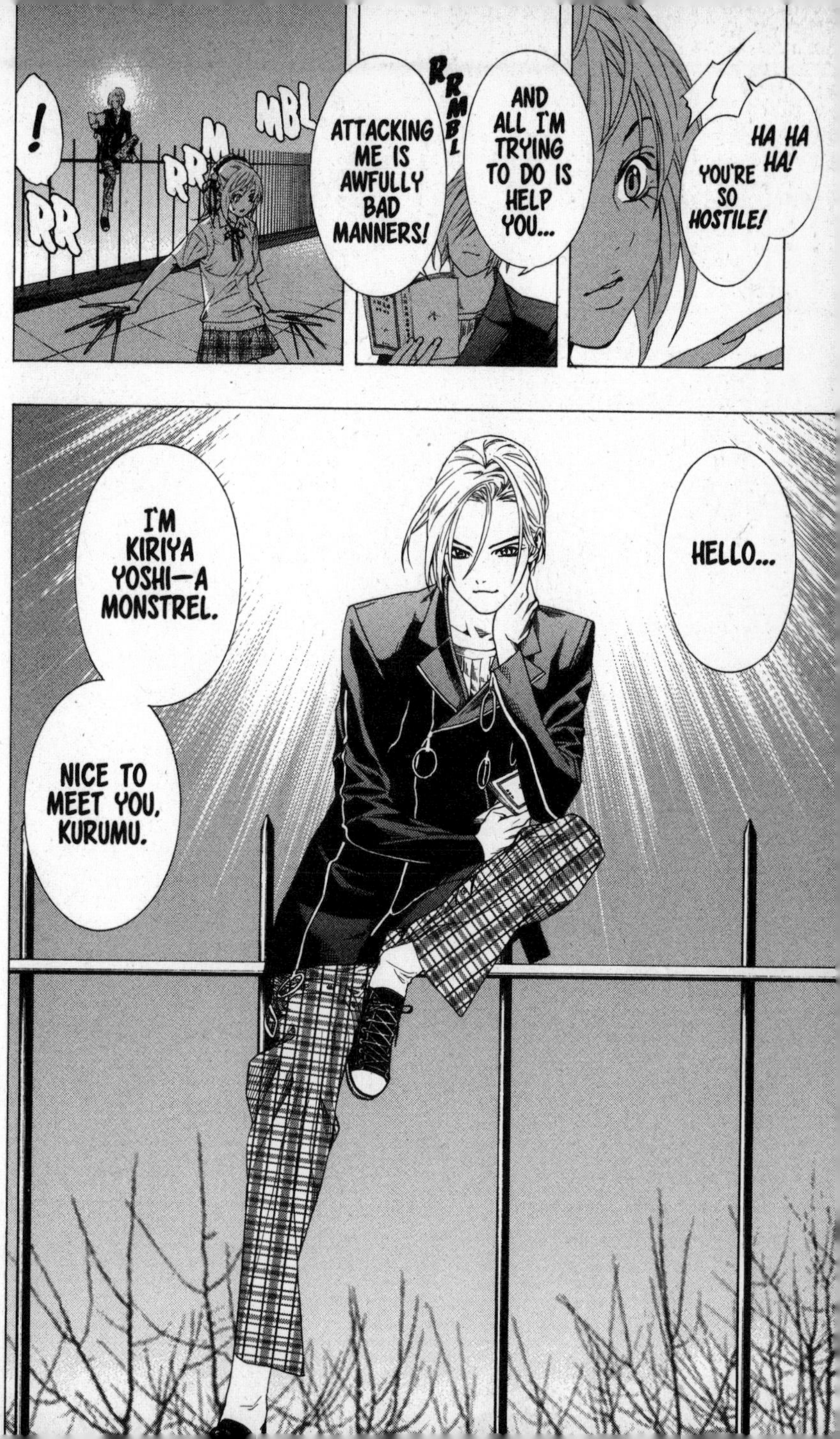
HA HA HA! YOU'RE SO HOSTILE!
AND ALL I'M TRYING TO DO IS HELP YOU...
RRMBL
ATTACKING ME IS AWFULLY BAD MANNERS!
!
RR RRM MBL
HELLO...
I'M KIRIYA YOSHI—A MONSTREL.
NICE TO MEET YOU, KURUMU.

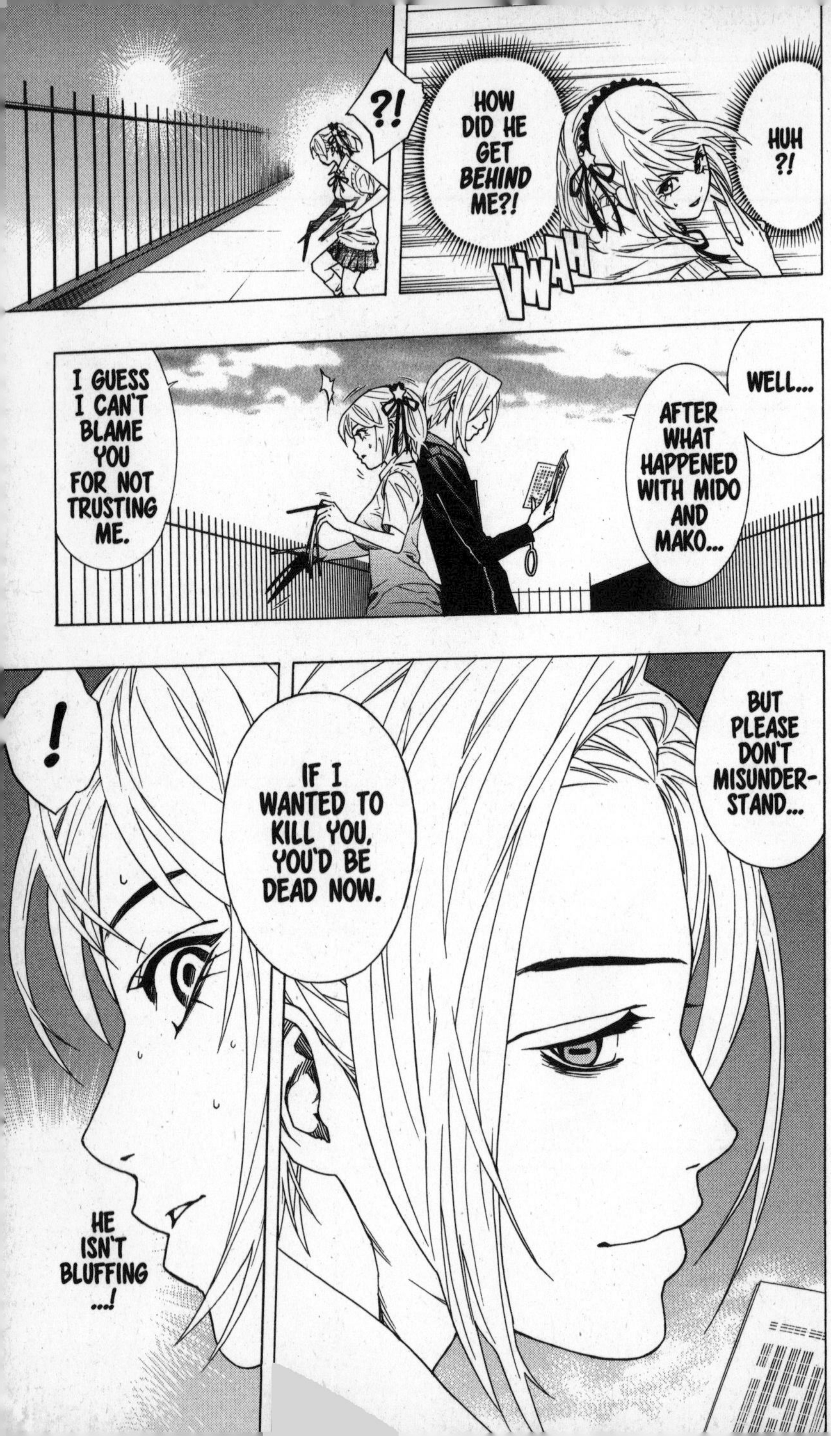
HUH ?!
HOW DID HE GET BEHIND ME?!
VWAH
?!
WELL...
AFTER WHAT HAPPENED WITH MIDO AND MAKO...
I GUESS I CAN'T BLAME YOU FOR NOT TRUSTING ME.
BUT PLEASE DON'T MISUNDERSTAND...
IF I WANTED TO KILL YOU, YOU'D BE DEAD NOW.
!
HE ISN'T BLUFFING ...!

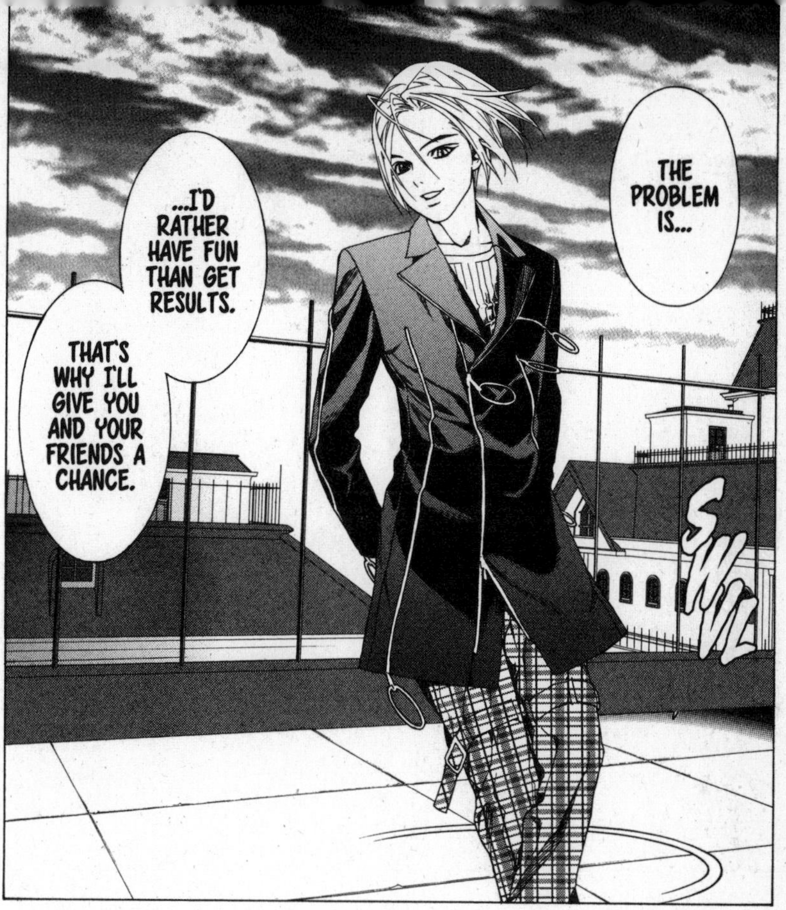
THE PROBLEM IS...
...I'D RATHER HAVE FUN THAN GET RESULTS.
THAT'S WHY I'LL GIVE YOU AND YOUR FRIENDS A CHANCE.
SWVL
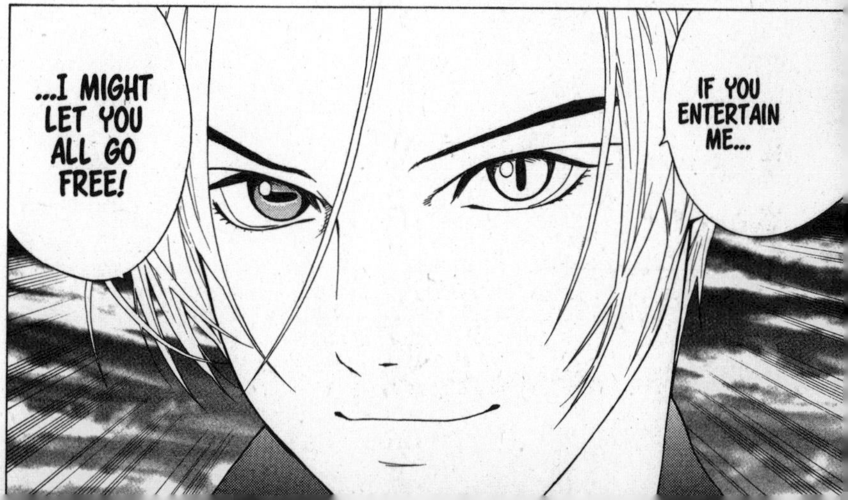
IF YOU ENTERTAIN ME...
...I MIGHT LET YOU ALL GO FREE!

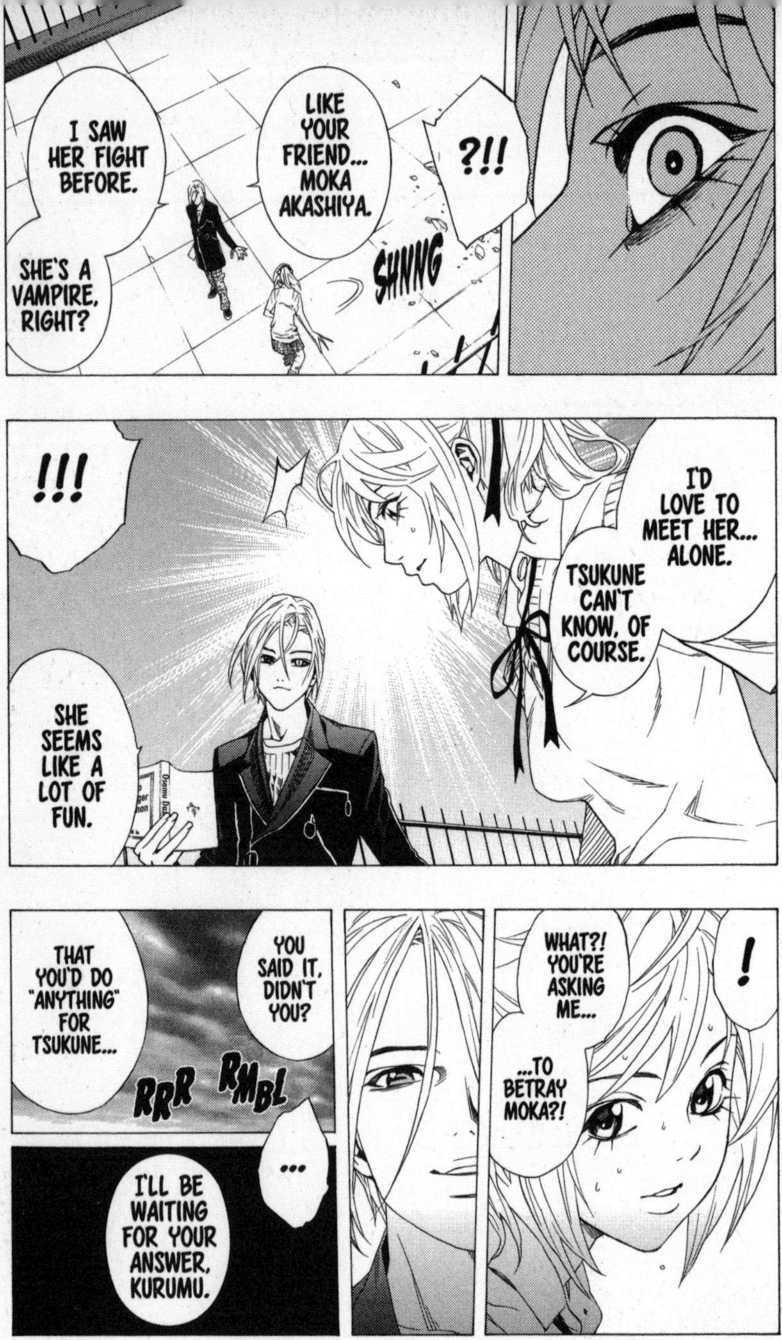
?!!
LIKE YOUR FRIEND... MOKA AKASHIYA.
SHNNG
I SAW HER FIGHT BEFORE.
SHE'S A VAMPIRE, RIGHT?
I'D LOVE TO MEET HER... ALONE.
TSUKUNE CAN'T KNOW, OF COURSE.
!!!
SHE SEEMS LIKE A LOT OF FUN.
!
WHAT?! YOU'RE ASKING ME...
...TO BETRAY MOKA?!
YOU SAID IT, DIDN'T YOU?
THAT YOU'D DO "ANYTHING" FOR TSUKUNE...
RRR RMBL
...
I'LL BE WAITING FOR YOUR ANSWER, KURUMU.

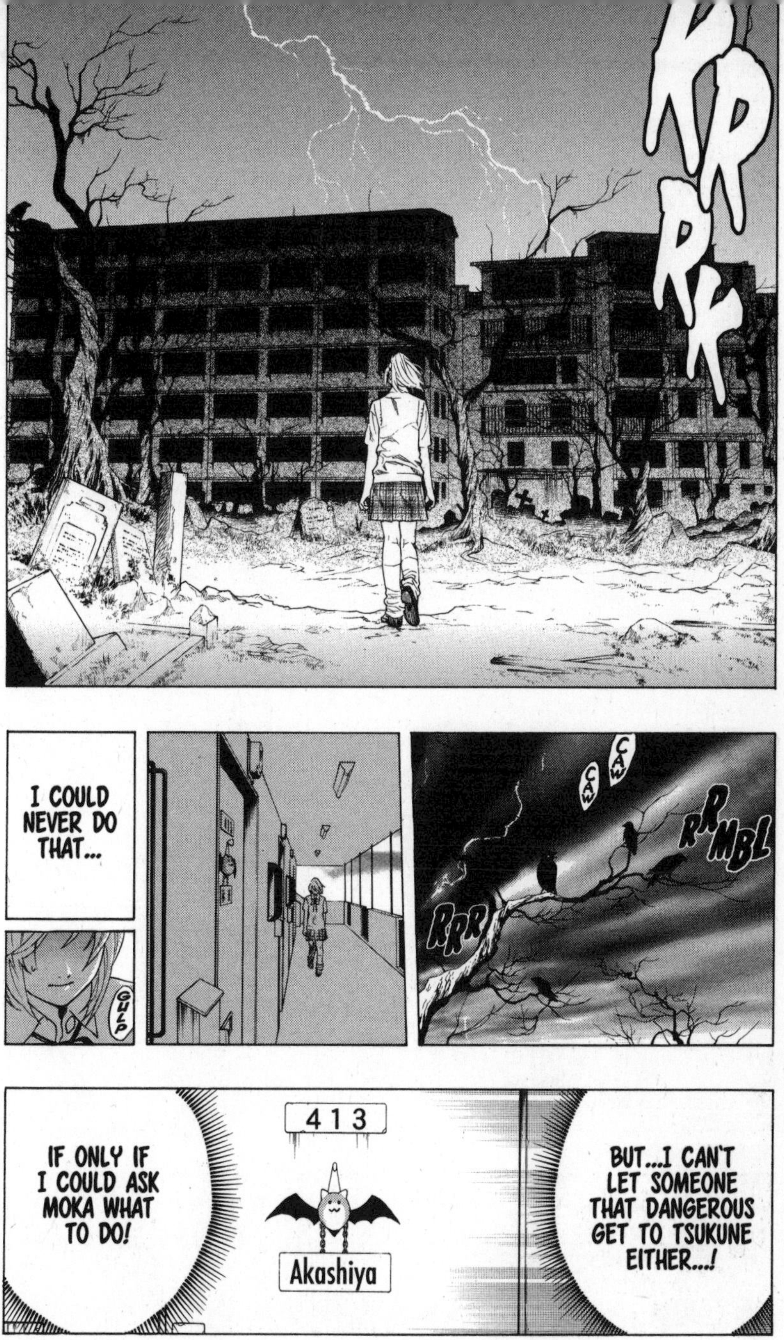
KRRRK
CAW
CAW
RRRMBL
RRR
I COULD NEVER DO THAT...
GULP
BUT...I CAN'T LET SOMEONE THAT DANGEROUS GET TO TSUKUNE EITHER...!
413
Akashiya
IF ONLY IF I COULD ASK MOKA WHAT TO DO!

READ THIS WAY

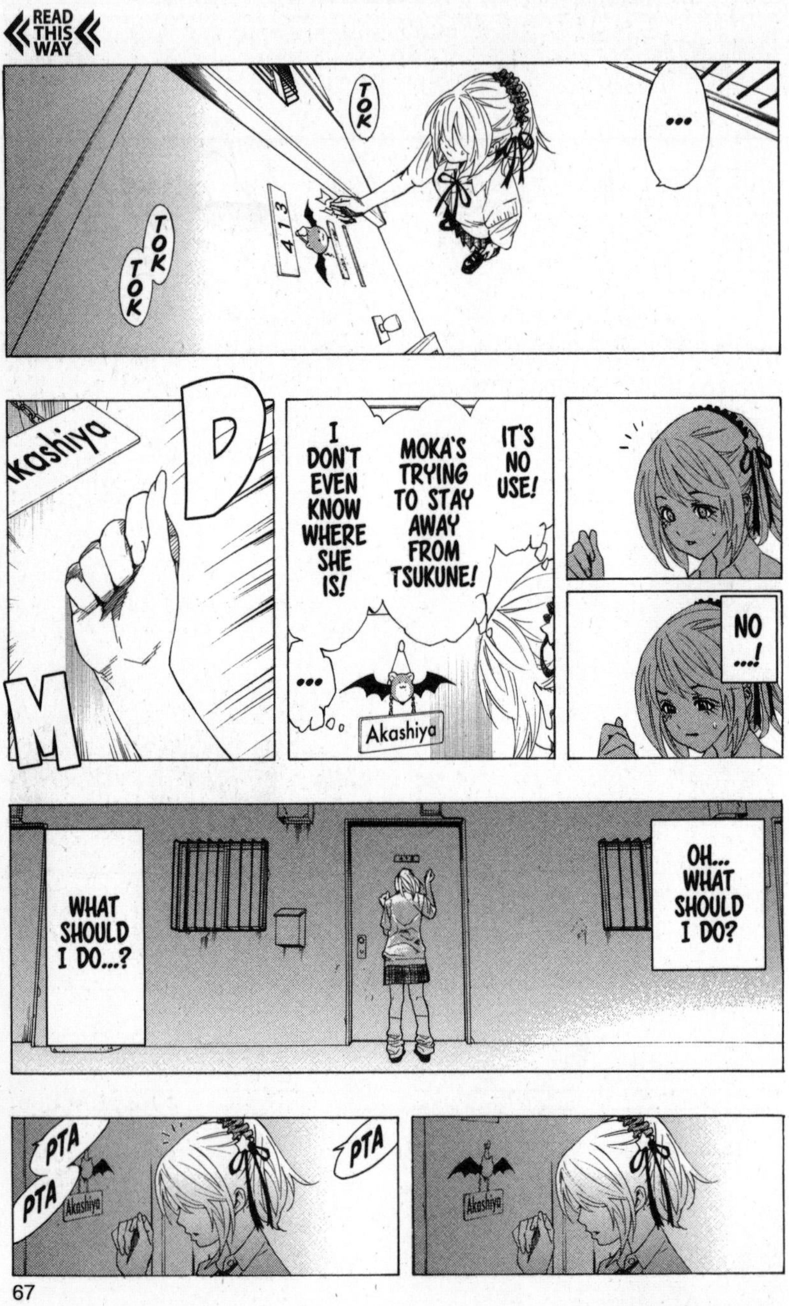

...
TOK
TOK TOK
413
NO ...!
IT'S NO USE!
MOKA'S TRYING TO STAY AWAY FROM TSUKUNE!
I DON'T EVEN KNOW WHERE SHE IS!
...
Akashiya
Akashiya
D
M
OH... WHAT SHOULD I DO?
WHAT SHOULD I DO...?
Akashiya
PTA
PTA
PTA
Akashiya

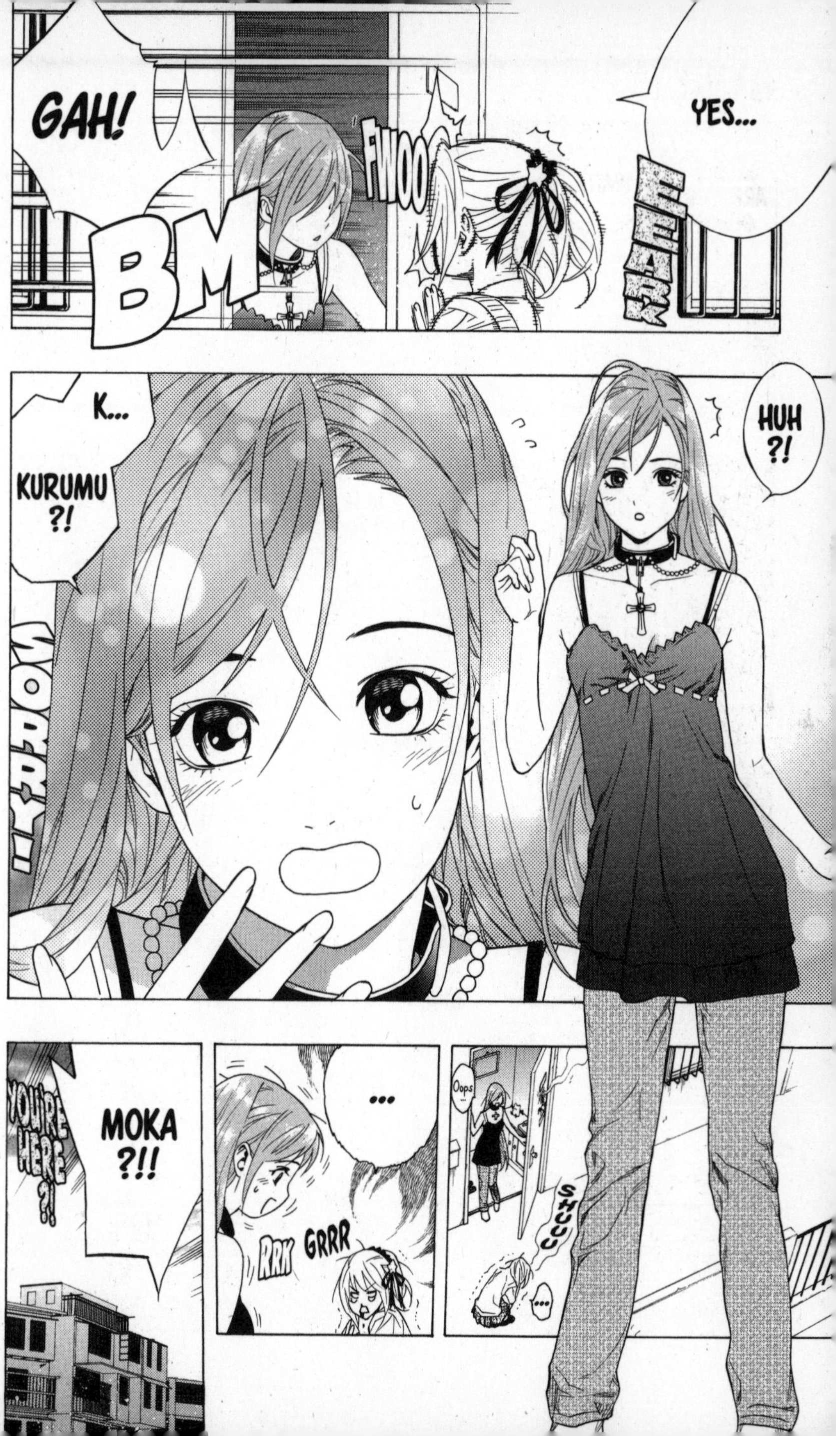
YES...
EEARK
FWOO
GAH!
BM
HUH ?!
K...
KURUMU ?!
SORRY!
Oops...
SHUUU
...
...
RRK
GRRR
MOKA ?!!
YOU'RE HERE ?!

READ THIS WAY

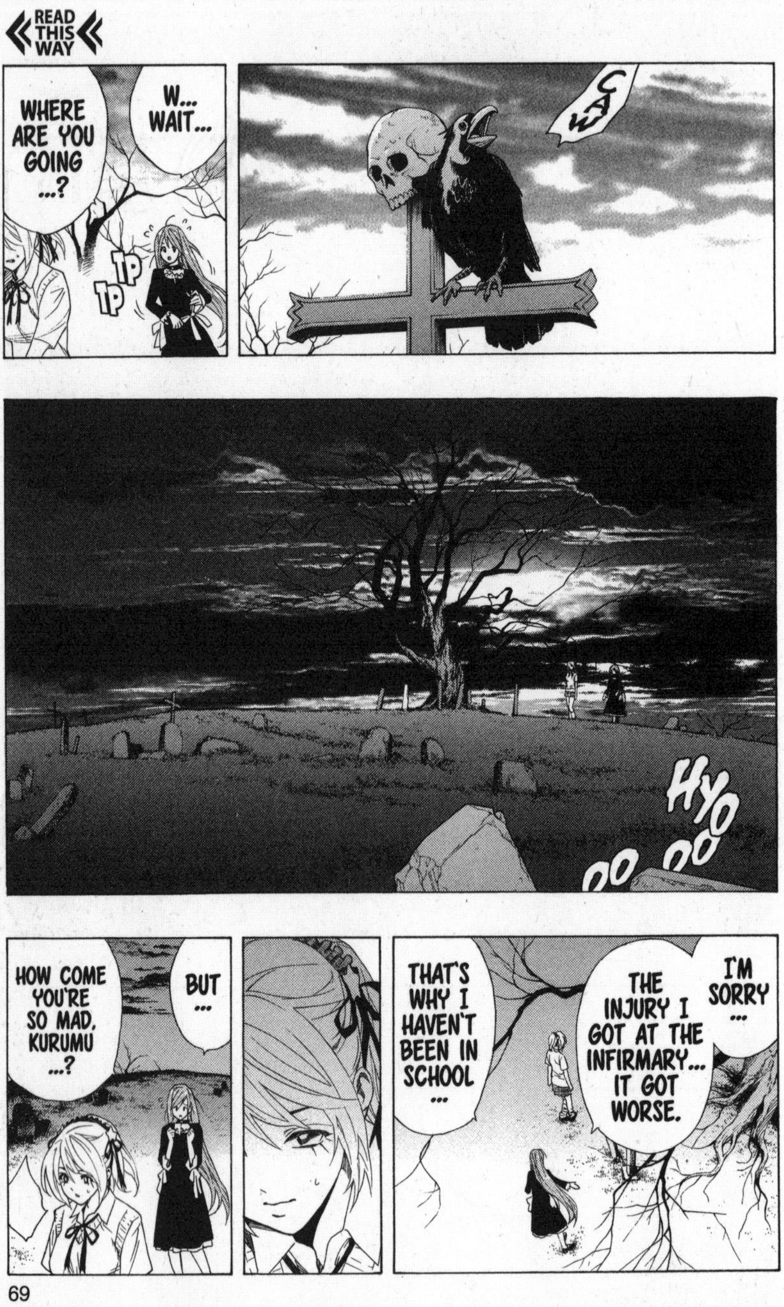
CAW
W... WAIT...
WHERE ARE YOU GOING ...?
TP
TP
HYOO OO OO
I'M SORRY ...
THE INJURY I GOT AT THE INFIRMARY... IT GOT WORSE.
THAT'S WHY I HAVEN'T BEEN IN SCHOOL ...
BUT ...
HOW COME YOU'RE SO MAD, KURUMU ...?

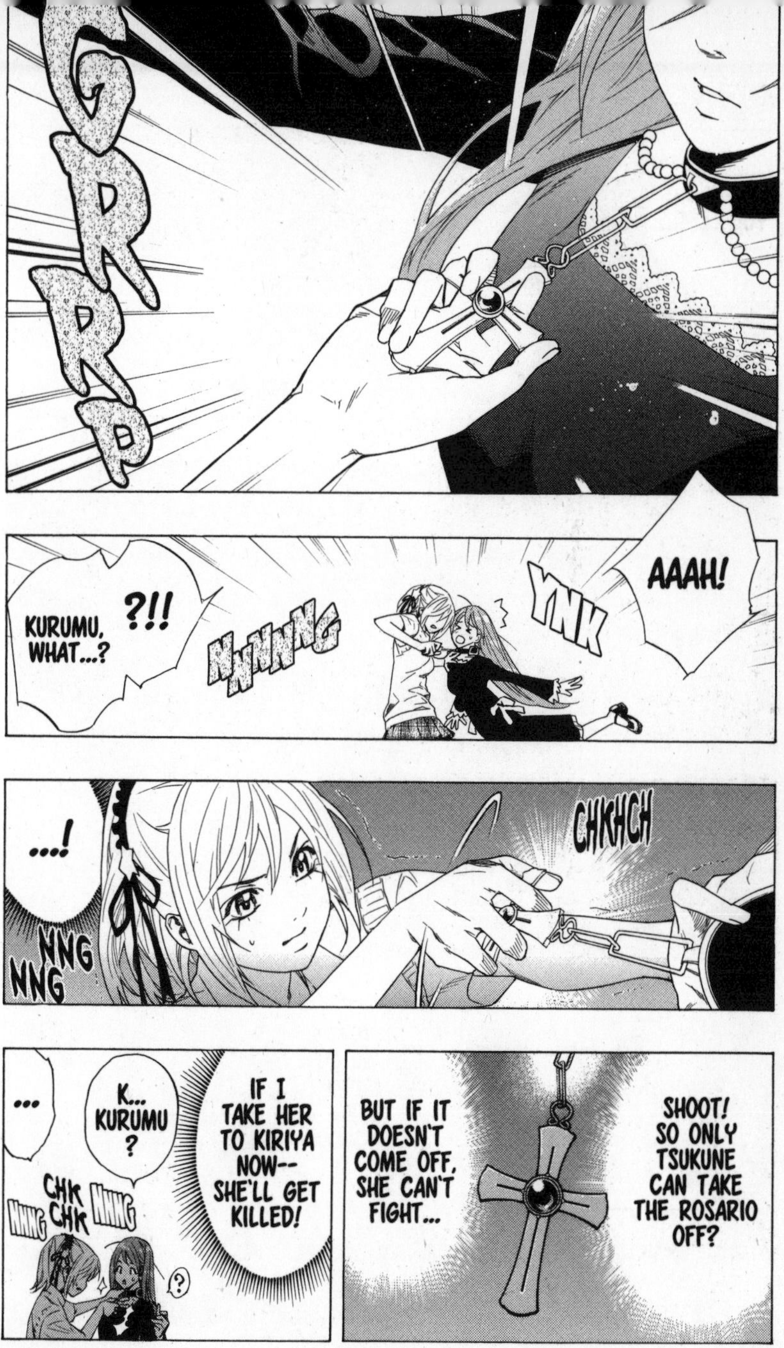
GRRRP
AAAH!
YNK
NNNNNG
?!!
KURUMU, WHAT...?
CHKHCH
...!
NNG NNG
SHOOT! SO ONLY TSUKUNE CAN TAKE THE ROSARIO OFF?
BUT IF IT DOESN'T COME OFF, SHE CAN'T FIGHT...
IF I TAKE HER TO KIRIYA NOW-- SHE'LL GET KILLED!
K... KURUMU?
...
NNNG
CHK CHK
NNNG
?

READ THIS WAY

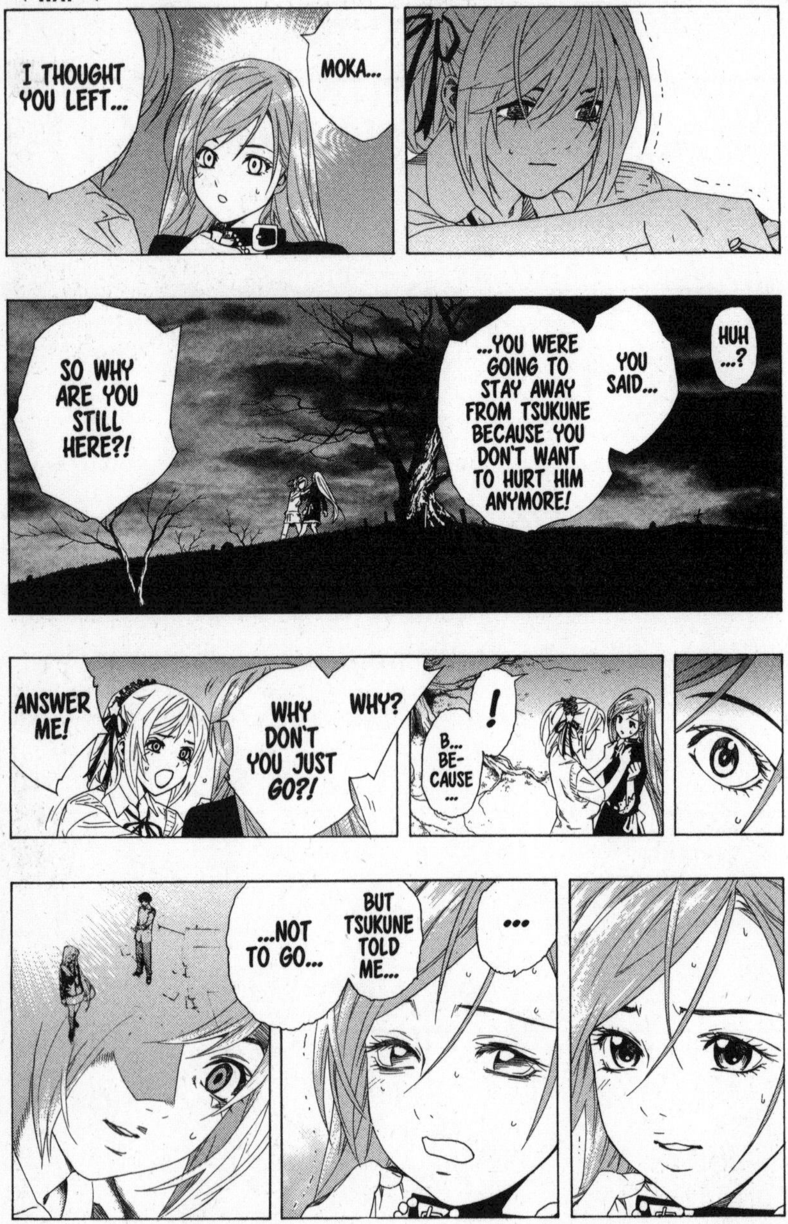

MOKA...
I THOUGHT YOU LEFT...
HUH ...?
YOU SAID...
...YOU WERE GOING TO STAY AWAY FROM TSUKUNE BECAUSE YOU DON'T WANT TO HURT HIM ANYMORE!
SO WHY ARE YOU STILL HERE?!
!
B... BE-CAUSE ...
WHY?
WHY DON'T YOU JUST GO?!
ANSWER ME!
...
BUT TSUKUNE TOLD ME...
...NOT TO GO...

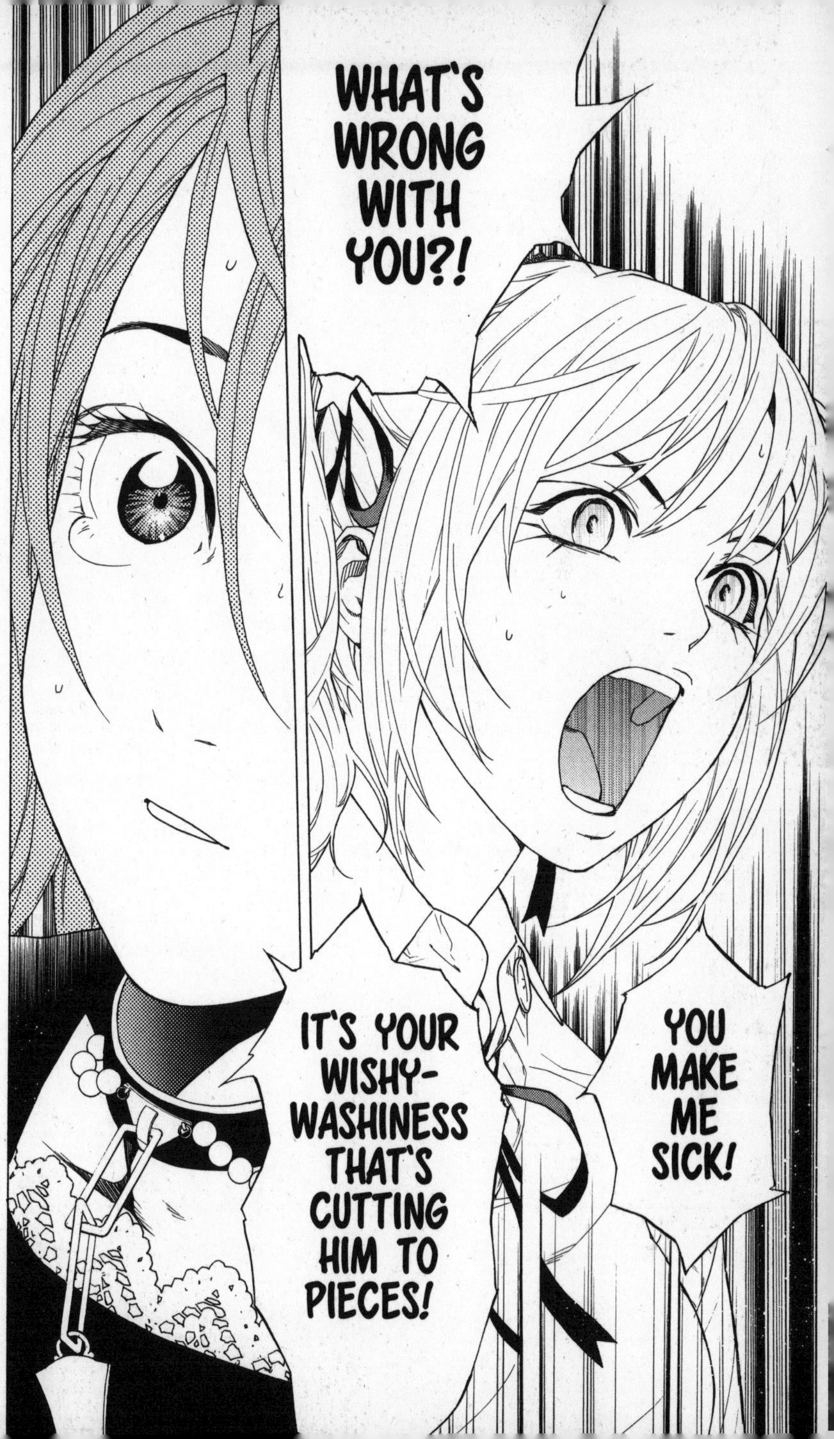
WHAT'S WRONG WITH YOU?!
YOU MAKE ME SICK!
IT'S YOUR WISHY-WASHINESS THAT'S CUTTING HIM TO PIECES!

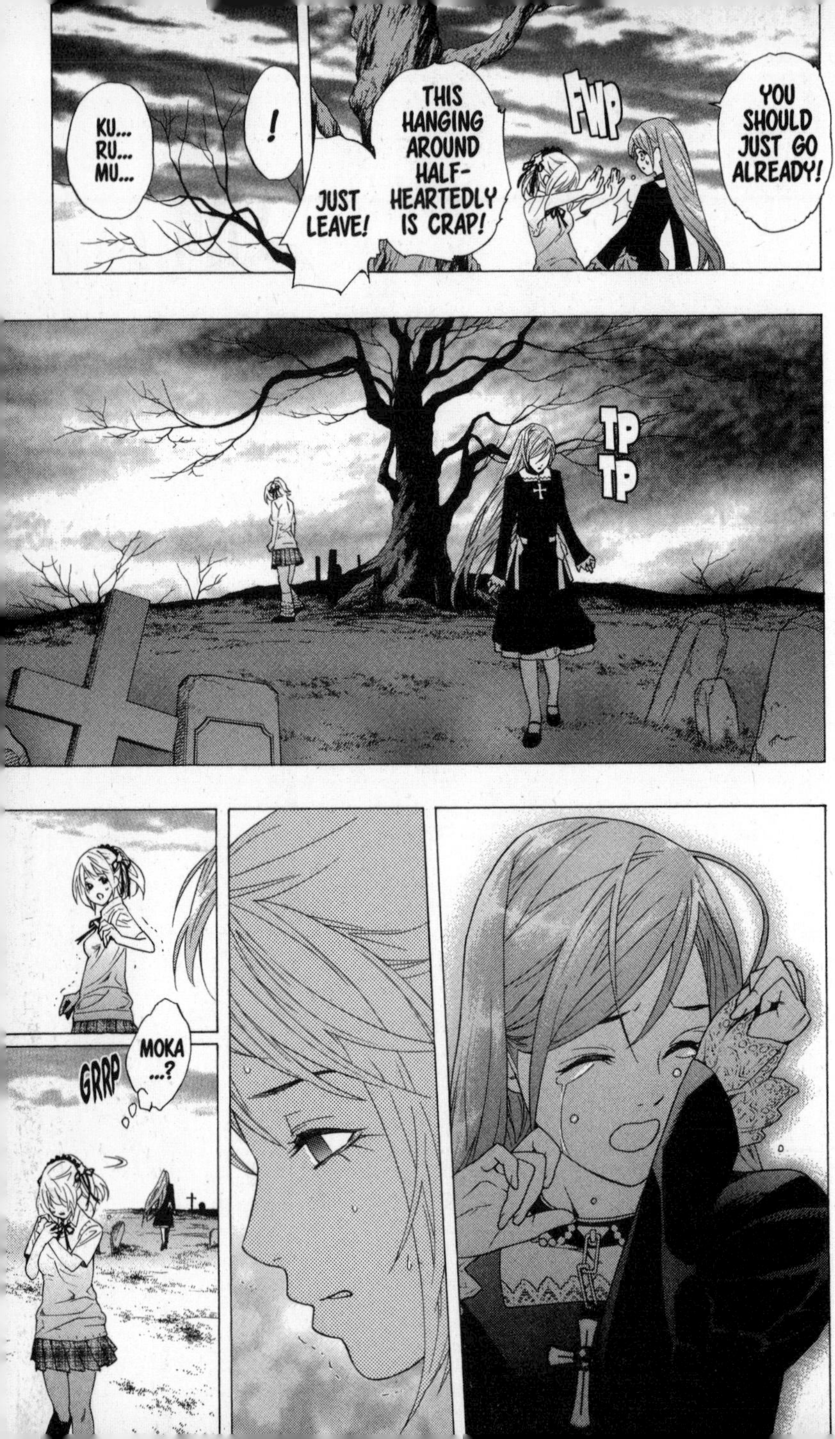
YOU SHOULD JUST GO ALREADY!
FWP
THIS HANGING AROUND HALF-HEARTEDLY IS CRAP!
JUST LEAVE!
!
KU... RU... MU...
TP TP
MOKA ...?
GRRP

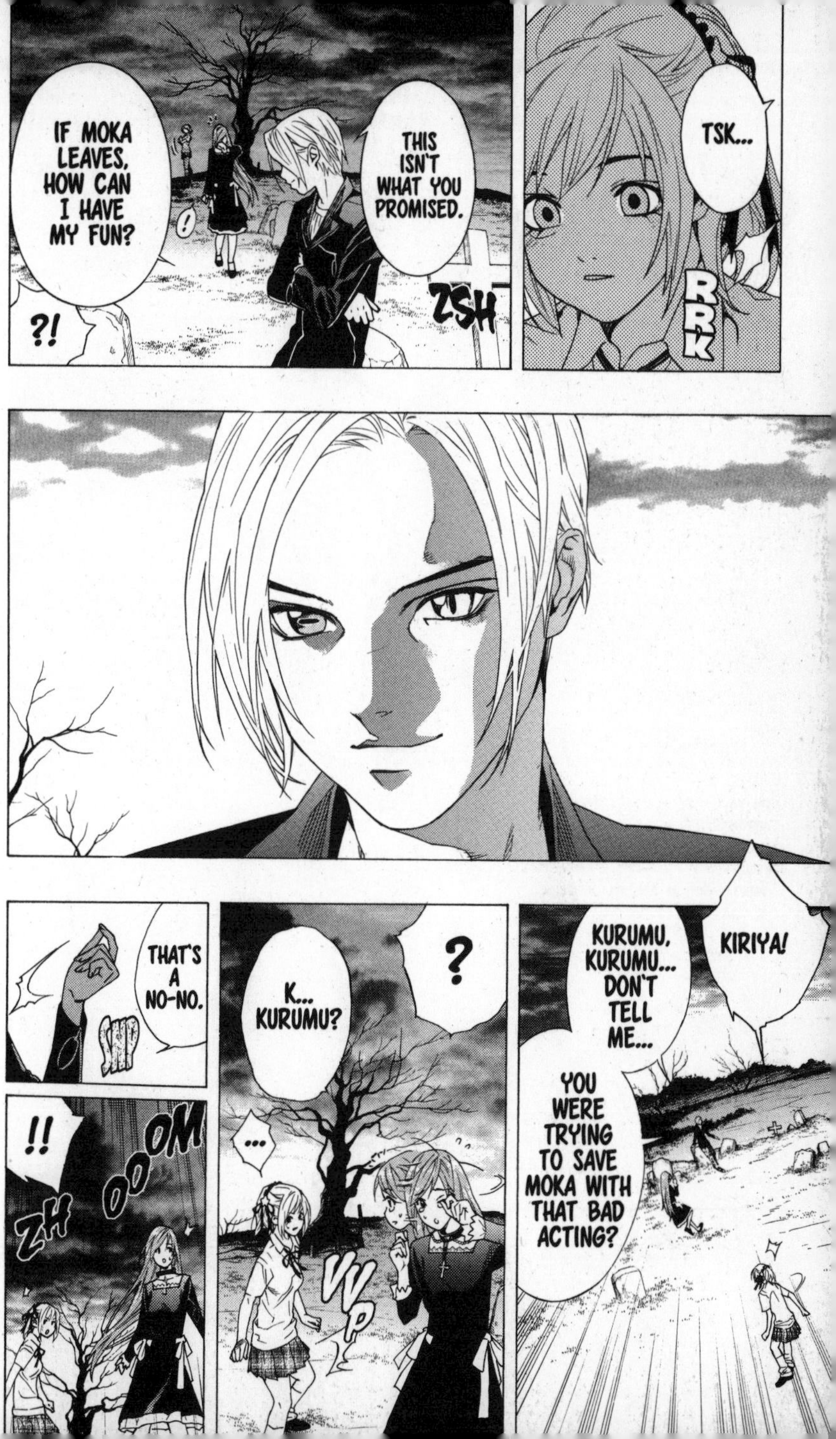
TSK...
RRK
THIS ISN'T WHAT YOU PROMISED.
ZSH
IF MOKA LEAVES, HOW CAN I HAVE MY FUN?
!
?!
KIRIYA!
KURUMU, KURUMU... DON'T TELL ME...
YOU WERE TRYING TO SAVE MOKA WITH THAT BAD ACTING?
?
K... KURUMU?
...
VVP
THAT'S A NO-NO.
!!
ZHOOOOM

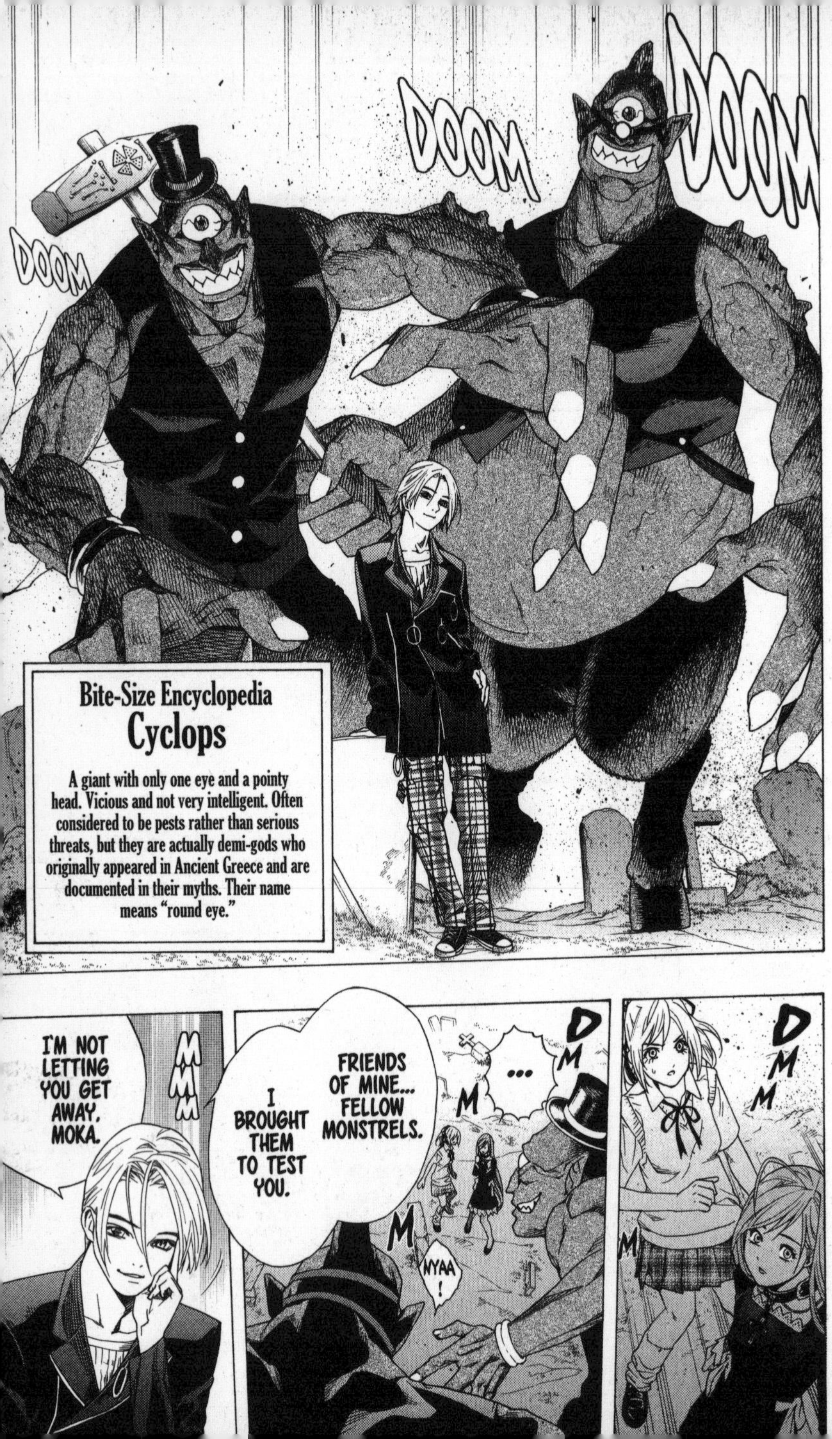
DOOM
DOOM
DOOM
Bite-Size Encyclopedia
Cyclops
A giant with only one eye and a pointy head. Vicious and not very intelligent. Often considered to be pests rather than serious threats, but they are actually demi-gods who originally appeared in Ancient Greece and are documented in their myths. Their name means "round eye."
DMM
M
...
DMM
M
FRIENDS OF MINE... FELLOW MONSTRELS.
I BROUGHT THEM TO TEST YOU.
M
NYAA!
MMM
I'M NOT LETTING YOU GET AWAY, MOKA.

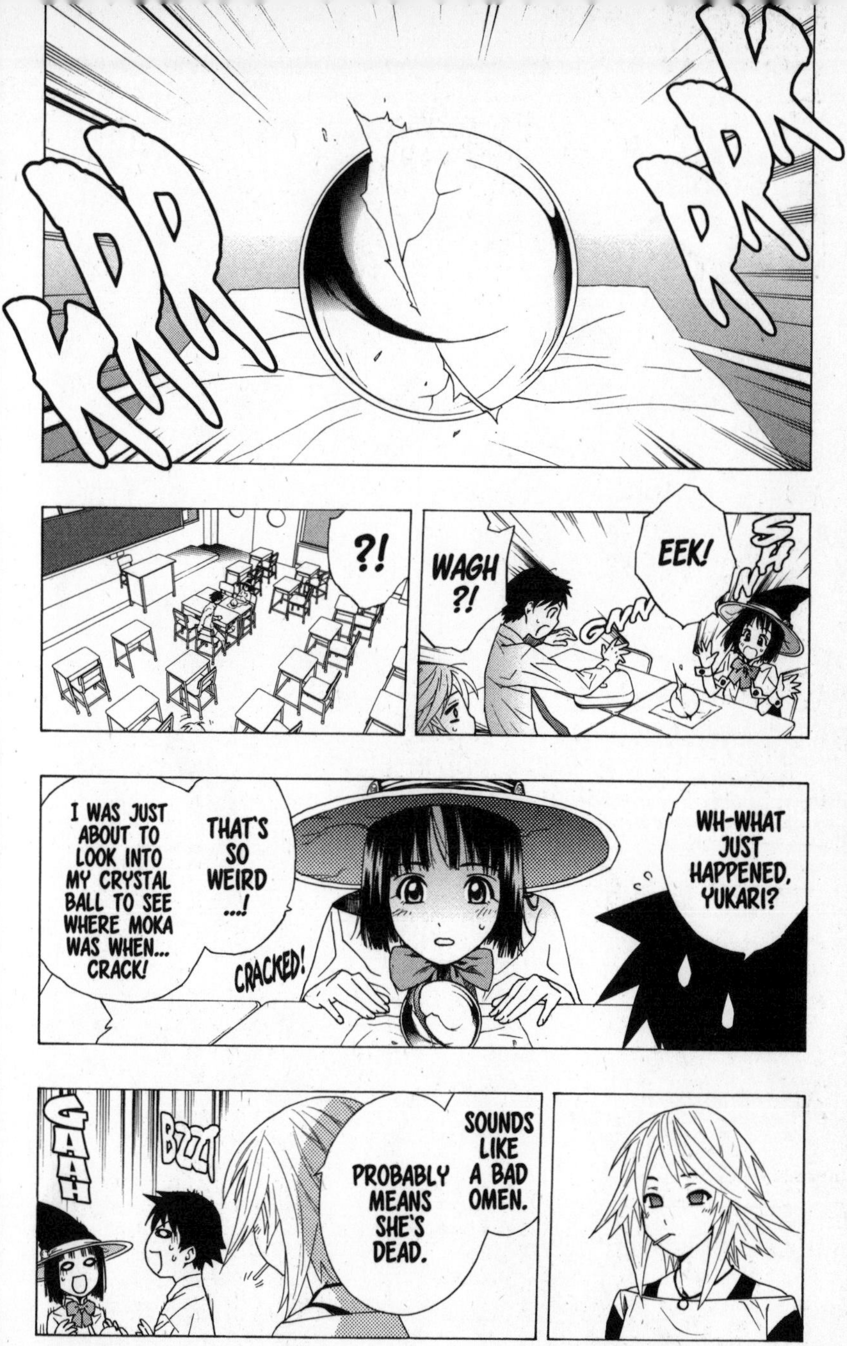
KRR
RRK
EEK!
SHN
GNN
WAGH ?!
?!
WH-WHAT JUST HAPPENED, YUKARI?
THAT'S SO WEIRD ...!
I WAS JUST ABOUT TO LOOK INTO MY CRYSTAL BALL TO SEE WHERE MOKA WAS WHEN... CRACK!
CRACKED!
SOUNDS LIKE A BAD OMEN.
PROBABLY MEANS SHE'S DEAD.
BZZT
GAAAH

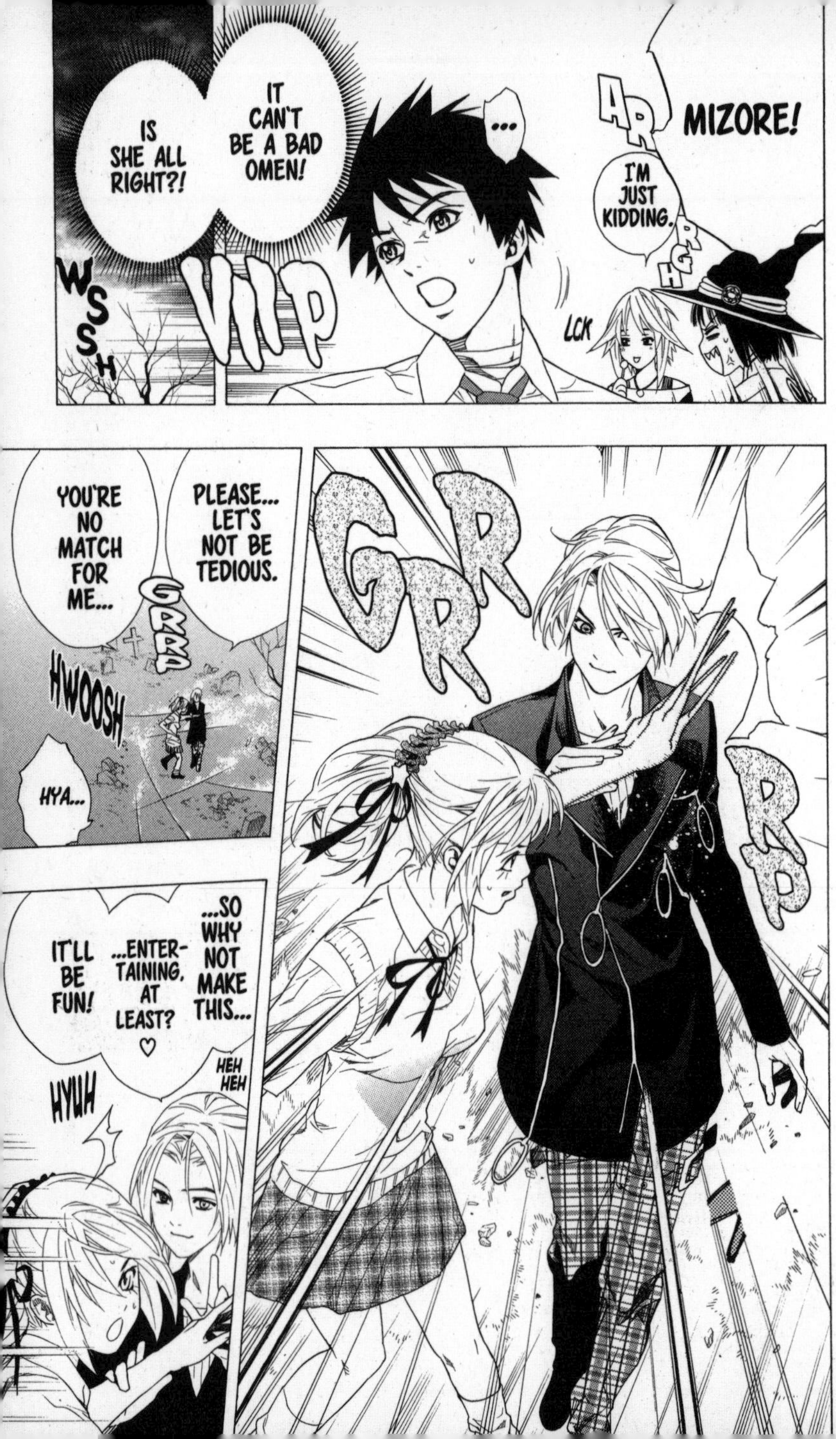
MIZORE!
ARRGH
I'M JUST KIDDING.
...
LCK
VIIP
IT CAN'T BE A BAD OMEN!
IS SHE ALL RIGHT?!
WSSH
GRR
RRP
PLEASE... LET'S NOT BE TEDIOUS.
YOU'RE NO MATCH FOR ME...
GRRR
HWOOSH
HYA...
...SO WHY NOT MAKE THIS...
...ENTER-TAINING, AT LEAST? ♡
IT'LL BE FUN!
HEH HEH
HYUH

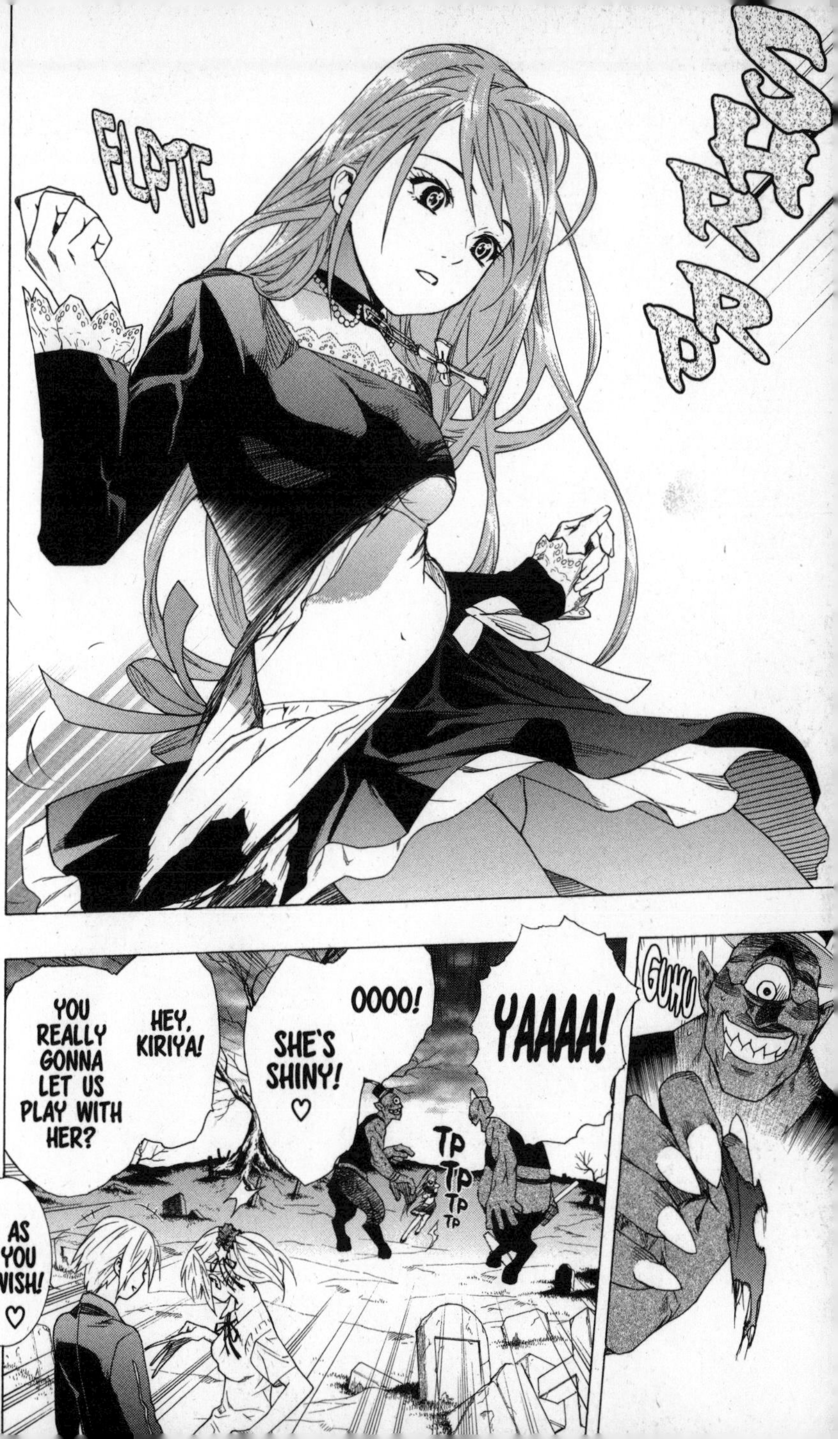
SHRRR
FLPTF
GUHU
YAAAA!
OOOO!
SHE'S SHINY! ♡
TP TP TP TP
HEY, KIRIYA!
YOU REALLY GONNA LET US PLAY WITH HER?
AS YOU WISH! ♡

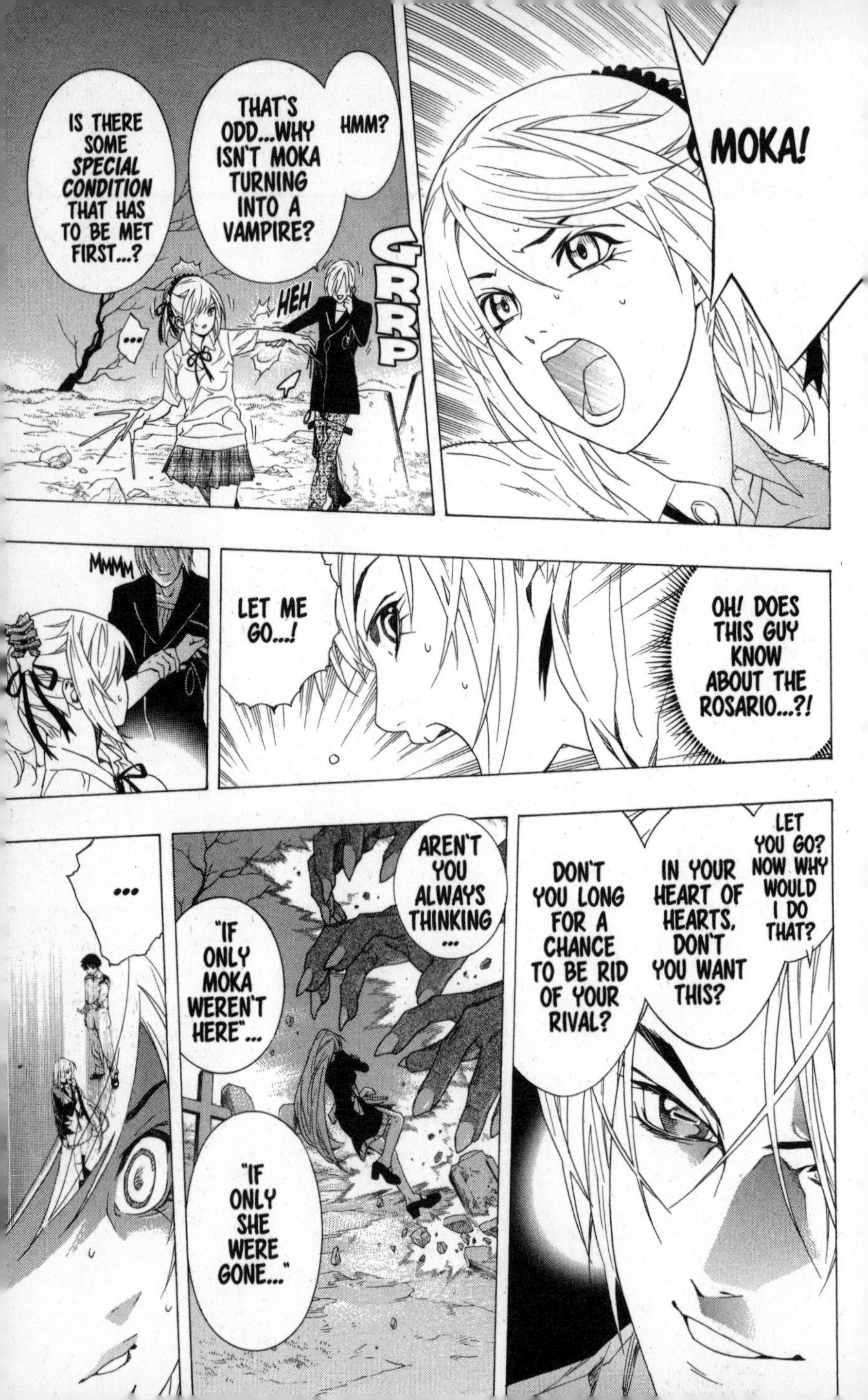
MOKA!
GRRP
HMM?
THAT'S ODD...WHY ISN'T MOKA TURNING INTO A VAMPIRE?
IS THERE SOME *SPECIAL CONDITION* THAT HAS TO BE MET FIRST...?
HEH
...
OH! DOES THIS GUY KNOW ABOUT THE ROSARIO...?!
LET ME GO...!
MMMM
LET YOU GO? NOW WHY WOULD I DO THAT?
IN YOUR HEART OF HEARTS, DON'T YOU WANT THIS?
DON'T YOU LONG FOR A CHANCE TO BE RID OF YOUR RIVAL?
AREN'T YOU ALWAYS THINKING...
"IF ONLY MOKA WEREN'T HERE"...
"IF ONLY SHE WERE GONE..."
...

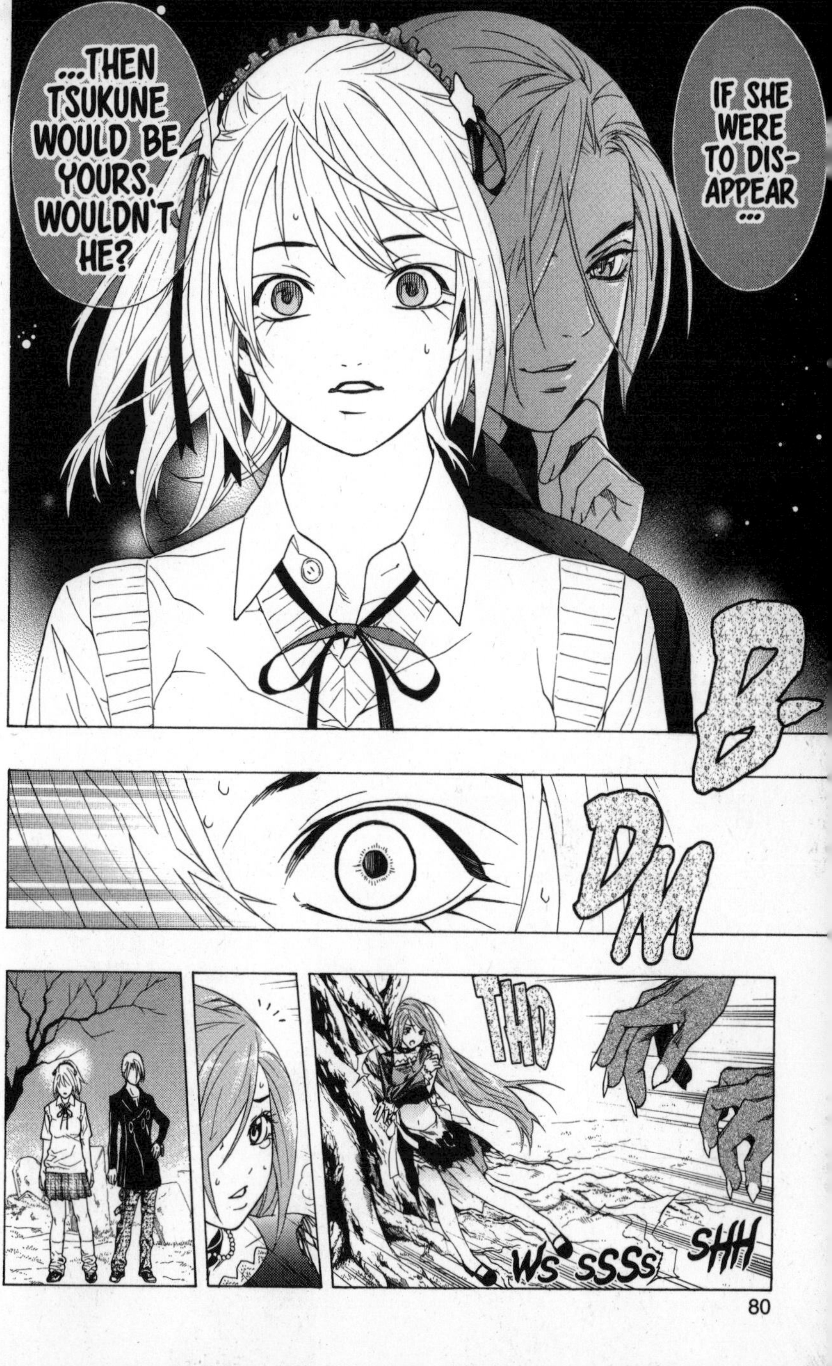
IF SHE WERE TO DIS-APPEAR ...
...THEN TSUKUNE WOULD BE YOURS, WOULDN'T HE?
B-
DM
SHH
THD
WS SSSS

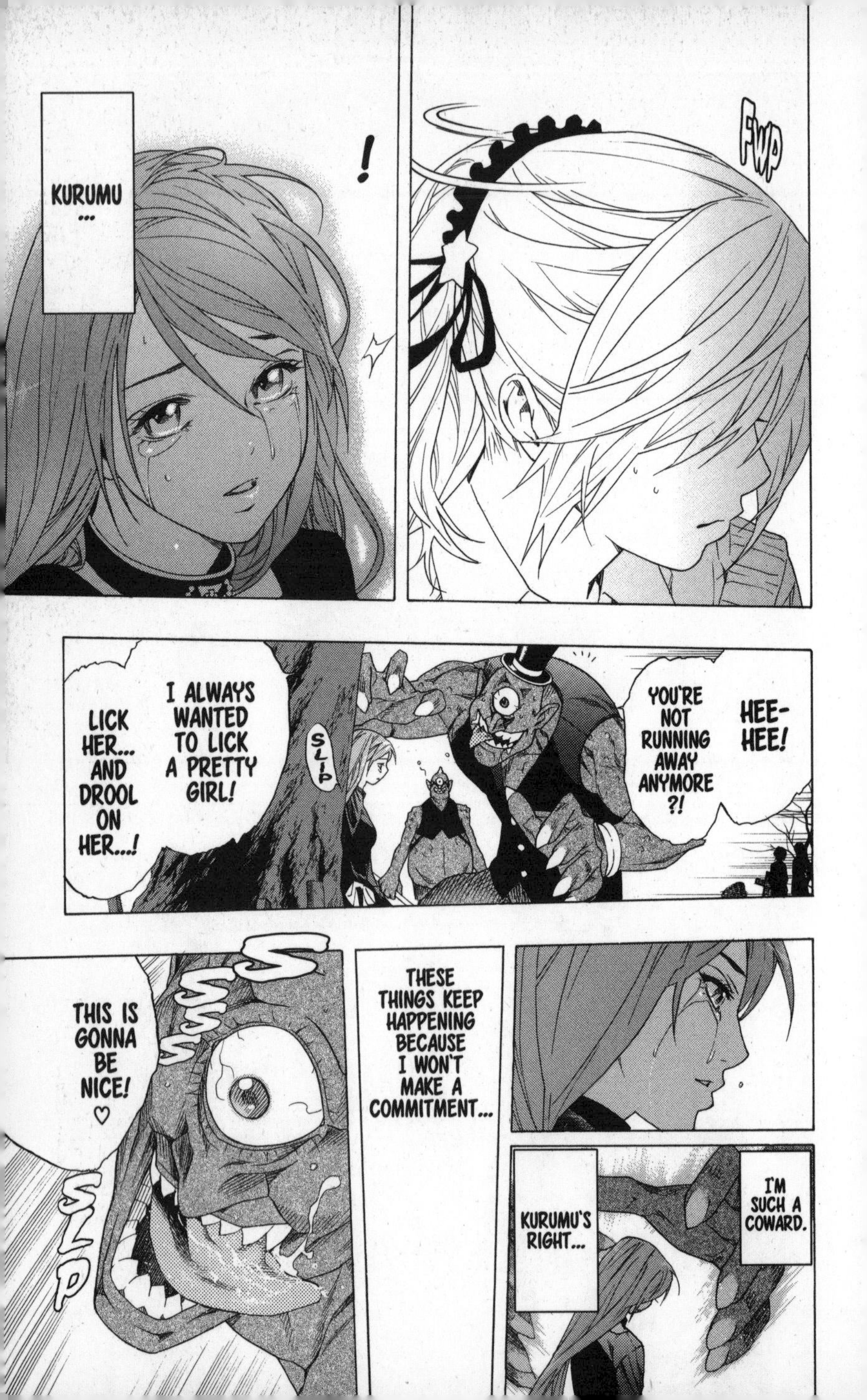
FWP
!
KURUMU ...
HEE-HEE!
YOU'RE NOT RUNNING AWAY ANYMORE ?!
SLIP
I ALWAYS WANTED TO LICK A PRETTY GIRL!
LICK HER... AND DROOL ON HER...!
I'M SUCH A COWARD.
KURUMU'S RIGHT...
THESE THINGS KEEP HAPPENING BECAUSE I WON'T MAKE A COMMITMENT...
SSSS
THIS IS GONNA BE NICE! ♡
SLP

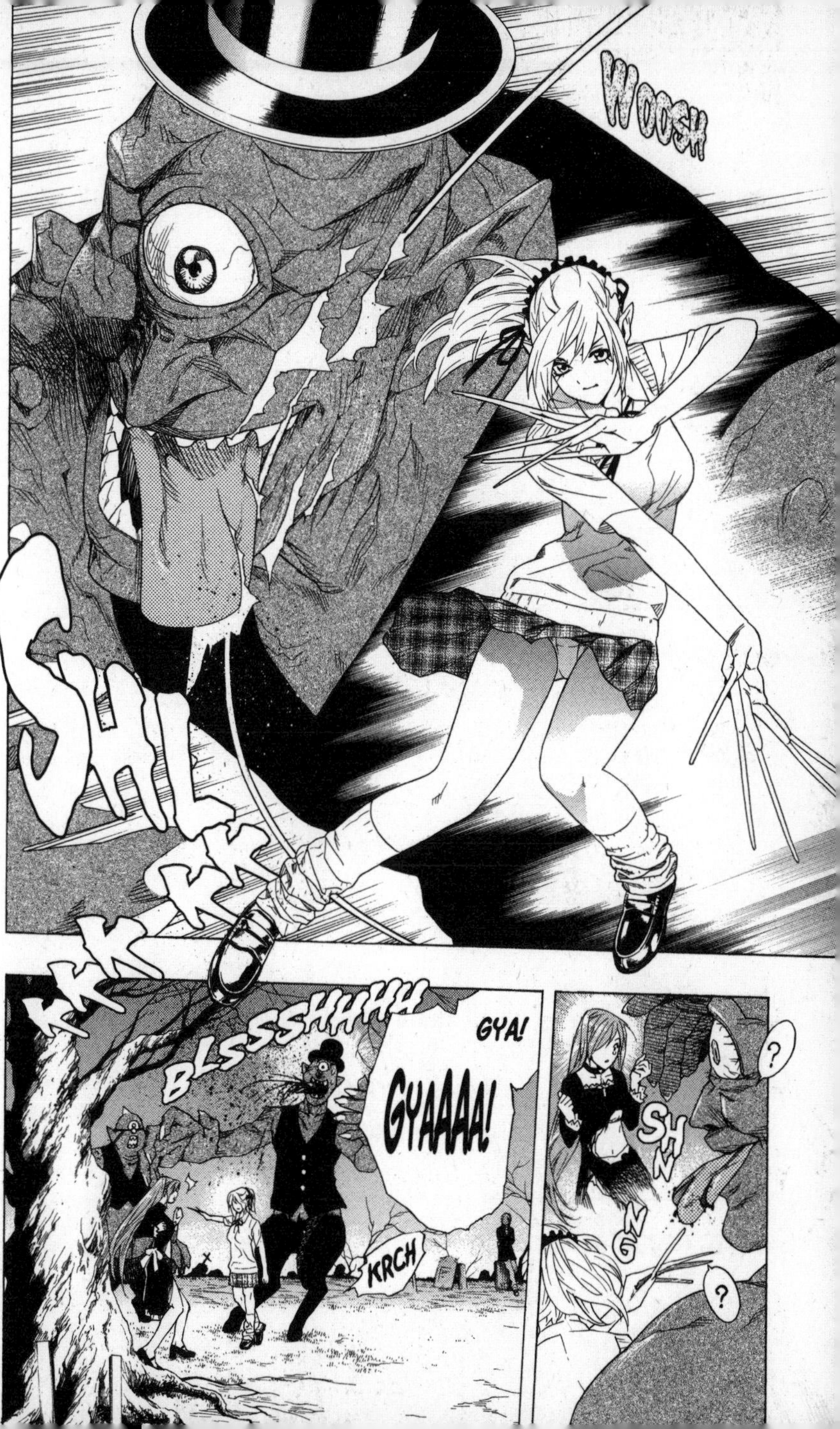
WOOSH
SHLKKKKKK
?
SHNNG
?
GYA!
GYAAAA!
BLSSSHHHH
KRCH

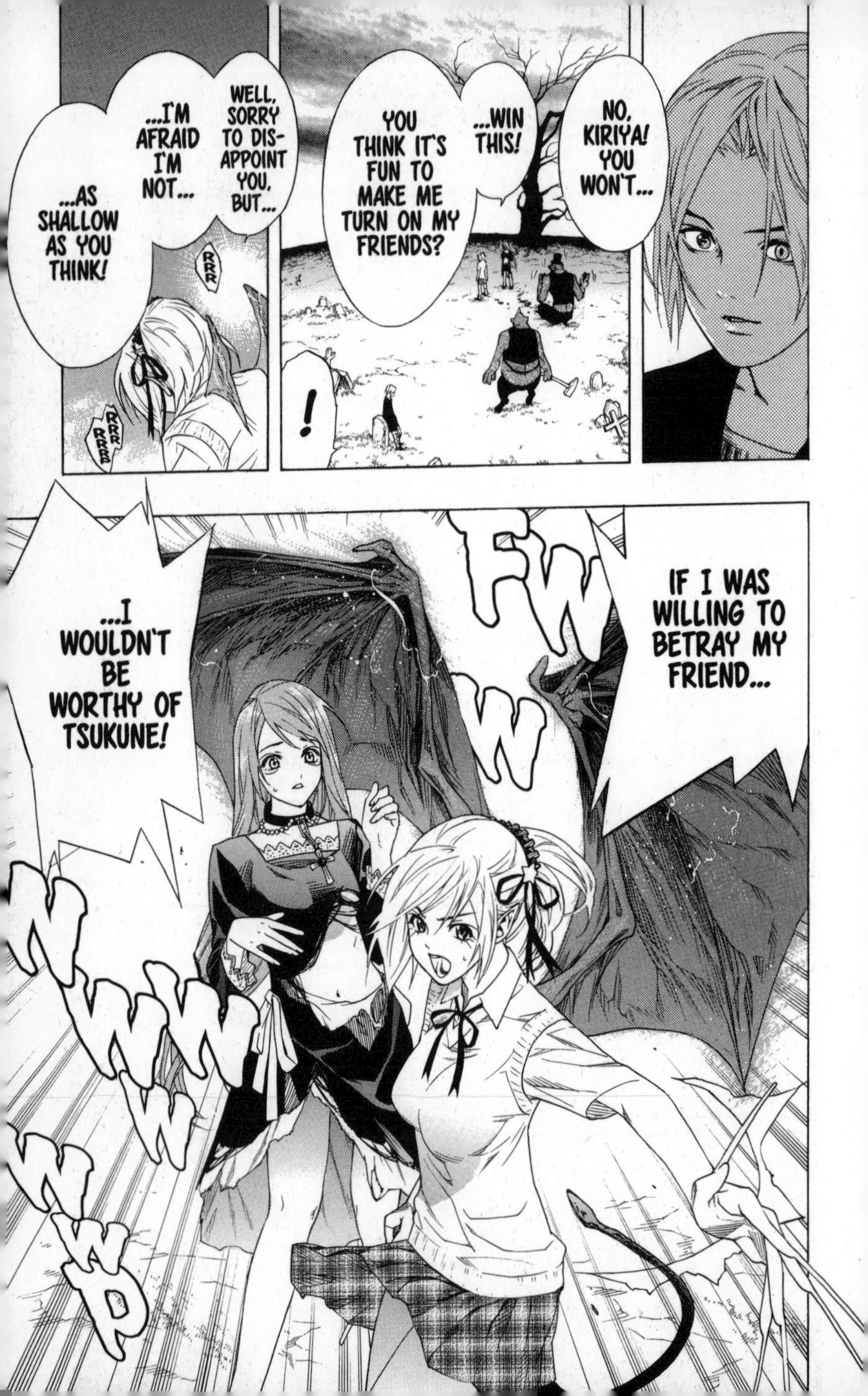
NO, KIRIYA! YOU WON'T...
...WIN THIS!
YOU THINK IT'S FUN TO MAKE ME TURN ON MY FRIENDS?
!
WELL, SORRY TO DIS-APPOINT YOU, BUT...
...I'M AFRAID I'M NOT...
...AS SHALLOW AS YOU THINK!
RRR
RRR
IF I WAS WILLING TO BETRAY MY FRIEND...
FWW
...I WOULDN'T BE WORTHY OF TSUKUNE!
WWWWWP

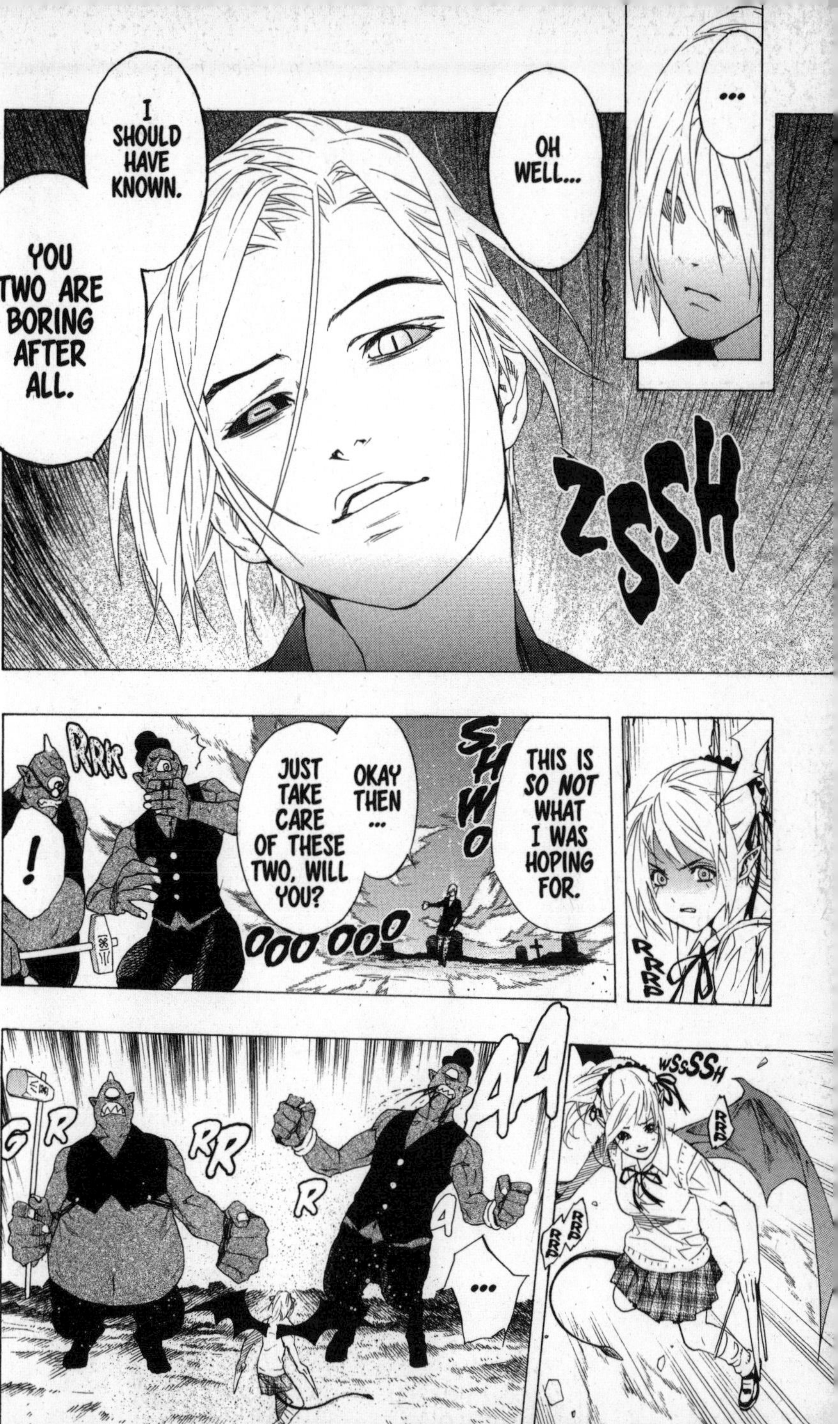
...
OH WELL...
I SHOULD HAVE KNOWN.
YOU TWO ARE BORING AFTER ALL.
ZSSH
RRRP
THIS IS SO NOT WHAT I WAS HOPING FOR.
SHWO
OKAY THEN ...
JUST TAKE CARE OF THESE TWO, WILL YOU?
OOO OOO
RRK
!
WSSSSH
RRP
AA
RRP
RRP
...
GR
RR
R

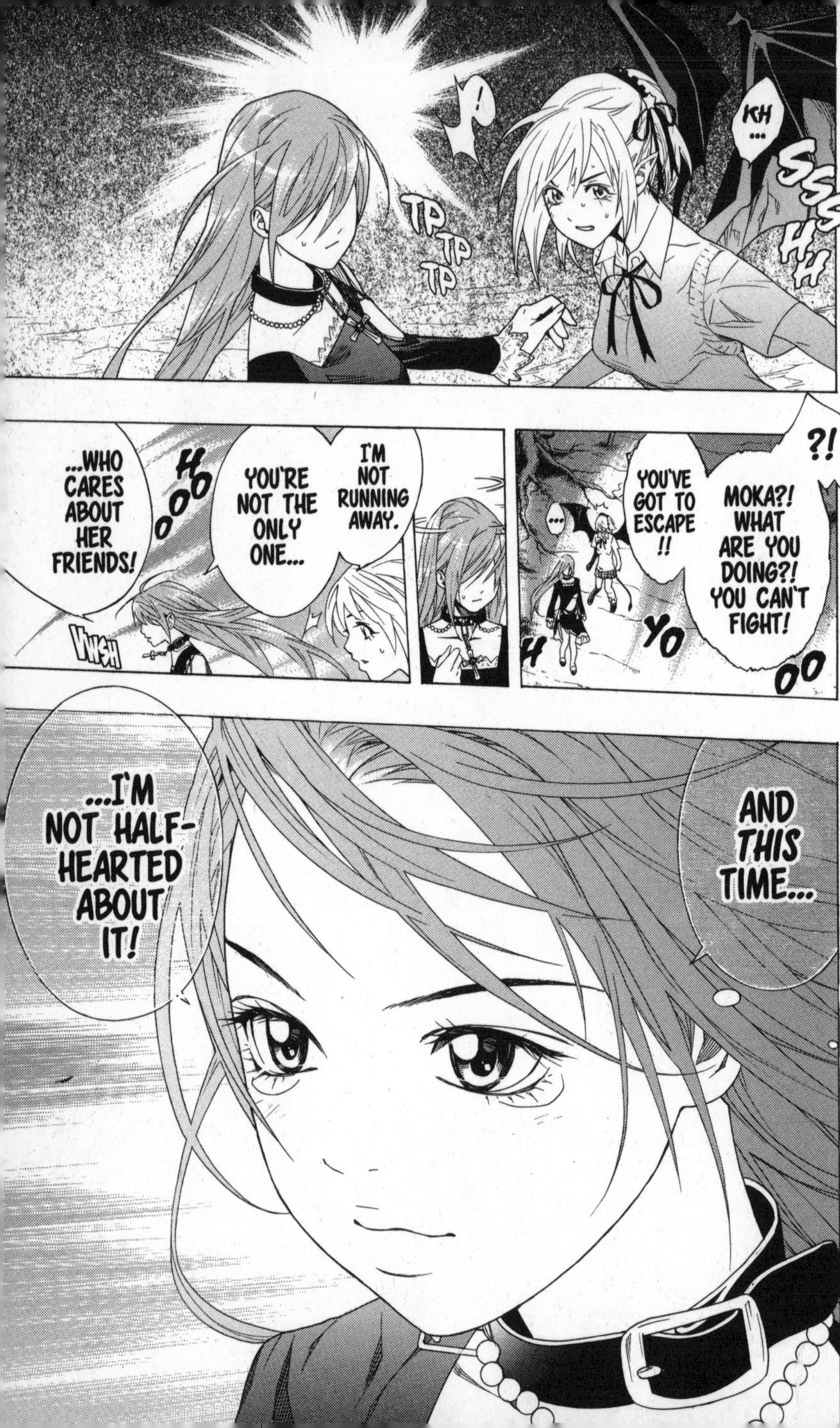
KH...
SSSHH
!
TP TP TP
?!
MOKA?! WHAT ARE YOU DOING?! YOU CAN'T FIGHT!
YOU'VE GOT TO ESCAPE!!
...
HYOOO
I'M NOT RUNNING AWAY.
YOU'RE NOT THE ONLY ONE...
HOOO
...WHO CARES ABOUT HER FRIENDS!
VWSH
AND THIS TIME...
...I'M NOT HALF-HEARTED ABOUT IT!

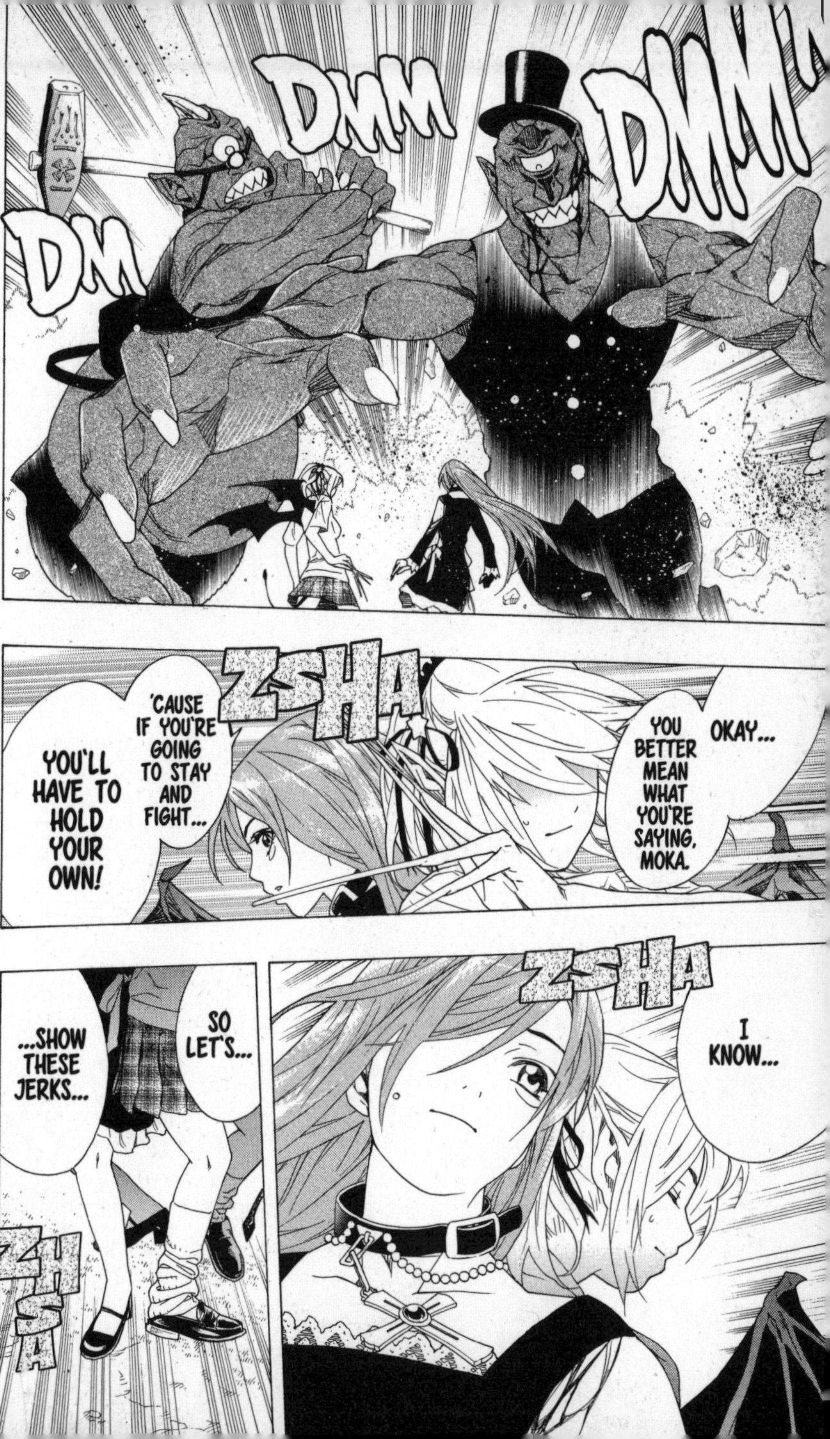
DMM
DMM
DM
OKAY...
YOU BETTER MEAN WHAT YOU'RE SAYING, MOKA.
ZSHA
'CAUSE IF YOU'RE GOING TO STAY AND FIGHT...
YOU'LL HAVE TO HOLD YOUR OWN!
ZSHA
I KNOW...
SO LET'S...
...SHOW THESE JERKS...
ZHSA

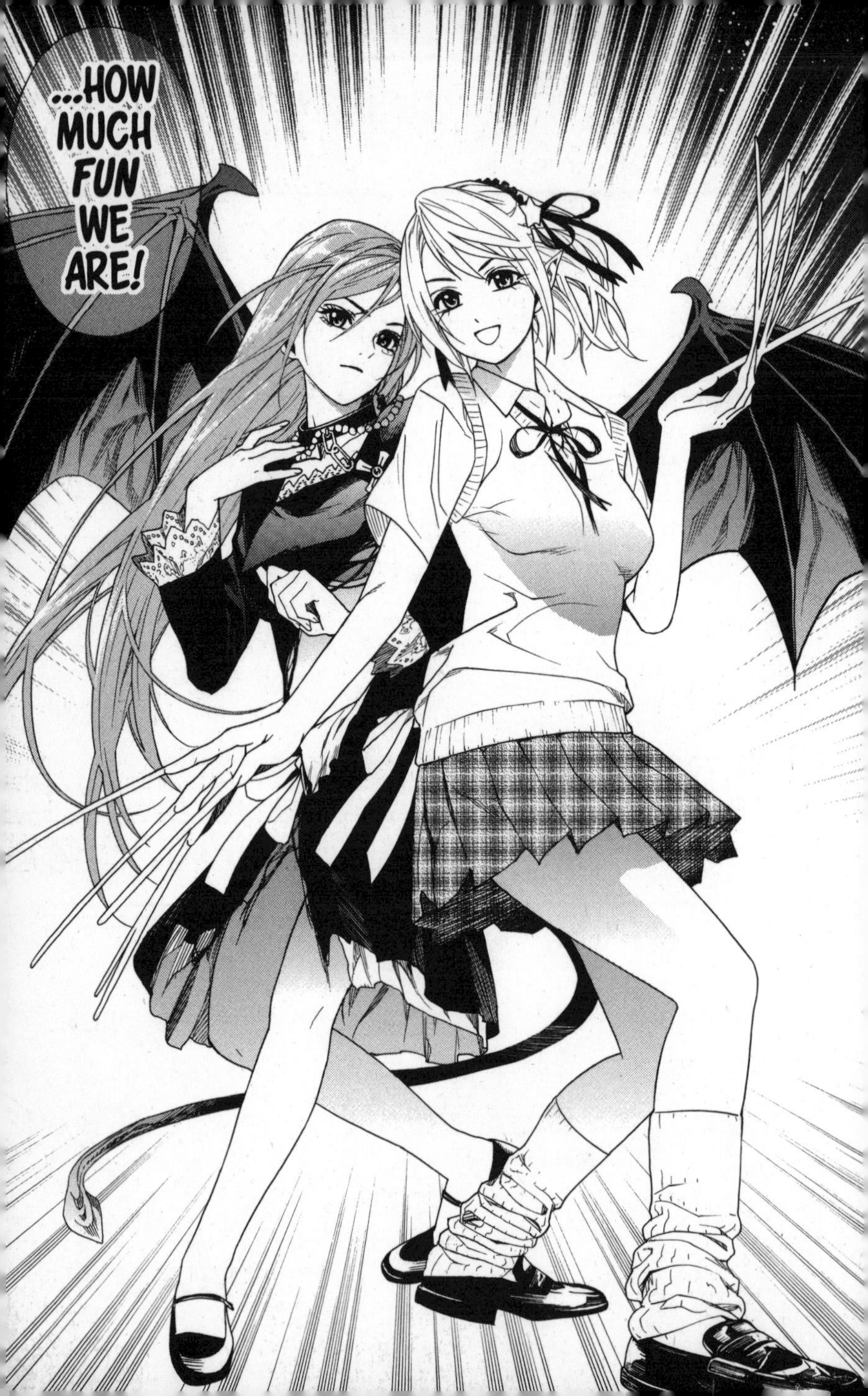
...HOW MUCH FUN WE ARE!

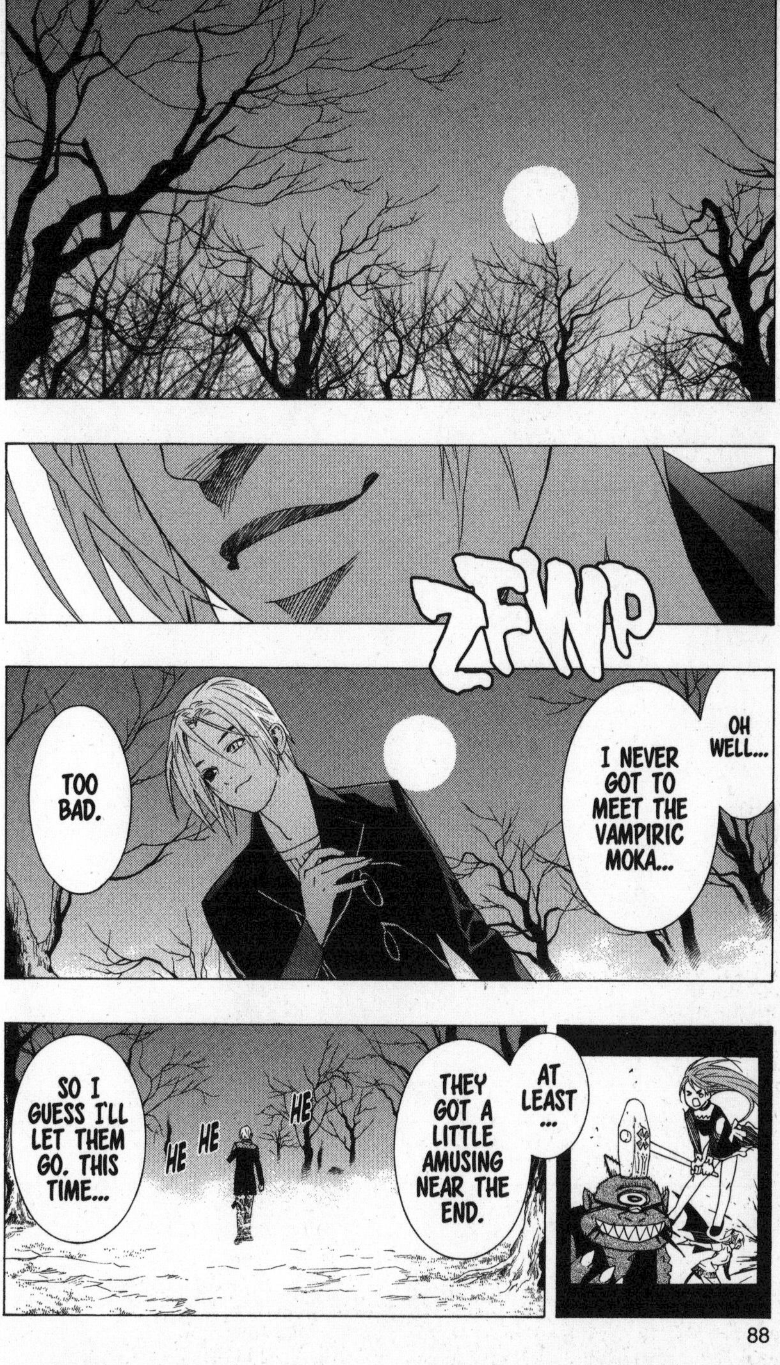
ZFWP
OH WELL...
I NEVER GOT TO MEET THE VAMPIRIC MOKA...
TOO BAD.
AT LEAST...
THEY GOT A LITTLE AMUSING NEAR THE END.
HE HE HE
SO I GUESS I'LL LET THEM GO. THIS TIME...

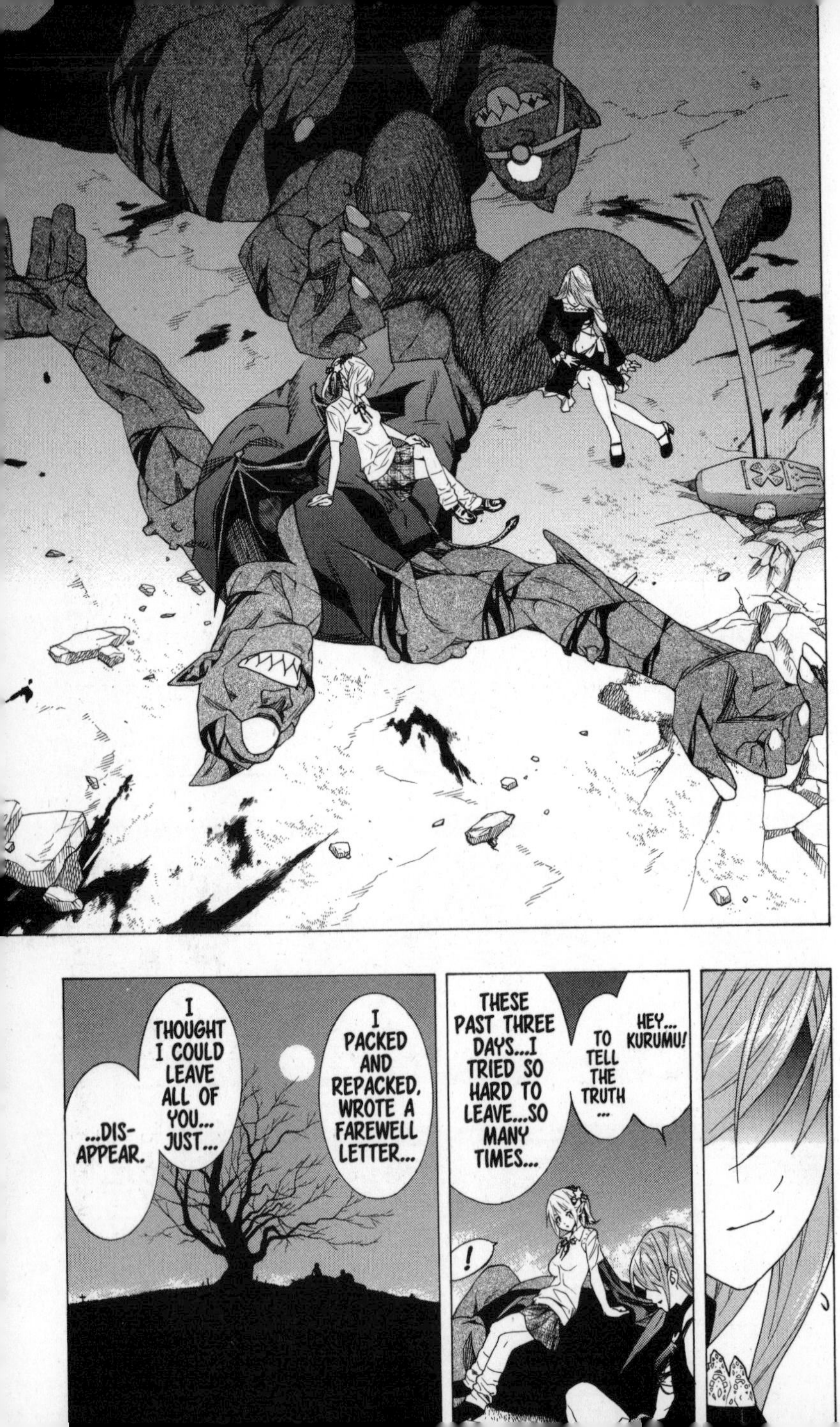
HEY... KURUMU!
TO TELL THE TRUTH...
THESE PAST THREE DAYS...I TRIED SO HARD TO LEAVE...SO MANY TIMES...
!
I PACKED AND REPACKED, WROTE A FAREWELL LETTER...
I THOUGHT I COULD LEAVE ALL OF YOU... JUST...
...DIS-APPEAR.

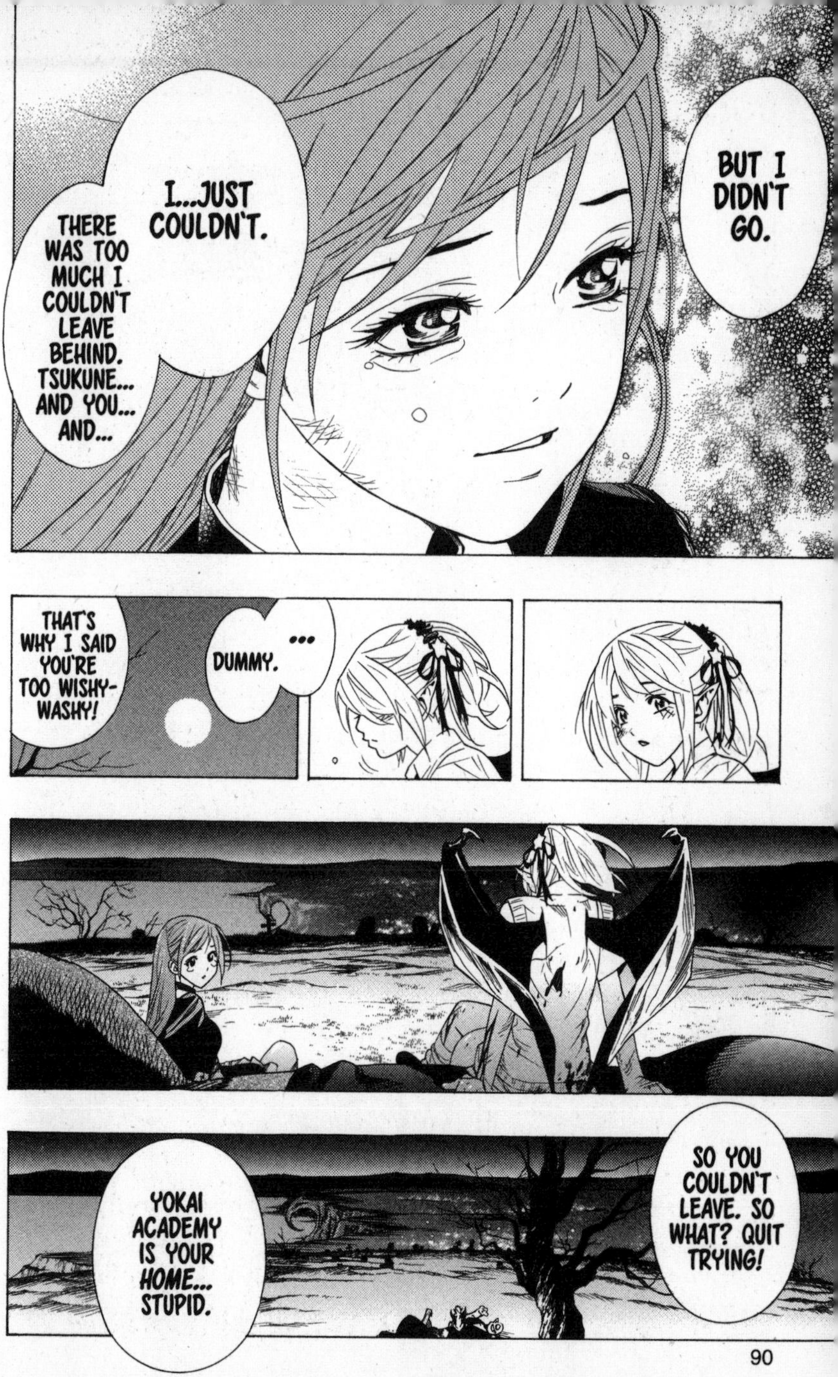
BUT I DIDN'T GO.
I...JUST COULDN'T.
THERE WAS TOO MUCH I COULDN'T LEAVE BEHIND. TSUKUNE... AND YOU... AND...
... DUMMY.
THAT'S WHY I SAID YOU'RE TOO WISHY-WASHY!
SO YOU COULDN'T LEAVE. SO WHAT? QUIT TRYING!
YOKAI ACADEMY IS YOUR HOME... STUPID.

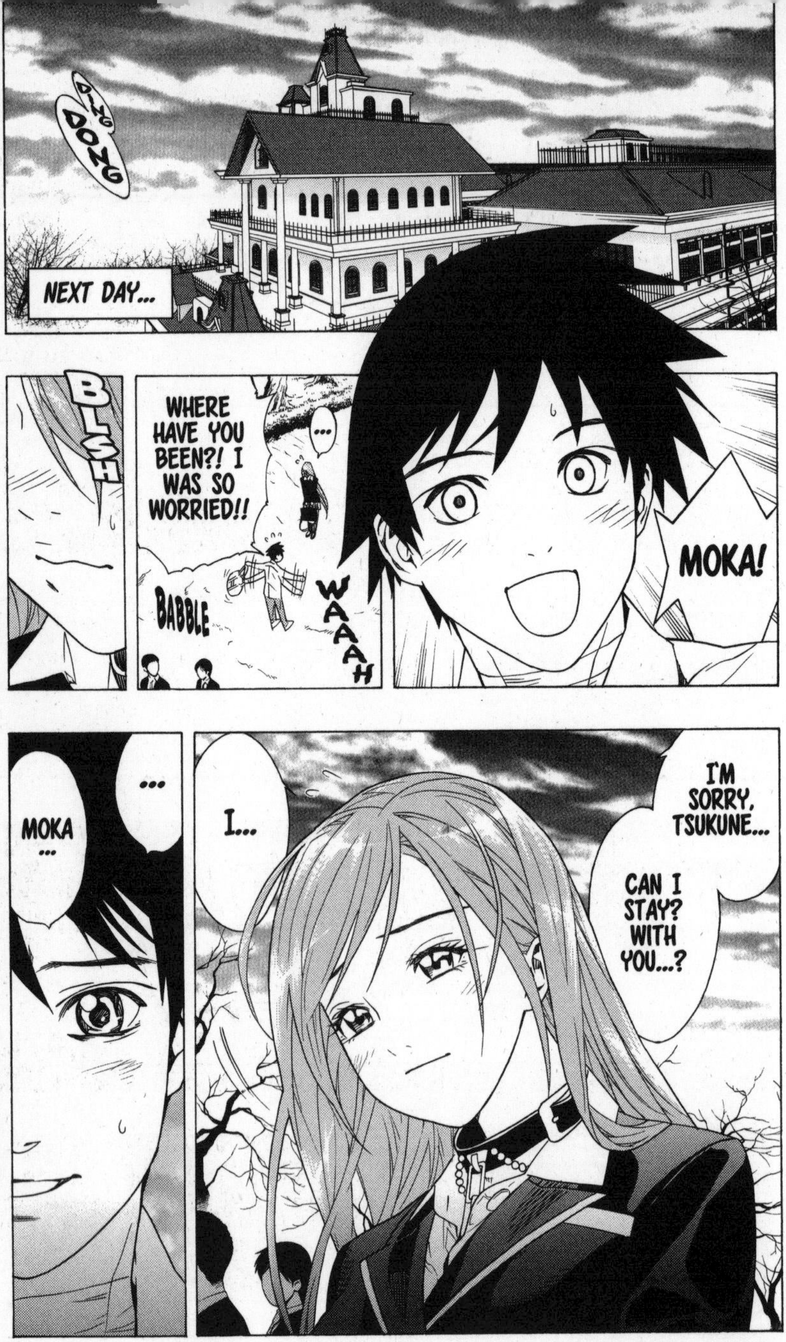
DING DONG
NEXT DAY...
MOKA!
WHERE HAVE YOU BEEN?! I WAS SO WORRIED!!
...
WAAAAH
BABBLE
BLSH
I'M SORRY, TSUKUNE...
CAN I STAY? WITH YOU...?
I...
...
MOKA ...

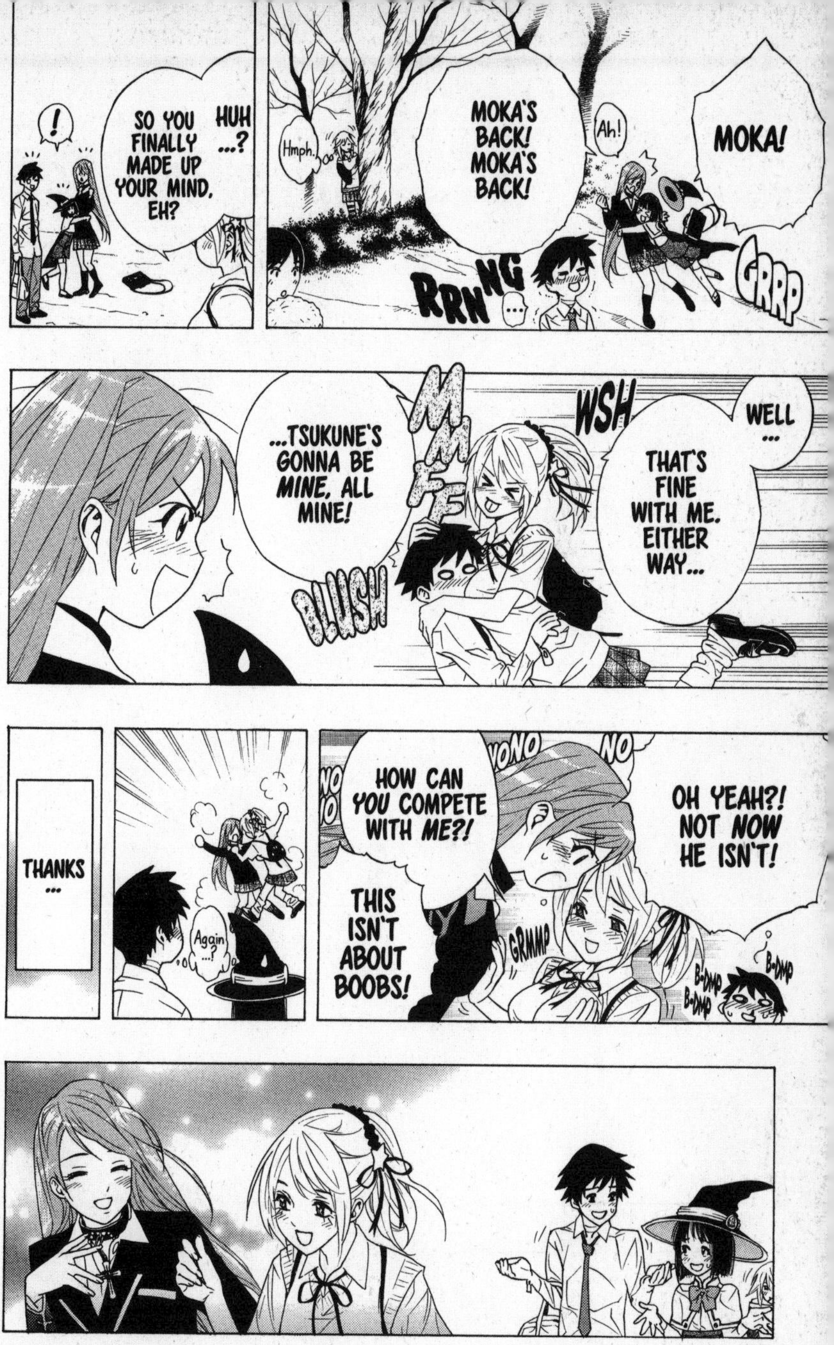
MOKA!
GRRP
Ah!
MOKA'S BACK! MOKA'S BACK!
RRNNG
...
Hmph.
HUH ...?
SO YOU FINALLY MADE UP YOUR MIND, EH?
!
WELL ...
THAT'S FINE WITH ME. EITHER WAY...
WSH
MMF
...TSUKUNE'S GONNA BE *MINE*, ALL MINE!
BLUSH
NO
OH YEAH?! NOT *NOW* HE ISN'T!
NONO
HOW CAN *YOU* COMPETE WITH *ME*?!
THIS ISN'T ABOUT BOOBS!
GRMMP
B-DMP B-DMP B-DMP
Again ...?
THANKS ...

# 27 : I Promise

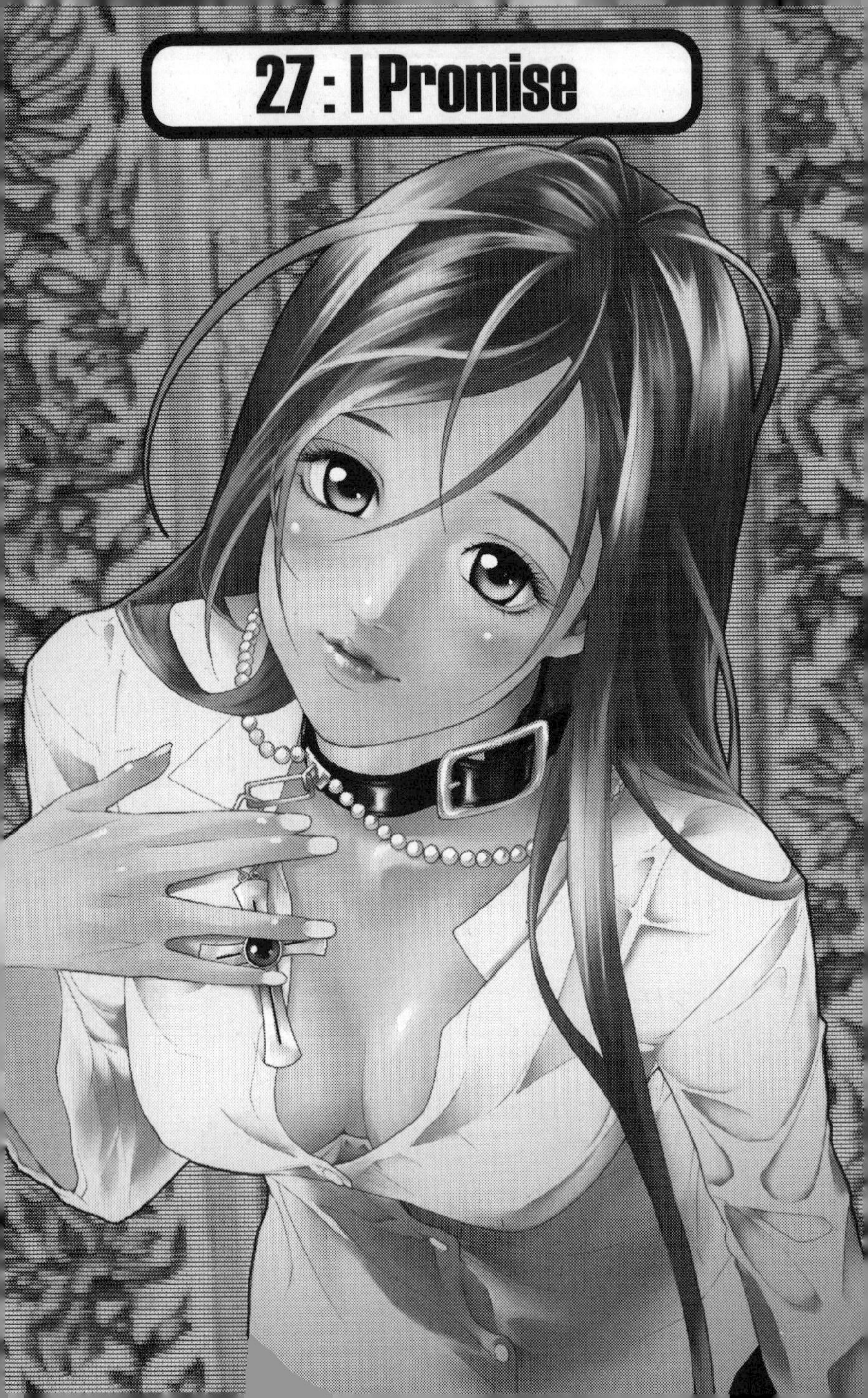

READ THIS WAY

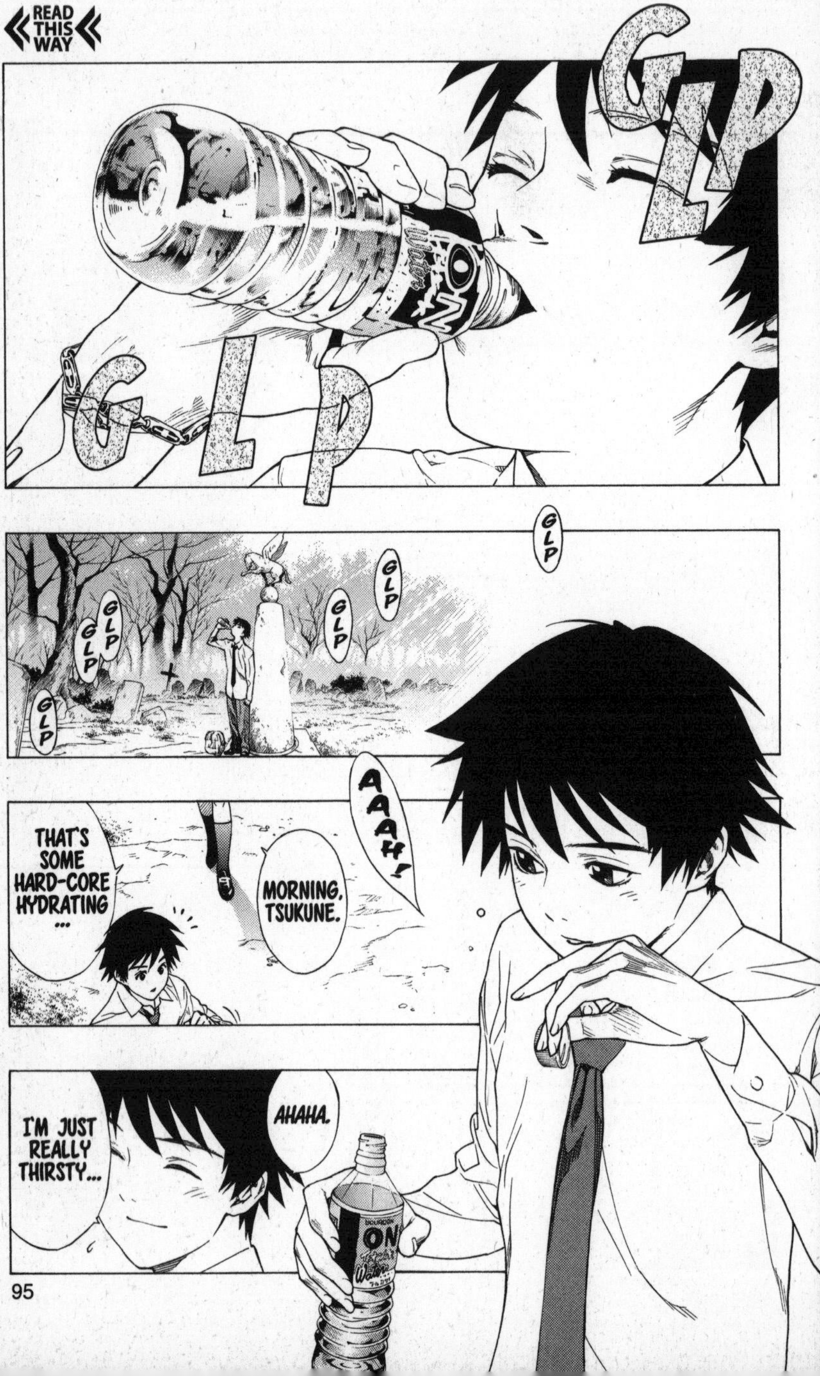
GLP
GLP
GLP
AAAH!
GLP
GLP
GLP
GLP
MORNING, TSUKUNE.
THAT'S SOME HARD-CORE HYDRATING...
AHAHA.
I'M JUST REALLY THIRSTY...

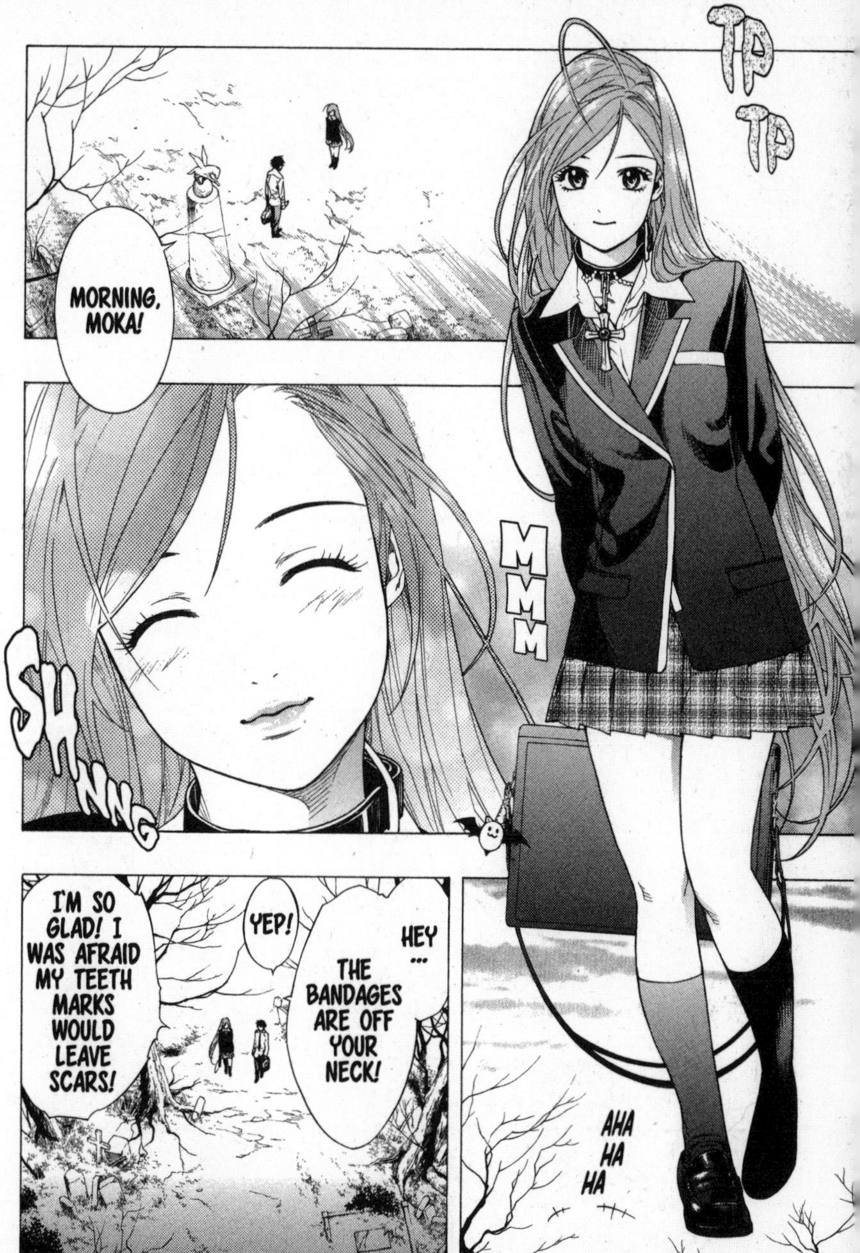
TP TP
MORNING, MOKA!
MMM
SHINNG
AHA HA HA
HEY... THE BANDAGES ARE OFF YOUR NECK!
YEP!
I'M SO GLAD! I WAS AFRAID MY TEETH MARKS WOULD LEAVE SCARS!

READ THIS WAY

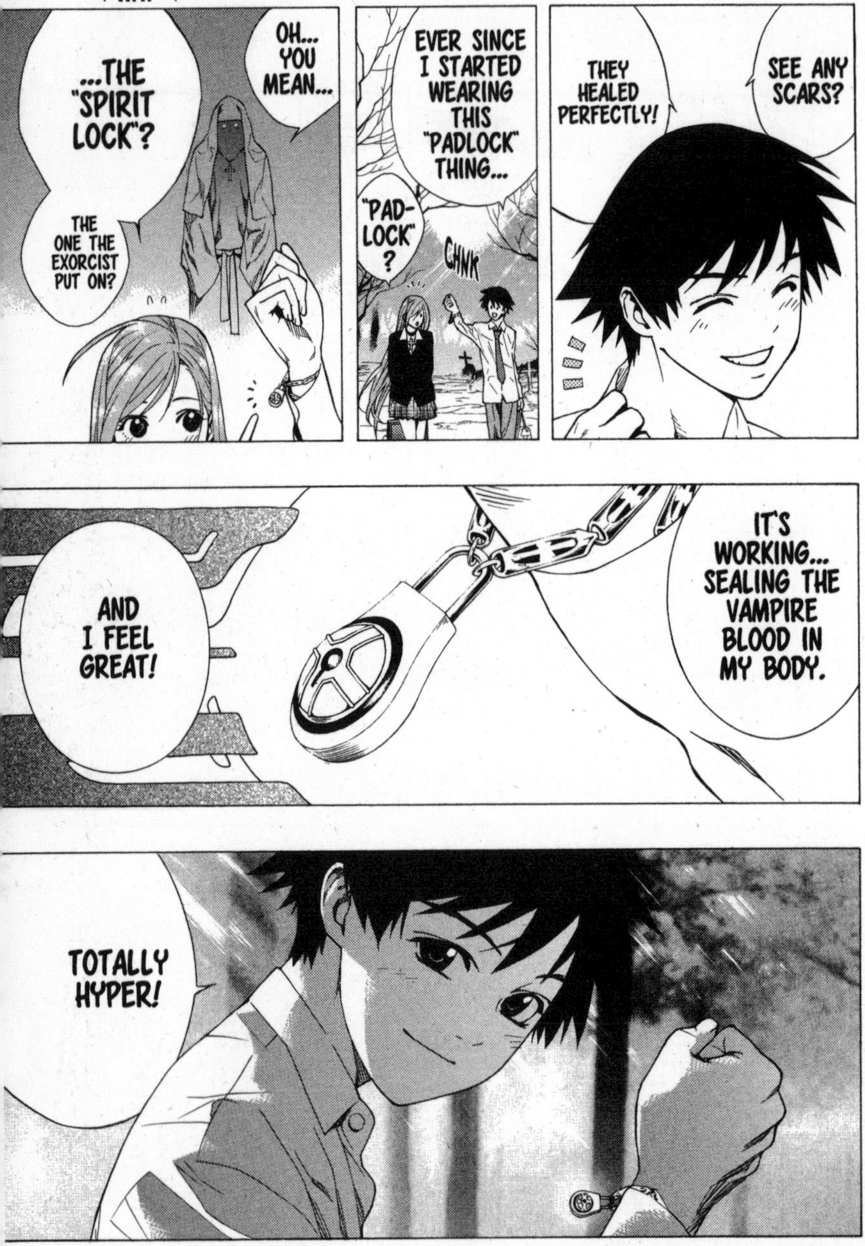
SEE ANY SCARS?
THEY HEALED PERFECTLY!
EVER SINCE I STARTED WEARING THIS "PADLOCK" THING...
CHNK
"PAD-LOCK"?
OH... YOU MEAN...
..THE "SPIRIT LOCK"?
THE ONE THE EXORCIST PUT ON?
IT'S WORKING... SEALING THE VAMPIRE BLOOD IN MY BODY.
AND I FEEL GREAT!
TOTALLY HYPER!

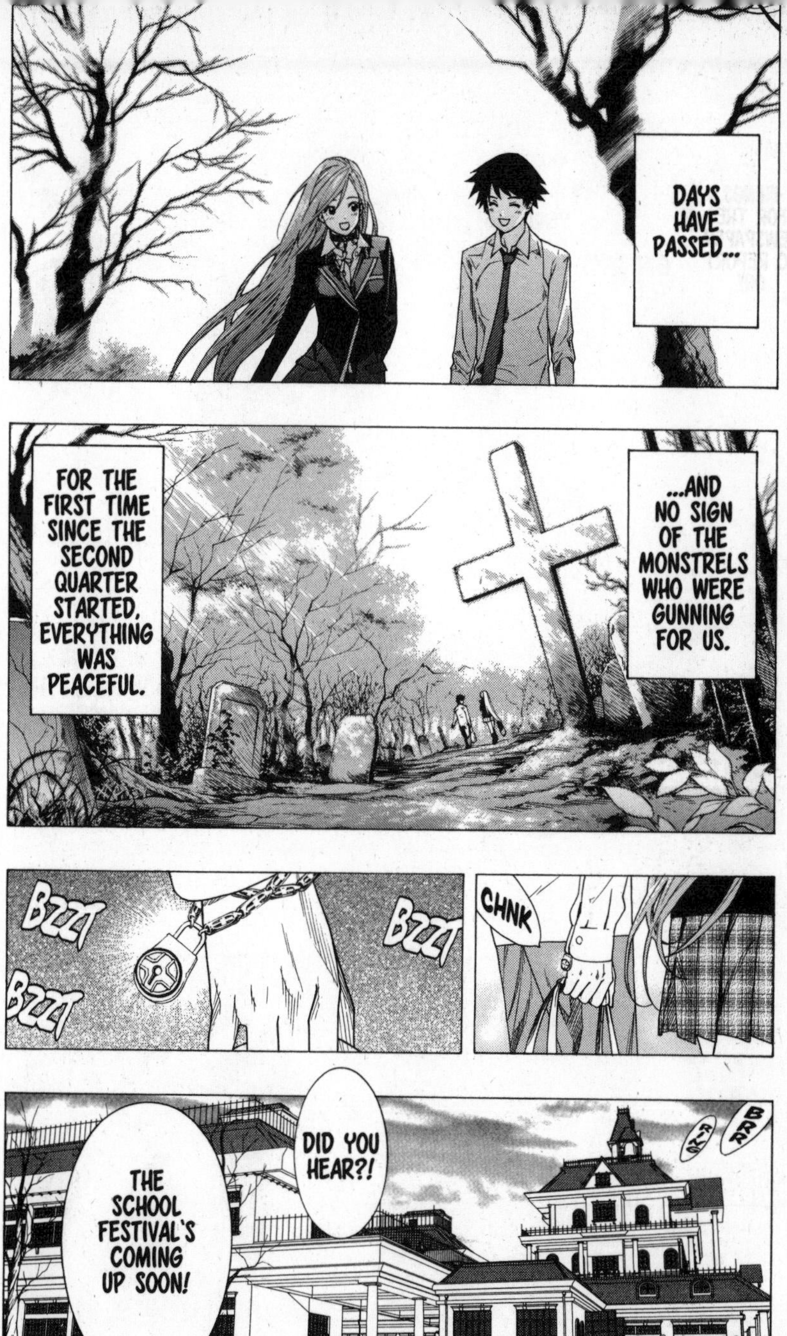
DAYS HAVE PASSED...
...AND NO SIGN OF THE MONSTRELS WHO WERE GUNNING FOR US.
FOR THE FIRST TIME SINCE THE SECOND QUARTER STARTED, EVERYTHING WAS PEACEFUL.
CHNK
BZZT
BZZT
BZZT
BRR
RING
DID YOU HEAR?!
THE SCHOOL FESTIVAL'S COMING UP SOON!

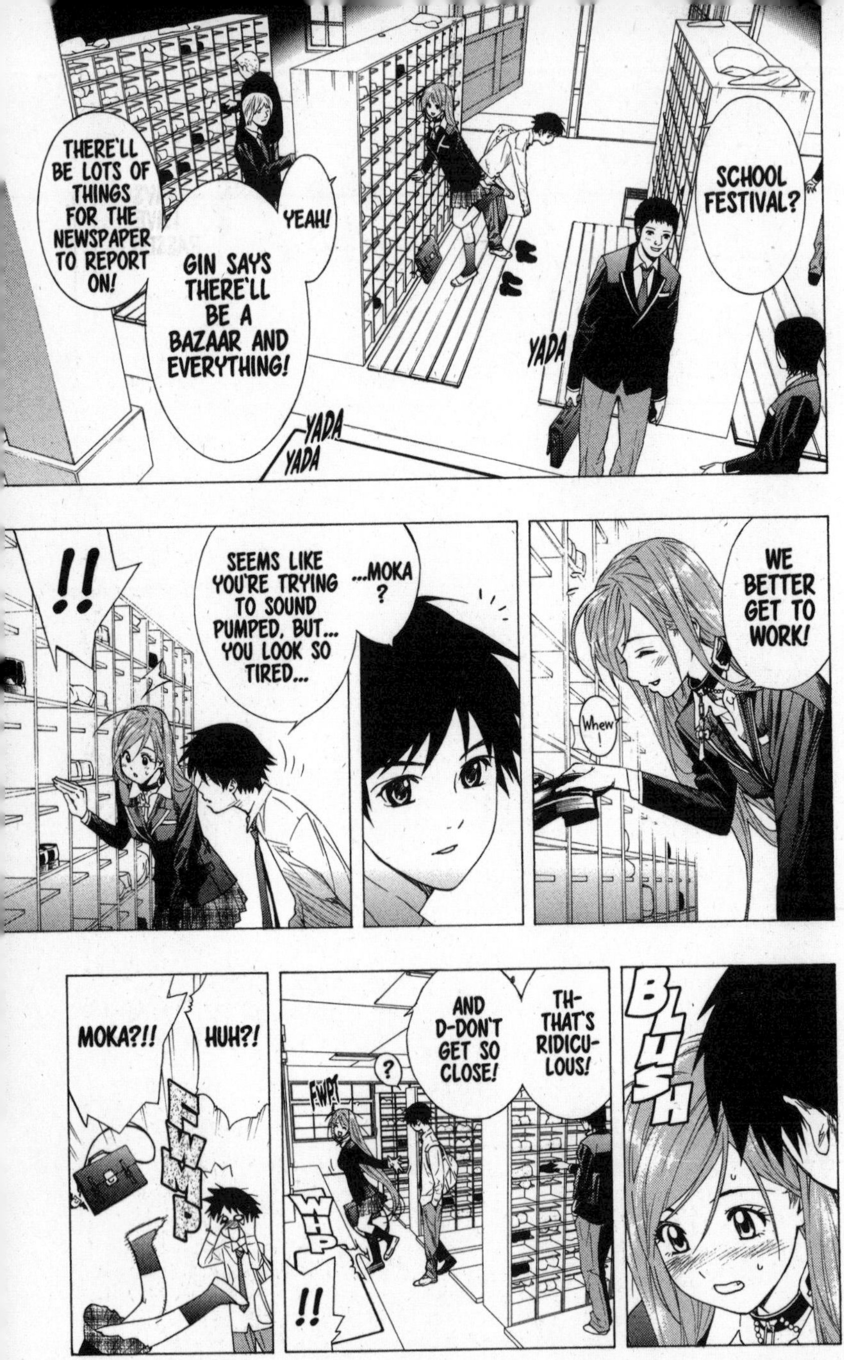
SCHOOL FESTIVAL?
YADA
YEAH!
GIN SAYS THERE'LL BE A BAZAAR AND EVERYTHING!
THERE'LL BE LOTS OF THINGS FOR THE NEWSPAPER TO REPORT ON!
YADA YADA
WE BETTER GET TO WORK!
Whew!
...MOKA?
SEEMS LIKE YOU'RE TRYING TO SOUND PUMPED, BUT... YOU LOOK SO TIRED...
!!
BLUSH
TH-THAT'S RIDICULOUS!
AND D-DON'T GET SO CLOSE!
?
FWP!
WHP!
!!
HUH?!
MOKA?!!
FWMP

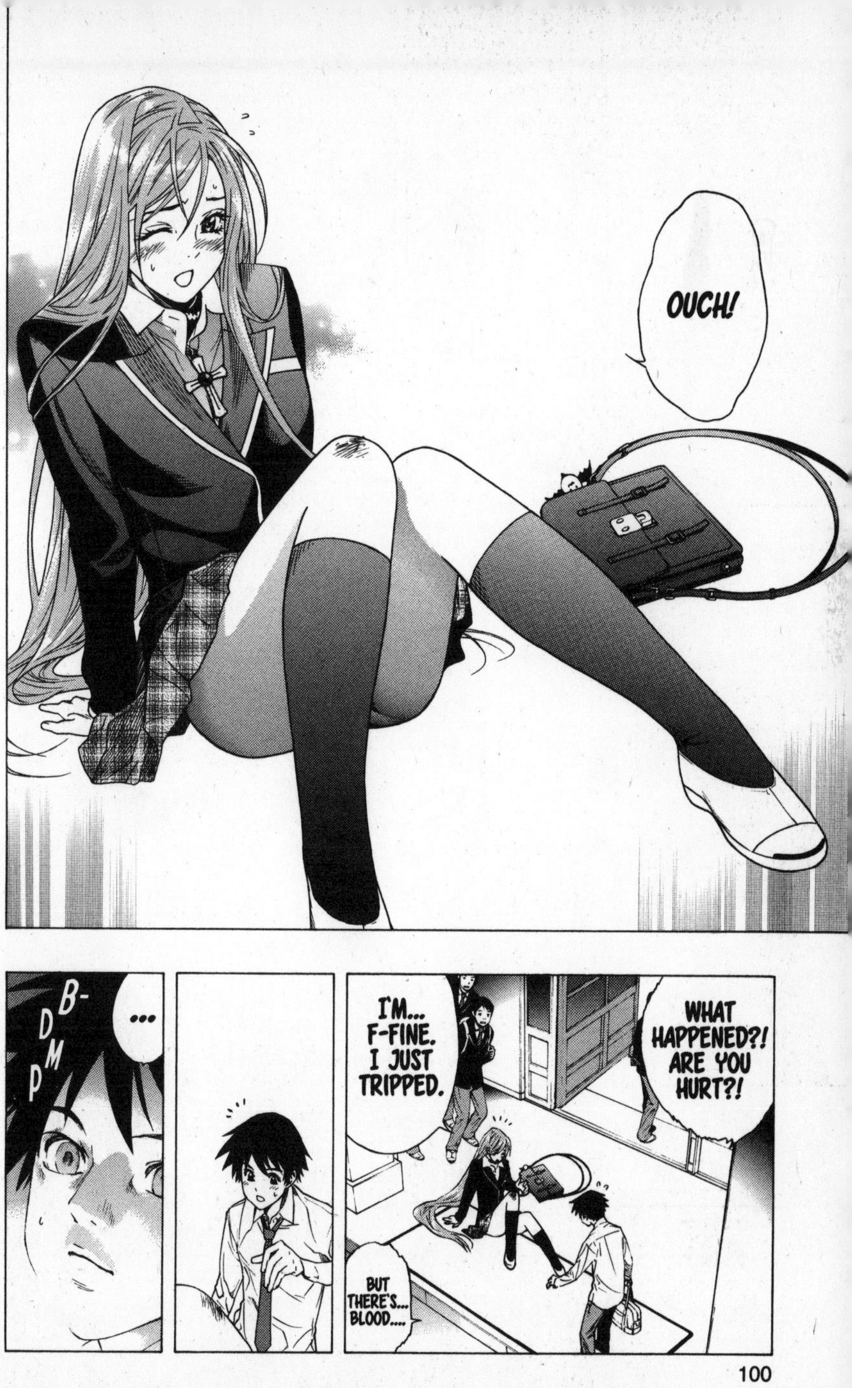
OUCH!
WHAT HAPPENED?! ARE YOU HURT?!
I'M... F-FINE. I JUST TRIPPED.
BUT THERE'S... BLOOD....
B-DMP
...

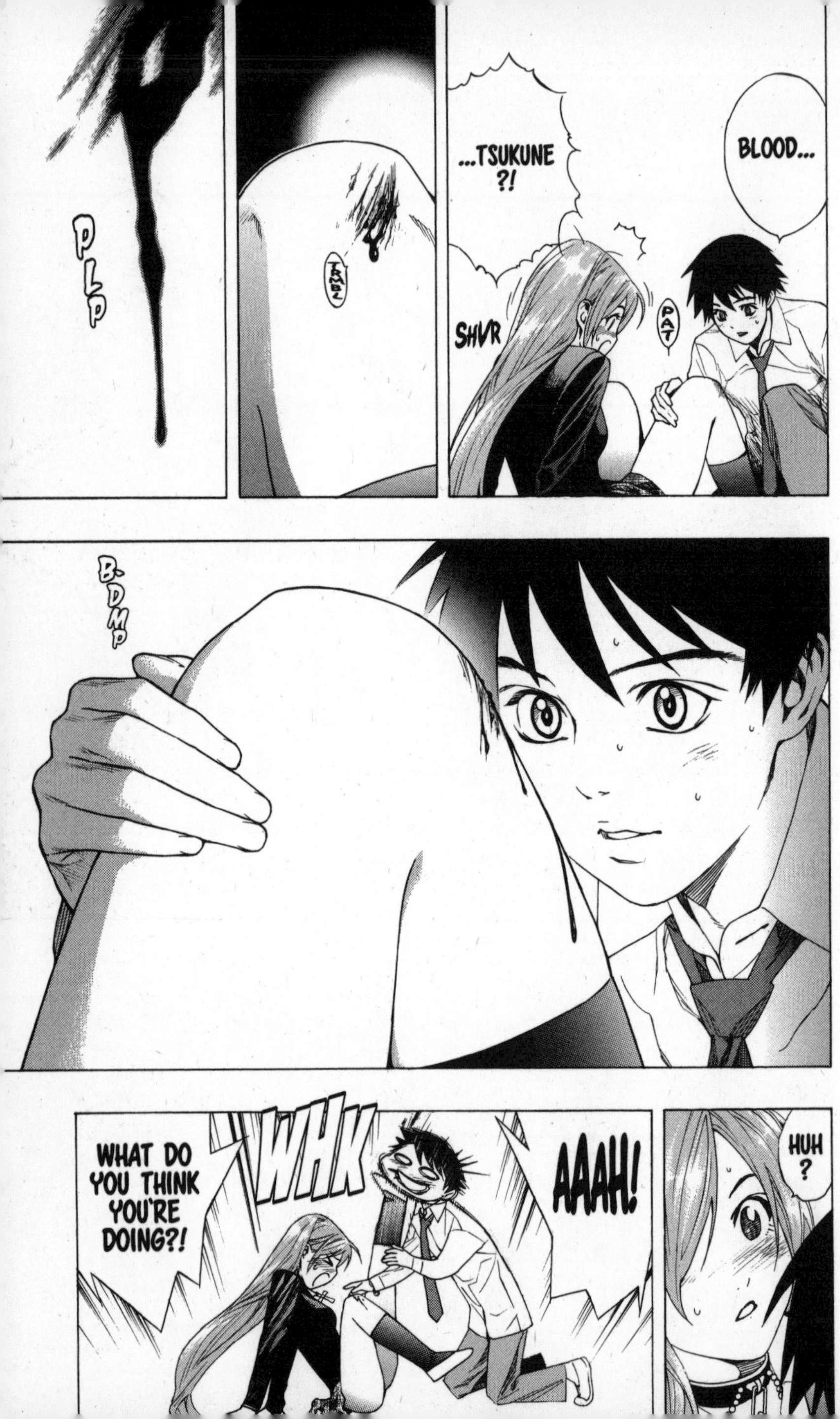
BLOOD...
...TSUKUNE ?!
PAT
SHVR
TRMBL
PLP
B-DMP
HUH ?
AAAH!
WHK
WHAT DO YOU THINK YOU'RE DOING?!

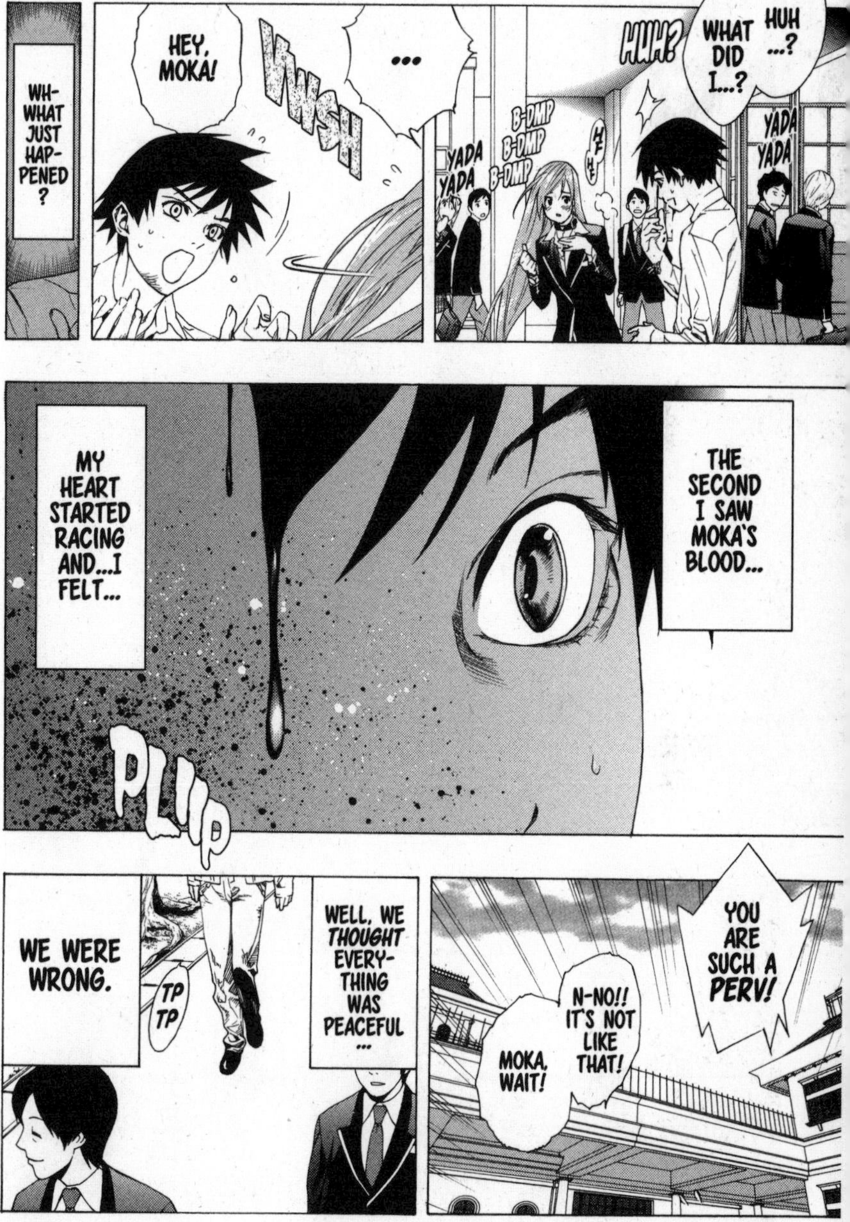

HUH ...?
WHAT DID I...?
HUH?
YADA YADA
B-DMP B-DMP B-DMP
YADA YADA
...
VWSH
HEY, MOKA!
WH-WHAT JUST HAP-PENED?
THE SECOND I SAW MOKA'S BLOOD...
MY HEART STARTED RACING AND...I FELT...
PLIP
YOU ARE SUCH A PERV!
N-NO!! IT'S NOT LIKE THAT!
MOKA, WAIT!
WELL, WE THOUGHT EVERY-THING WAS PEACEFUL...
TP TP
WE WERE WRONG.

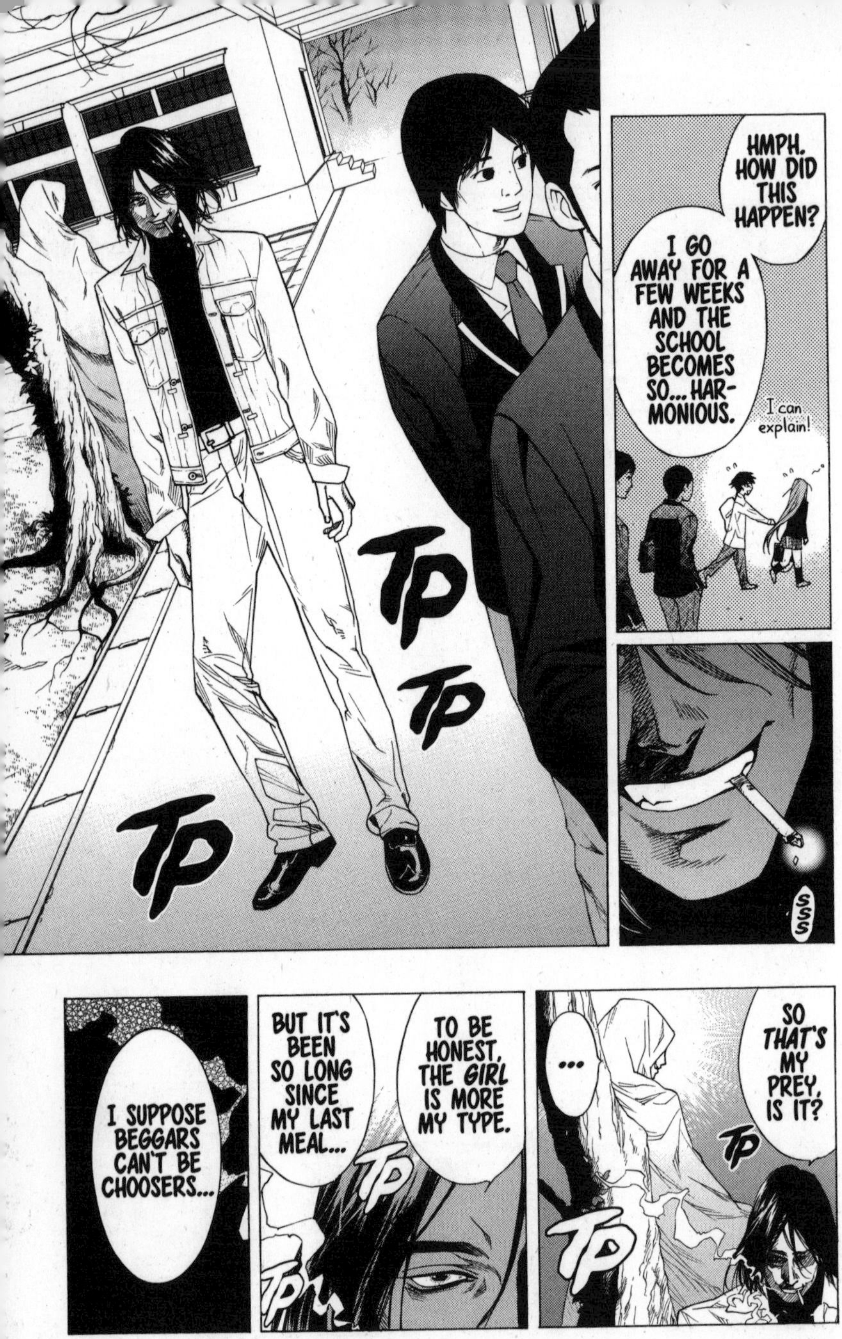
HMPH. HOW DID THIS HAPPEN?
I GO AWAY FOR A FEW WEEKS AND THE SCHOOL BECOMES SO... HARMONIOUS.
I can explain!
SSS
TP
TP
TP
SO *THAT'S* MY PREY, IS IT?
...
TP
TP
TO BE HONEST, THE *GIRL* IS MORE MY TYPE.
BUT IT'S BEEN SO LONG SINCE MY LAST MEAL...
TP
TP
I SUPPOSE BEGGARS CAN'T BE CHOOSERS...

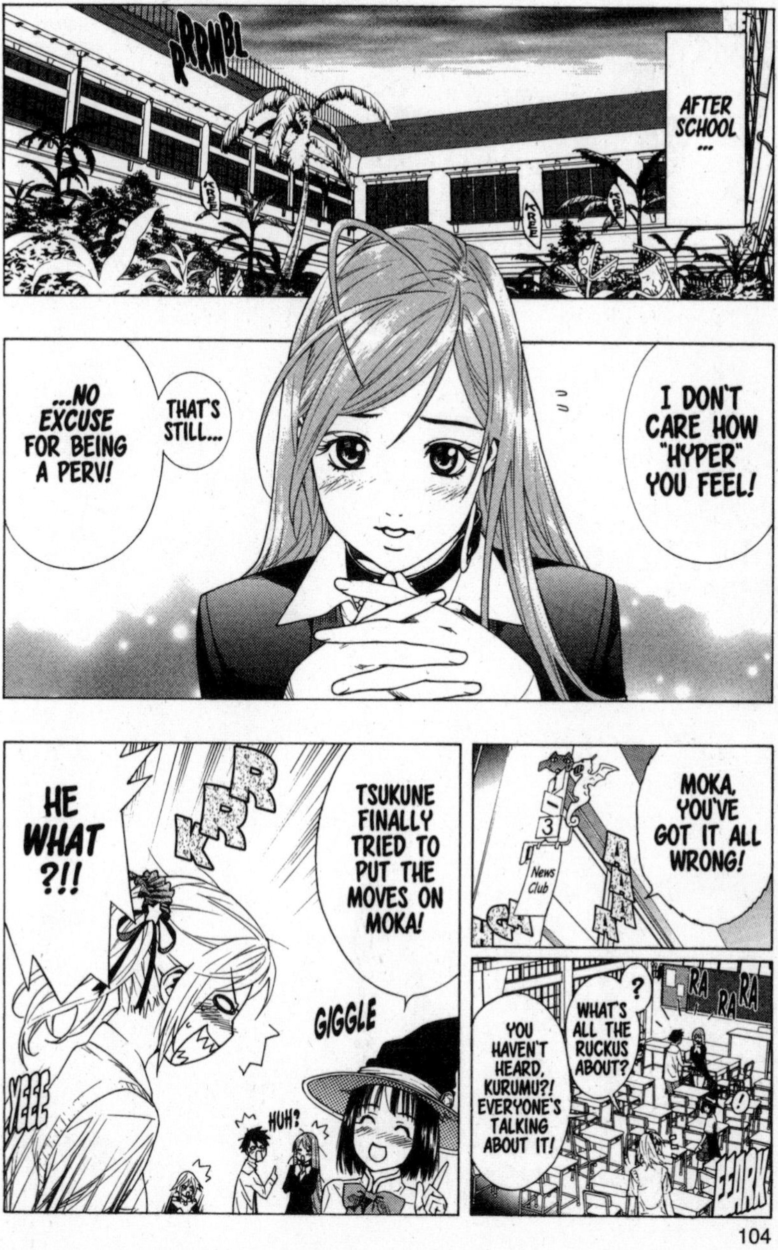
RRRMBL
AFTER SCHOOL...
KREE
KREE
KREE
I DON'T CARE HOW "HYPER" YOU FEEL!
THAT'S STILL...
...NO EXCUSE FOR BEING A PERV!
MOKA, YOU'VE GOT IT ALL WRONG!
News Club
RA RA RA
?
WHAT'S ALL THE RUCKUS ABOUT?
YOU HAVEN'T HEARD, KURUMU?! EVERYONE'S TALKING ABOUT IT!
TSUKUNE FINALLY TRIED TO PUT THE MOVES ON MOKA!
GIGGLE
HUH?
RRRK
HE WHAT?!!
YEEE

READ THIS WAY

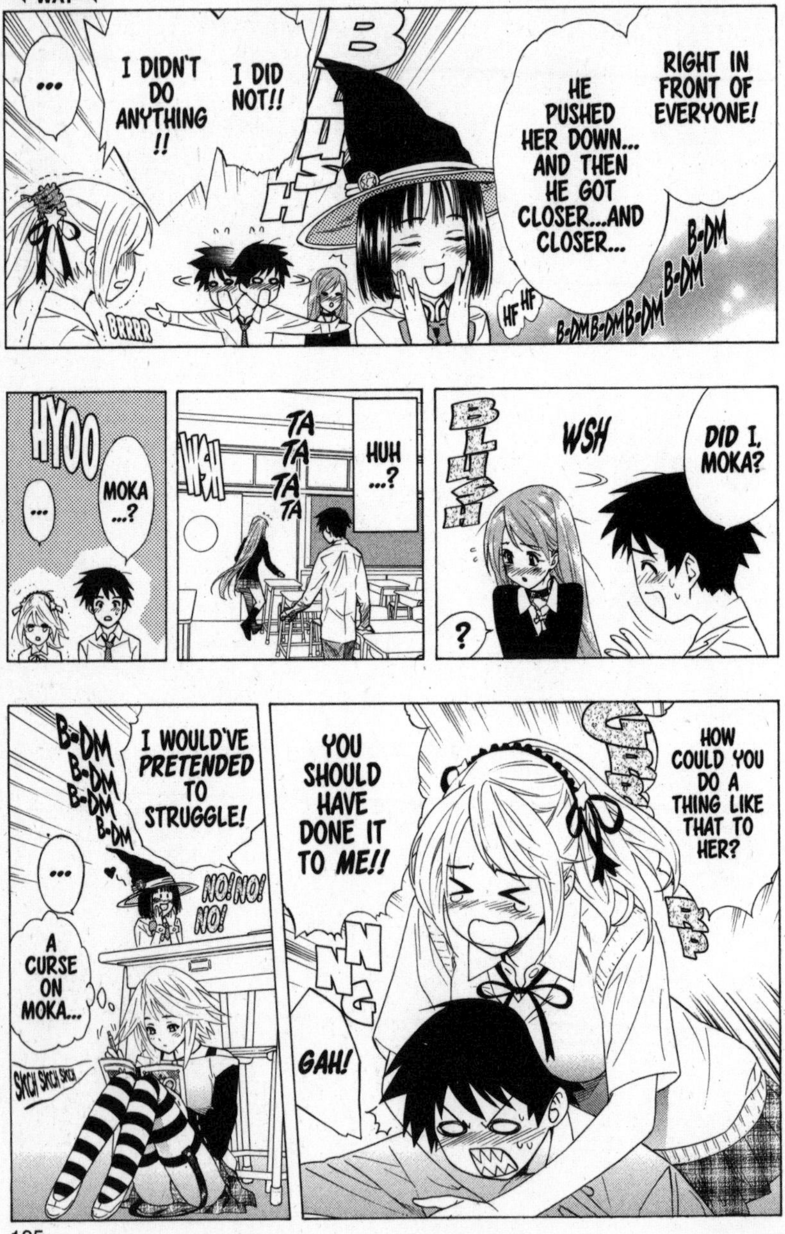
RIGHT IN FRONT OF EVERYONE!
HE PUSHED HER DOWN... AND THEN HE GOT CLOSER...AND CLOSER...
B-DM B-DM
HF HF
B-DM B-DM B-DM
BLUSH
I DID NOT!!
I DIDN'T DO ANYTHING !!
...
BRRRR
DID I, MOKA?
WSH
BLUSH
?
HUH ...?
TA TA TA TA
WSH
HYOO
MOKA ...?
...
HOW COULD YOU DO A THING LIKE THAT TO HER?
YOU SHOULD HAVE DONE IT TO ME!!
NNG
GAH!
I WOULD'VE PRETENDED TO STRUGGLE!
B-DM B-DM B-DM B-DM
NO! NO! NO!
...
A CURSE ON MOKA...

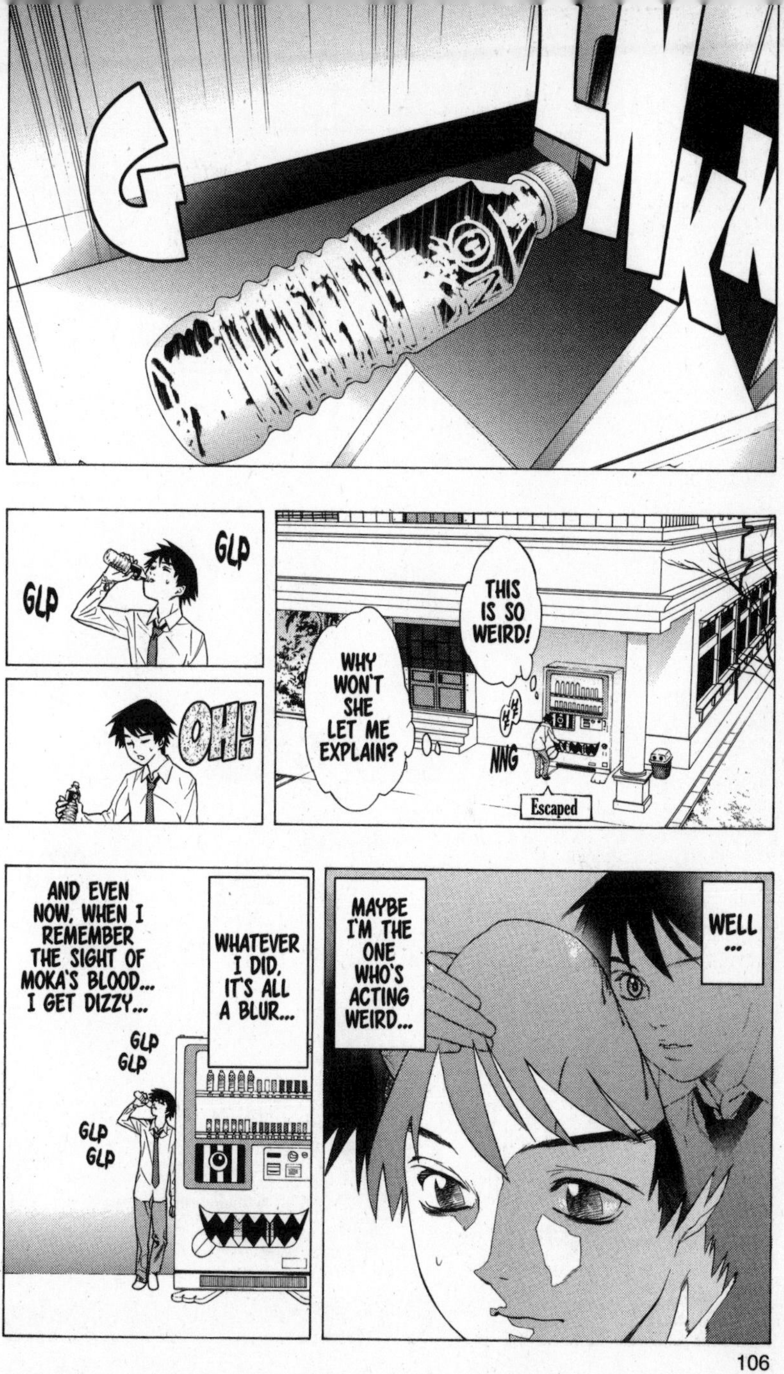
G
LNKK
THIS IS SO WEIRD!
WHY WON'T SHE LET ME EXPLAIN?
NNG
Escaped
GLP
GLP
OH!
WELL...
MAYBE I'M THE ONE WHO'S ACTING WEIRD...
WHATEVER I DID, IT'S ALL A BLUR...
AND EVEN NOW, WHEN I REMEMBER THE SIGHT OF MOKA'S BLOOD... I GET DIZZY...
GLP GLP
GLP GLP

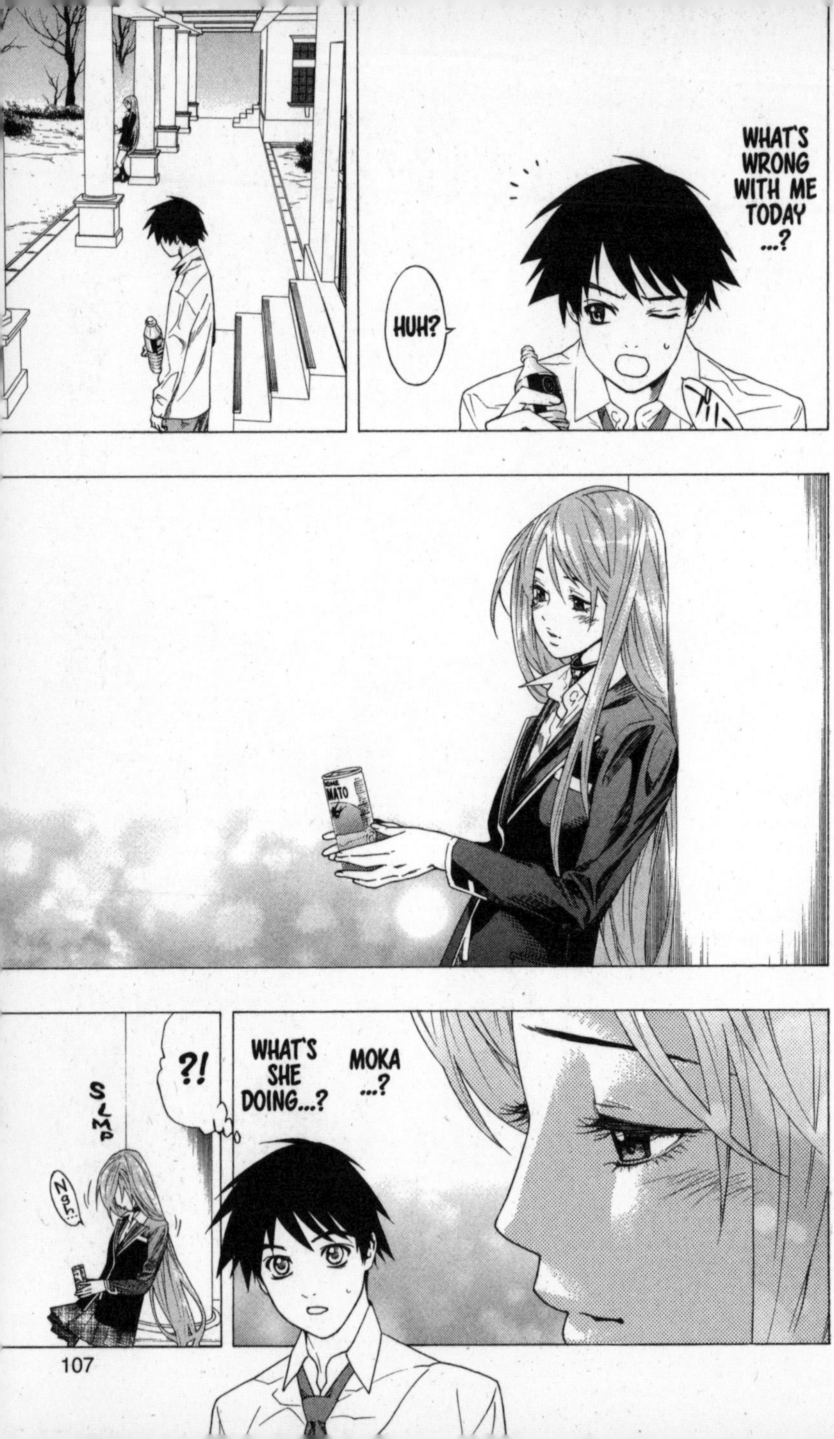
WHAT'S WRONG WITH ME TODAY ...?
HUH?
MOKA ...?
WHAT'S SHE DOING...?
?!
SLMP
Nsh...

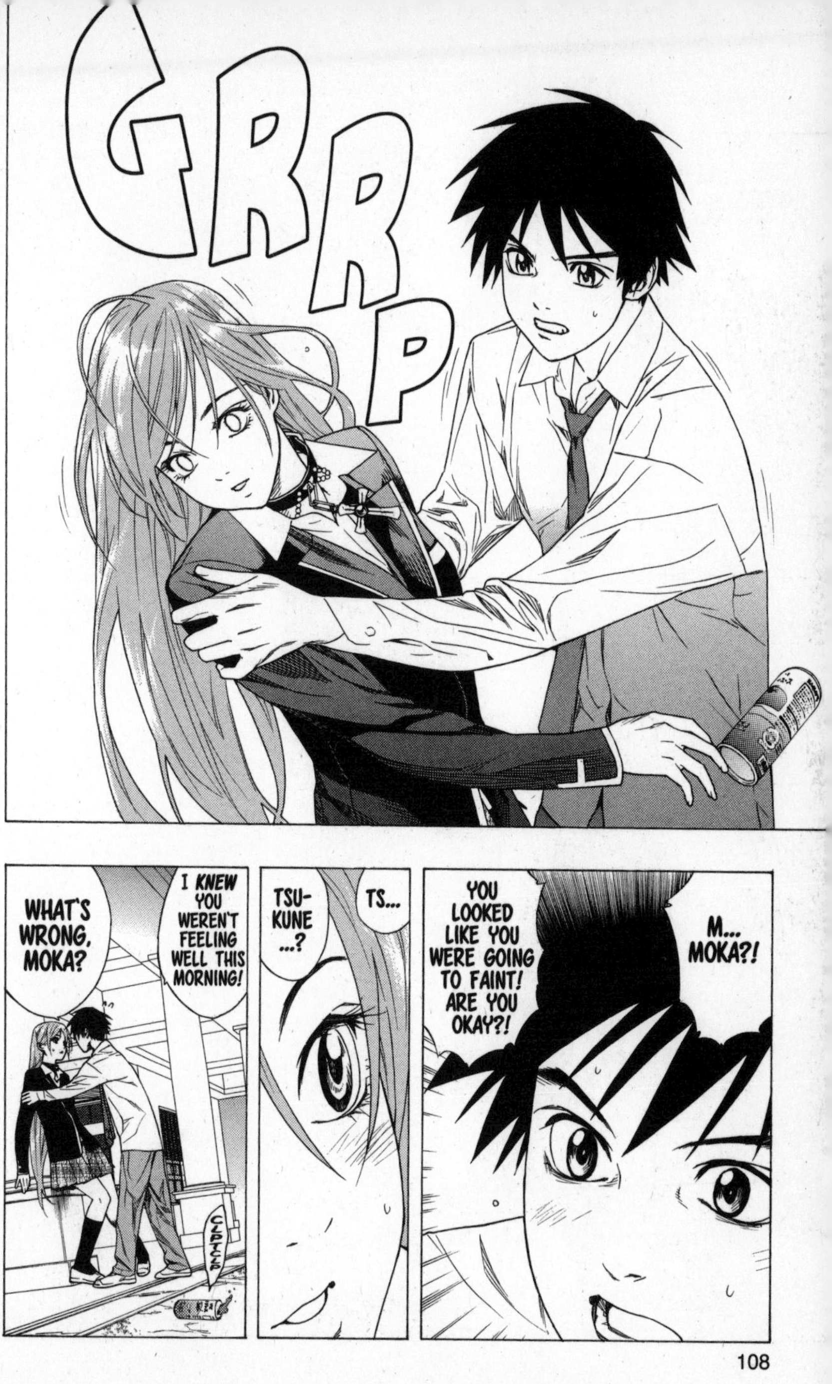
GRRRP
M... MOKA?!
YOU LOOKED LIKE YOU WERE GOING TO FAINT! ARE YOU OKAY?!
TS...
TSU-KUNE ...?
I KNEW YOU WEREN'T FEELING WELL THIS MORNING!
WHAT'S WRONG, MOKA?
CLPTCLP

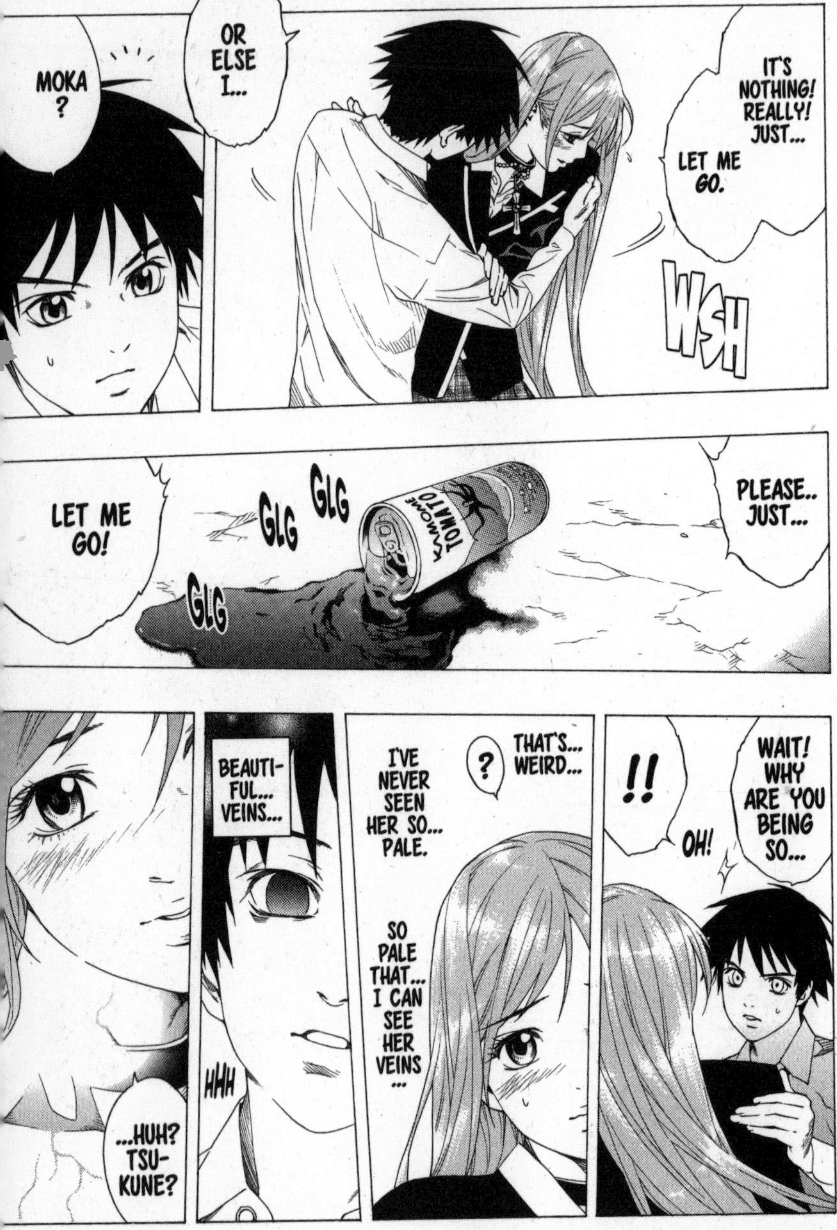
IT'S NOTHING! REALLY! JUST...
LET ME GO.
WSH
OR ELSE I...
MOKA ?
PLEASE.. JUST...
GLG
GLG
KAMOME TOMATO
GLG
LET ME GO!
WAIT! WHY ARE YOU BEING SO...
OH!
!!
THAT'S... WEIRD...
?
I'VE NEVER SEEN HER SO... PALE.
SO PALE THAT... I CAN SEE HER VEINS ...
BEAUTI-FUL... VEINS...
HHH
...HUH? TSU-KUNE?

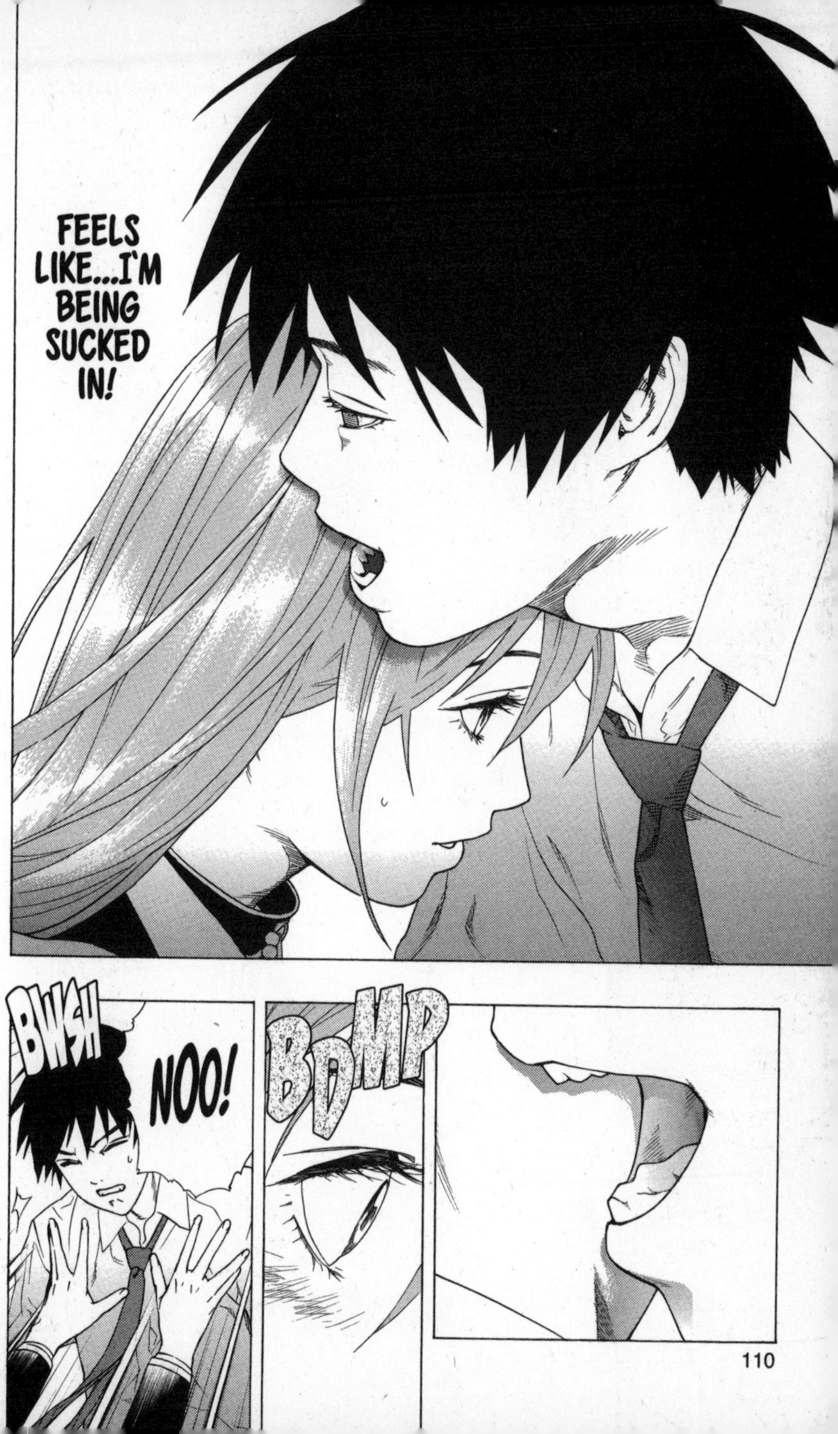
FEELS LIKE...I'M BEING SUCKED IN!
BDMP
BWSH
NOO!

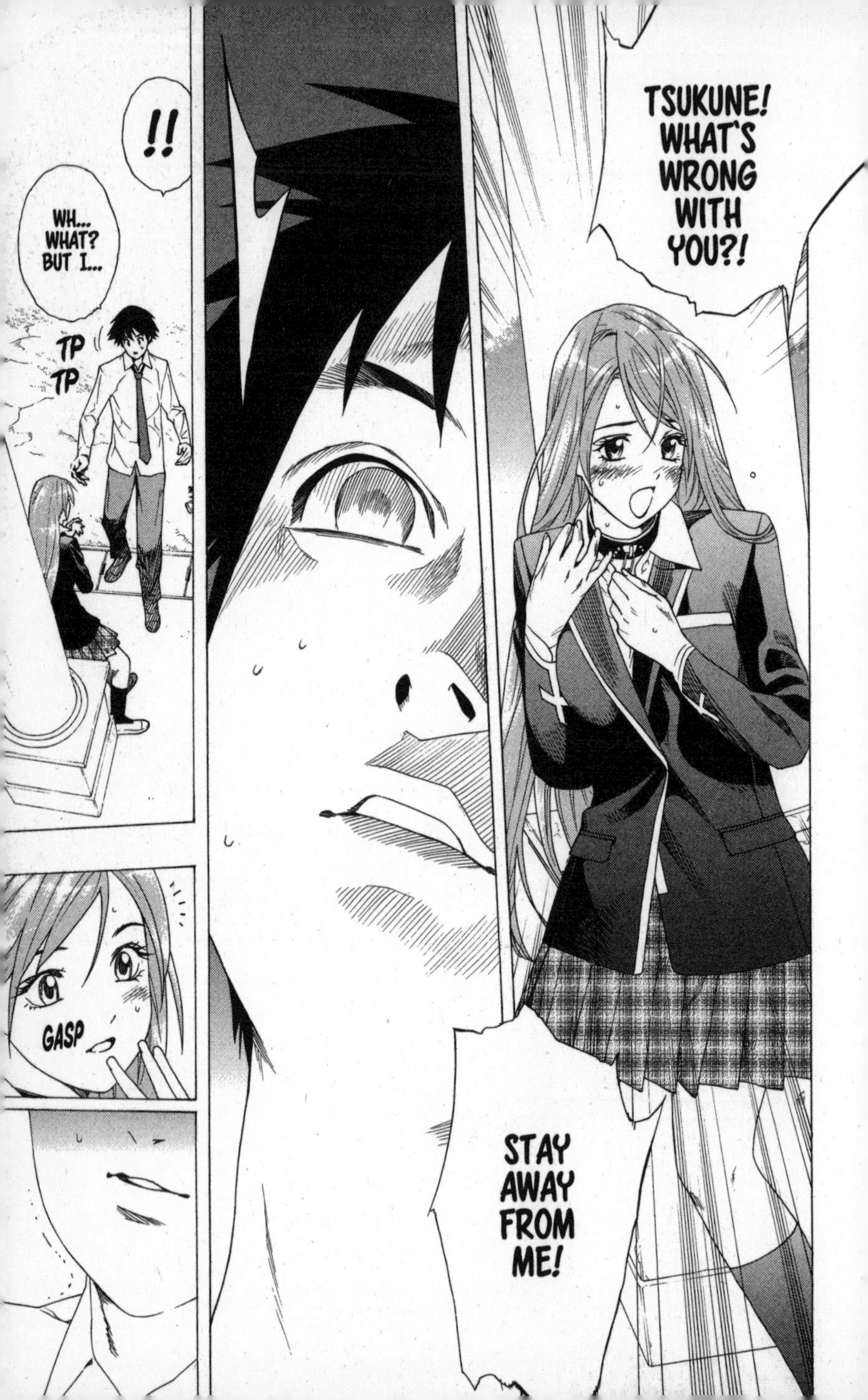
TSUKUNE! WHAT'S WRONG WITH YOU?!
STAY AWAY FROM ME!
!!
WH... WHAT? BUT I...
TP TP
GASP

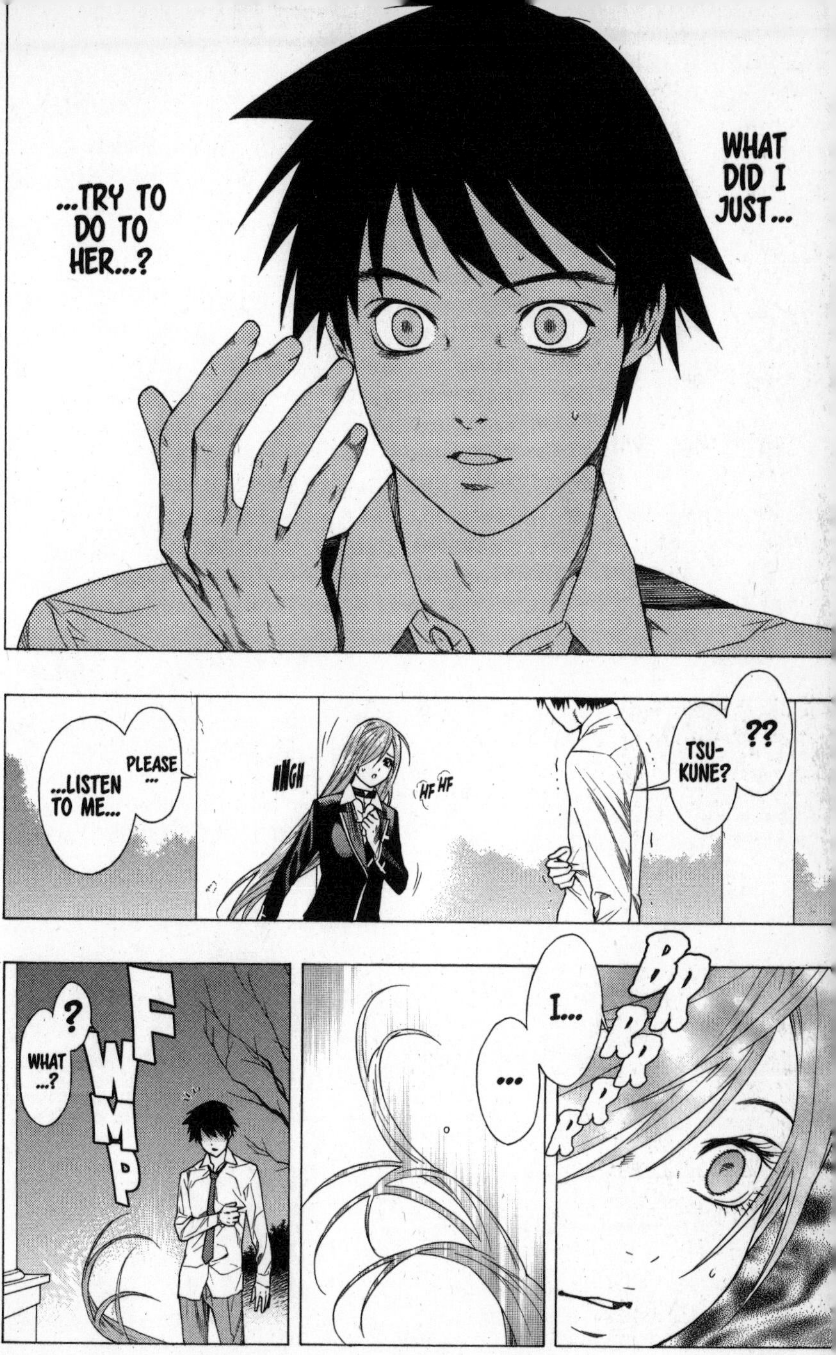
WHAT DID I JUST...
...TRY TO DO TO HER...?
??
TSU-KUNE?
HF HF
NNGH
PLEASE...
...LISTEN TO ME...
BRRRRR
I...
...
FWMP
?
WHAT...?

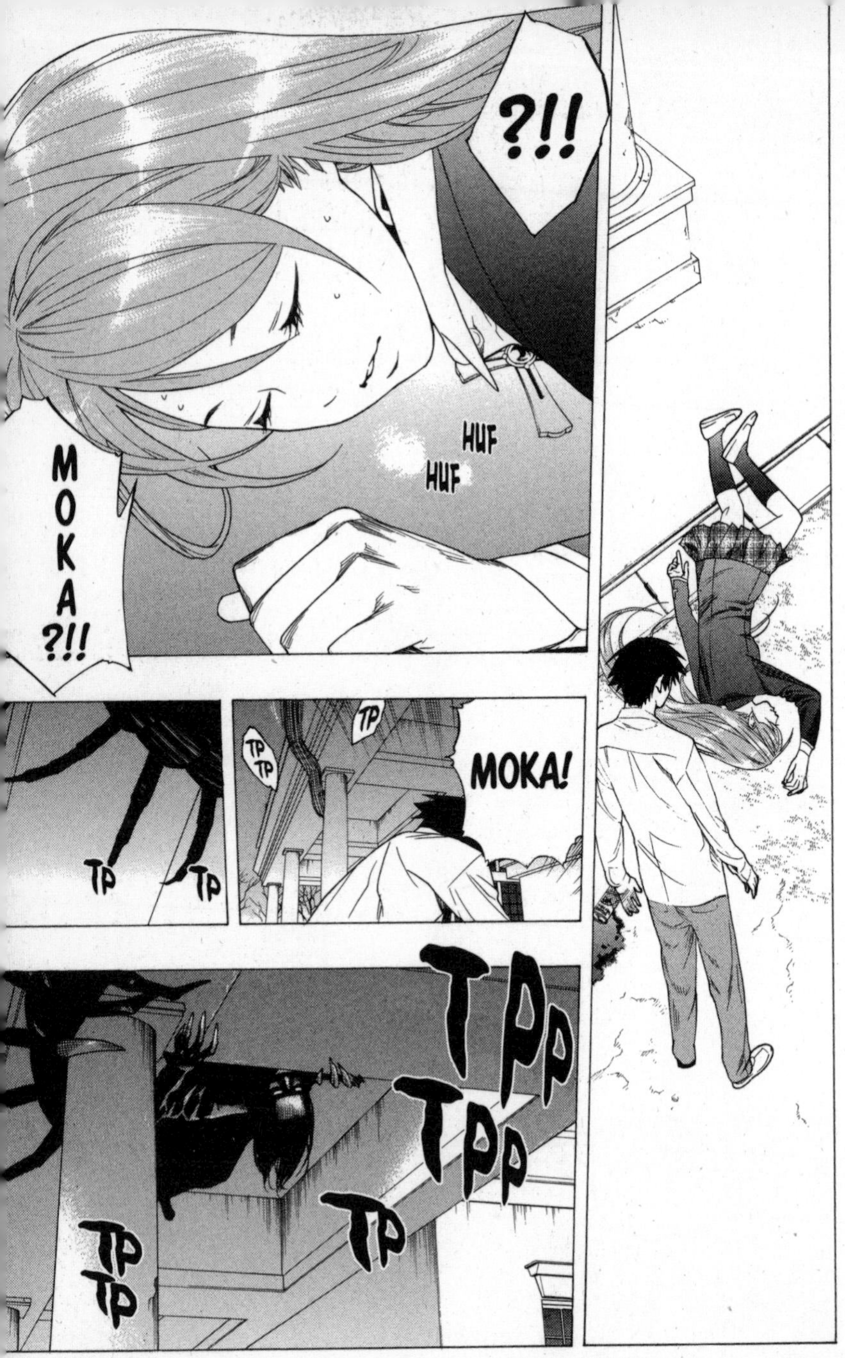

?!!
HUF
HUF
MOKA?!!
MOKA!
TP
TP TP
TP
TP
TPP
TPP
TP
TP TP

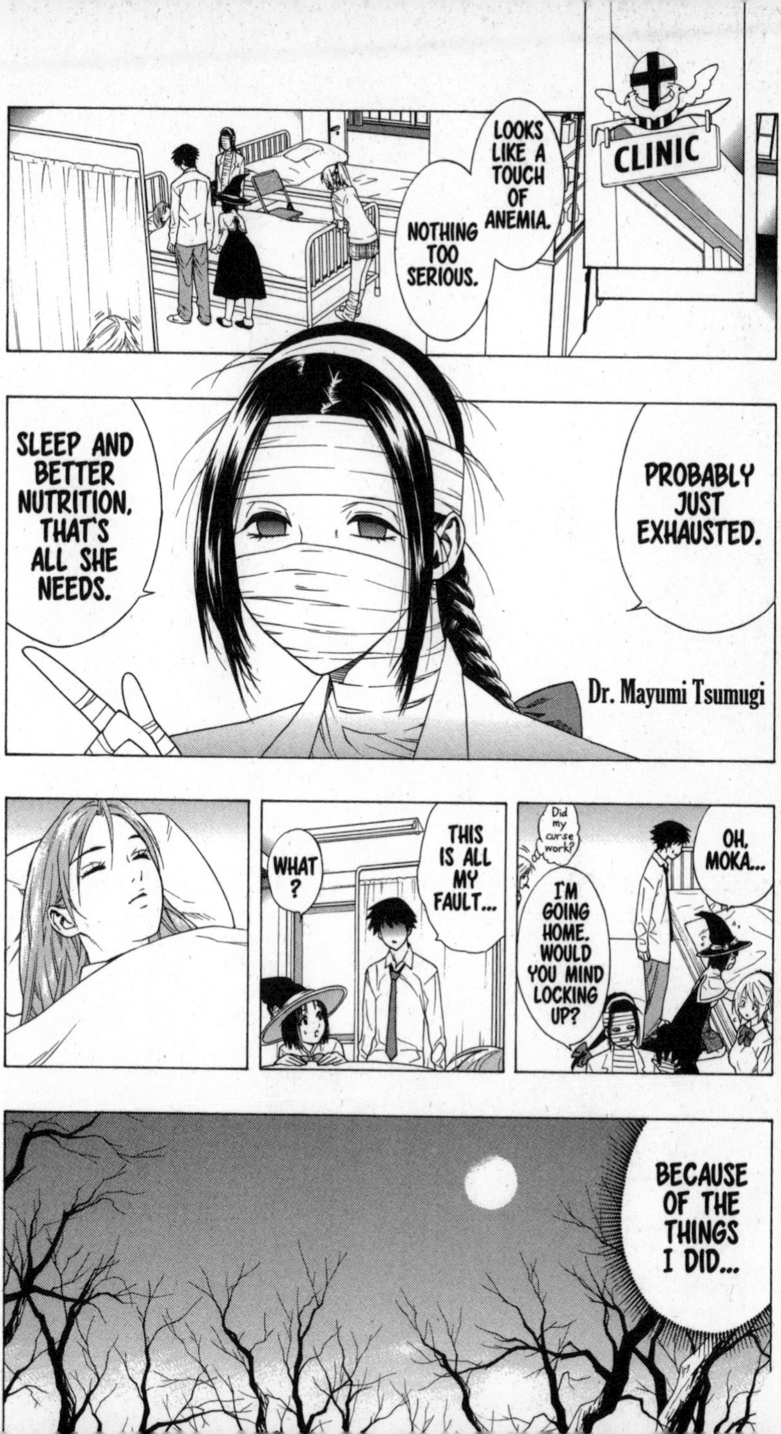
CLINIC
LOOKS LIKE A TOUCH OF ANEMIA.
NOTHING TOO SERIOUS.
PROBABLY JUST EXHAUSTED.
Dr. Mayumi Tsumugi
SLEEP AND BETTER NUTRITION, THAT'S ALL SHE NEEDS.
OH, MOKA...
Did my curse work?
I'M GOING HOME. WOULD YOU MIND LOCKING UP?
THIS IS ALL MY FAULT...
WHAT?
BECAUSE OF THE THINGS I DID...

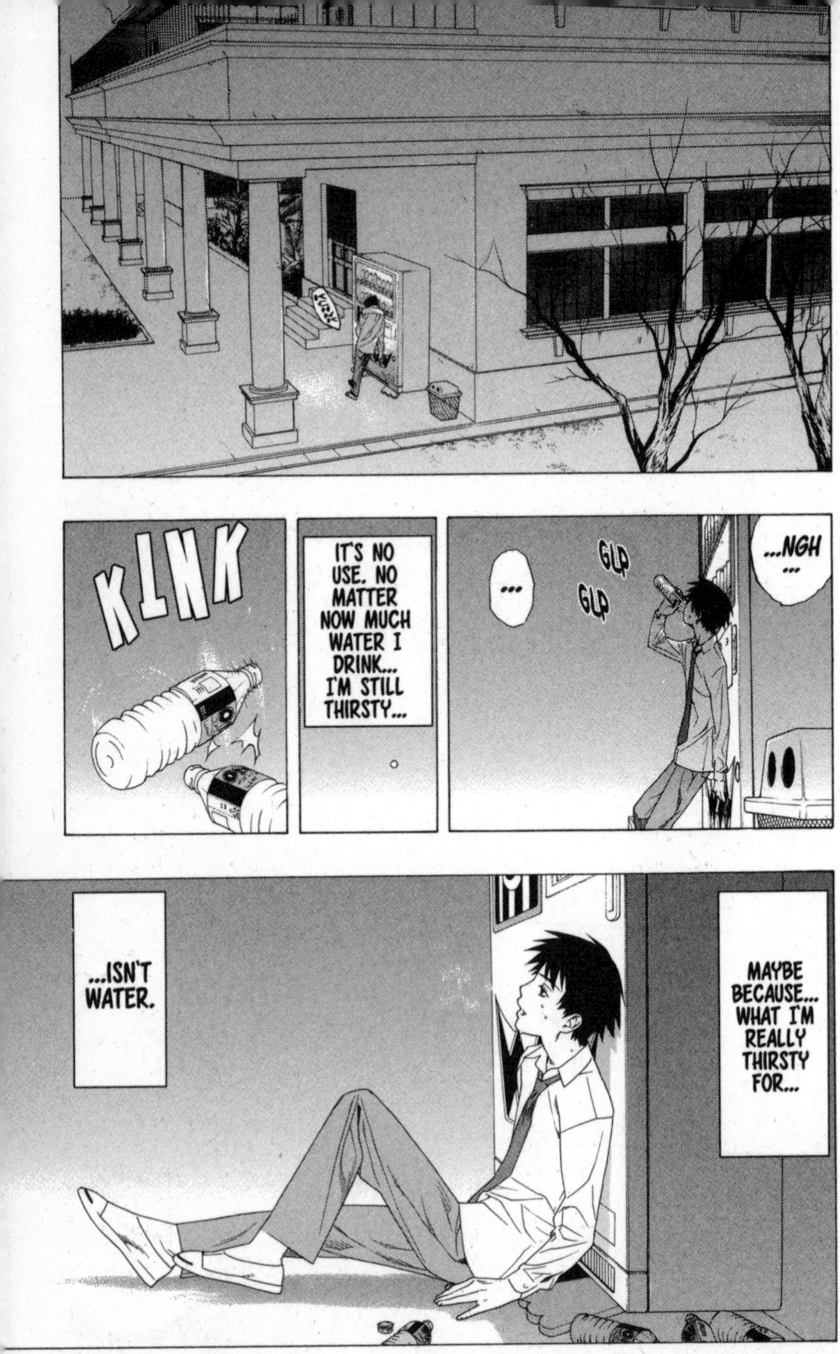
...NGH ...
GLP
GLP
...
IT'S NO USE. NO MATTER NOW MUCH WATER I DRINK... I'M STILL THIRSTY...
KLNK
MAYBE BECAUSE... WHAT I'M REALLY THIRSTY FOR...
...ISN'T WATER.

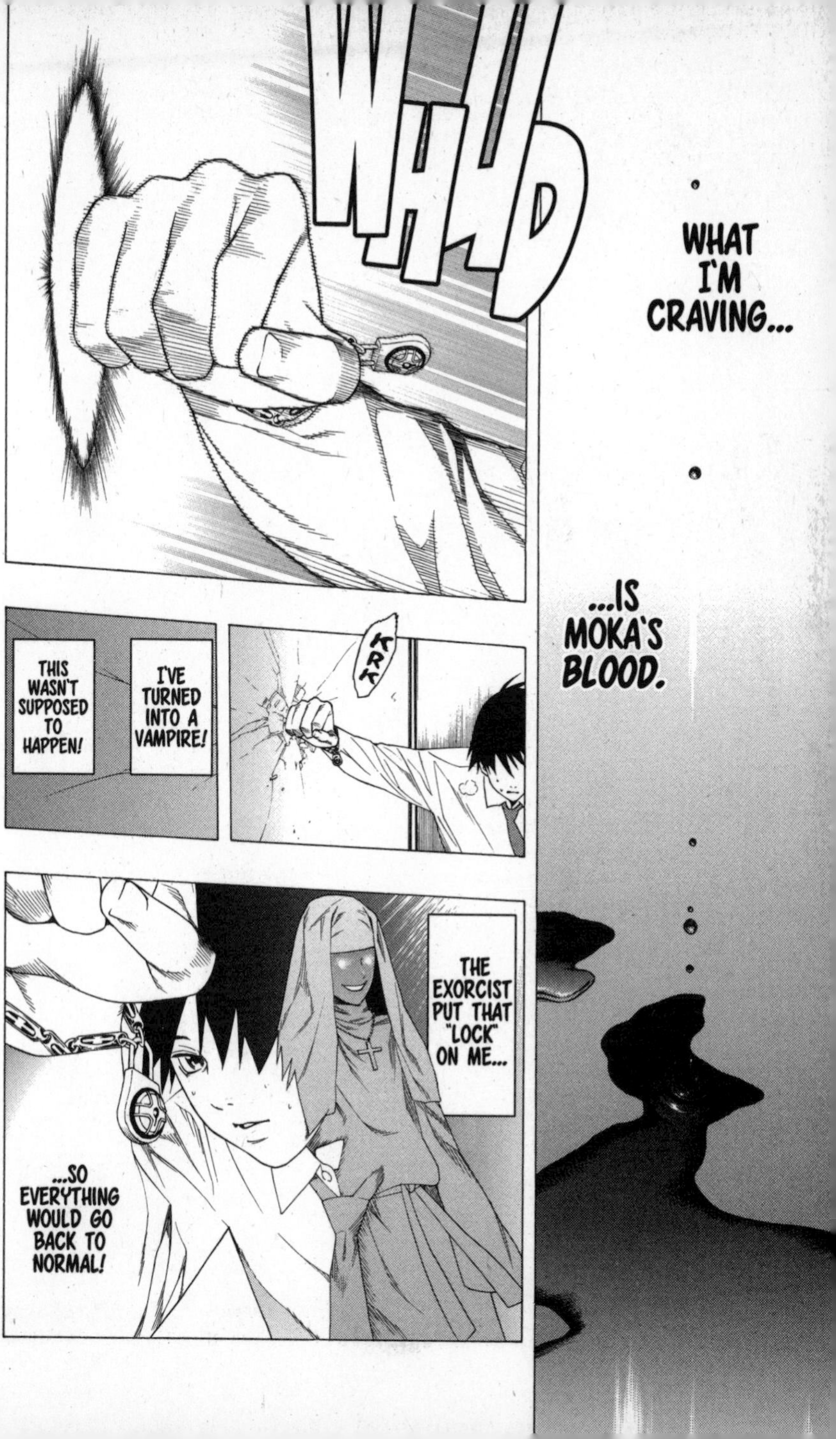
WHAT I'M CRAVING...
...IS MOKA'S BLOOD.
WHUD
KRK
I'VE TURNED INTO A VAMPIRE!
THIS WASN'T SUPPOSED TO HAPPEN!
THE EXORCIST PUT THAT "LOCK" ON ME...
...SO EVERYTHING WOULD GO BACK TO NORMAL!

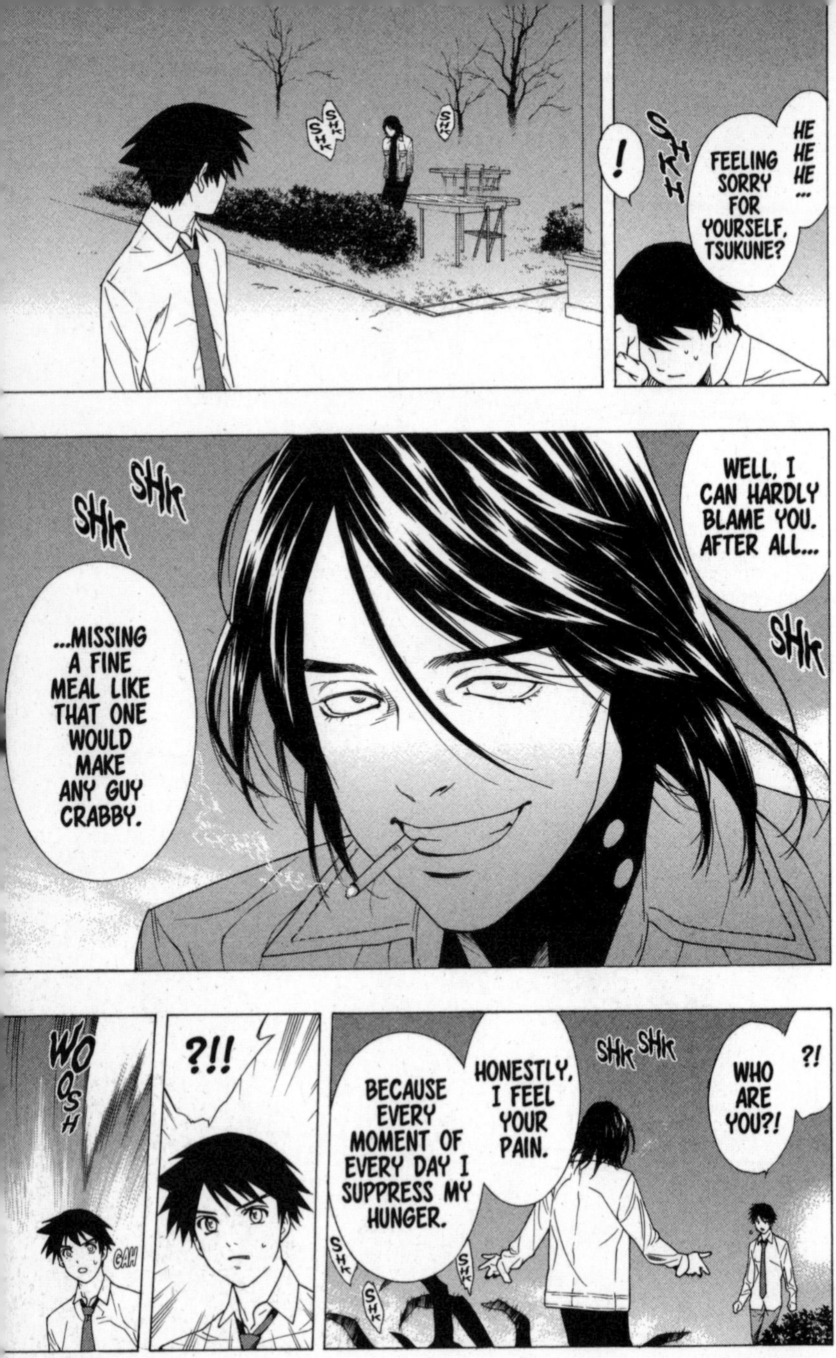
HE HE HE...
FEELING SORRY FOR YOURSELF, TSUKUNE?
SHKK
!
SHK
SHK SHK
WELL, I CAN HARDLY BLAME YOU. AFTER ALL...
SHK
SHK SHK
...MISSING A FINE MEAL LIKE THAT ONE WOULD MAKE ANY GUY CRABBY.
?!
WHO ARE YOU?!
SHK SHK
HONESTLY, I FEEL YOUR PAIN.
BECAUSE EVERY MOMENT OF EVERY DAY I SUPPRESS MY HUNGER.
SHK
SHK
SHK
?!!
WOOSH
GAH

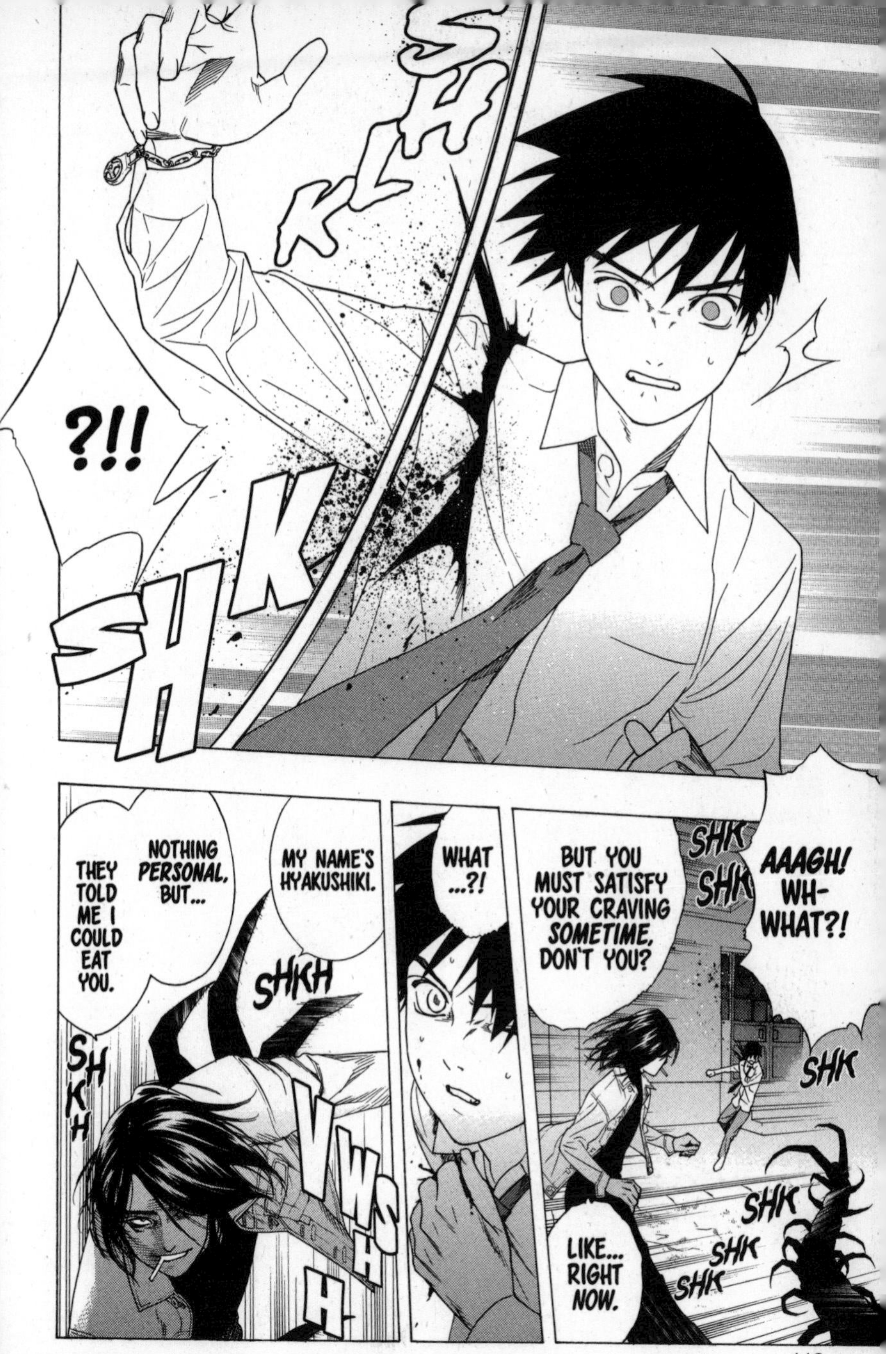
SHLK
?!!
SHK
BUT YOU MUST SATISFY YOUR CRAVING SOMETIME, DON'T YOU?
SHK SHK
AAAGH! WH-WHAT?!
SHK
LIKE... RIGHT NOW.
SHK
SHK
SHK
WHAT ...?!
MY NAME'S HYAKUSHIKI.
NOTHING PERSONAL, BUT...
THEY TOLD ME I COULD EAT YOU.
SHKH
SHKH
VWSHH

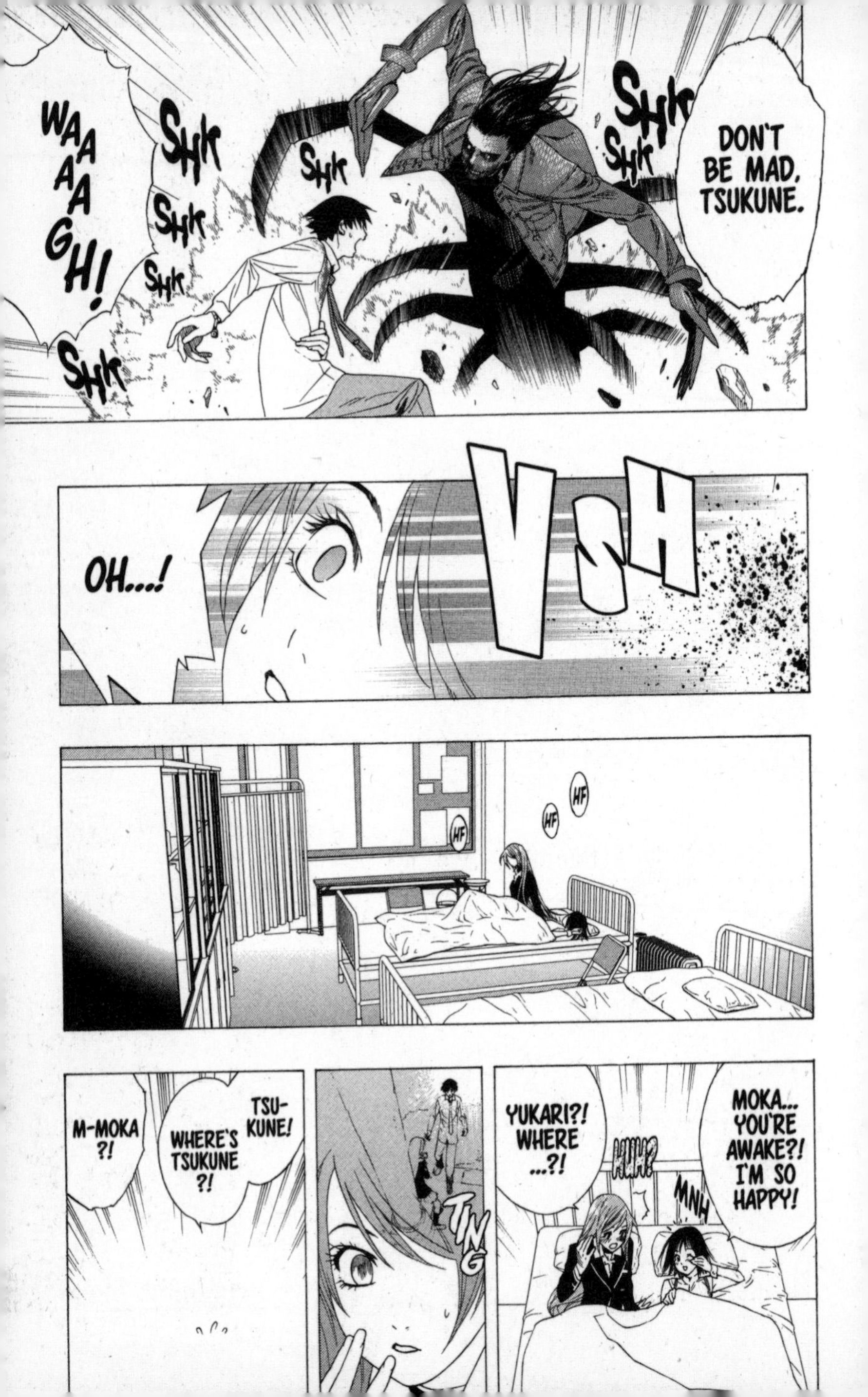
DON'T BE MAD, TSUKUNE.
SHK
SHK
SHK
SHK
SHK
SHK
WAAAAAGH!
SHK
VSH
OH...!
HF
HF
HF
MOKA... YOU'RE AWAKE?! I'M SO HAPPY!
MNH
HUH?
YUKARI?! WHERE ...?!
TING
TSU-KUNE!
WHERE'S TSUKUNE?!
M-MOKA?!

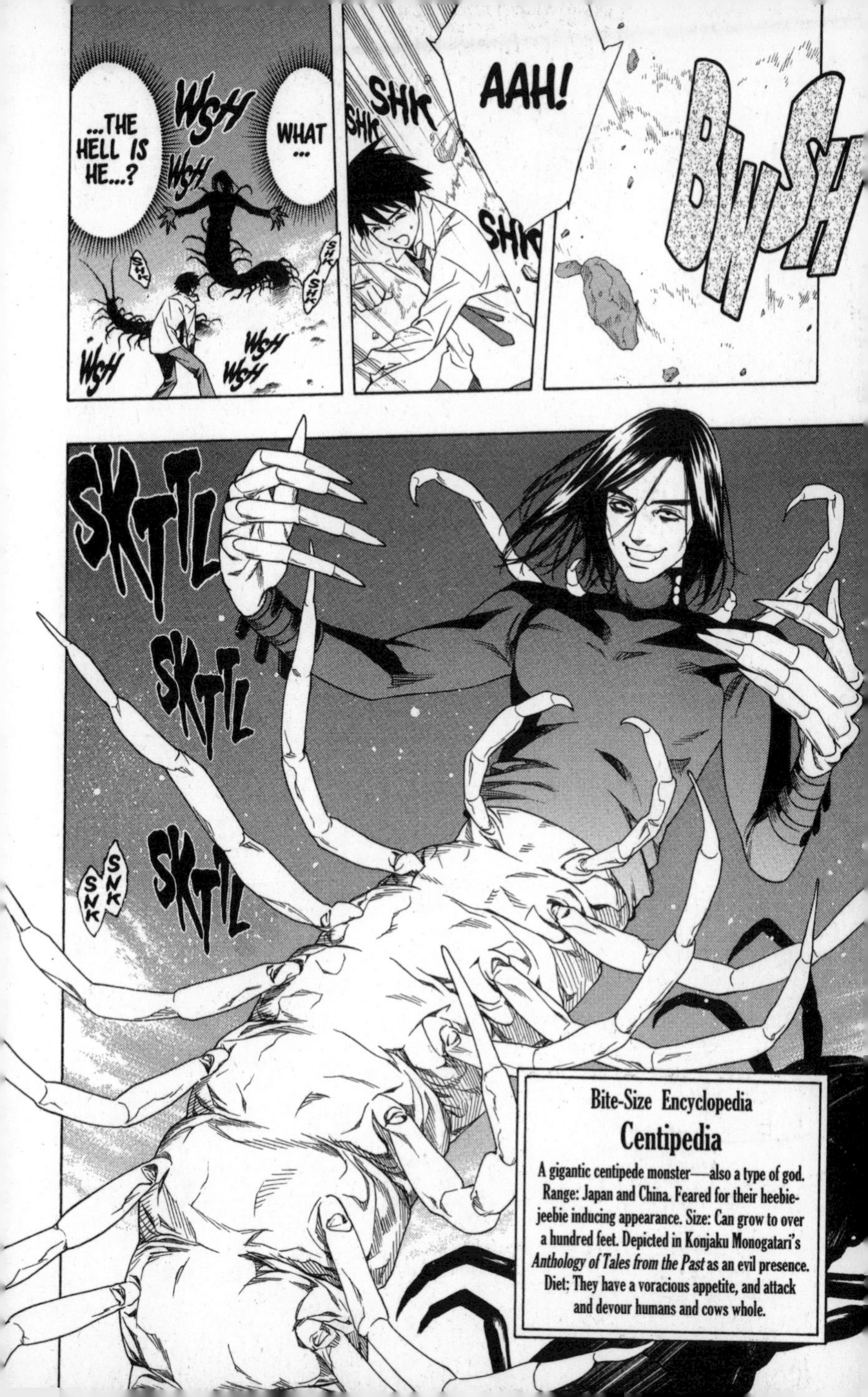
BWSH
AAH!
SHK
SHK
SHK
WHAT...
...THE HELL IS HE...?
WSH
WSH
SHK
SHK
SHK
WSH
WSH
WSH
SKTTL
SKTTL
SKTTL
SNK
SNK
Bite-Size Encyclopedia
Centipedia
A gigantic centipede monster—also a type of god. Range: Japan and China. Feared for their heebie-jeebie inducing appearance. Size: Can grow to over a hundred feet. Depicted in Konjaku Monogatari's *Anthology of Tales from the Past* as an evil presence. Diet: They have a voracious appetite, and attack and devour humans and cows whole.

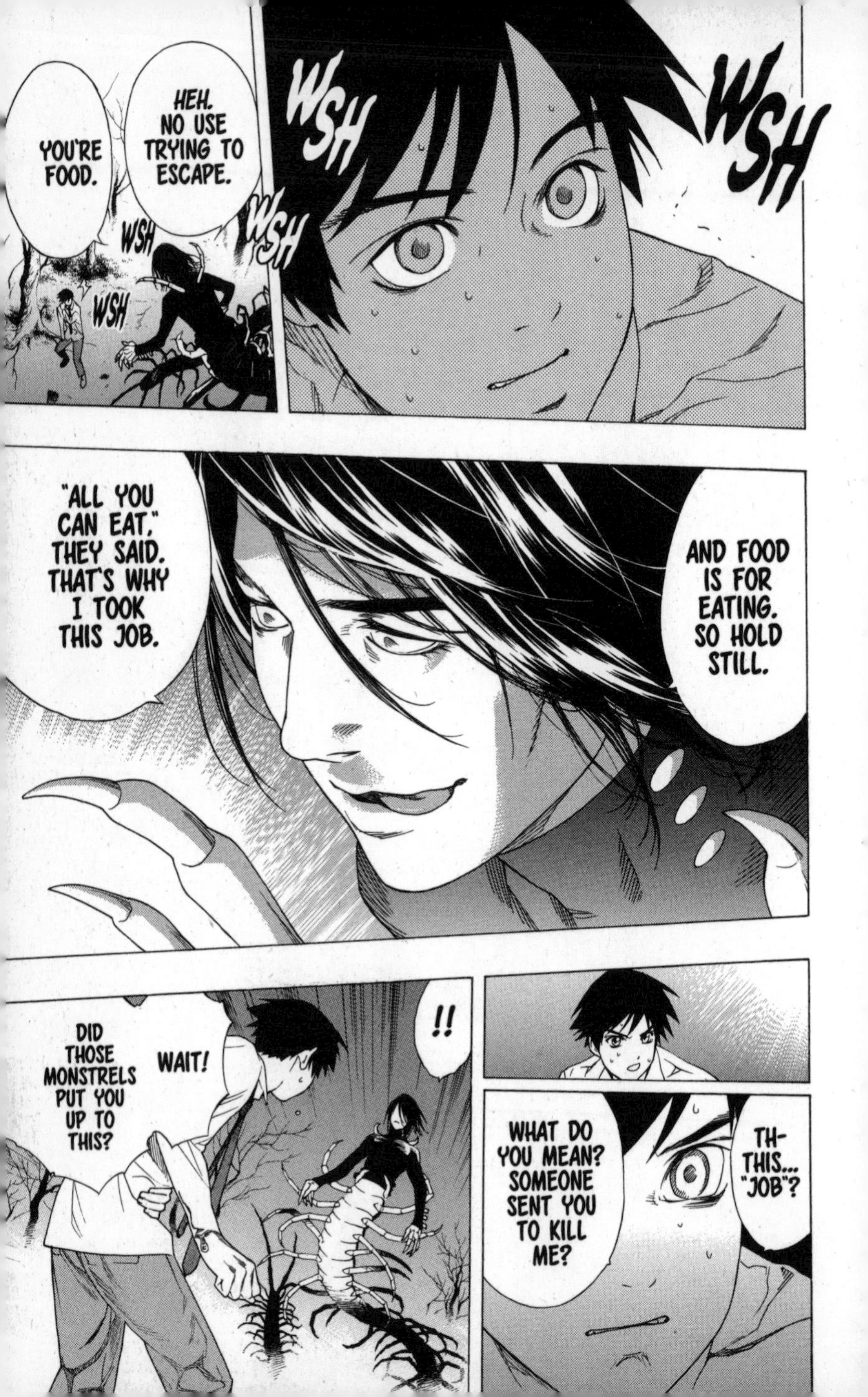
WSH
WSH
WSH
HEH. NO USE TRYING TO ESCAPE.
YOU'RE FOOD.
WSH
WSH
AND FOOD IS FOR EATING. SO HOLD STILL.
"ALL YOU CAN EAT," THEY SAID. THAT'S WHY I TOOK THIS JOB.
TH-THIS... "JOB"?
WHAT DO YOU MEAN? SOMEONE SENT YOU TO KILL ME?
!!
WAIT!
DID THOSE MONSTRELS PUT YOU UP TO THIS?

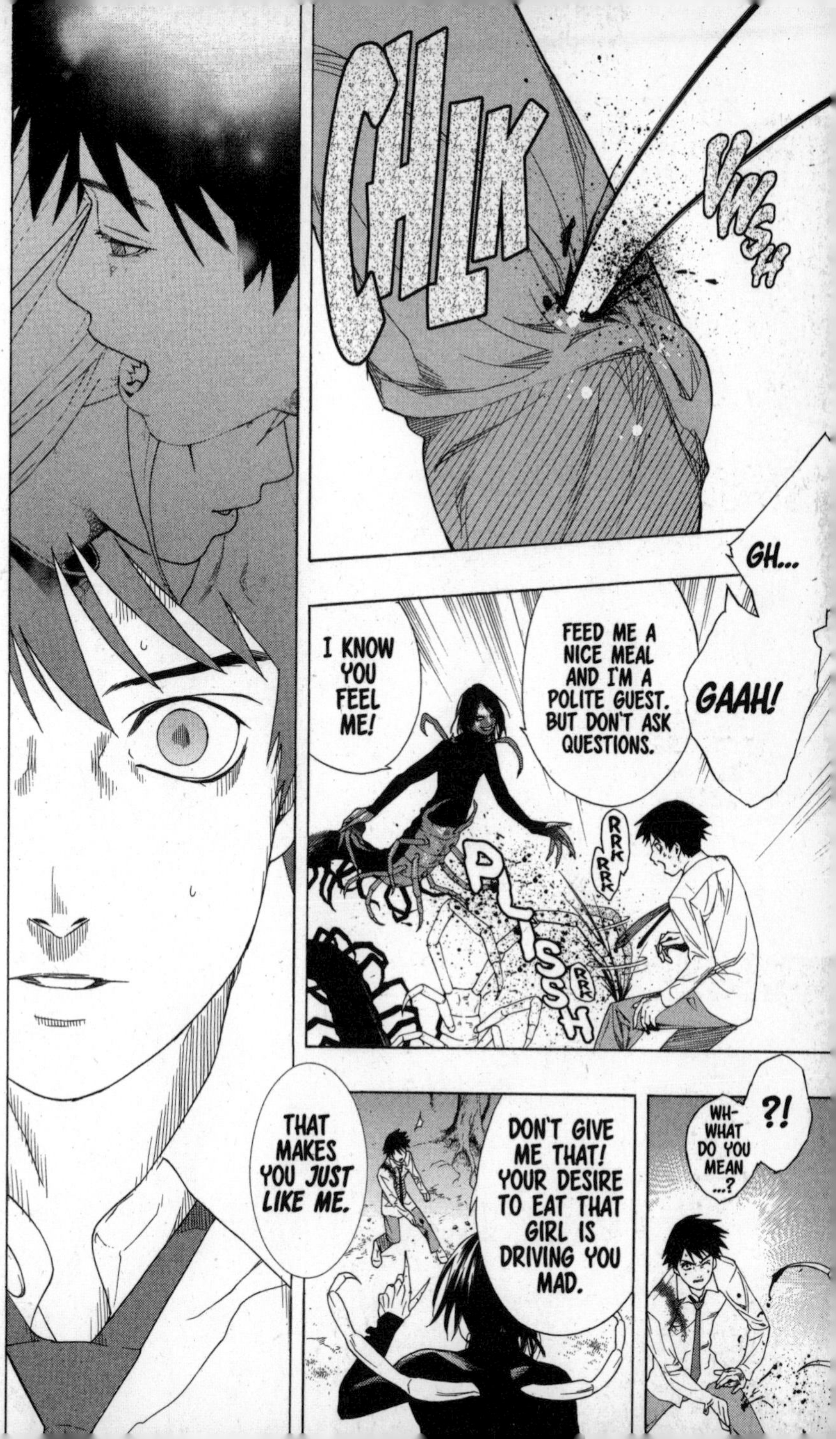
VWSH
CHLK
GH...
GAAH!
FEED ME A NICE MEAL AND I'M A POLITE GUEST. BUT DON'T ASK QUESTIONS.
I KNOW YOU FEEL ME!
RRK RRK RRK
PLISH
RRK
?!
WH-WHAT DO YOU MEAN ...?
DON'T GIVE ME THAT! YOUR DESIRE TO EAT THAT GIRL IS DRIVING YOU MAD.
THAT MAKES YOU JUST LIKE ME.

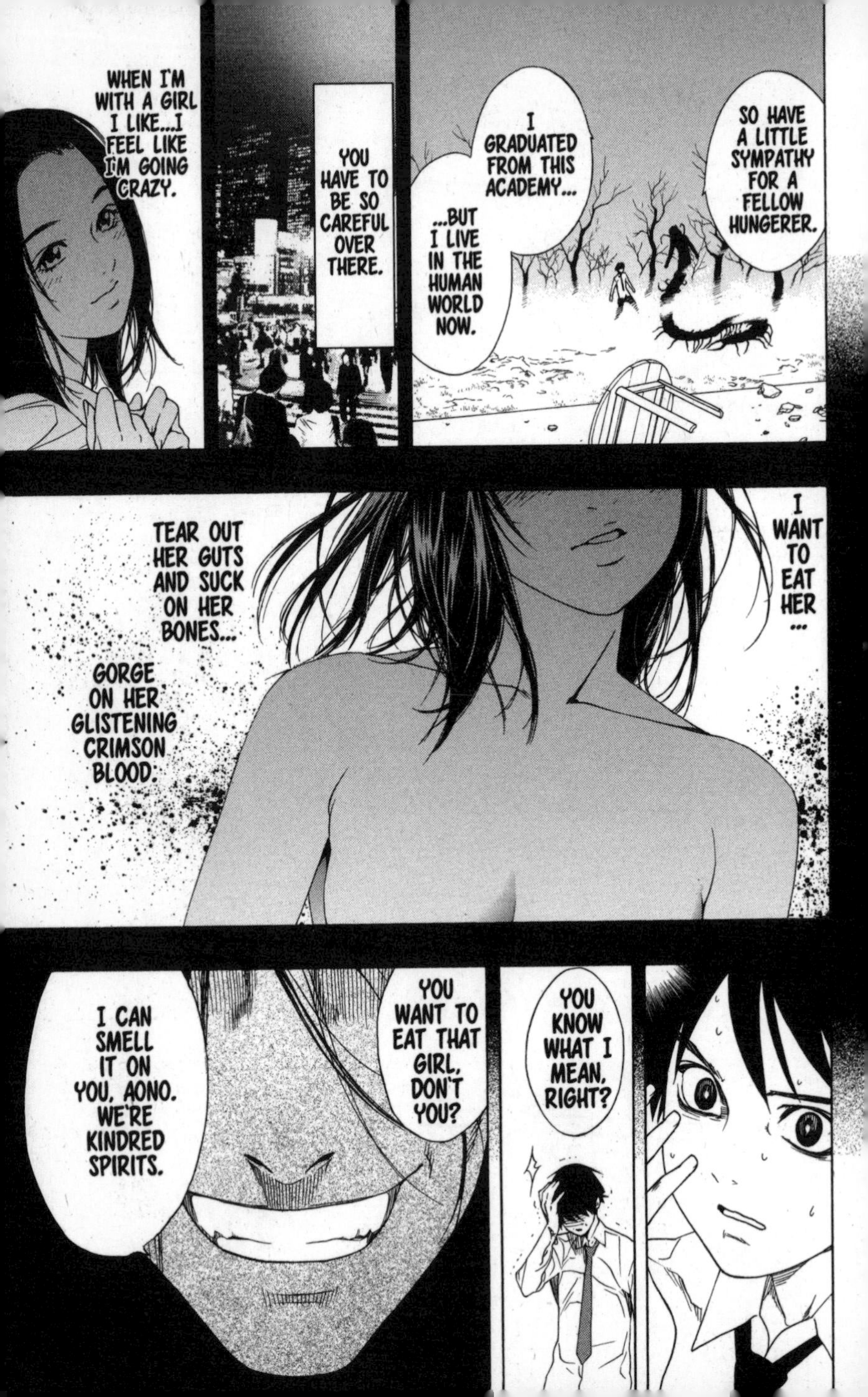
SO HAVE A LITTLE SYMPATHY FOR A FELLOW HUNGERER.
I GRADUATED FROM THIS ACADEMY...
...BUT I LIVE IN THE HUMAN WORLD NOW.
YOU HAVE TO BE SO CAREFUL OVER THERE.
WHEN I'M WITH A GIRL I LIKE...I FEEL LIKE I'M GOING CRAZY.
I WANT TO EAT HER...
TEAR OUT HER GUTS AND SUCK ON HER BONES...
GORGE ON HER GLISTENING CRIMSON BLOOD.
YOU KNOW WHAT I MEAN, RIGHT?
YOU WANT TO EAT THAT GIRL, DON'T YOU?
I CAN SMELL IT ON YOU, AONO. WE'RE KINDRED SPIRITS.

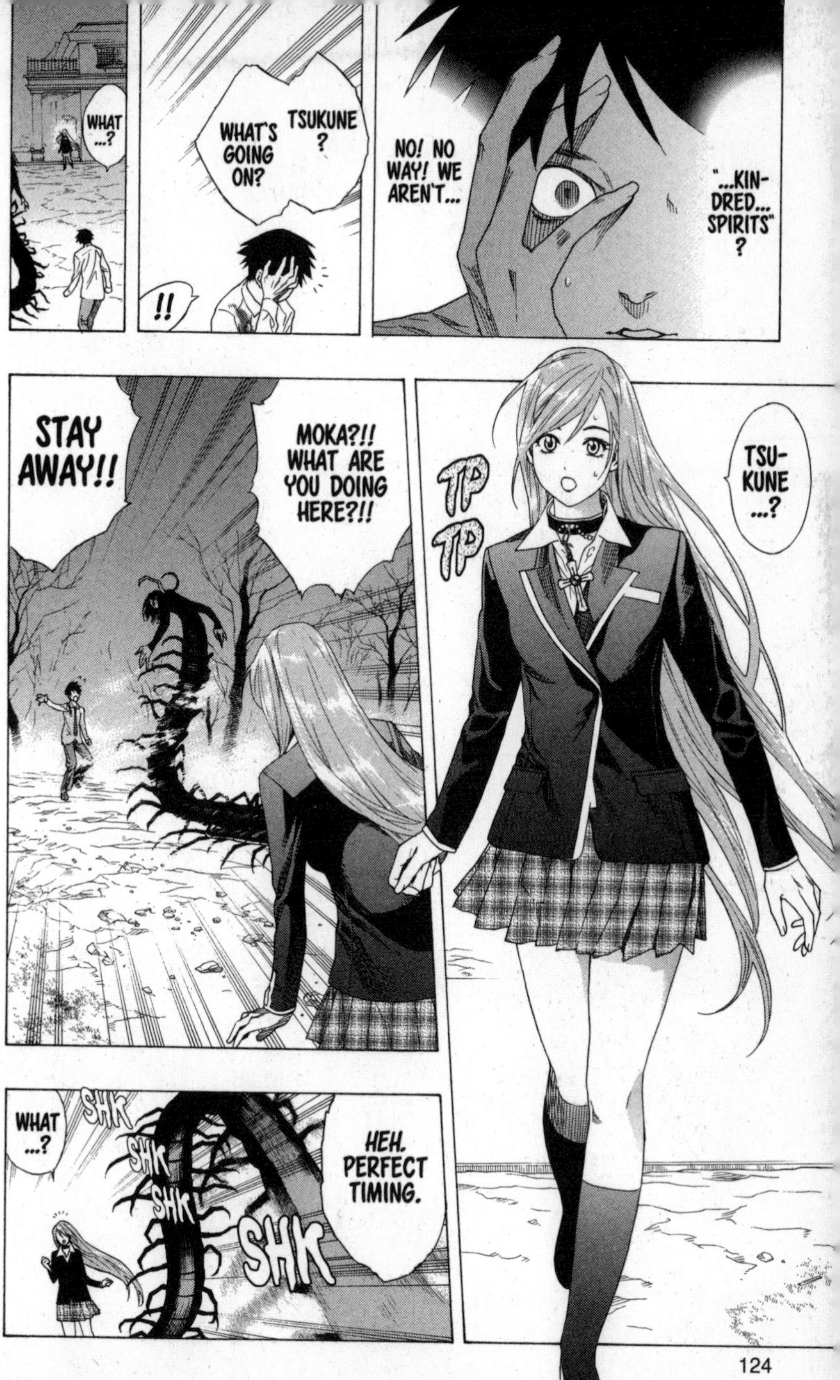

"...KIN-DRED... SPIRITS" ?
NO! NO WAY! WE AREN'T...
TSUKUNE ?
WHAT'S GOING ON?
!!
WHAT ...?
TSU-KUNE ...?
TP TP
MOKA?!! WHAT ARE YOU DOING HERE?!!
STAY AWAY!!
HEH. PERFECT TIMING.
SHK
SHK
SHK
SHK
WHAT ...?

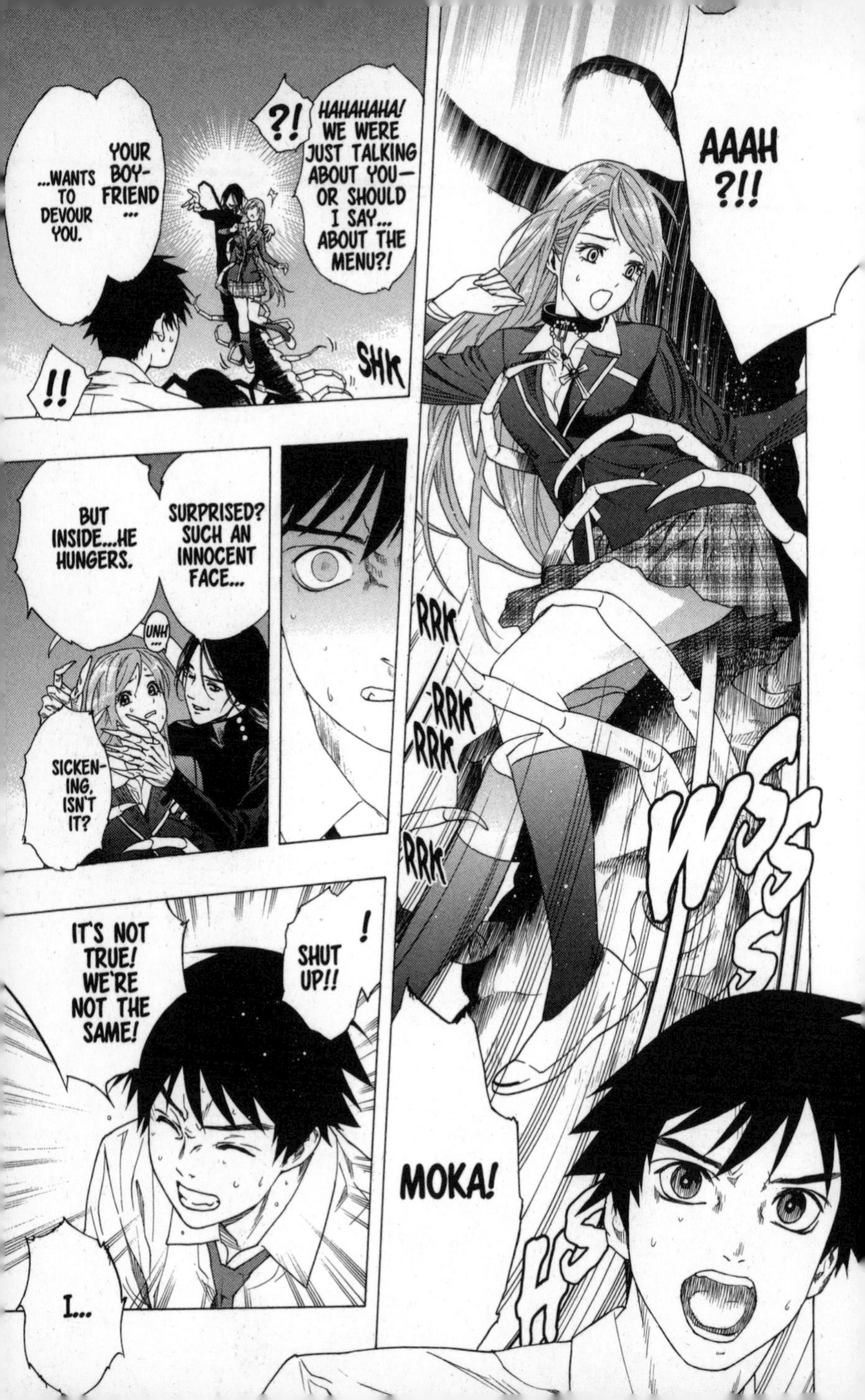
AAAH ?!!
RRK
RRK
RRK
RRK
MOKA!
HAHAHAHA! WE WERE JUST TALKING ABOUT YOU— OR SHOULD I SAY... ABOUT THE MENU?!
?!
YOUR BOY-FRIEND...
...WANTS TO DEVOUR YOU.
SHK
!!
SURPRISED? SUCH AN INNOCENT FACE...
BUT INSIDE...HE HUNGERS.
UNH...
SICKEN-ING, ISN'T IT?
!
SHUT UP!!
IT'S NOT TRUE! WE'RE NOT THE SAME!
I...

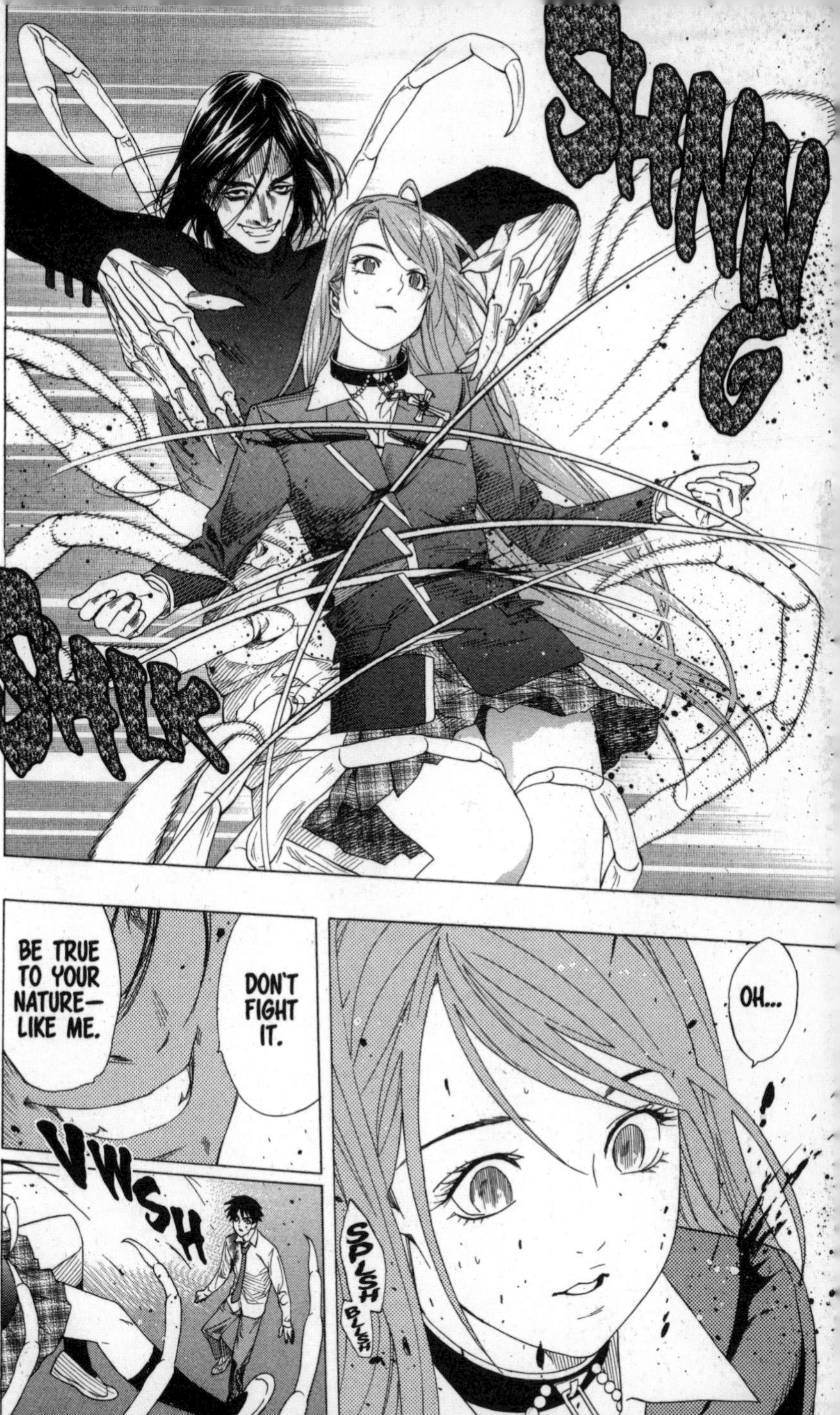
SHINNG
SHLIK
OH...
SPLSH
BLISH
DON'T FIGHT IT.
BE TRUE TO YOUR NATURE— LIKE ME.
VWSH

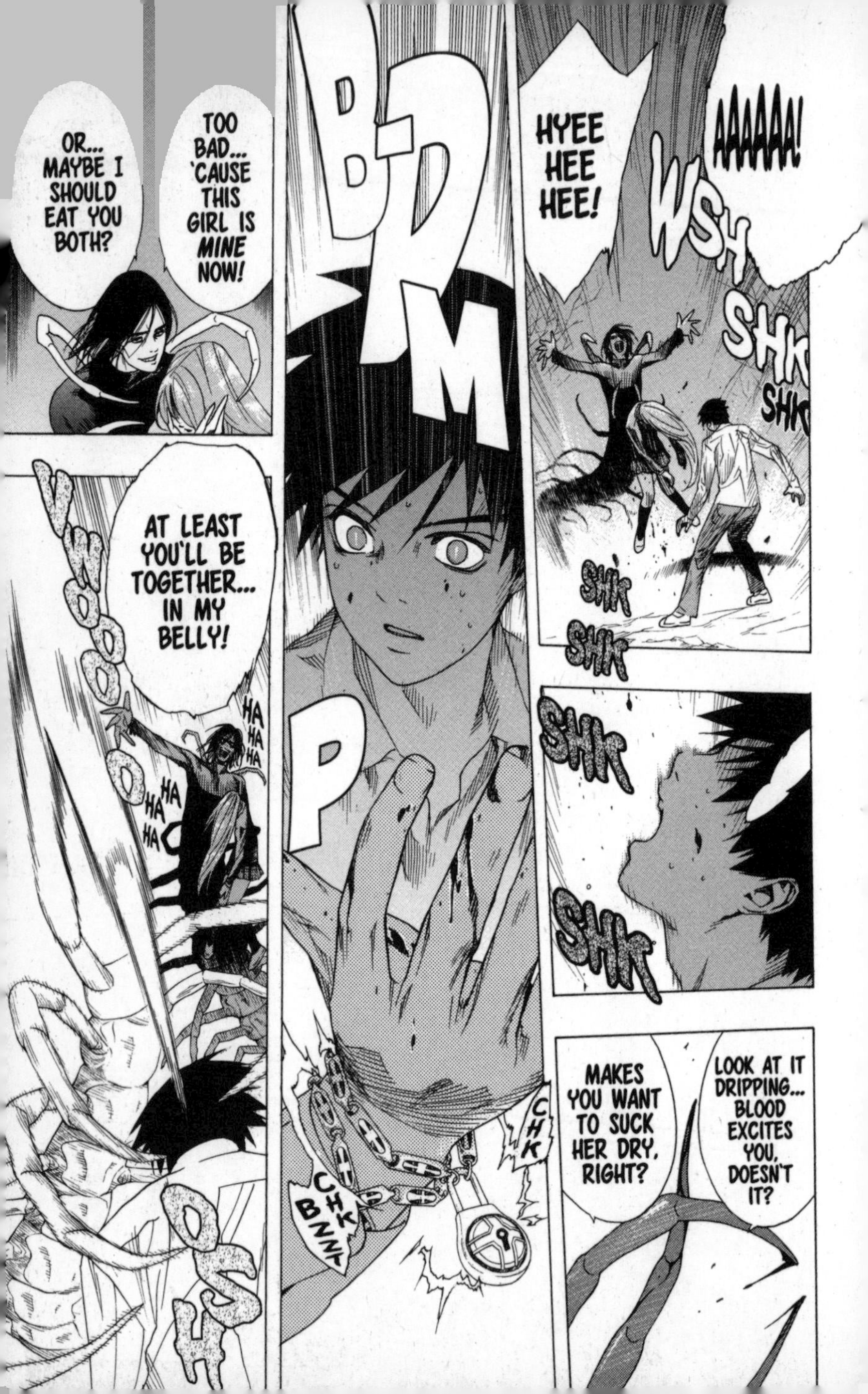
AAAAAA!
HYEE HEE HEE!
WSH
SHK
SHK
SHK
SHK
SHK
SHK
LOOK AT IT DRIPPING... BLOOD EXCITES YOU, DOESN'T IT?
MAKES YOU WANT TO SUCK HER DRY, RIGHT?
BA-DUMP
CHK
CHK
BZZT
TOO BAD... 'CAUSE THIS GIRL IS MINE NOW!
OR... MAYBE I SHOULD EAT YOU BOTH?
AT LEAST YOU'LL BE TOGETHER... IN MY BELLY!
VWOOOOOO
HA HA HA
HA HA HA
OOSH

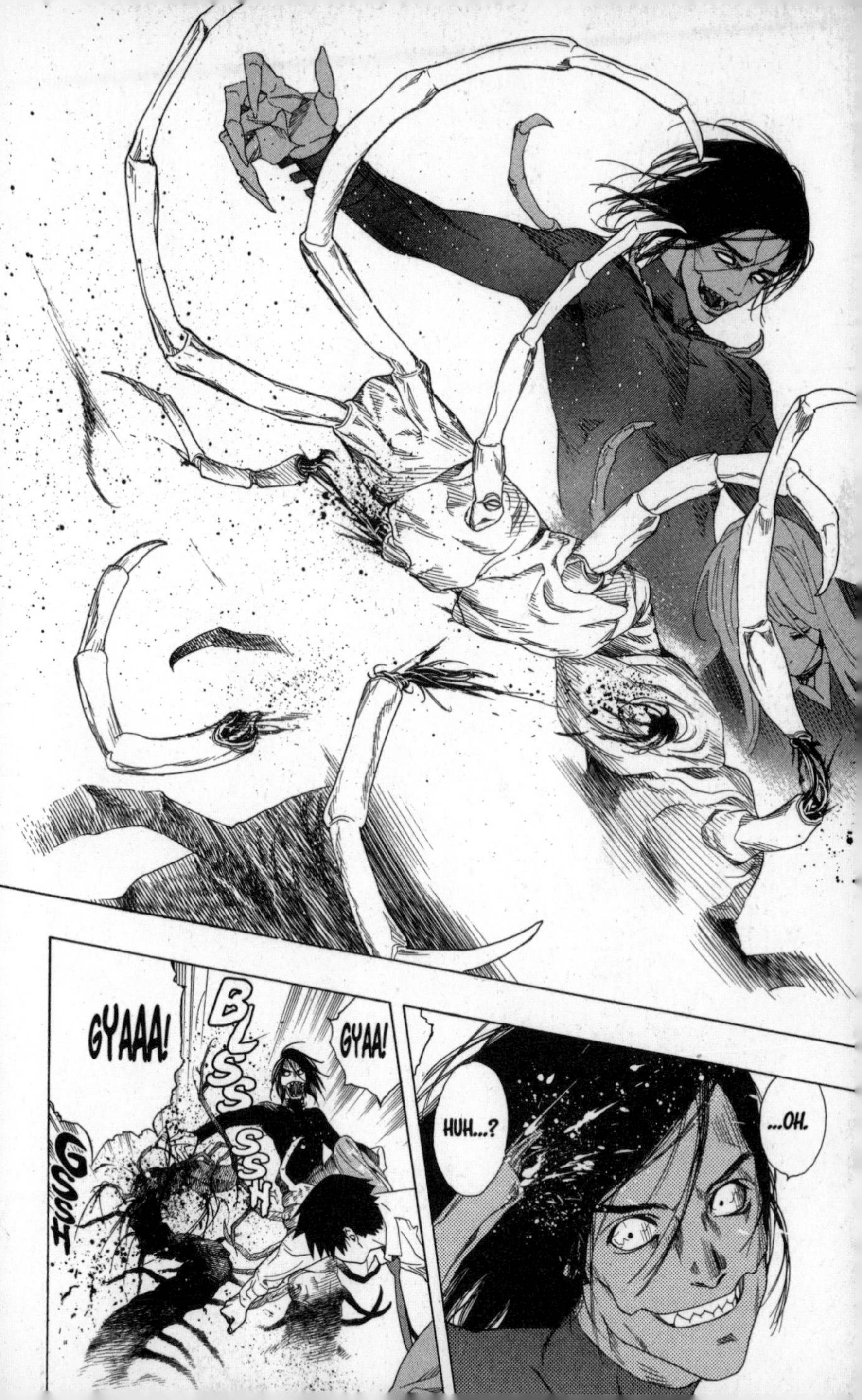
...OH.
HUH...?
GYAA!
BLSSSSH
GYAAA!
GUSH

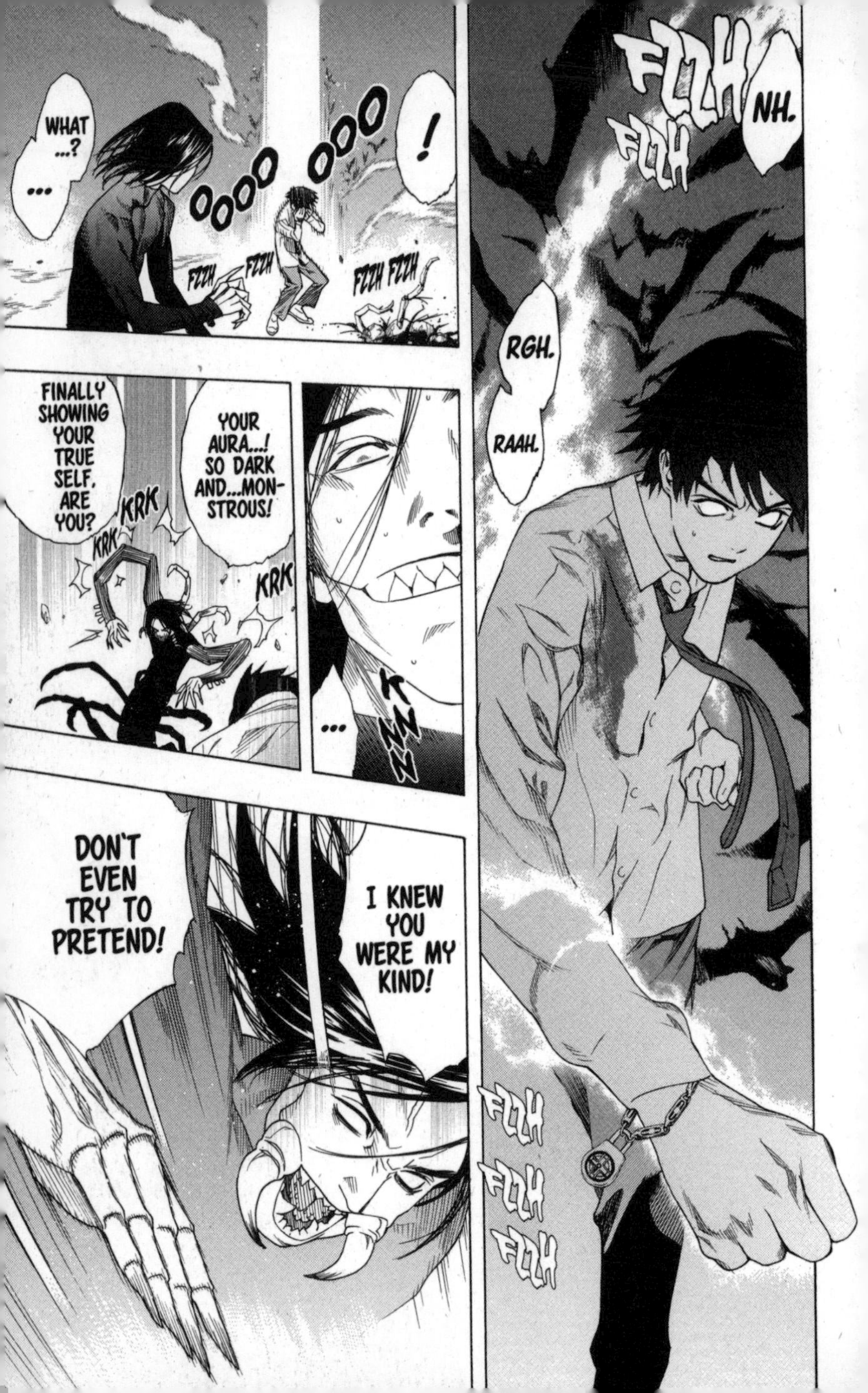
NH.
FZZH
FZZH
RGH.
RAAH.
FZZH
FZZH
FZZH
!
OOOO OOO
FZZH FZZH
WHAT ...? ...
FZZH FZZH
...
KNNN
YOUR AURA...! SO DARK AND...MON-STROUS!
FINALLY SHOWING YOUR TRUE SELF, ARE YOU?
KRK
KRK
KRK
I KNEW YOU WERE MY KIND!
DON'T EVEN TRY TO PRETEND!

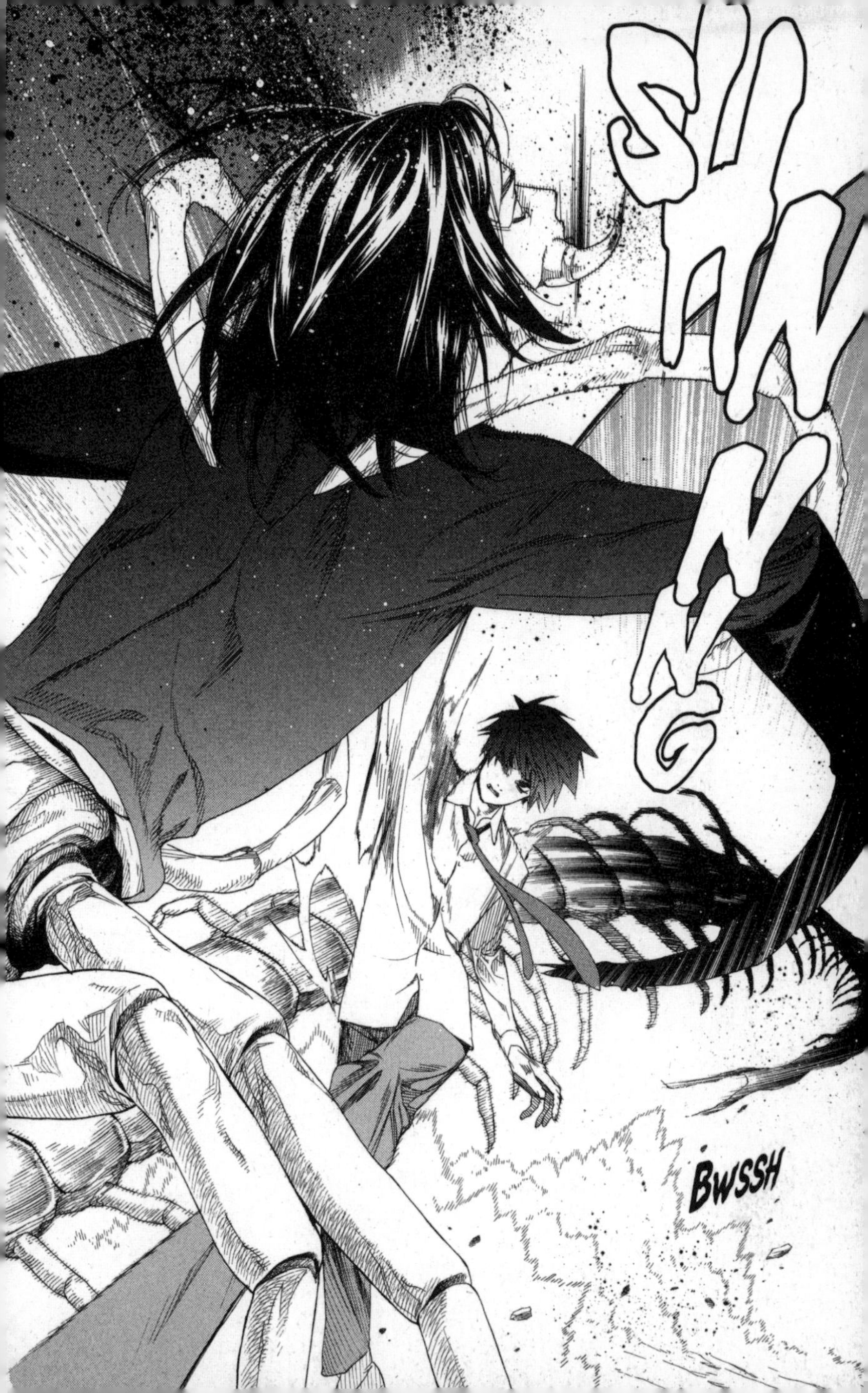
SHWNNG
BWSSH

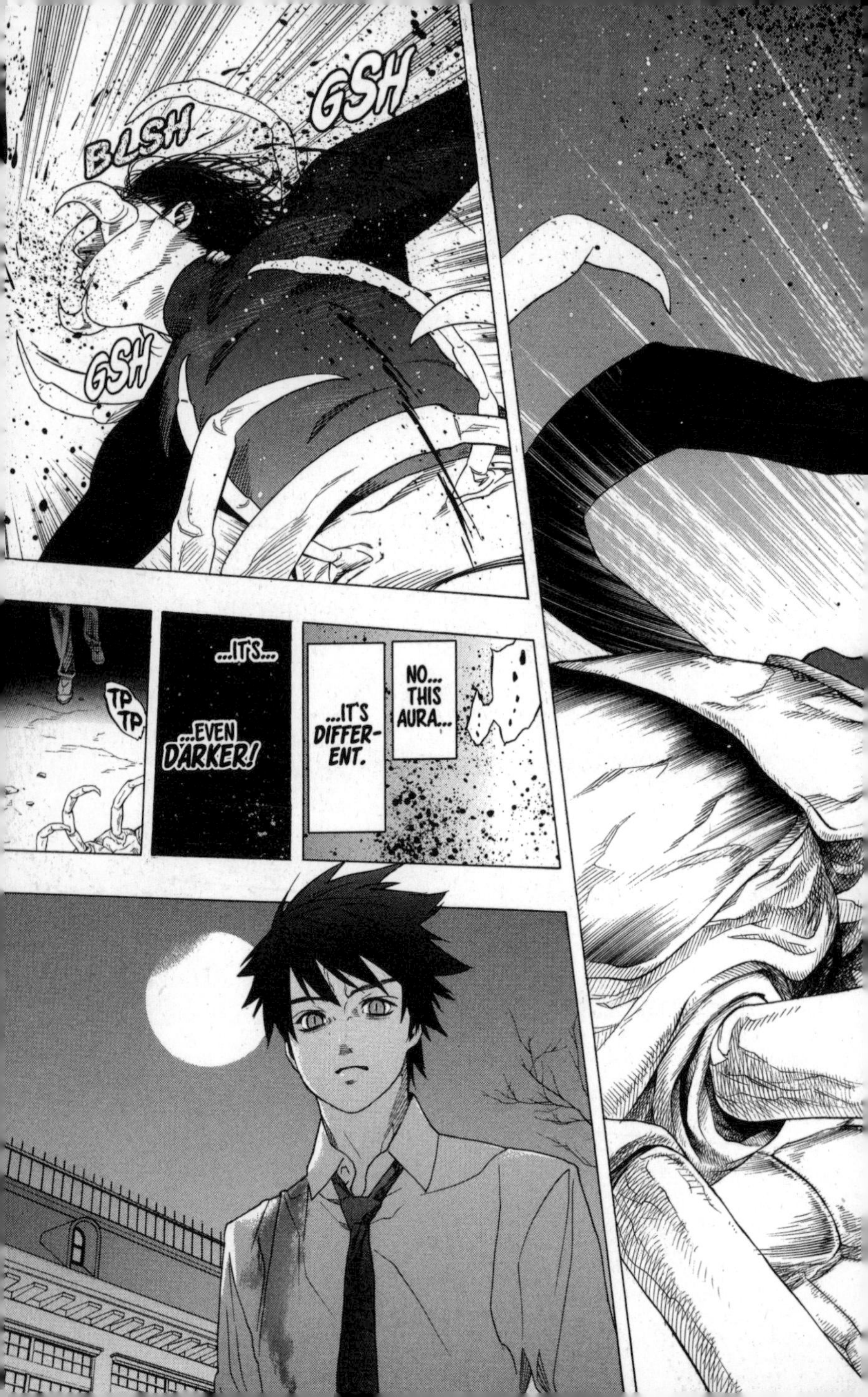
GSH
BLSH
GSH
NO... THIS AURA...
...IT'S DIFFER-ENT.
...IT'S...
...EVEN DARKER!
TP TP

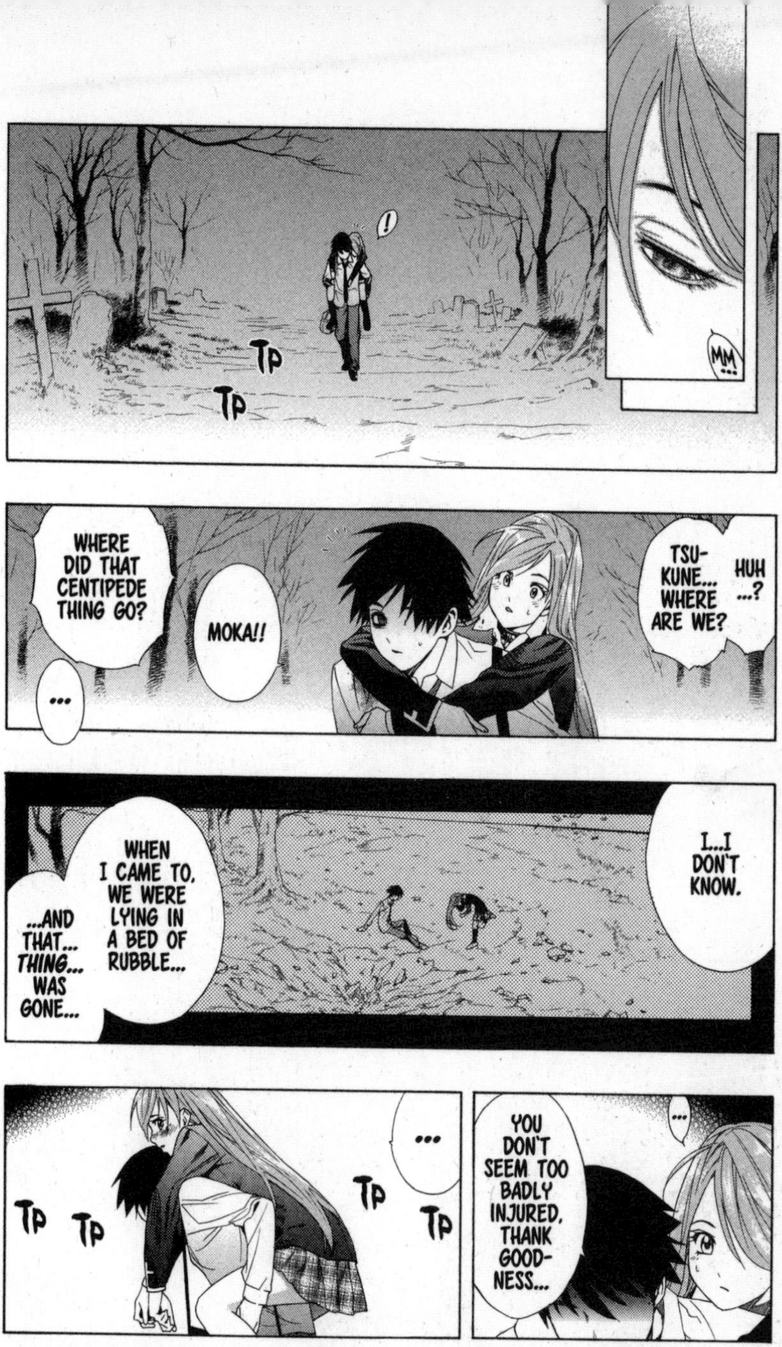
MM...
!
TP
TP
HUH...?
TSU-KUNE... WHERE ARE WE?
MOKA!!
WHERE DID THAT CENTIPEDE THING GO?
...
I...I DON'T KNOW.
WHEN I CAME TO, WE WERE LYING IN A BED OF RUBBLE...
...AND THAT... *THING*... WAS GONE...
...
YOU DON'T SEEM TOO BADLY INJURED, THANK GOOD-NESS...
...
TP
TP
TP
TP

READ THIS WAY

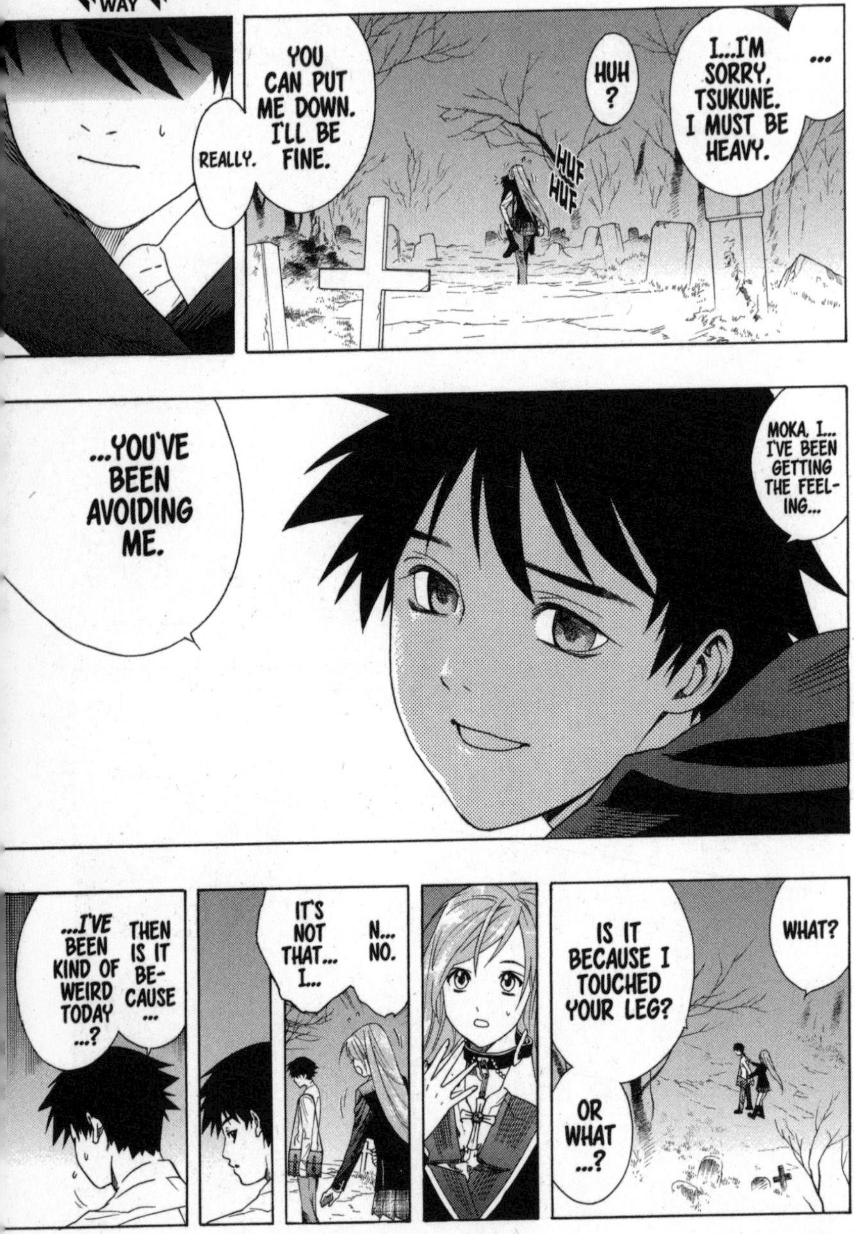
...
I...I'M SORRY, TSUKUNE. I MUST BE HEAVY.
HUH?
HUF HUF
YOU CAN PUT ME DOWN. I'LL BE FINE.
REALLY.
MOKA, I... I'VE BEEN GETTING THE FEEL-ING...
...YOU'VE BEEN AVOIDING ME.
WHAT?
IS IT BECAUSE I TOUCHED YOUR LEG?
OR WHAT...?
N... NO.
IT'S NOT THAT... I...
THEN IS IT BE-CAUSE ...
...I'VE BEEN KIND OF WEIRD TODAY ...?

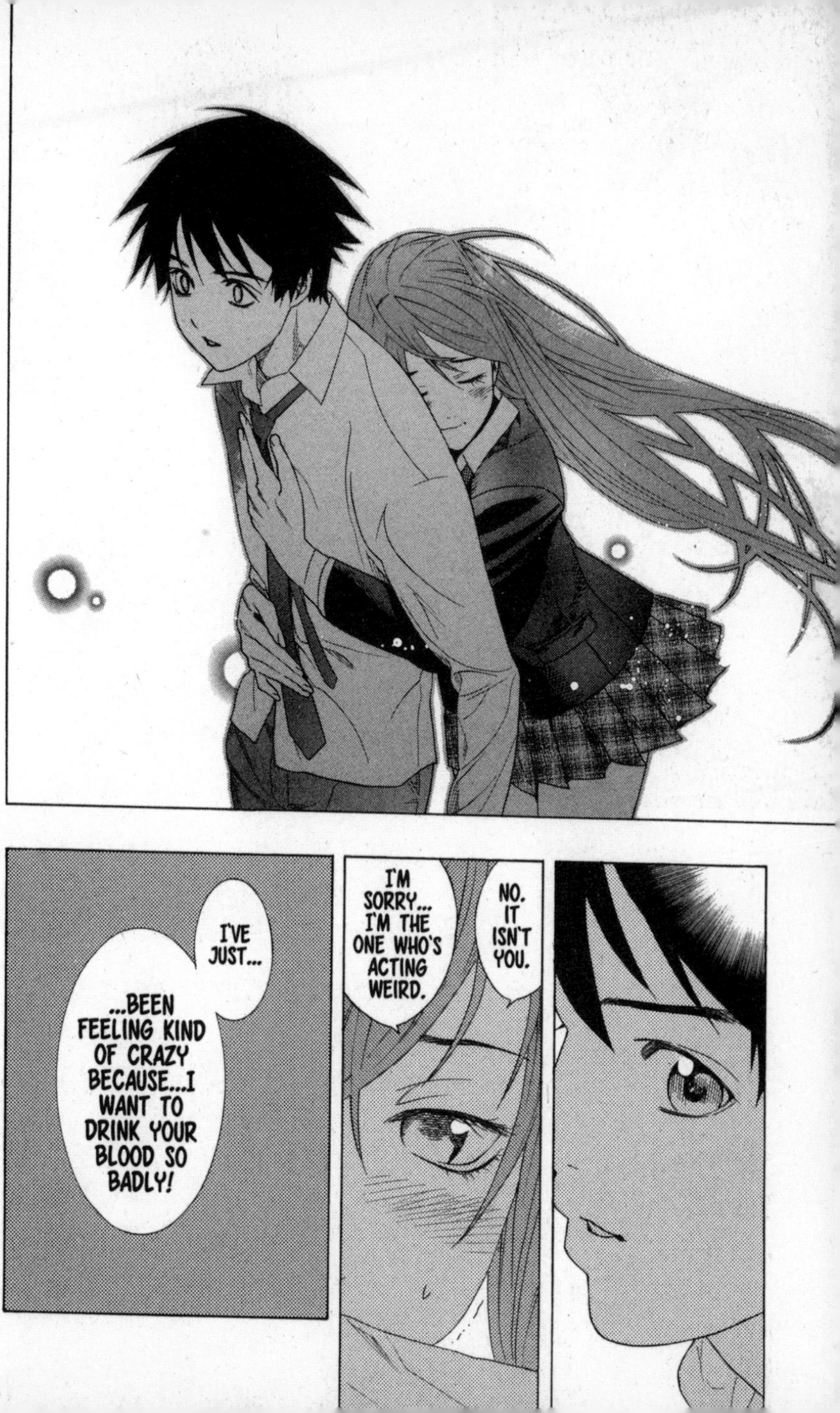
NO. IT ISN'T YOU.
I'M SORRY... I'M THE ONE WHO'S ACTING WEIRD.
I'VE JUST...
...BEEN FEELING KIND OF CRAZY BECAUSE...I WANT TO DRINK YOUR BLOOD SO BADLY!

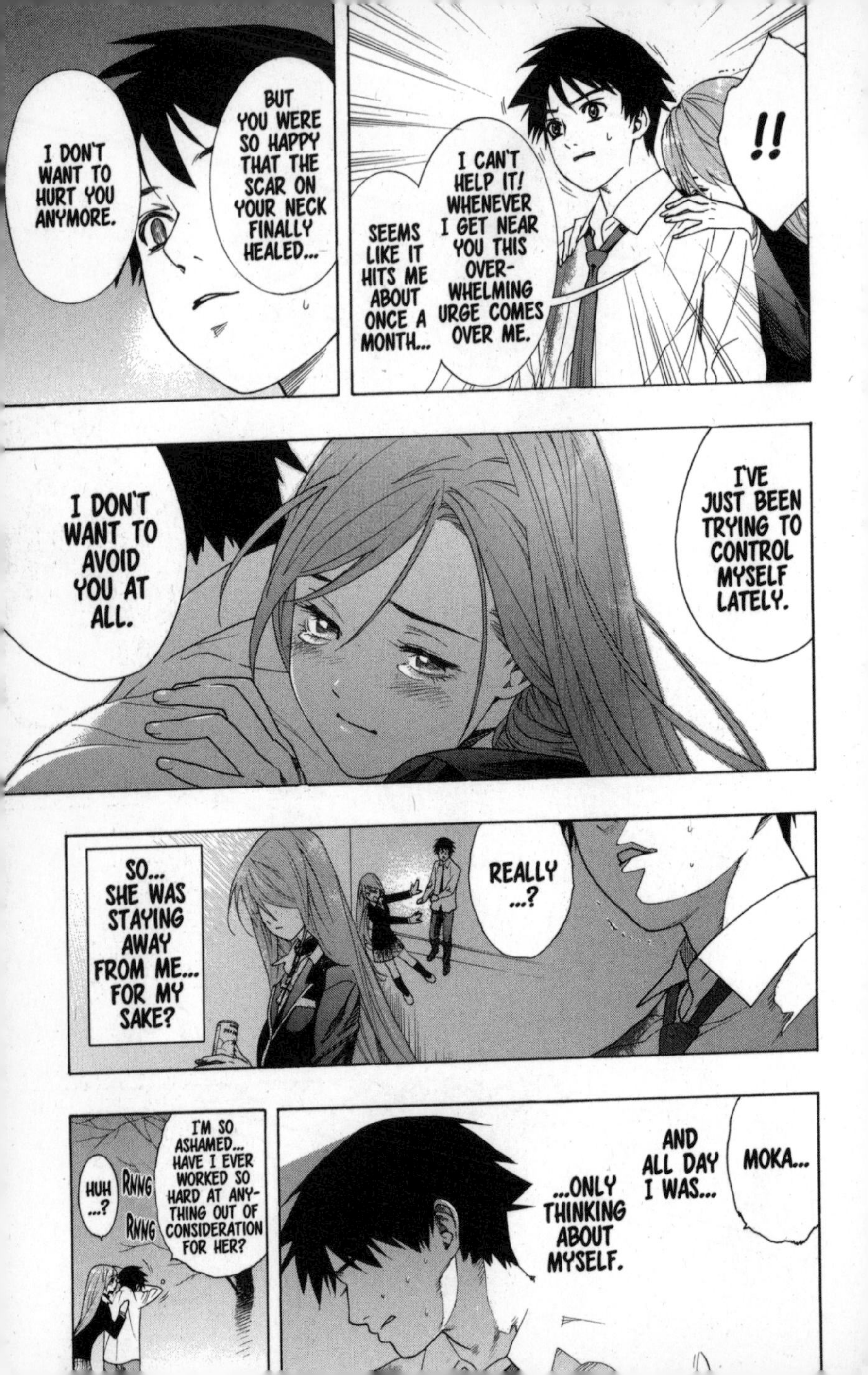
!!
I CAN'T HELP IT! WHENEVER I GET NEAR YOU THIS OVER-WHELMING URGE COMES OVER ME.
SEEMS LIKE IT HITS ME ABOUT ONCE A MONTH...
BUT YOU WERE SO HAPPY THAT THE SCAR ON YOUR NECK FINALLY HEALED...
I DON'T WANT TO HURT YOU ANYMORE.
I'VE JUST BEEN TRYING TO CONTROL MYSELF LATELY.
I DON'T WANT TO AVOID YOU AT ALL.
REALLY ...?
SO... SHE WAS STAYING AWAY FROM ME... FOR MY SAKE?
MOKA...
AND ALL DAY I WAS...
...ONLY THINKING ABOUT MYSELF.
I'M SO ASHAMED... HAVE I EVER WORKED SO HARD AT ANY-THING OUT OF CONSIDERATION FOR HER?
RNNG
RNNG
HUH ...?

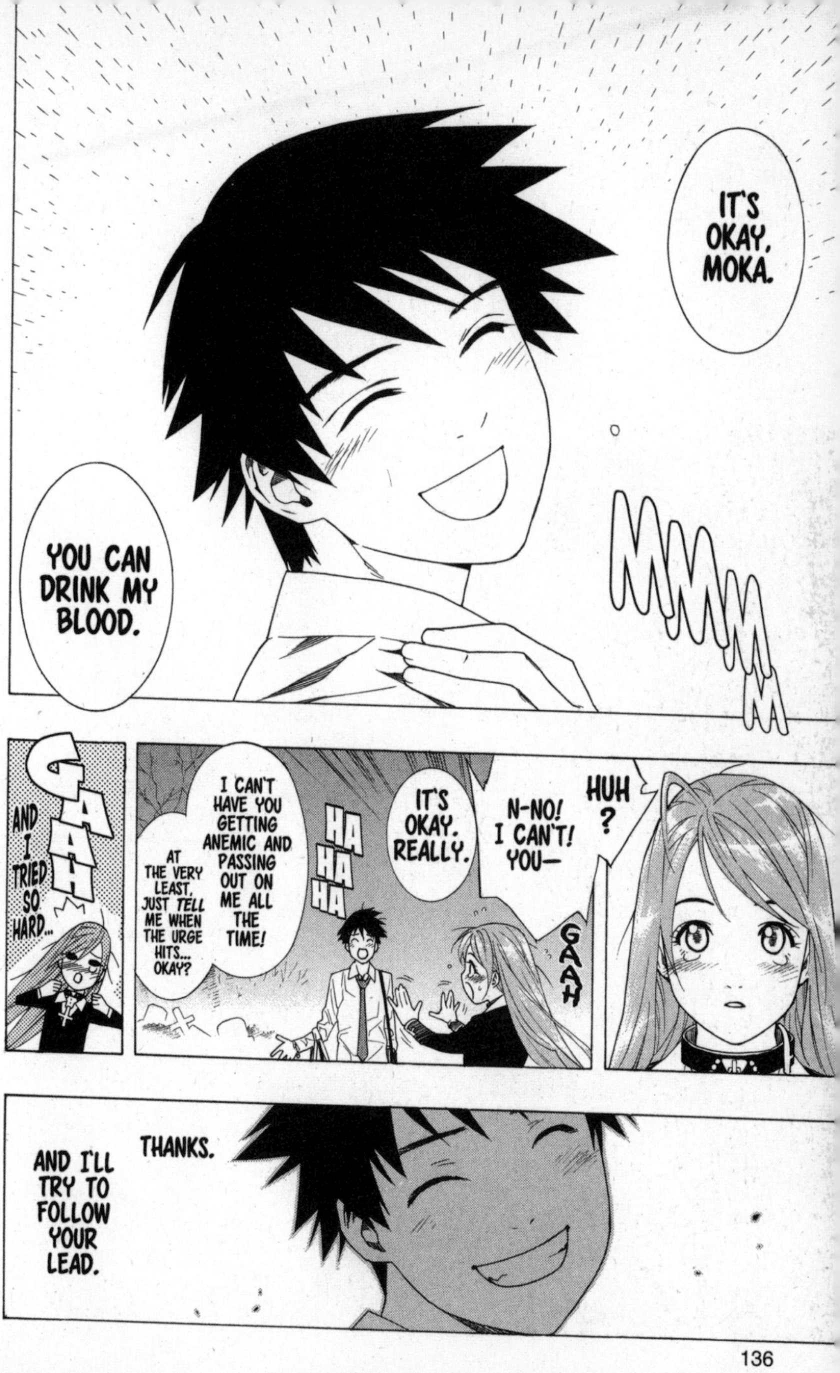
IT'S OKAY, MOKA.
MMMMM
YOU CAN DRINK MY BLOOD.
HUH?
N-NO! I CAN'T! YOU—
GAAH
IT'S OKAY. REALLY.
HA HA HA
I CAN'T HAVE YOU GETTING ANEMIC AND PASSING OUT ON ME ALL THE TIME!
AT THE VERY LEAST, JUST *TELL* ME WHEN THE URGE HITS... OKAY?
GAAAH
AND I TRIED SO HARD...
THANKS.
AND I'LL TRY TO FOLLOW YOUR LEAD.

READ THIS WAY

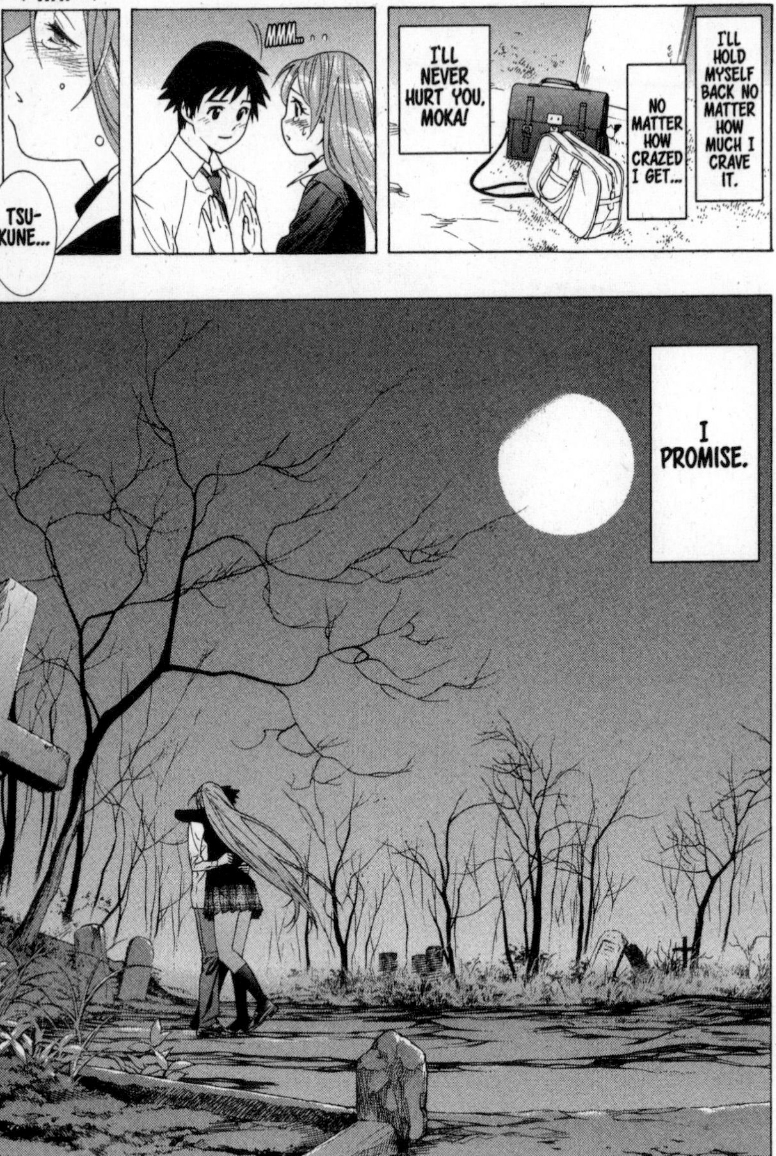
I'LL HOLD MYSELF BACK NO MATTER HOW MUCH I CRAVE IT.
NO MATTER HOW CRAZED I GET...
I'LL NEVER HURT YOU, MOKA!
MMM...
TSU-KUNE...
I PROMISE.

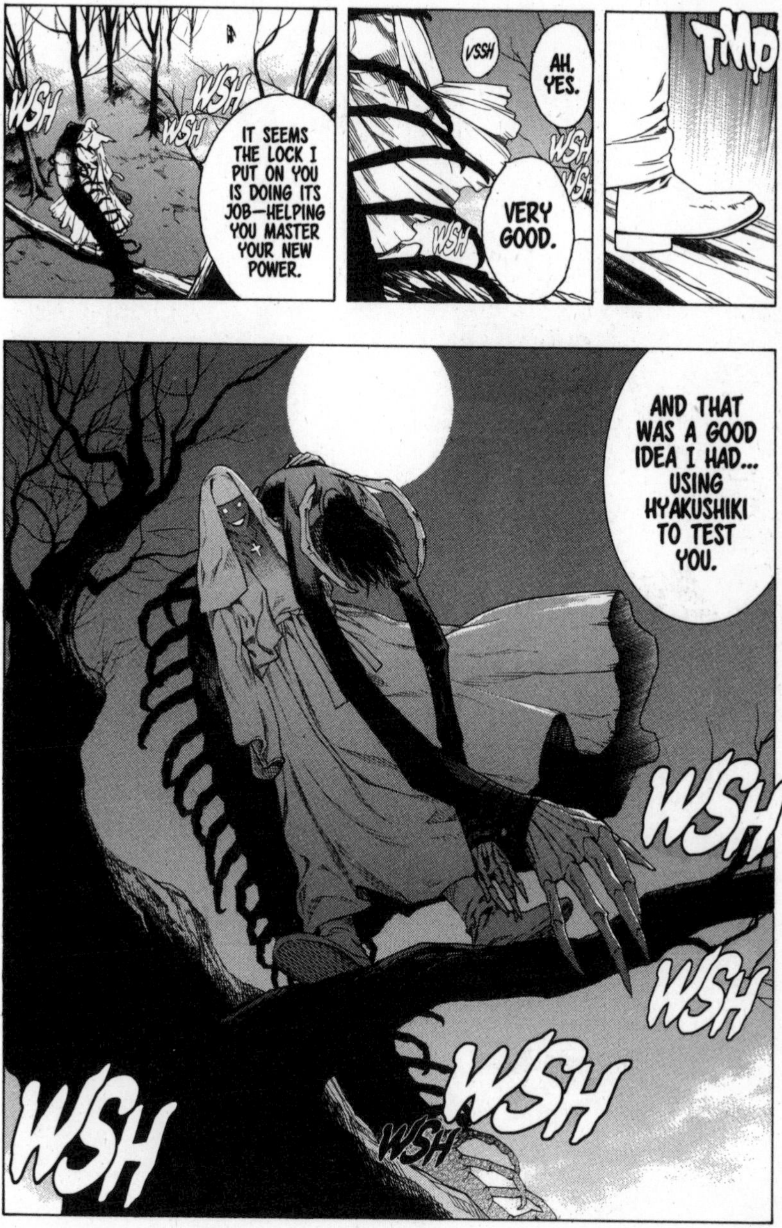
TMP
VSSH
AH, YES.
WSH
WSH
VERY GOOD.
WSH
WSH
WSH
WSH
IT SEEMS THE LOCK I PUT ON YOU IS DOING ITS JOB—HELPING YOU MASTER YOUR NEW POWER.
AND THAT WAS A GOOD IDEA I HAD... USING HYAKUSHIKI TO TEST YOU.
WSH
WSH
WSH
WSH
WSH

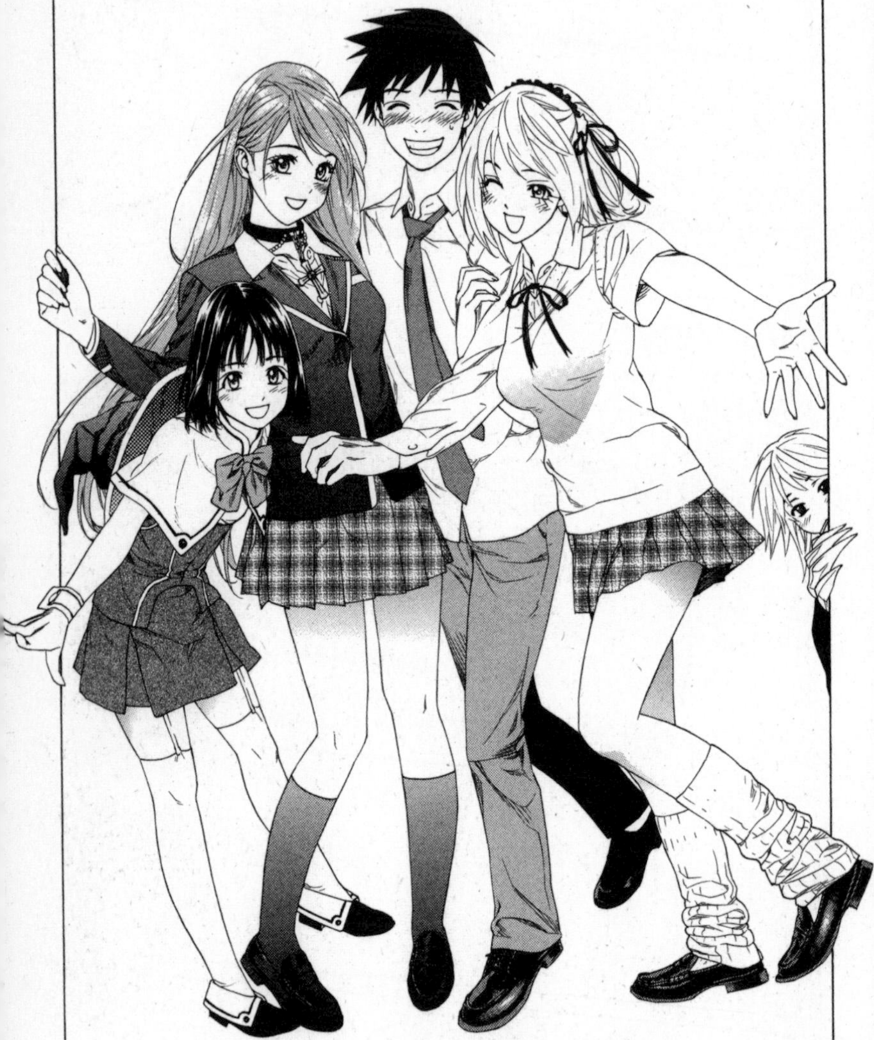

# 28 : Our Choice

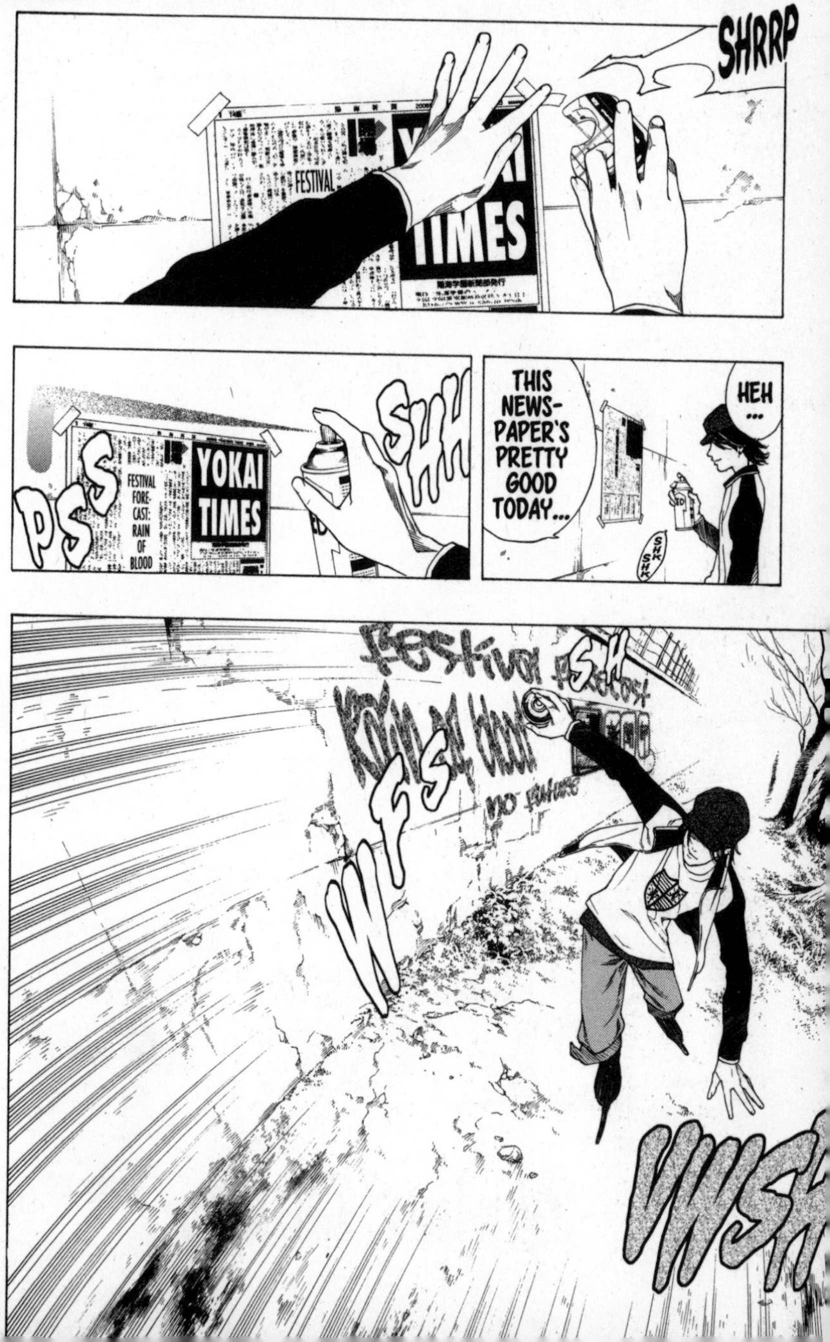
SHRRP
FESTIVAL
YOKAI TIMES
HEH ...
THIS NEWS-PAPER'S PRETTY GOOD TODAY...
SHK SHK
SHH
YOKAI TIMES
FESTIVAL FORE-CAST: RAIN OF BLOOD
PSSS
FSH
VWSH

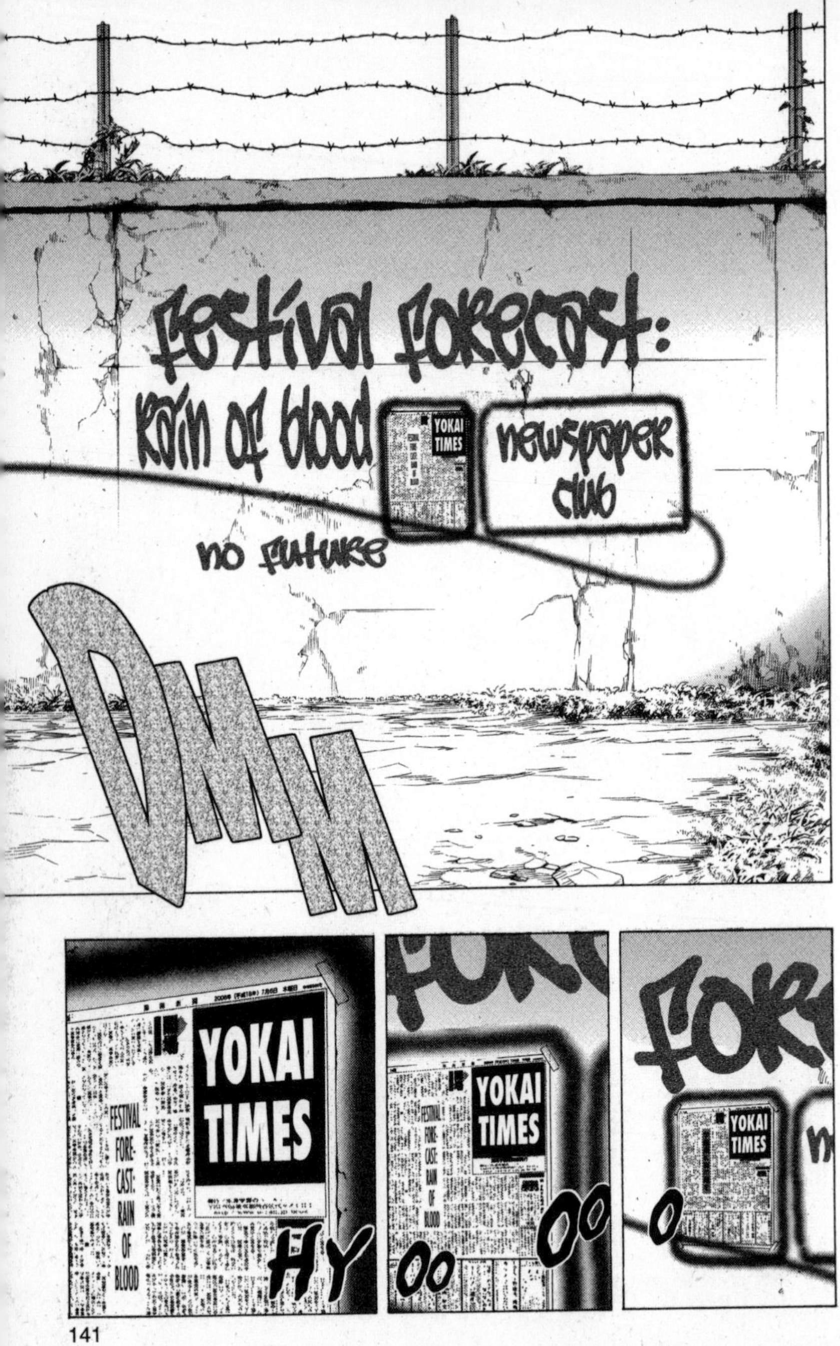
festival forecast:
rain of blood
YOKAI TIMES
newspaper club
no future
DMMM
FORE
YOKAI TIMES
o
FORE
YOKAI TIMES
FESTIVAL FORE-CAST: RAIN OF BLOOD
oo OO
YOKAI TIMES
FESTIVAL FORE-CAST: RAIN OF BLOOD
HY

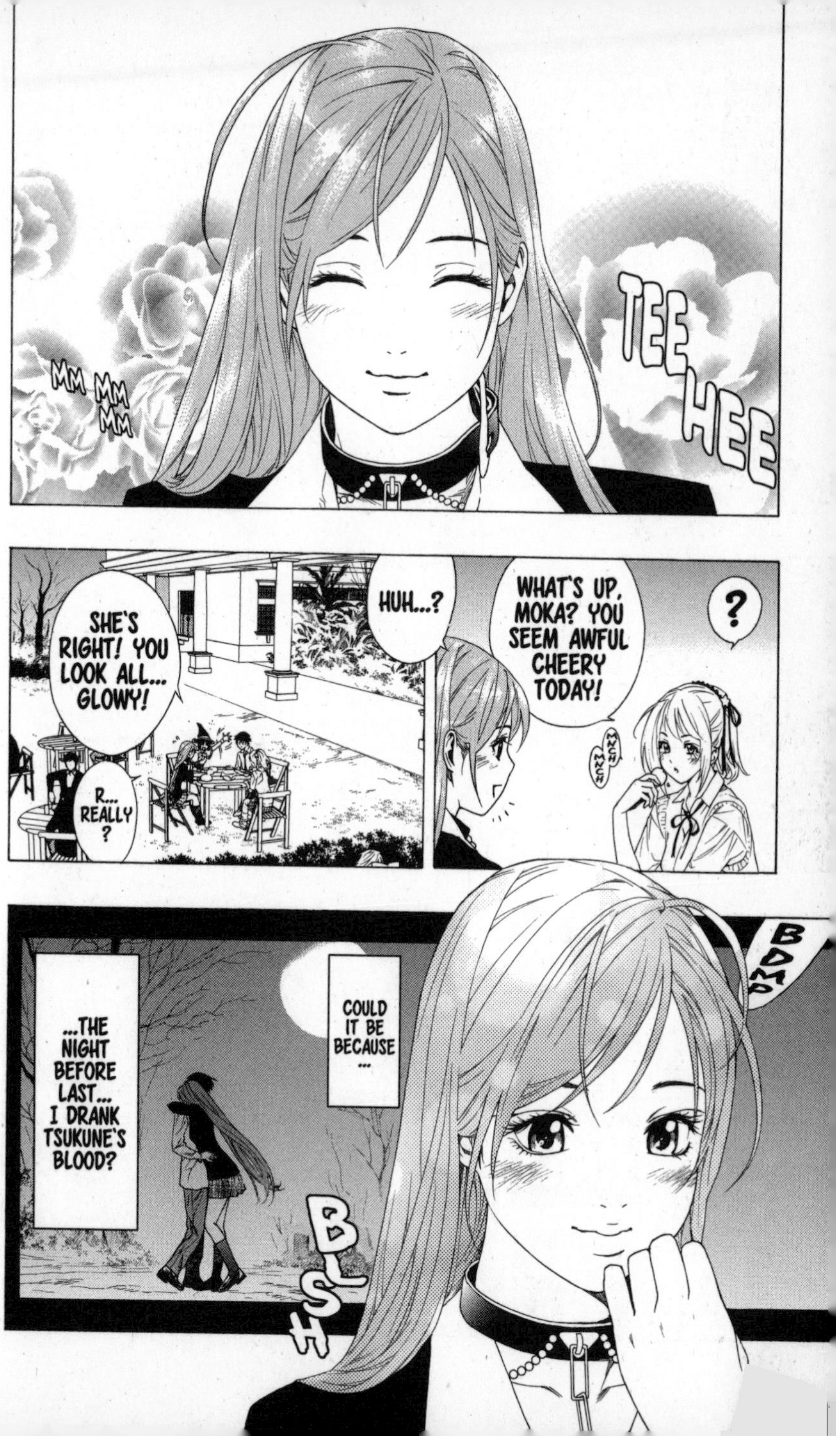
TEE HEE
MM MM MM
?
WHAT'S UP, MOKA? YOU SEEM AWFUL CHEERY TODAY!
MNCH MNCH
HUH...?
SHE'S RIGHT! YOU LOOK ALL... GLOWY!
R... REALLY ?
BDMP
COULD IT BE BECAUSE ...
...THE NIGHT BEFORE LAST... I DRANK TSUKUNE'S BLOOD?
BLSH

READ THIS WAY

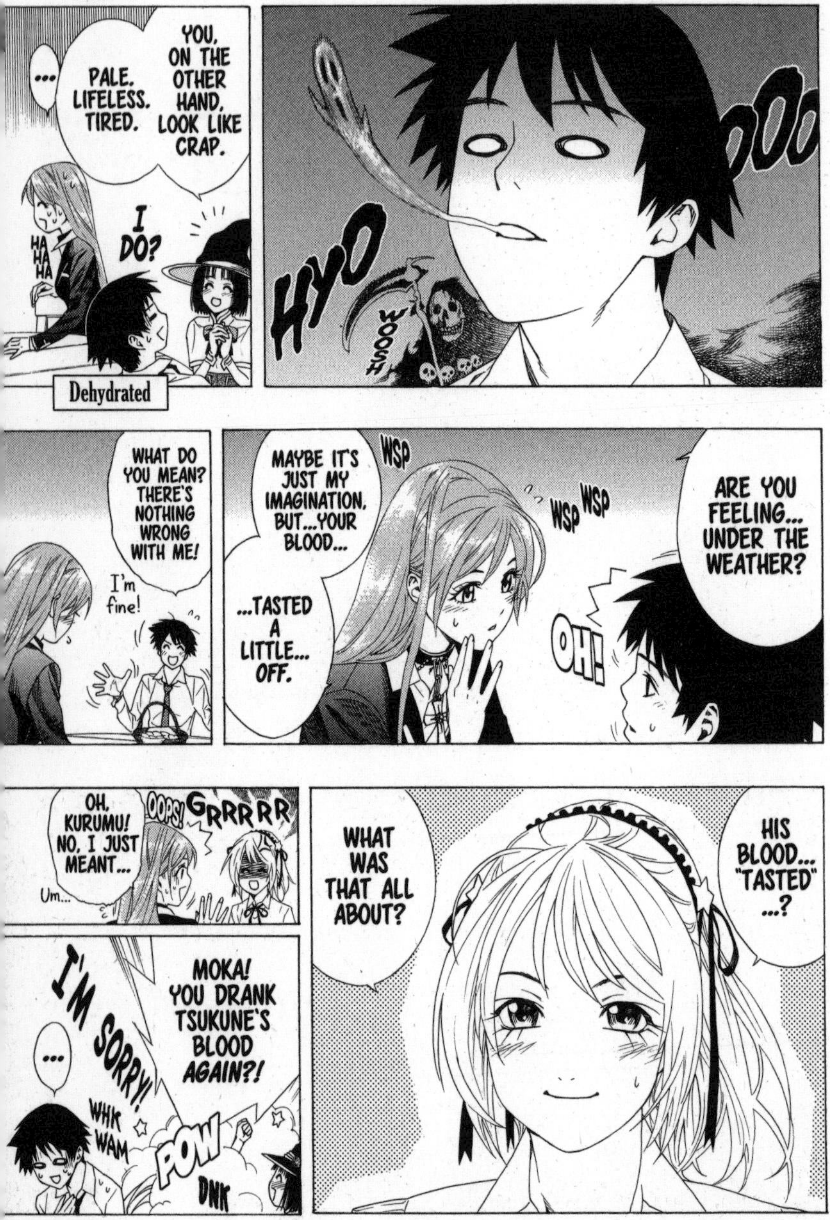
OOO
HYO
WOOSH
YOU, ON THE OTHER HAND, LOOK LIKE CRAP.
PALE. LIFELESS. TIRED.
...
I DO?
HA HA HA
Dehydrated
ARE YOU FEELING... UNDER THE WEATHER?
OH!
WSP WSP
WSP
MAYBE IT'S JUST MY IMAGINATION, BUT...YOUR BLOOD...
...TASTED A LITTLE... OFF.
WHAT DO YOU MEAN? THERE'S NOTHING WRONG WITH ME!
I'm fine!
HIS BLOOD... "TASTED" ...?
WHAT WAS THAT ALL ABOUT?
GRRRRR
OOPS!
OH, KURUMU! NO, I JUST MEANT...
Um...
MOKA! YOU DRANK TSUKUNE'S BLOOD AGAIN?!
I'M SORRY!
...
WHK WAM
POW
DNK

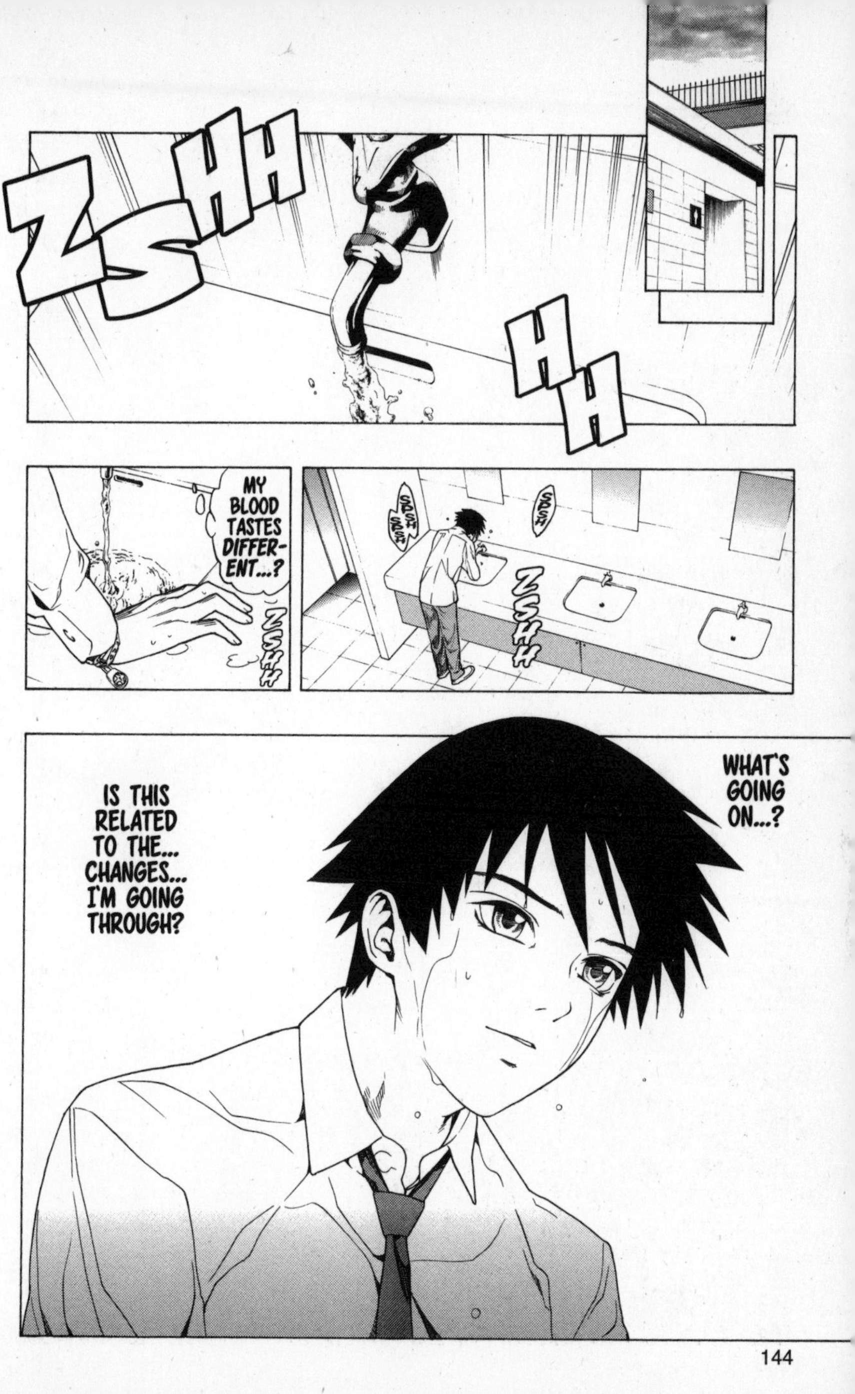
ZSHH
HH
SPSH SPSH
SPSH
ZSHH
MY BLOOD TASTES DIFFERENT...?
ZSHH
WHAT'S GOING ON...?
IS THIS RELATED TO THE... CHANGES... I'M GOING THROUGH?

READ THIS WAY

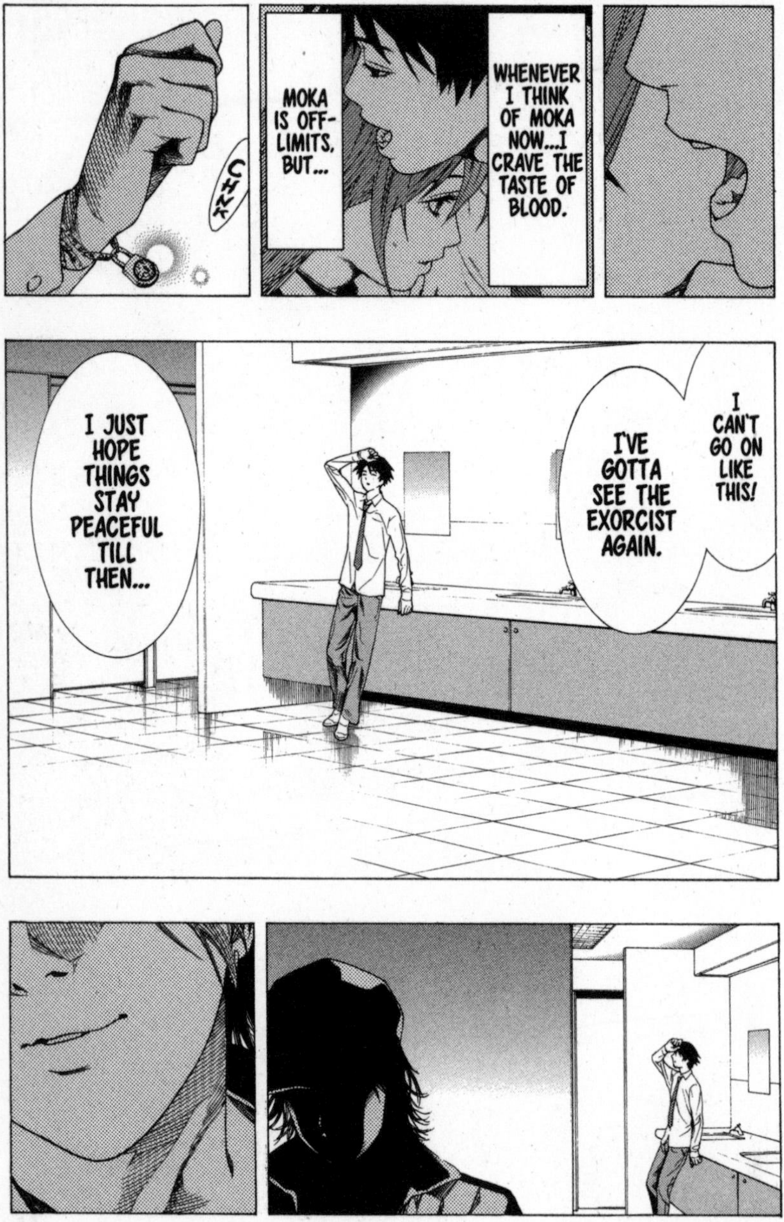

WHENEVER I THINK OF MOKA NOW...I CRAVE THE TASTE OF BLOOD.
MOKA IS OFF-LIMITS, BUT...
CHNK
I CAN'T GO ON LIKE THIS!
I'VE GOTTA SEE THE EXORCIST AGAIN.
I JUST HOPE THINGS STAY PEACEFUL TILL THEN...

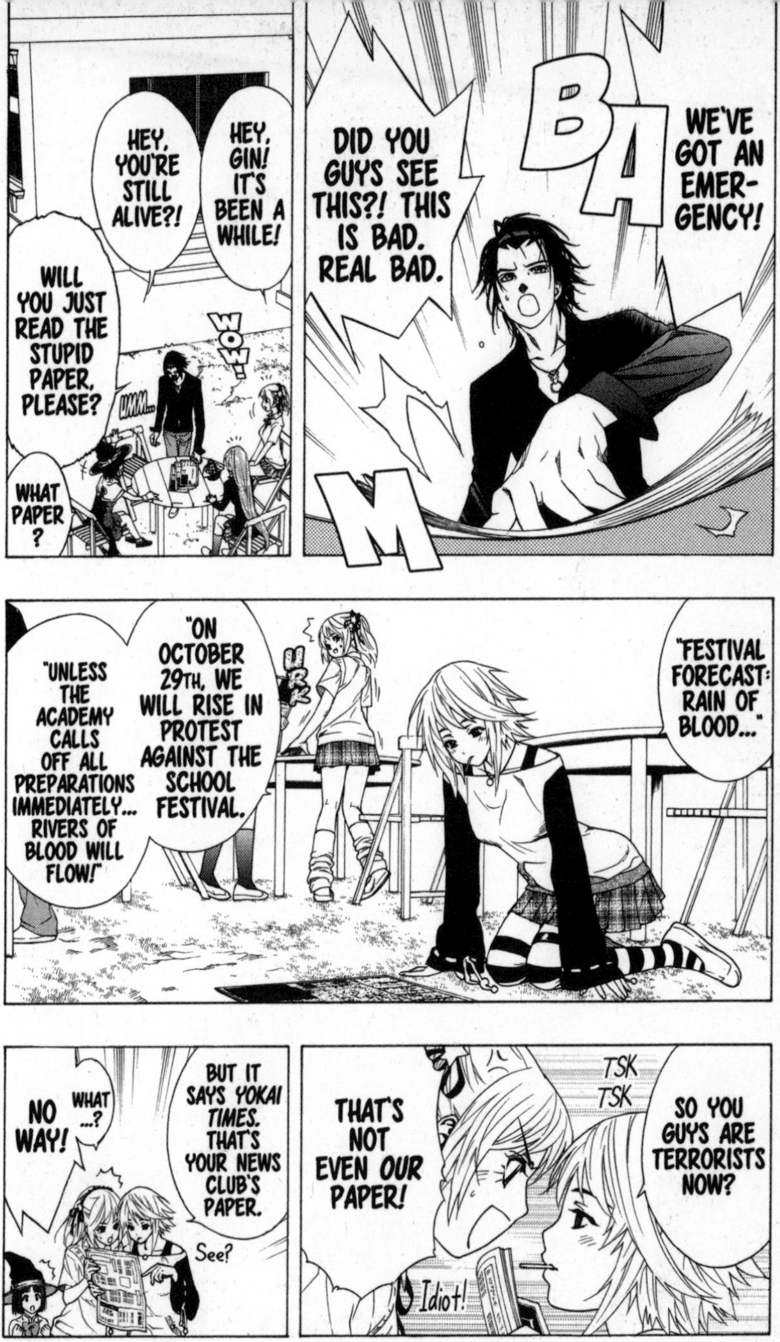
BAM
WE'VE GOT AN EMERGENCY!
DID YOU GUYS SEE THIS?! THIS IS BAD. REAL BAD.
HEY, GIN! IT'S BEEN A WHILE!
HEY, YOU'RE STILL ALIVE?!
WOW!
WILL YOU JUST READ THE STUPID PAPER, PLEASE?
UMM...
WHAT PAPER?
"FESTIVAL FORECAST: RAIN OF BLOOD..."
URK
"ON OCTOBER 29TH, WE WILL RISE IN PROTEST AGAINST THE SCHOOL FESTIVAL.
"UNLESS THE ACADEMY CALLS OFF ALL PREPARATIONS IMMEDIATELY... RIVERS OF BLOOD WILL FLOW!"
TSK TSK
SO YOU GUYS ARE TERRORISTS NOW?
THAT'S NOT EVEN OUR PAPER!
Idiot!
BUT IT SAYS YOKAI TIMES. THAT'S YOUR NEWS CLUB'S PAPER.
WHAT ...?
NO WAY!
See?

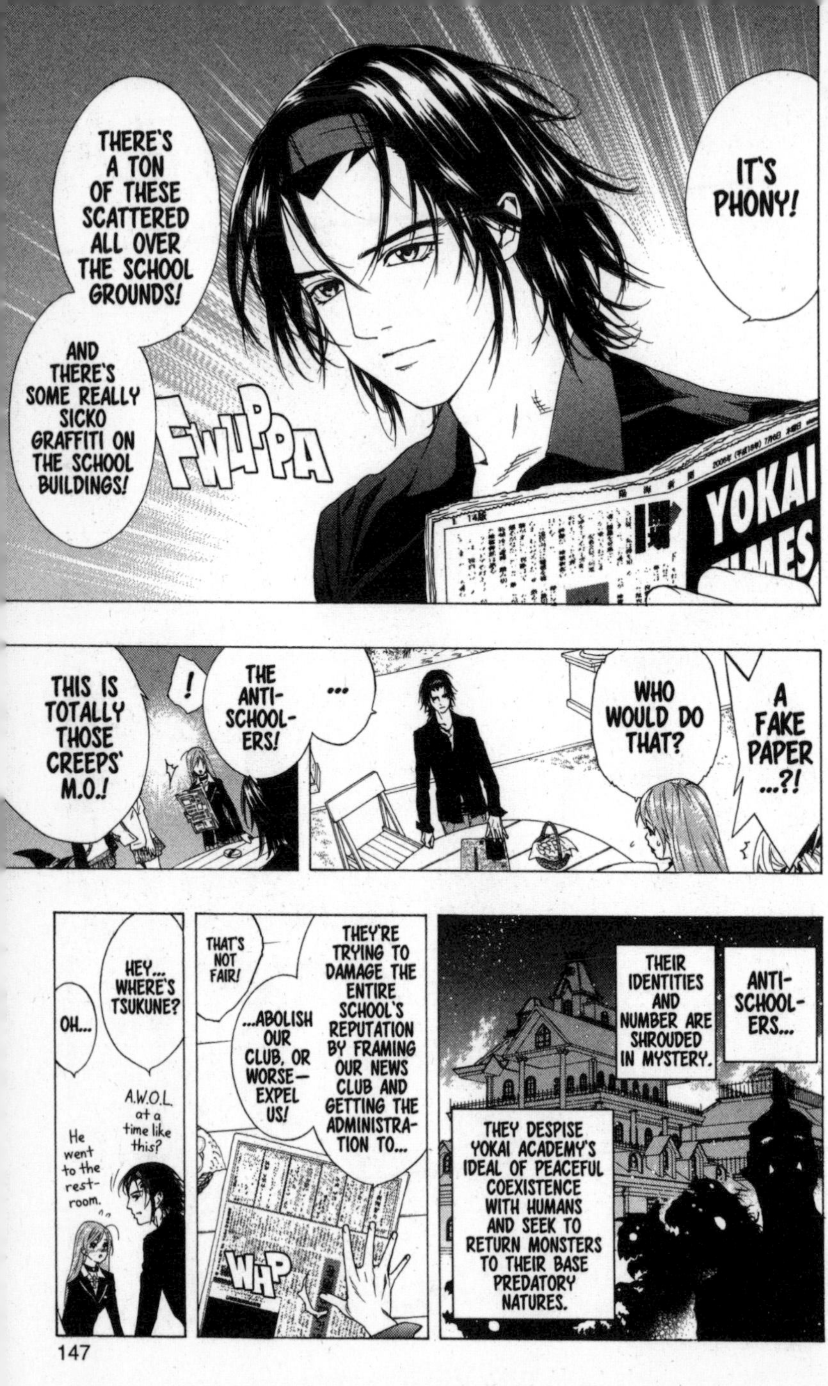
IT'S PHONY!
THERE'S A TON OF THESE SCATTERED ALL OVER THE SCHOOL GROUNDS!
AND THERE'S SOME REALLY SICKO GRAFFITI ON THE SCHOOL BUILDINGS!
FWUPPA
YOKAI
A FAKE PAPER...?!
WHO WOULD DO THAT?
...
THE ANTI-SCHOOLERS!
!
THIS IS TOTALLY THOSE CREEPS' M.O.!
ANTI-SCHOOLERS...
THEIR IDENTITIES AND NUMBER ARE SHROUDED IN MYSTERY.
THEY DESPISE YOKAI ACADEMY'S IDEAL OF PEACEFUL COEXISTENCE WITH HUMANS AND SEEK TO RETURN MONSTERS TO THEIR BASE PREDATORY NATURES.
THEY'RE TRYING TO DAMAGE THE ENTIRE SCHOOL'S REPUTATION BY FRAMING OUR NEWS CLUB AND GETTING THE ADMINISTRATION TO...
...ABOLISH OUR CLUB, OR WORSE—EXPEL US!
THAT'S NOT FAIR!
WHP
HEY... WHERE'S TSUKUNE?
OH...
A.W.O.L. at a time like this?
He went to the restroom.

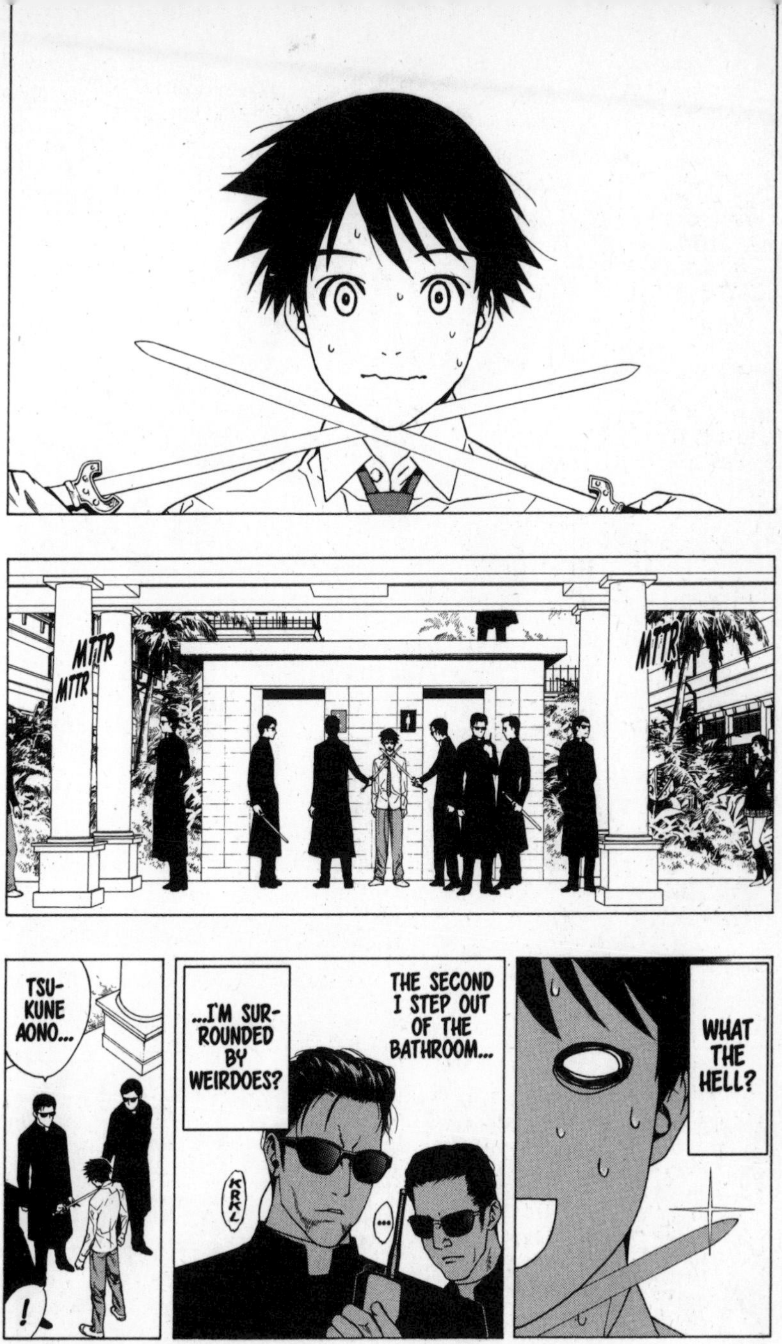
MTTR
MTTR
MTTR
WHAT THE HELL?
THE SECOND I STEP OUT OF THE BATHROOM...
...I'M SURROUNDED BY WEIRDOES?
KRKL
...
TSU-KUNE AONO...
!

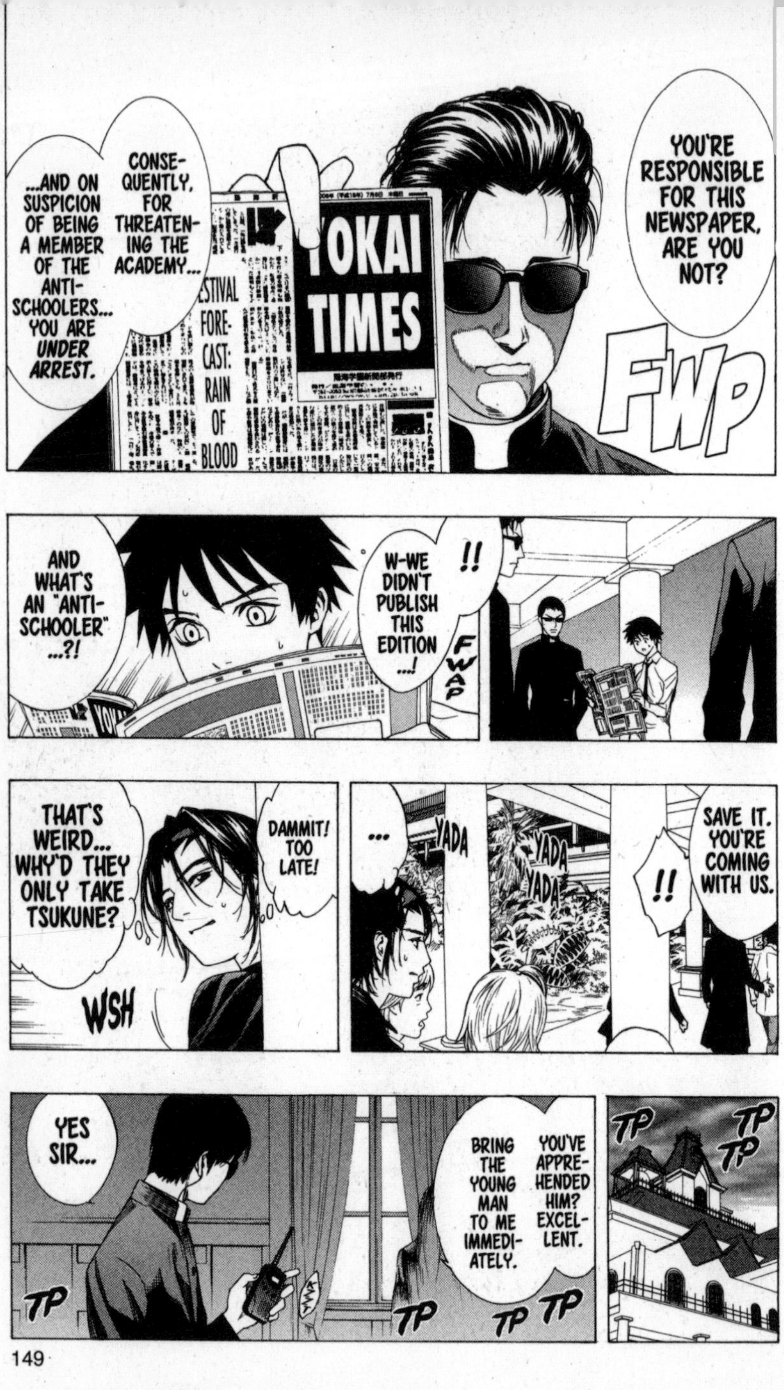
YOU'RE RESPONSIBLE FOR THIS NEWSPAPER, ARE YOU NOT?
FWP
YOKAI TIMES
ESTIVAL FORE-CAST: RAIN OF BLOOD
CONSE-QUENTLY, FOR THREATEN-ING THE ACADEMY...
...AND ON SUSPICION OF BEING A MEMBER OF THE ANTI-SCHOOLERS... YOU ARE *UNDER ARREST.*
!!
W-WE DIDN'T PUBLISH THIS EDITION...!
FWAP
AND WHAT'S AN "ANTI-SCHOOLER" ...?!
SAVE IT. YOU'RE COMING WITH US.
!!
YADA
YADA
YADA
YADA
...
DAMMIT! TOO LATE!
THAT'S WEIRD... WHY'D THEY ONLY TAKE TSUKUNE?
WSH
TP
TP
TP
YOU'VE APPRE-HENDED HIM? EXCEL-LENT.
BRING THE YOUNG MAN TO ME IMMEDI-ATELY.
TP
TP
TP
YES SIR...
TP

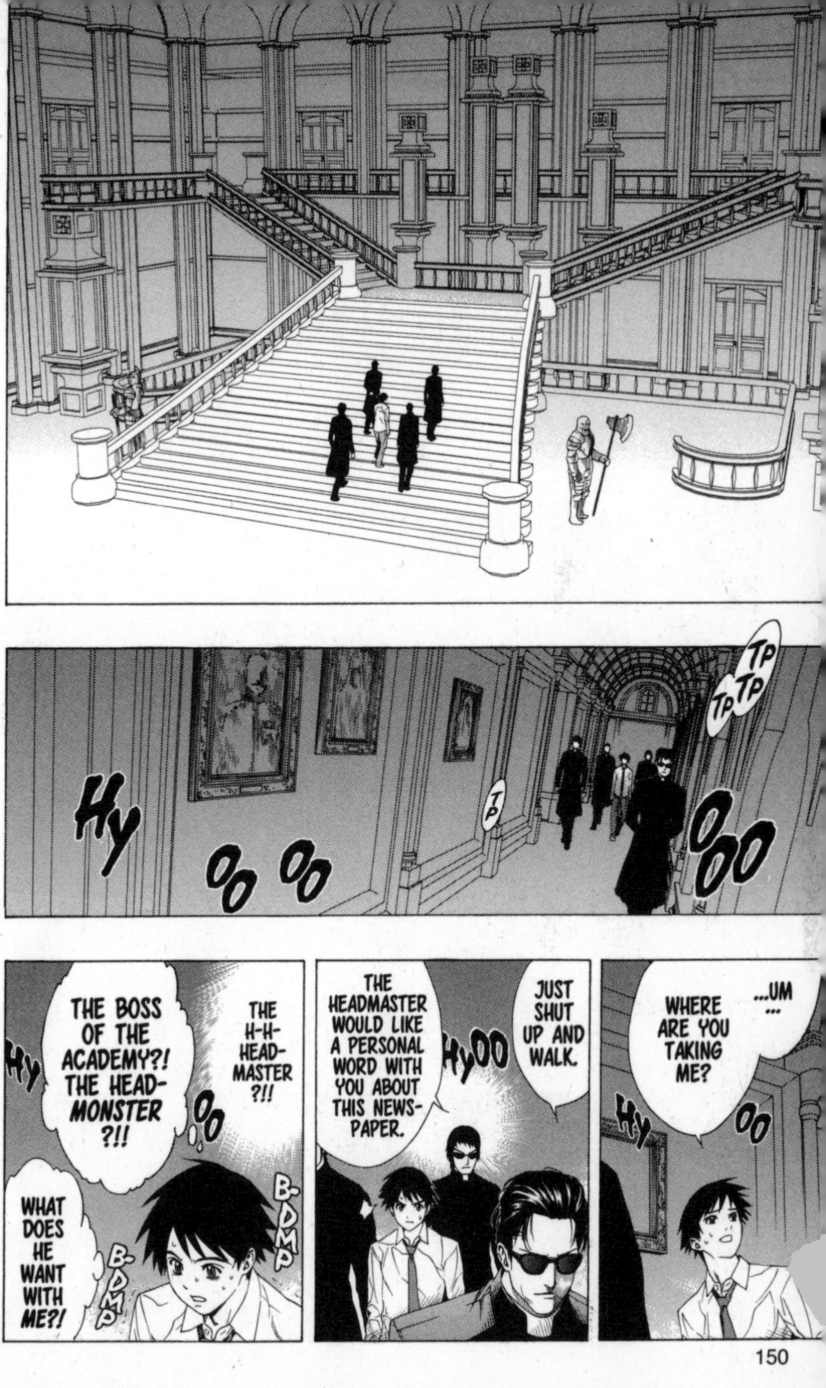
TP TP TP
OOO
TP
OO OO
HY
...UM ...
WHERE ARE YOU TAKING ME?
HY OO
JUST SHUT UP AND WALK.
THE HEADMASTER WOULD LIKE A PERSONAL WORD WITH YOU ABOUT THIS NEWSPAPER.
HYOO
THE H-H-HEAD-MASTER?!!
THE BOSS OF THE ACADEMY?! THE HEAD-*MONSTER*?!!
HY OO
B-DMP
B-DMP
WHAT DOES HE WANT WITH *ME*?!

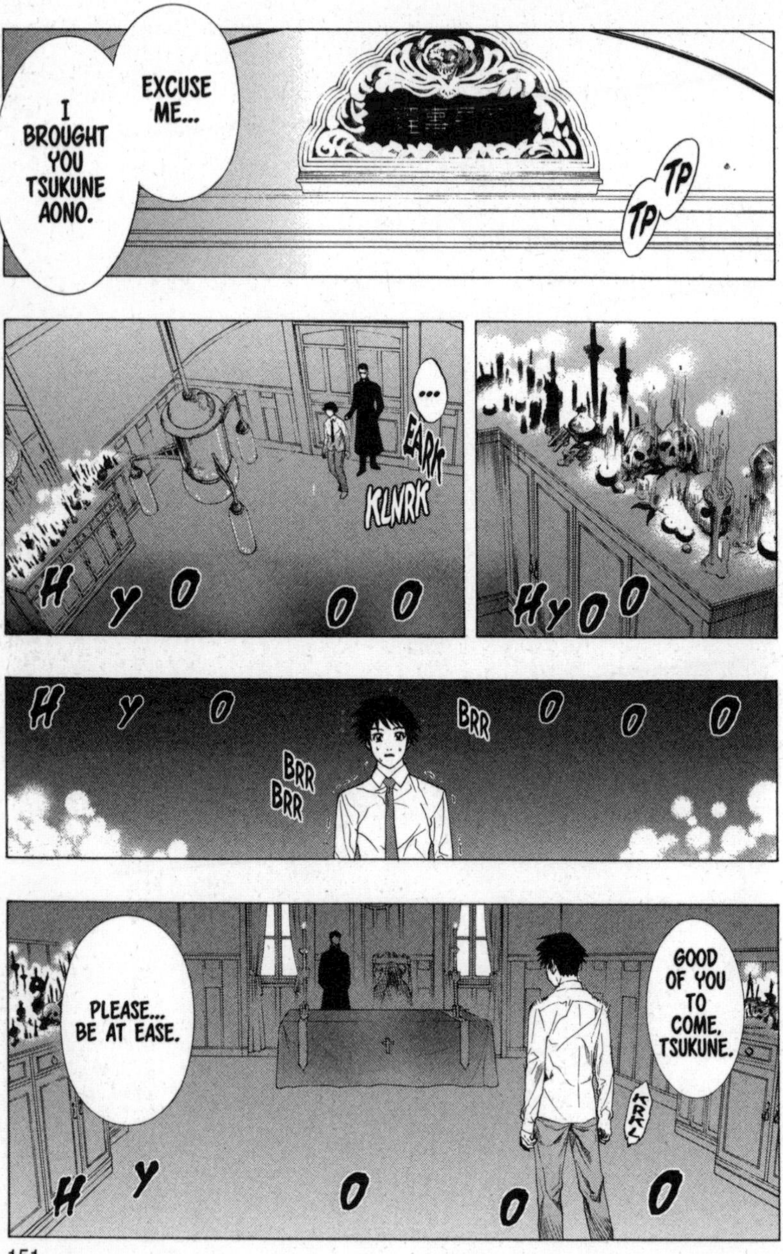
TP TP
EXCUSE ME...
I BROUGHT YOU TSUKUNE AONO.
HyOOO
...
EARK
KLNRK
HyOOOO
HyOOOOO
BRR
BRR BRR
GOOD OF YOU TO COME, TSUKUNE.
KRKL
PLEASE... BE AT EASE.
HyOOOO

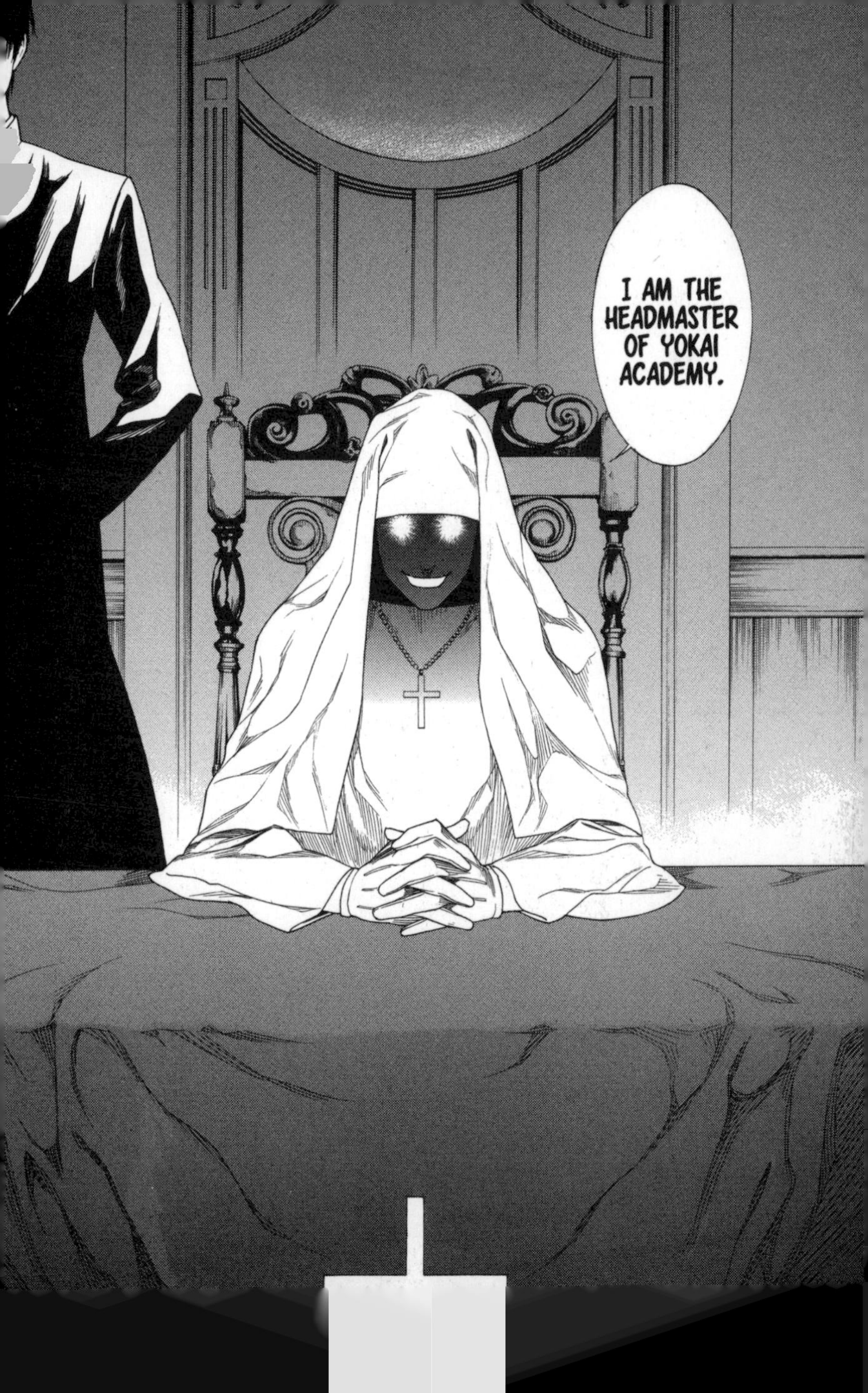
I AM THE HEADMASTER OF YOKAI ACADEMY.

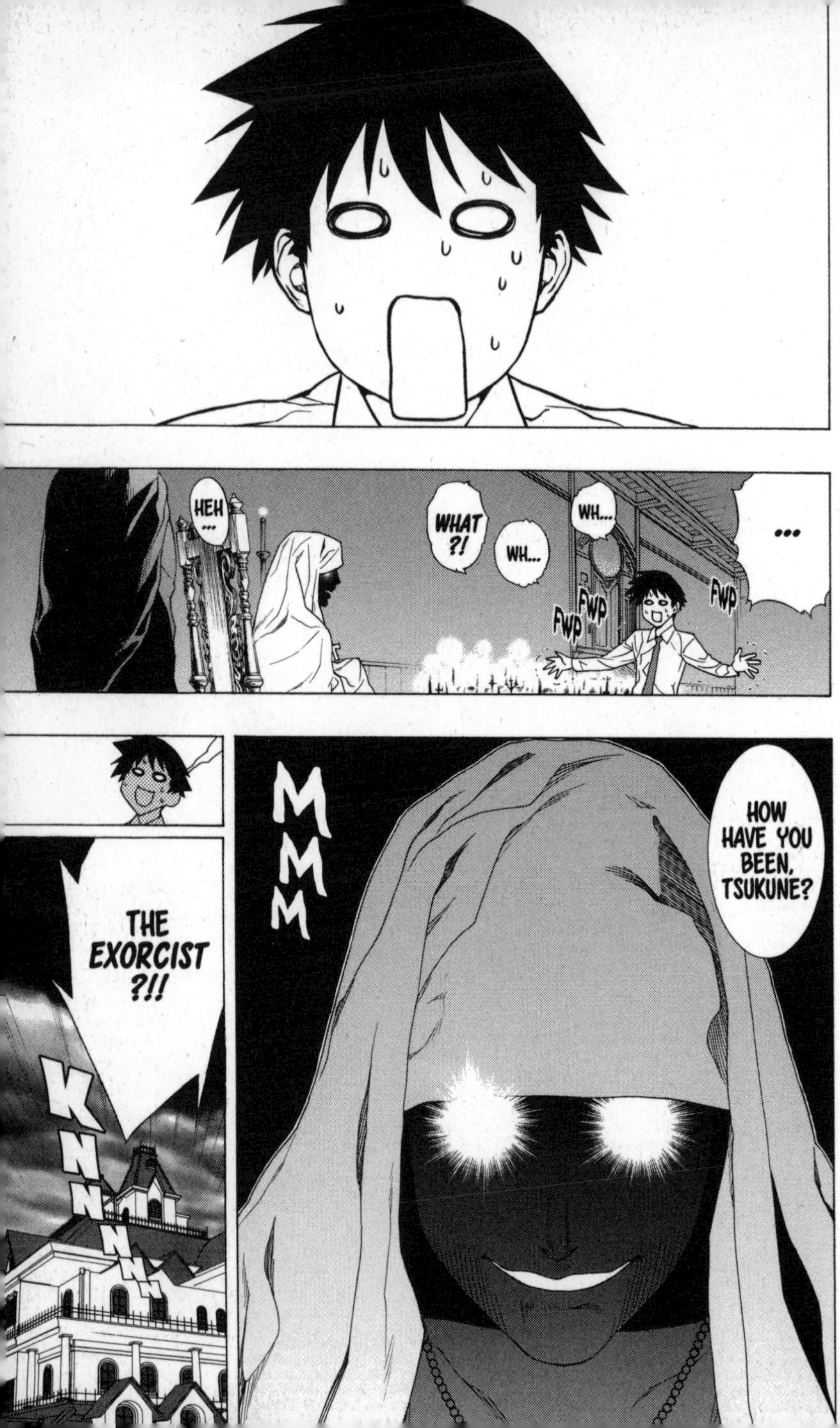
...
FWP
WH...
FWP FWP
WH...
WHAT ?!
HEH ...
HOW HAVE YOU BEEN, TSUKUNE?
MMM
THE EXORCIST ?!!
KNNNNNN

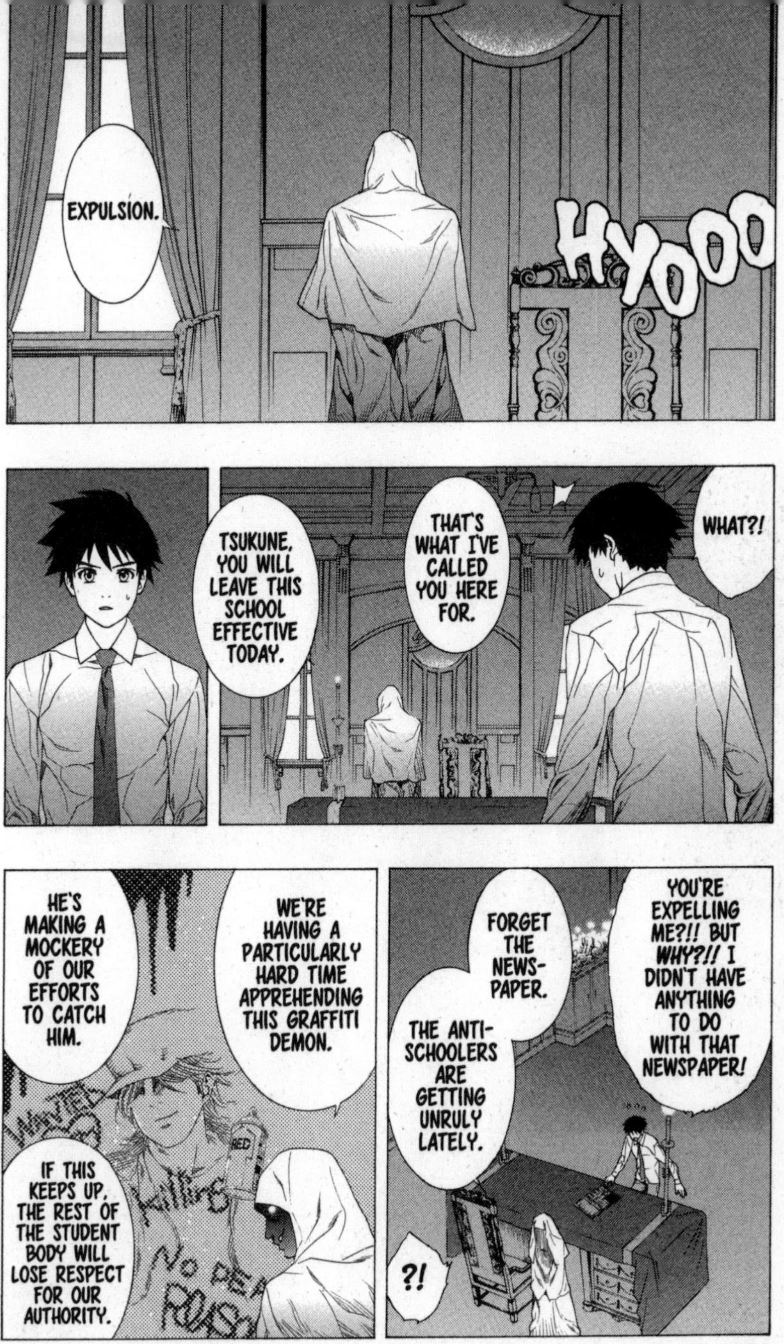
HYOOO
EXPULSION.
WHAT?!
THAT'S WHAT I'VE CALLED YOU HERE FOR.
TSUKUNE, YOU WILL LEAVE THIS SCHOOL EFFECTIVE TODAY.
YOU'RE EXPELLING ME?!! BUT WHY?!! I DIDN'T HAVE ANYTHING TO DO WITH THAT NEWSPAPER!
FORGET THE NEWS-PAPER.
THE ANTI-SCHOOLERS ARE GETTING UNRULY LATELY.
?!
WE'RE HAVING A PARTICULARLY HARD TIME APPREHENDING THIS GRAFFITI DEMON.
HE'S MAKING A MOCKERY OF OUR EFFORTS TO CATCH HIM.
RED
IF THIS KEEPS UP, THE REST OF THE STUDENT BODY WILL LOSE RESPECT FOR OUR AUTHORITY.

READ THIS WAY

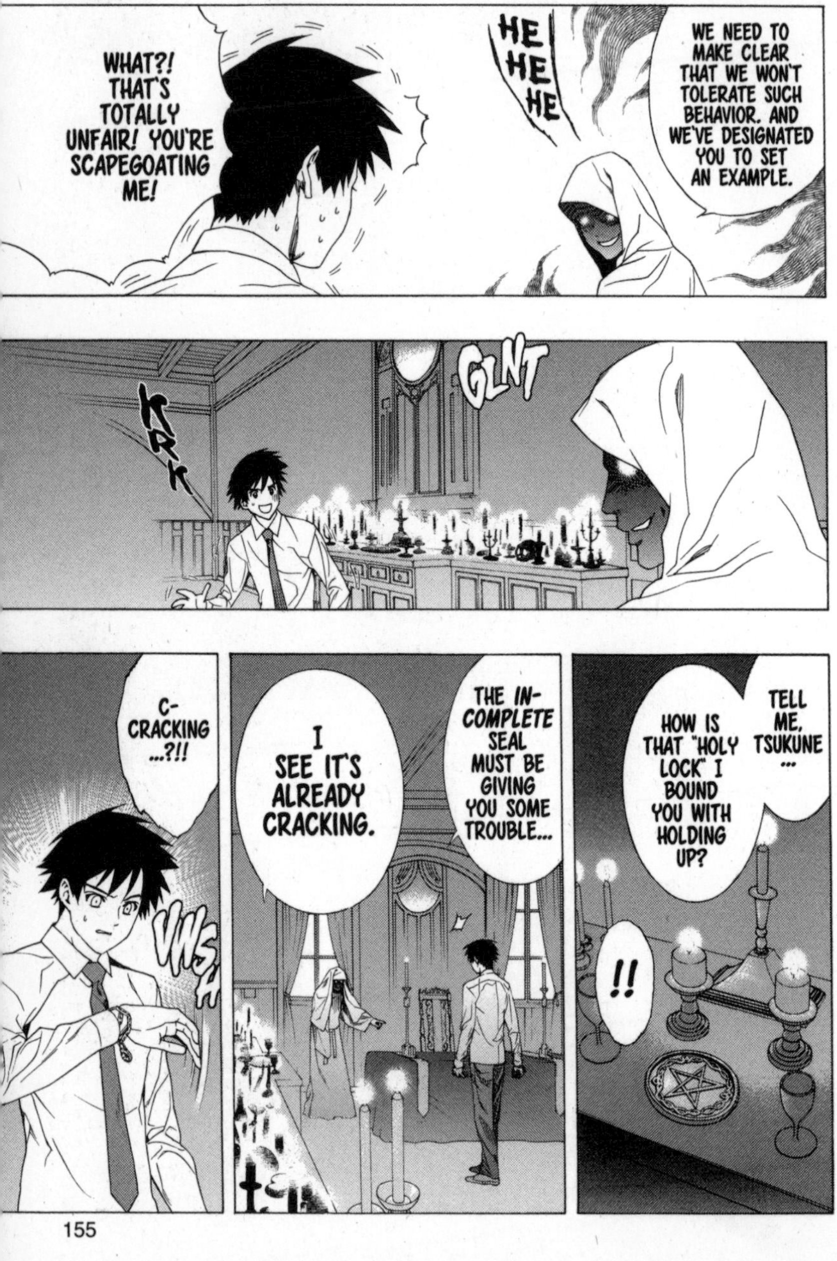
WE NEED TO MAKE CLEAR THAT WE WON'T TOLERATE SUCH BEHAVIOR. AND WE'VE DESIGNATED YOU TO SET AN EXAMPLE.
HE HE HE
WHAT?! THAT'S TOTALLY UNFAIR! YOU'RE SCAPEGOATING ME!
GLNT
KRK
TELL ME, TSUKUNE...
HOW IS THAT "HOLY LOCK" I BOUND YOU WITH HOLDING UP?
!!
THE IN-COMPLETE SEAL MUST BE GIVING YOU SOME TROUBLE...
I SEE IT'S ALREADY CRACKING.
C-CRACKING...?!!
VWSH

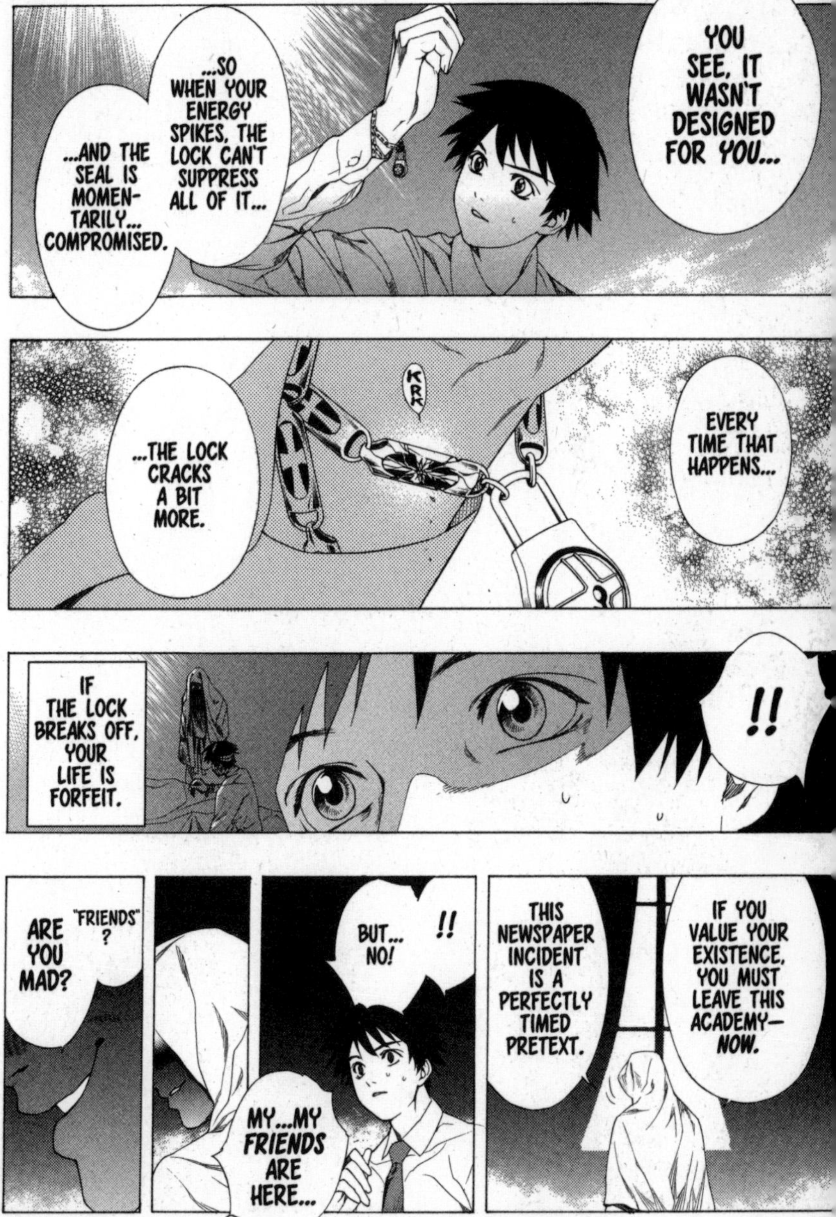
YOU SEE, IT WASN'T DESIGNED FOR *YOU*...
...SO WHEN YOUR ENERGY SPIKES, THE LOCK CAN'T SUPPRESS ALL OF IT...
...AND THE SEAL IS MOMENTARILY... COMPROMISED.
EVERY TIME THAT HAPPENS...
KRK
...THE LOCK CRACKS A BIT MORE.
!!
IF THE LOCK BREAKS OFF, YOUR LIFE IS FORFEIT.
IF YOU VALUE YOUR EXISTENCE, YOU MUST LEAVE THIS ACADEMY—*NOW.*
THIS NEWSPAPER INCIDENT IS A PERFECTLY TIMED PRETEXT.
!!
BUT... NO!
MY...MY *FRIENDS* ARE HERE...
"FRIENDS"?
ARE YOU MAD?

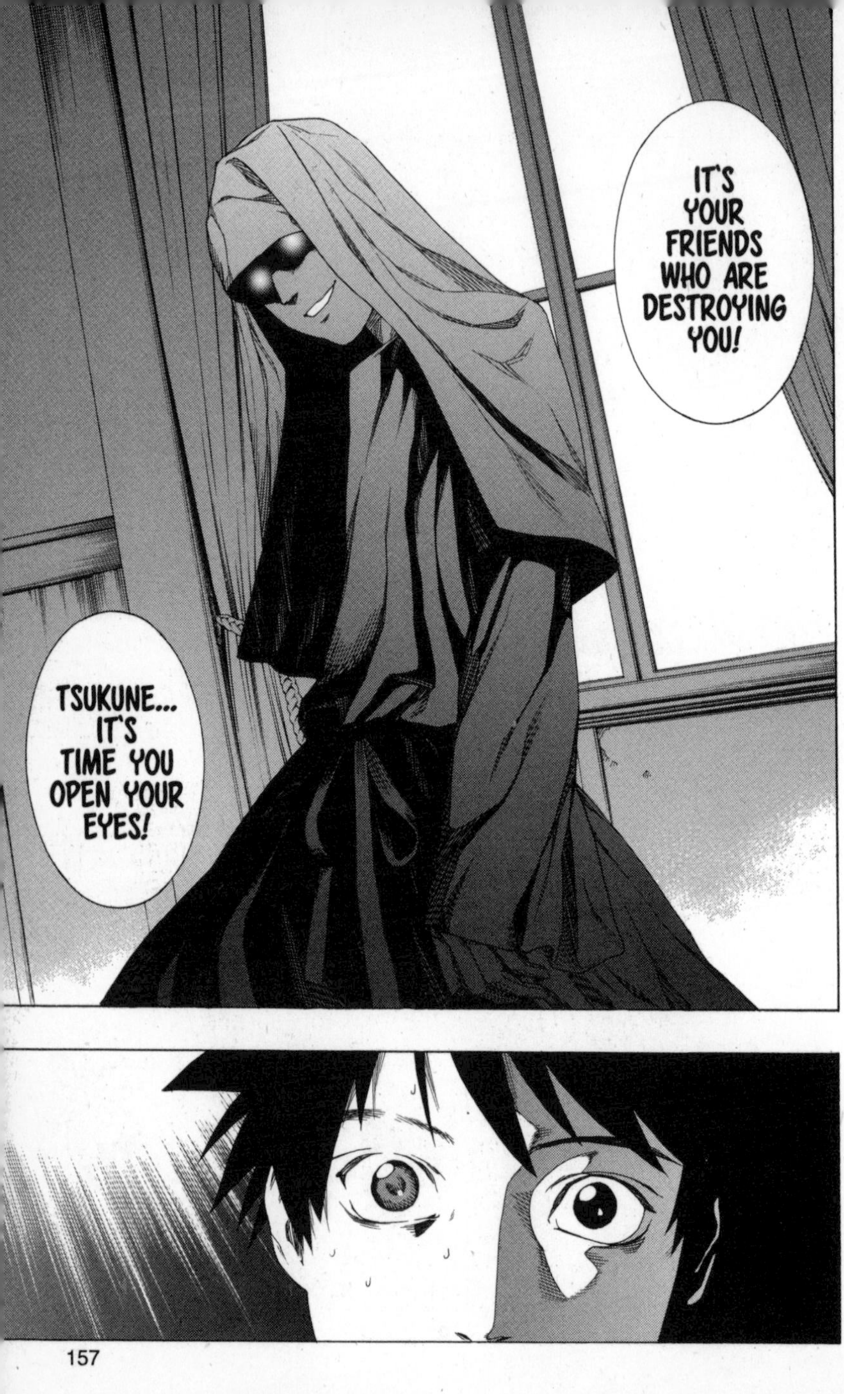
IT'S YOUR FRIENDS WHO ARE DESTROYING YOU!
TSUKUNE... IT'S TIME YOU OPEN YOUR EYES!

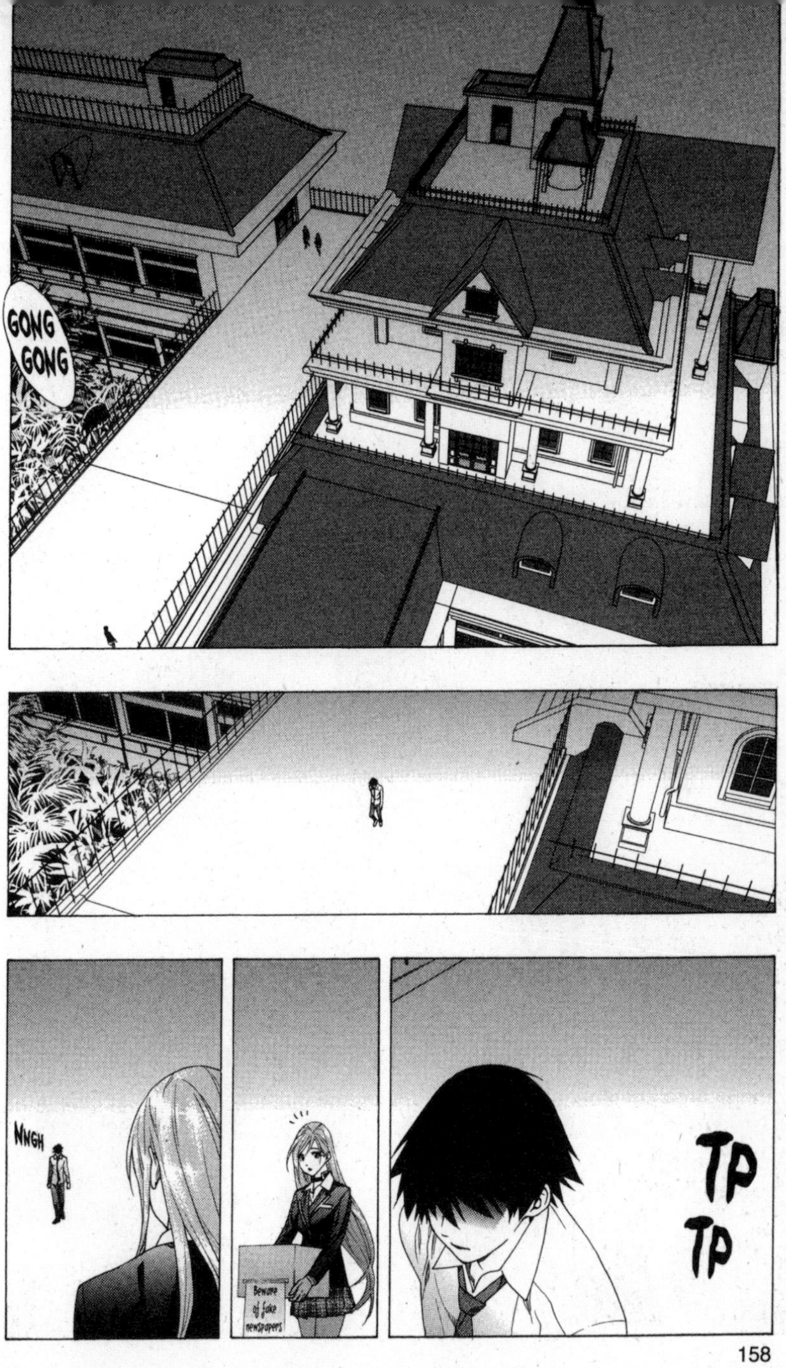
GONG GONG
TP TP
Beware of fake newspapers
NNGH

READ THIS WAY

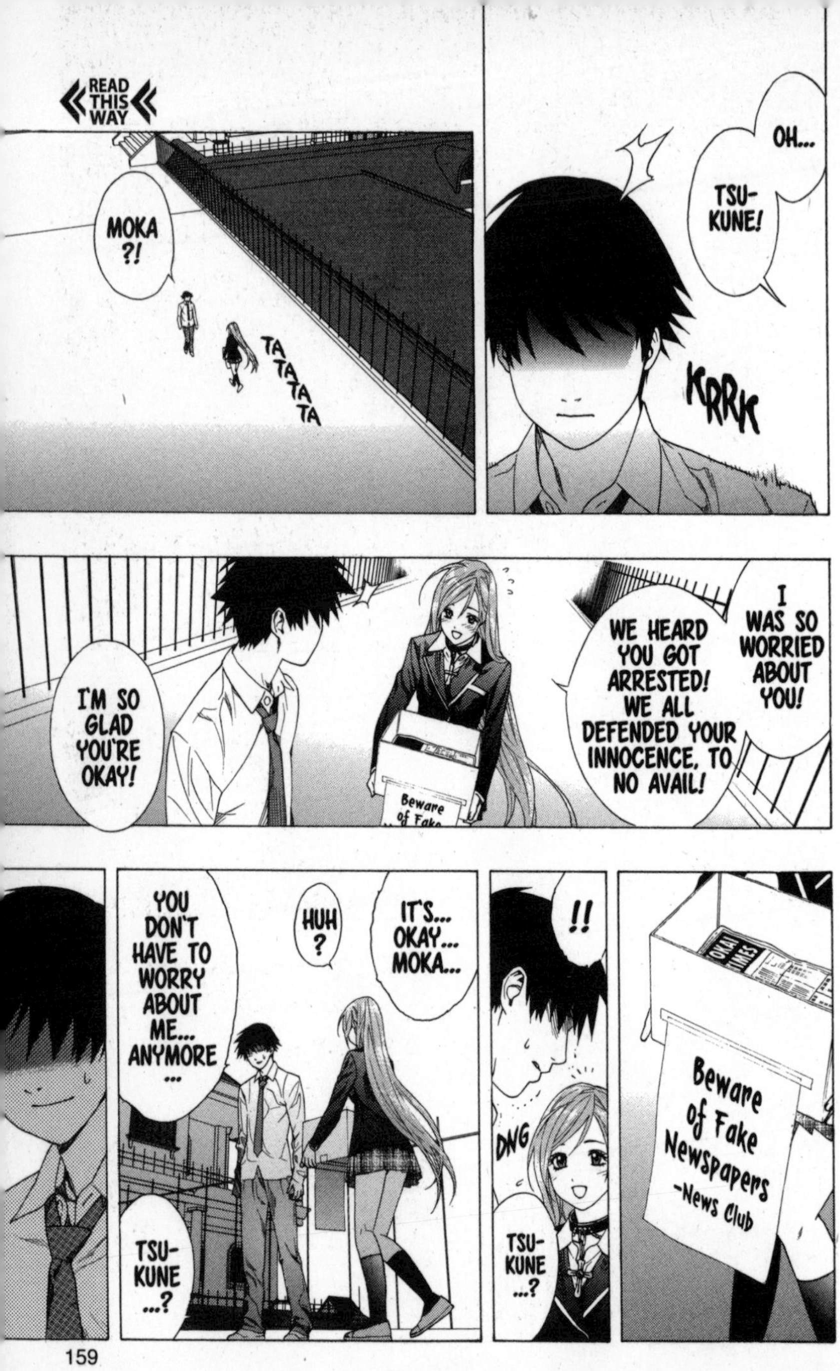

OH... TSU-KUNE!
KRRK
MOKA ?!
TA TA TA TA
I WAS SO WORRIED ABOUT YOU!
WE HEARD YOU GOT ARRESTED! WE ALL DEFENDED YOUR INNOCENCE, TO NO AVAIL!
I'M SO GLAD YOU'RE OKAY!
Beware of Fake Newspapers -News Club
!!
DNG
TSU-KUNE ...?
IT'S... OKAY... MOKA...
HUH ?
YOU DON'T HAVE TO WORRY ABOUT ME... ANYMORE ...
TSU-KUNE ...?

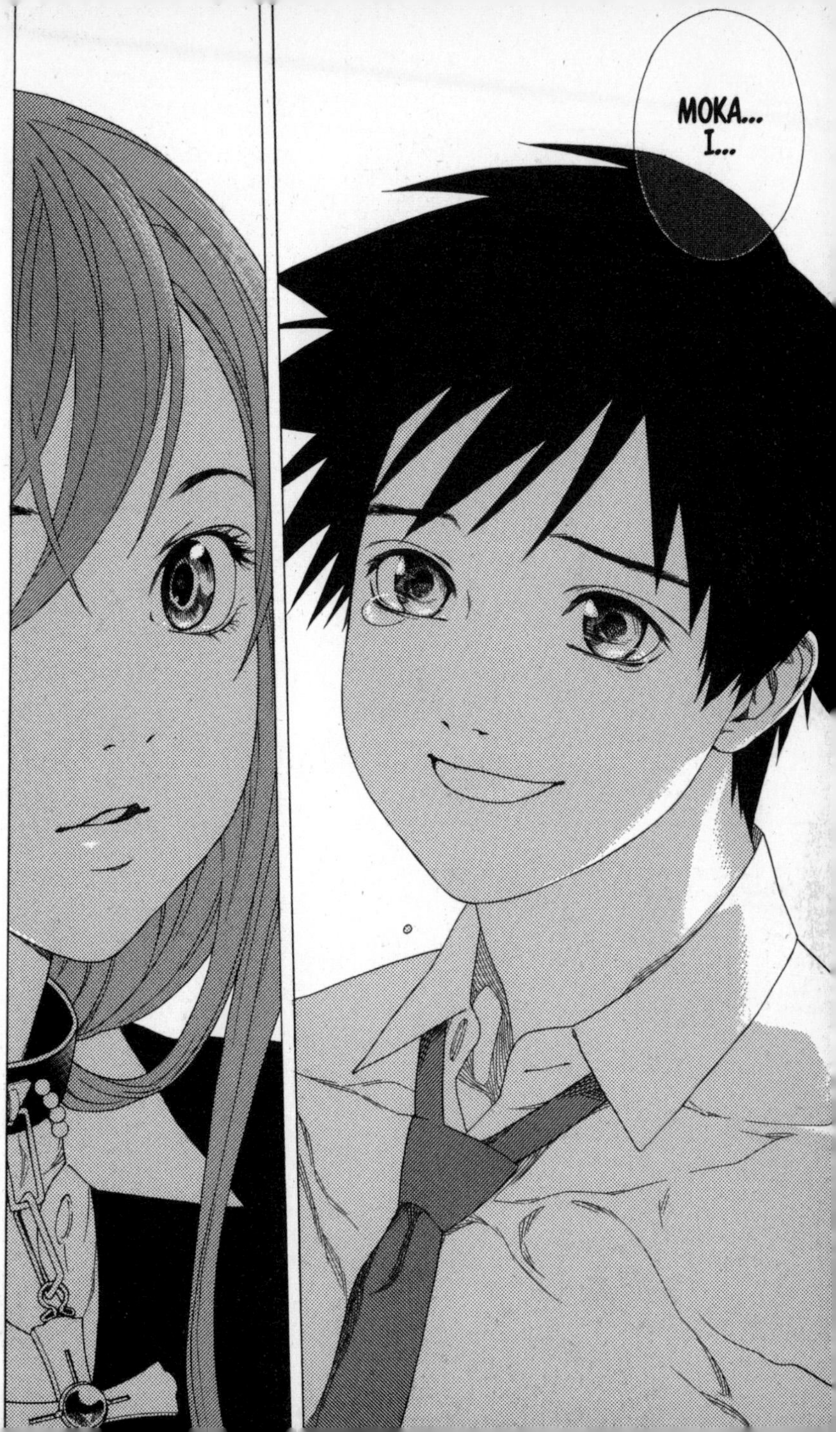
MOKA... I...

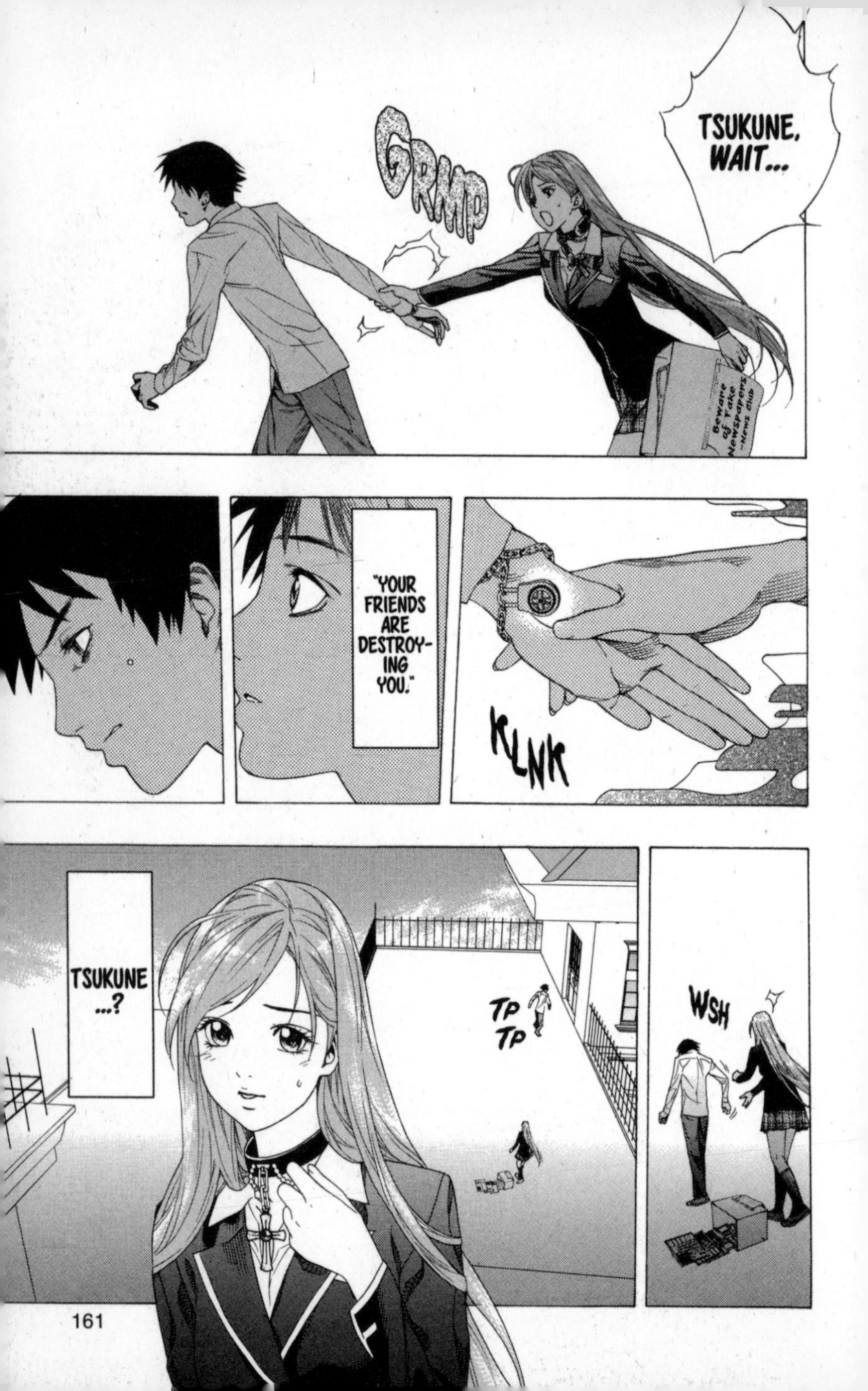
TSUKUNE, WAIT...
GRMP
Beware of Fake Newspapers -News Club
KLNK
"YOUR FRIENDS ARE DESTROY-ING YOU."
WSH
TP TP
TSUKUNE ...?

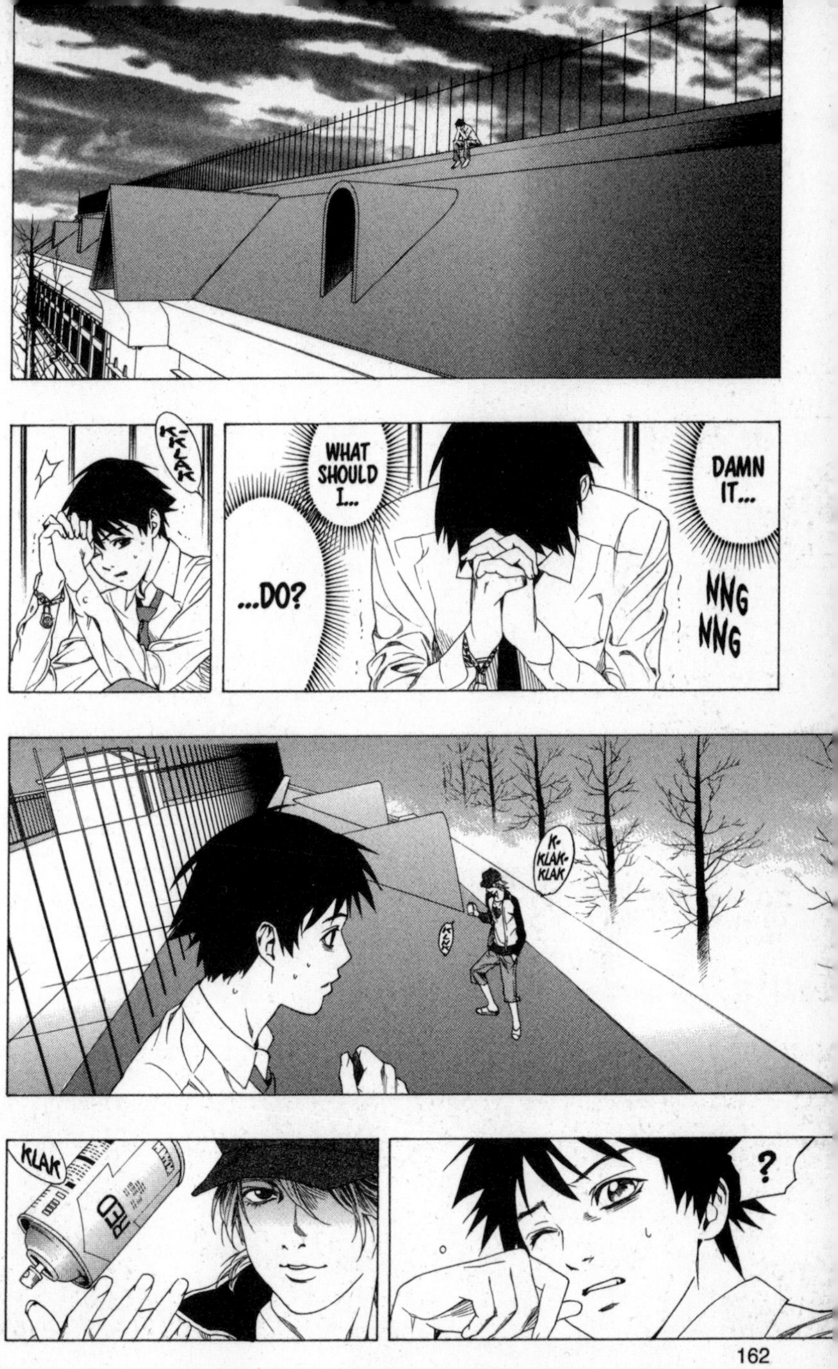
DAMN IT...
NNG NNG
WHAT SHOULD I...
...DO?
K-KLAK
K-KLAK-KLAK
KLAK
?
KLAK
RED

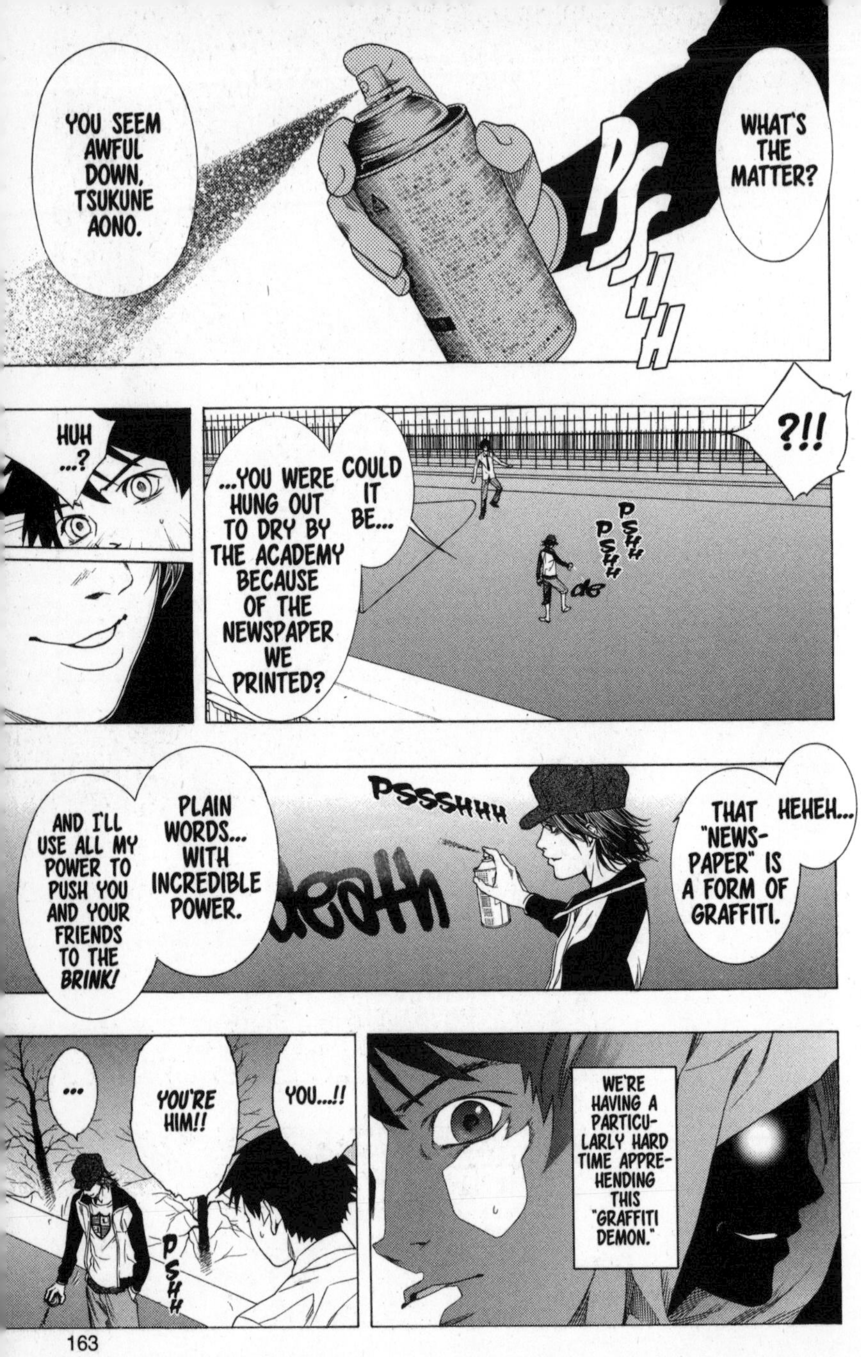
WHAT'S THE MATTER?
PSSHHH
YOU SEEM AWFUL DOWN, TSUKUNE AONO.
?!!
PSHH PSHH
COULD IT BE...
...YOU WERE HUNG OUT TO DRY BY THE ACADEMY BECAUSE OF THE NEWSPAPER WE PRINTED?
HUH ...?
HEHEH...
THAT "NEWS-PAPER" IS A FORM OF GRAFFITI.
PSSSHHH
PLAIN WORDS... WITH INCREDIBLE POWER.
AND I'LL USE ALL MY POWER TO PUSH YOU AND YOUR FRIENDS TO THE BRINK!
WE'RE HAVING A PARTICU-LARLY HARD TIME APPRE-HENDING THIS "GRAFFITI DEMON."
YOU...!!
YOU'RE HIM!!
...
PSHH

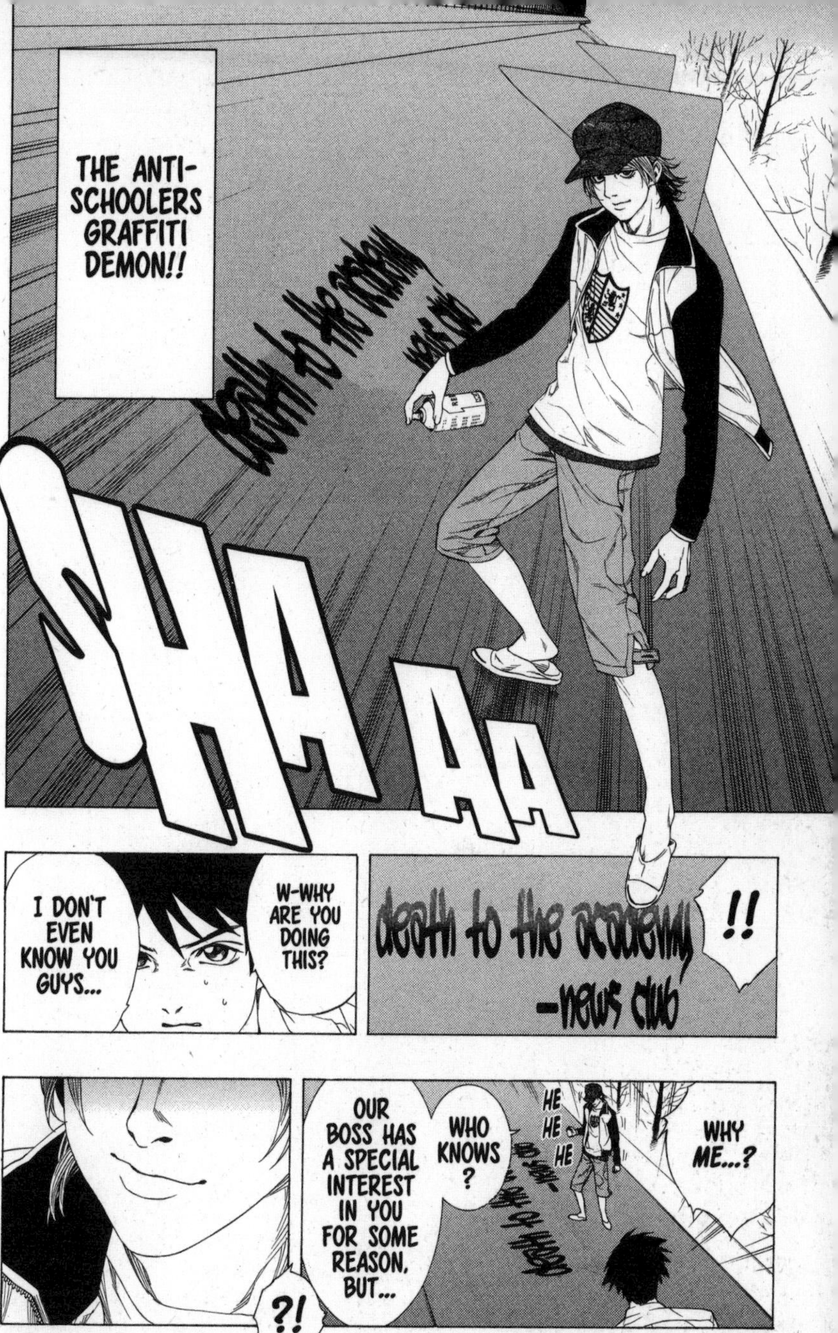
THE ANTI-SCHOOLERS GRAFFITI DEMON!!
SHAAA
death to the academy
-news club
!!
W-WHY ARE YOU DOING THIS?
I DON'T EVEN KNOW YOU GUYS...
WHY ME...?
HE HE HE
WHO KNOWS?
OUR BOSS HAS A SPECIAL INTEREST IN YOU FOR SOME REASON, BUT...
?!

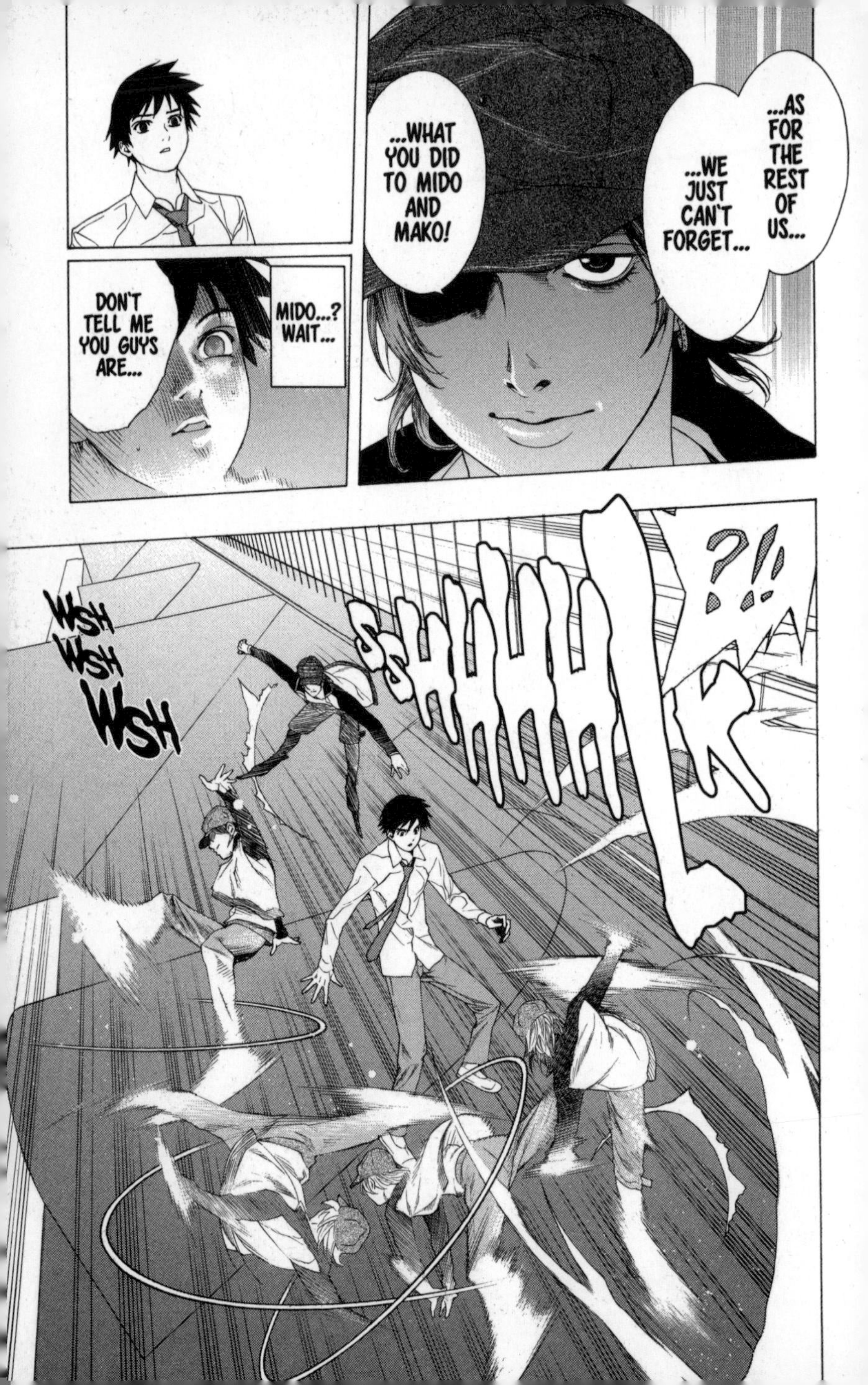
...AS FOR THE REST OF US...
...WE JUST CAN'T FORGET...
...WHAT YOU DID TO MIDO AND MAKO!
MIDO...? WAIT...
DON'T TELL ME YOU GUYS ARE...
?!!
SSHHHHK
WSH WSH WSH

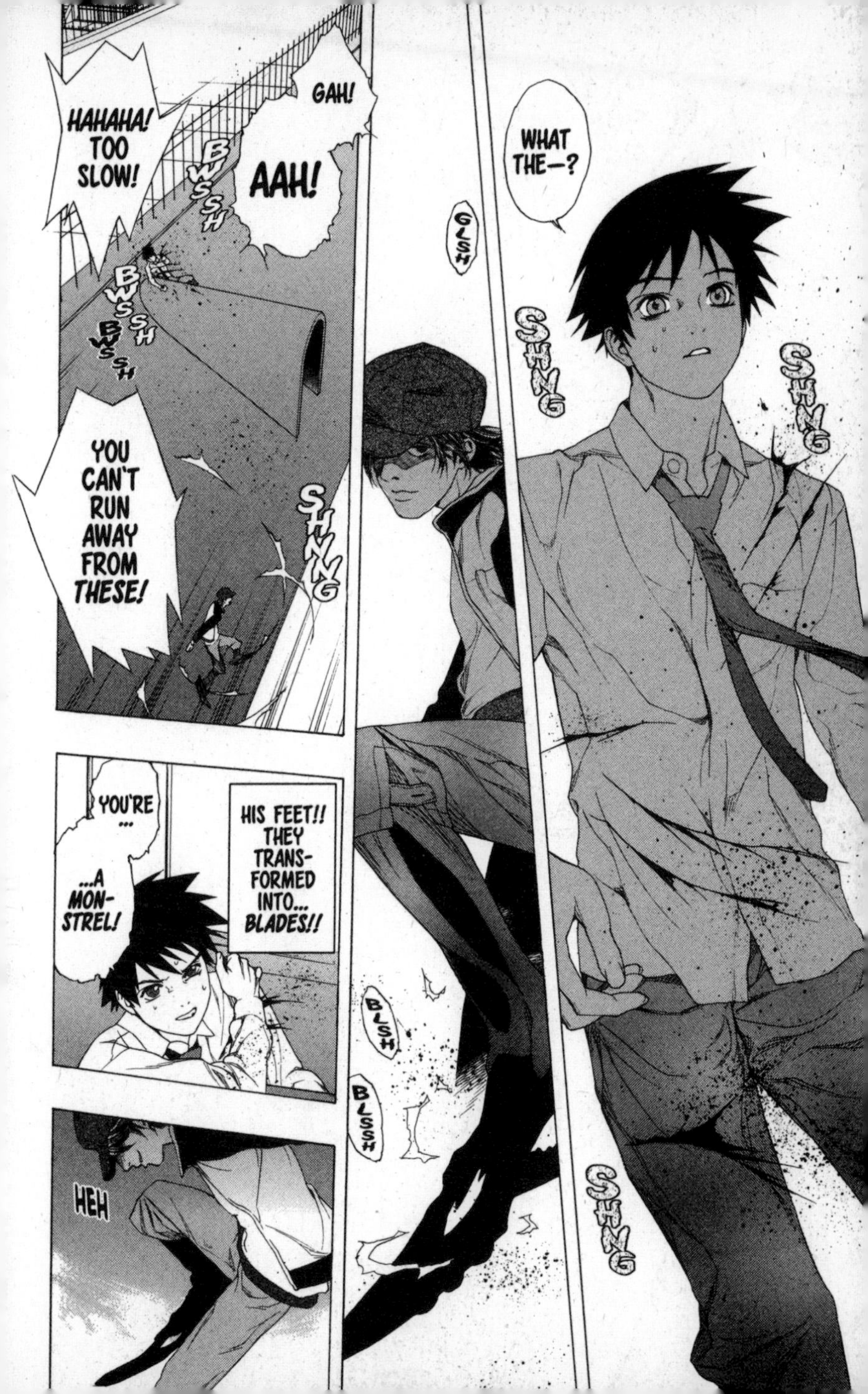
WHAT THE—?
SHNG
SHNG
SHNG
GLSH
BLSH
BLSSH
GAH!
HAHAHA! TOO SLOW!
AAH!
BWSSH
BWSSH
BWSSH
YOU CAN'T RUN AWAY FROM THESE!
SHNNG
HIS FEET!! THEY TRANS-FORMED INTO... BLADES!!
YOU'RE ...
...A MON-STREL!
HEH

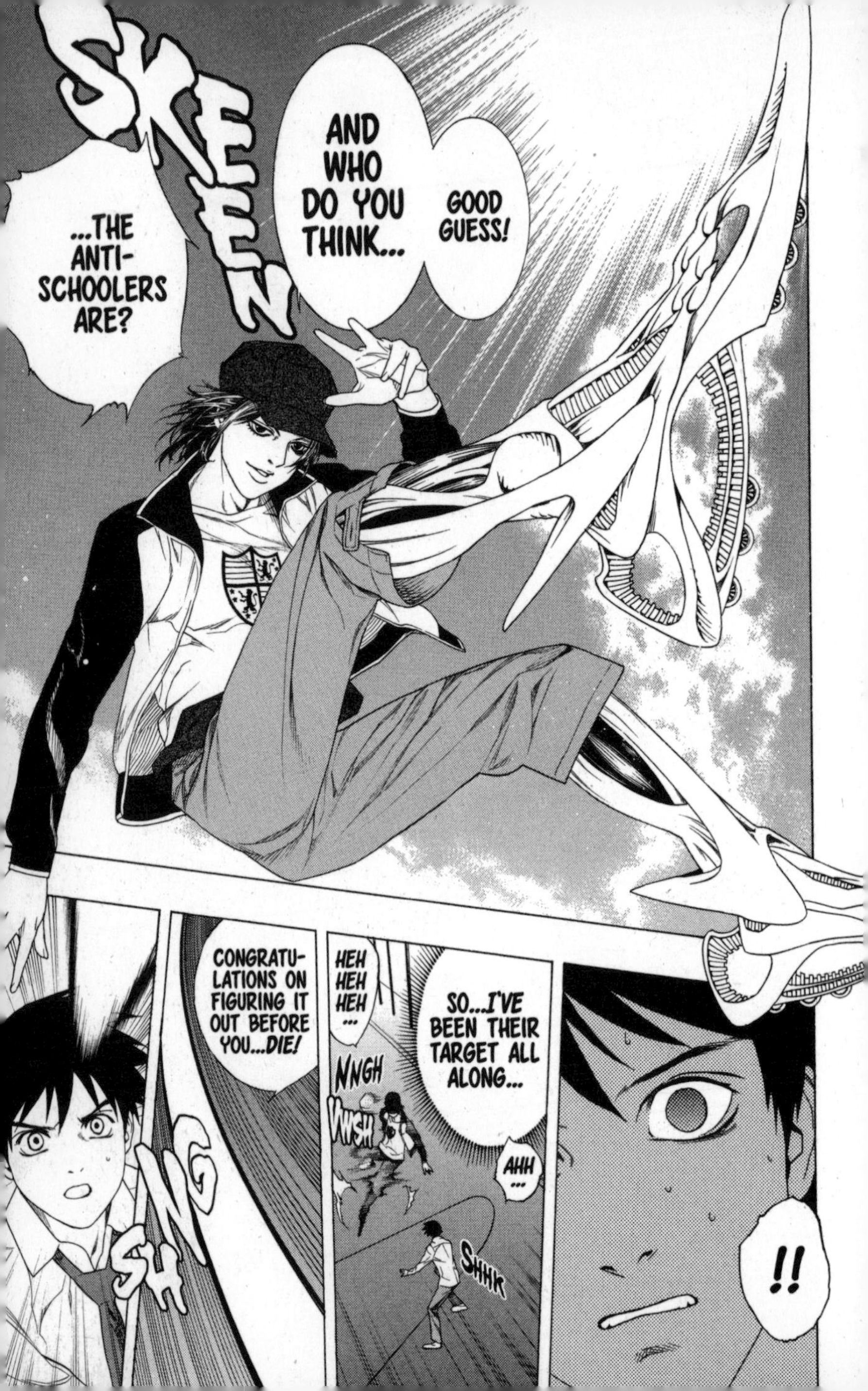
SKEEEN
GOOD GUESS!
AND WHO DO YOU THINK...
...THE ANTI-SCHOOLERS ARE?
AHH...
!!
SO...I'VE BEEN THEIR TARGET ALL ALONG...
HEH HEH HEH...
NNGH
VWISH
SHHK
CONGRATULATIONS ON FIGURING IT OUT BEFORE YOU...DIE!

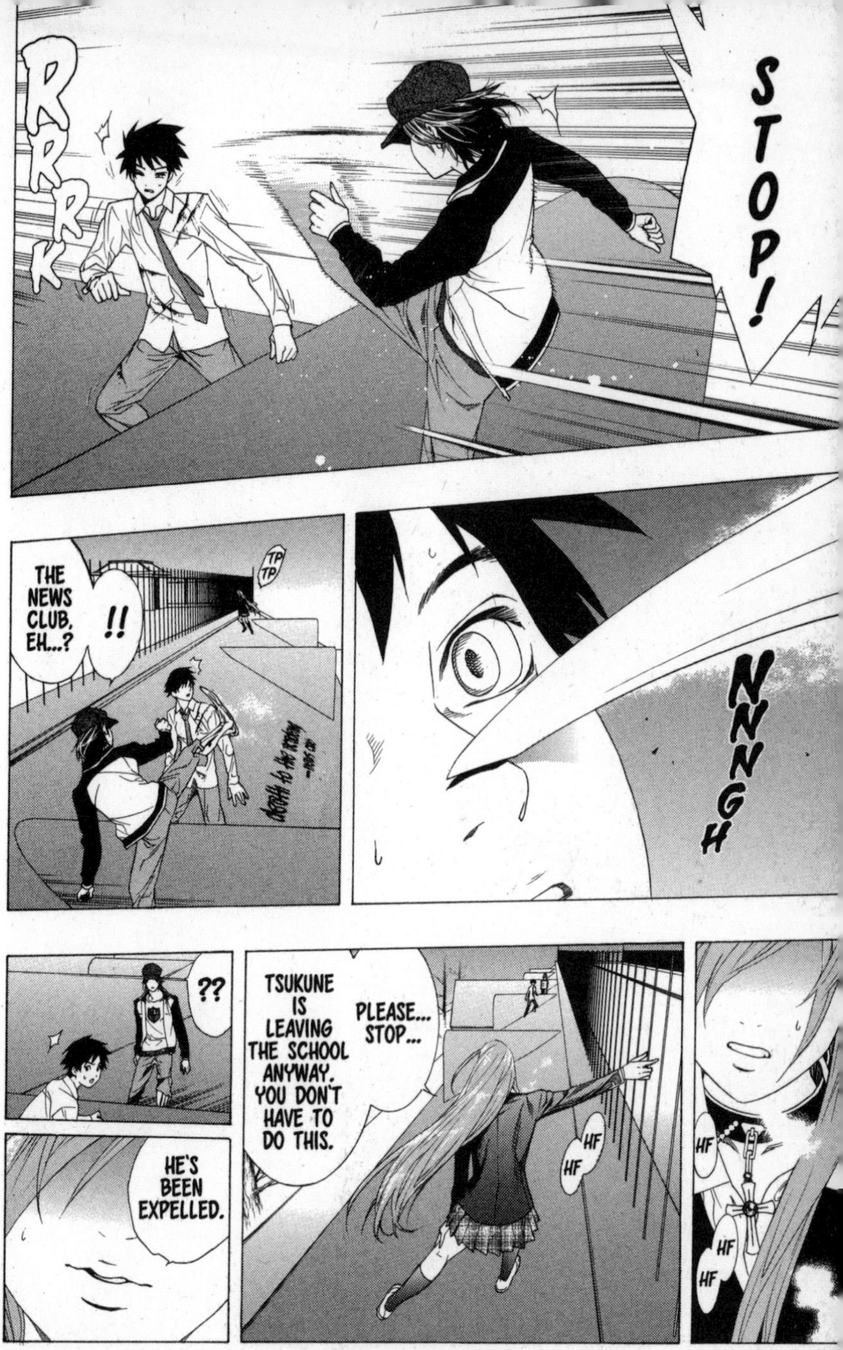
STOP!
RRRK
NNNGH
THE NEWS CLUB, EH...?
!!
TP TP
HF
HF
HF
HF
PLEASE... STOP...
HF
HF
??
TSUKUNE IS LEAVING THE SCHOOL ANYWAY. YOU DON'T HAVE TO DO THIS.
HE'S BEEN EXPELLED.

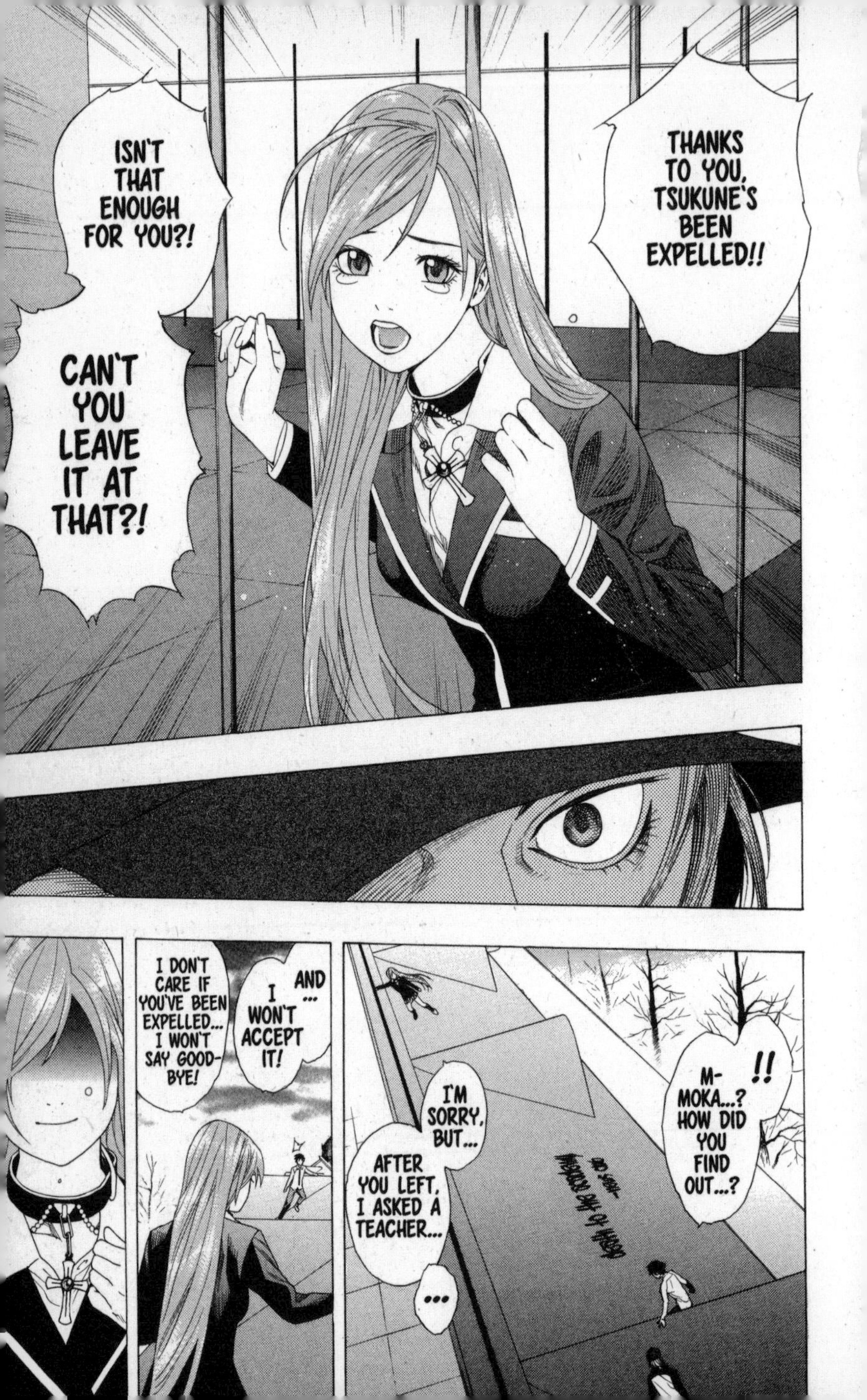
THANKS TO YOU, TSUKUNE'S BEEN EXPELLED!!
ISN'T THAT ENOUGH FOR YOU?!
CAN'T YOU LEAVE IT AT THAT?!
!!
M-MOKA...? HOW DID YOU FIND OUT...?
I'M SORRY, BUT...
AFTER YOU LEFT, I ASKED A TEACHER...
...
AND ...
I WON'T ACCEPT IT!
I DON'T CARE IF YOU'VE BEEN EXPELLED... I WON'T SAY GOOD-BYE!

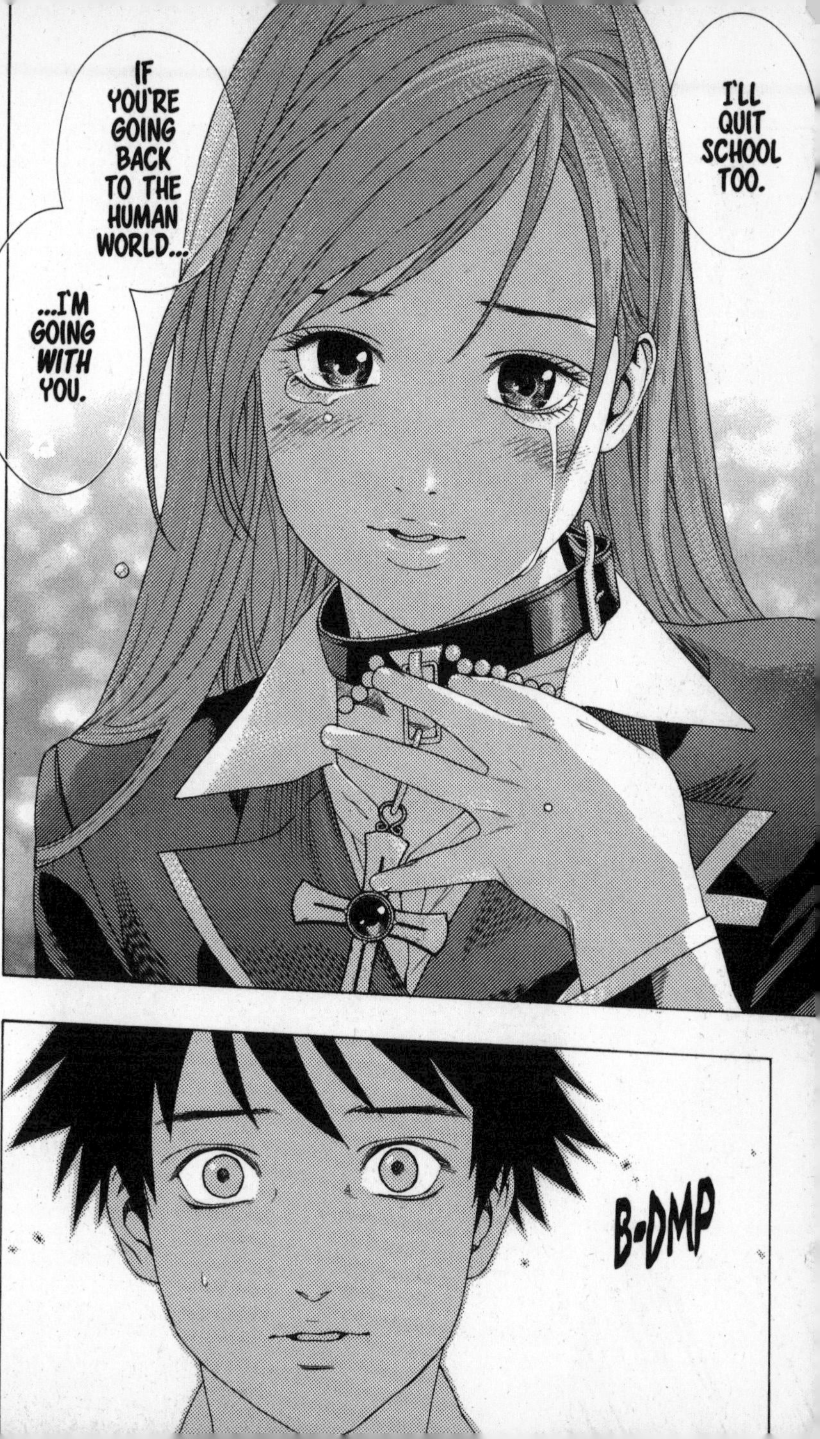
I'LL QUIT SCHOOL TOO.
IF YOU'RE GOING BACK TO THE HUMAN WORLD...
...I'M GOING WITH YOU.
B-DMP

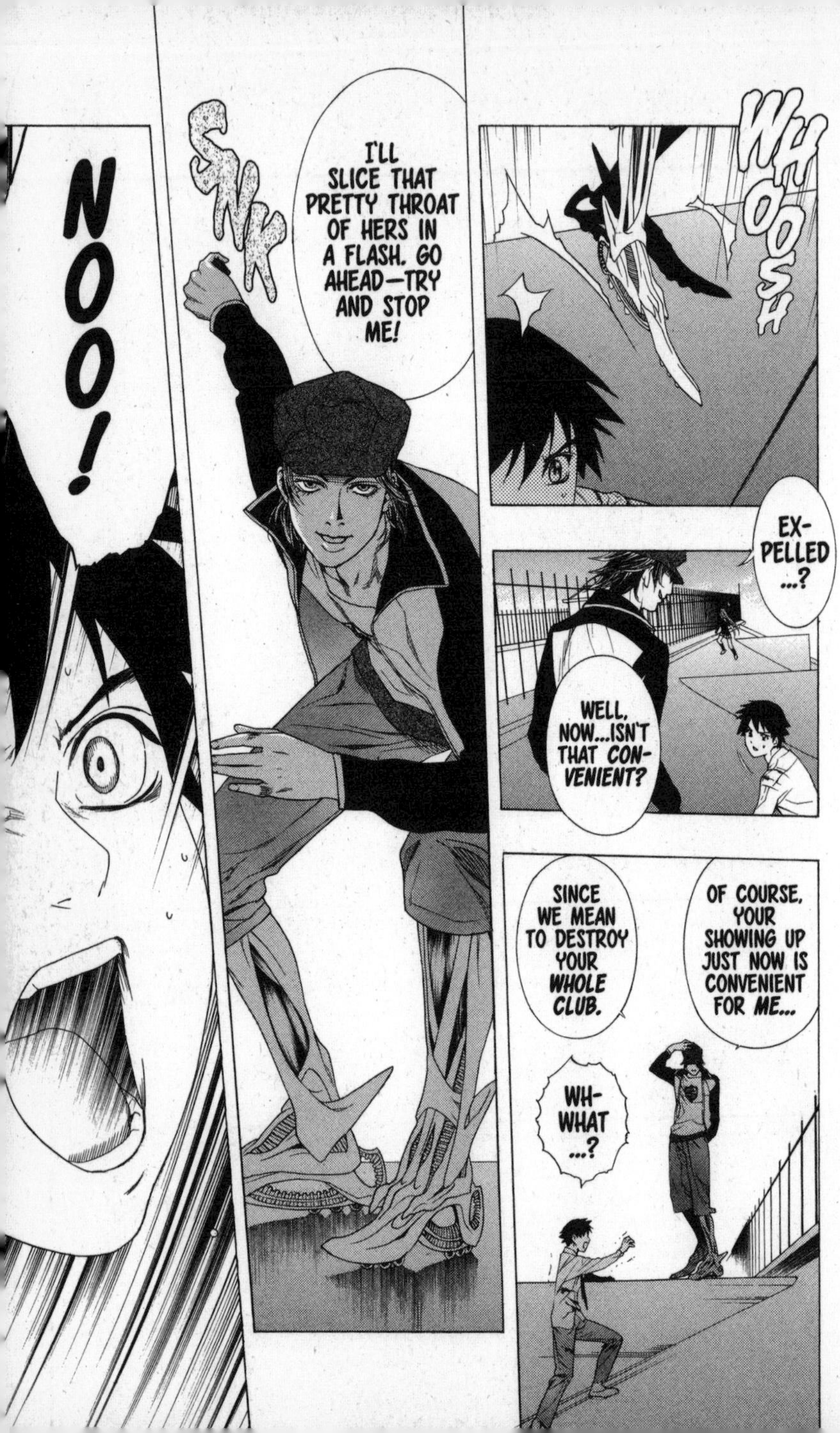
WHOOSH
EX-PELLED ...?
WELL, NOW...ISN'T THAT CON-VENIENT?
OF COURSE, YOUR SHOWING UP JUST NOW IS CONVENIENT FOR ME...
SINCE WE MEAN TO DESTROY YOUR WHOLE CLUB.
WH-WHAT ...?
SNK
I'LL SLICE THAT PRETTY THROAT OF HERS IN A FLASH. GO AHEAD—TRY AND STOP ME!
NOOO!

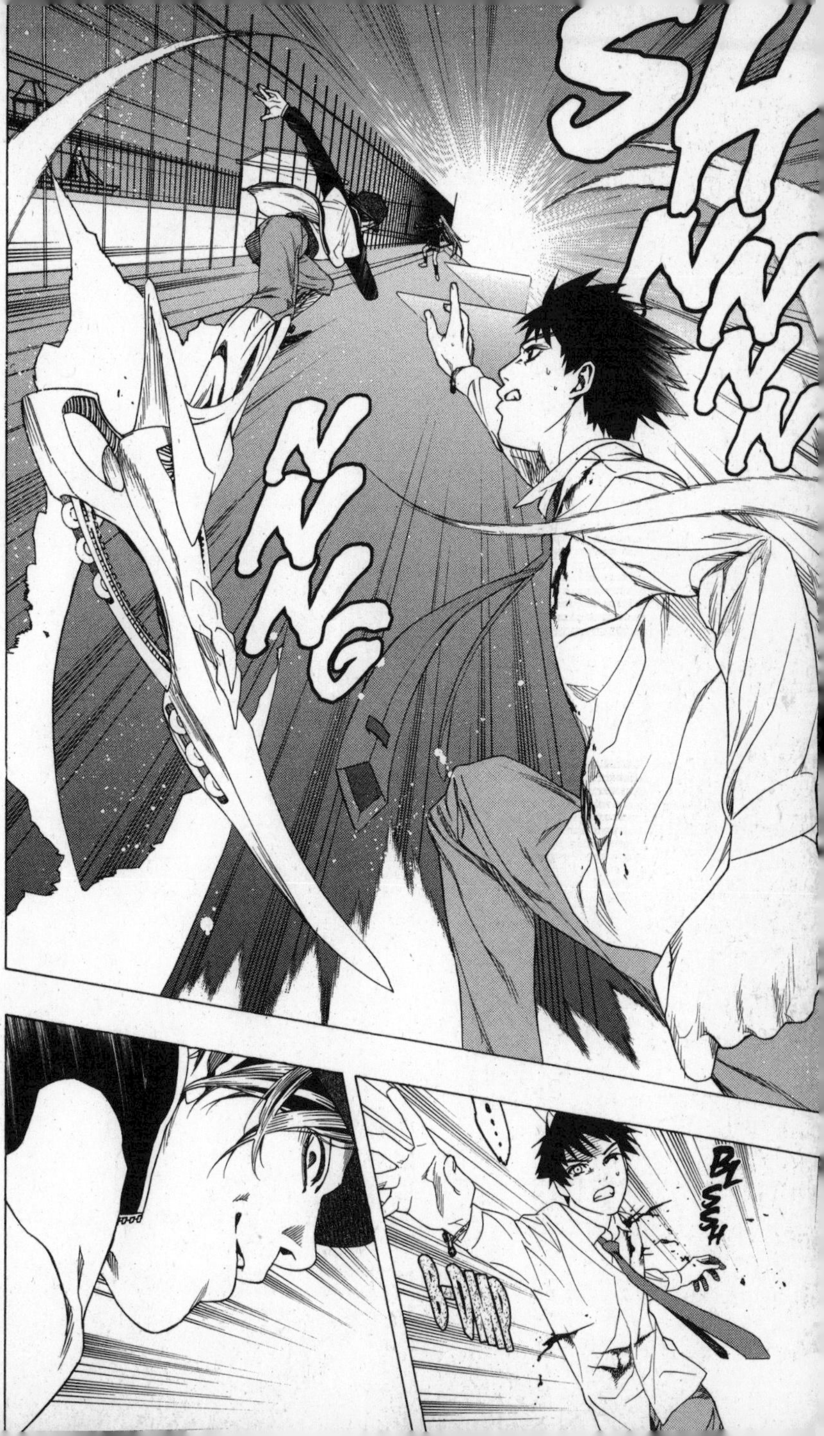

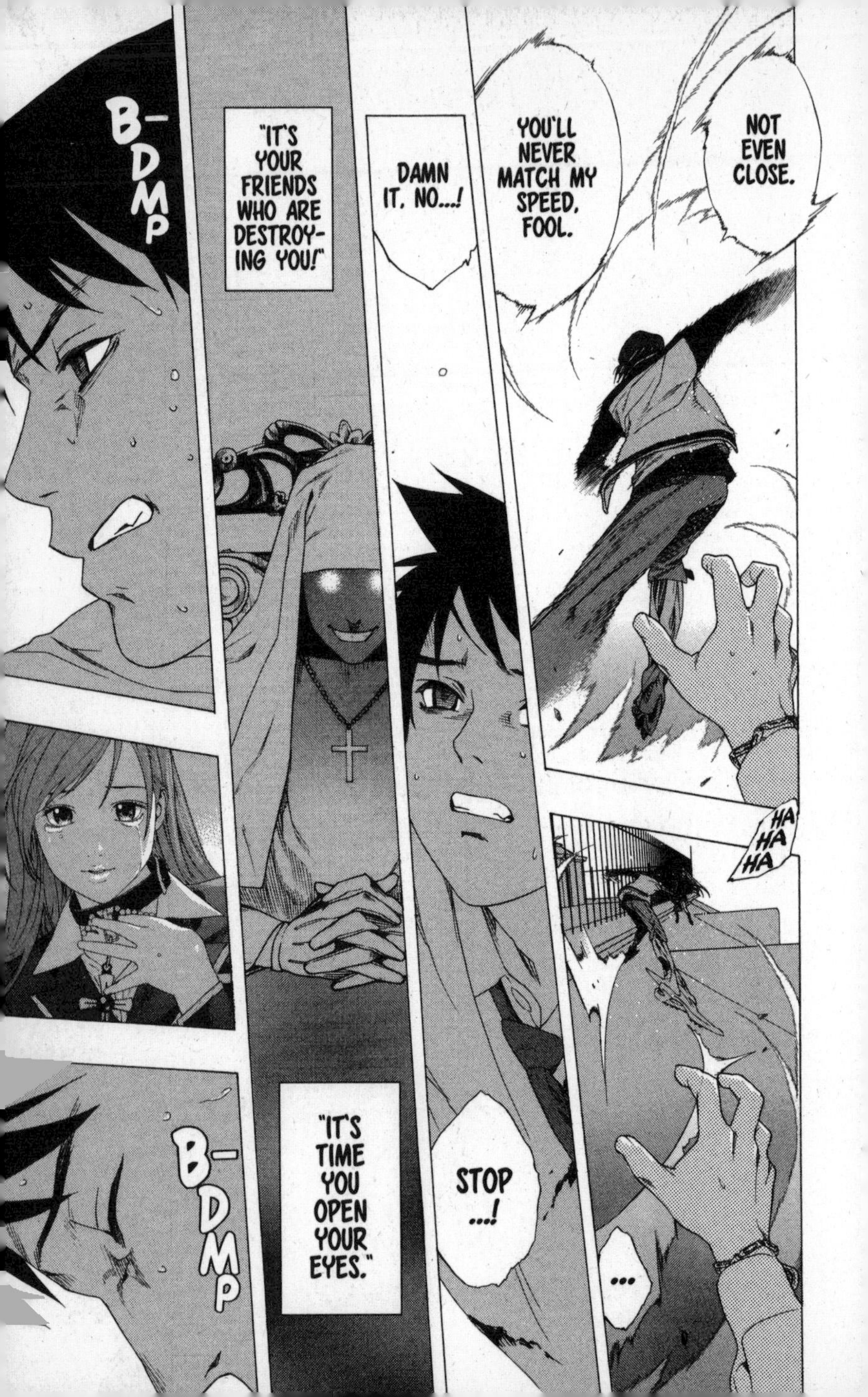

NOT EVEN CLOSE.
YOU'LL NEVER MATCH MY SPEED, FOOL.
HA HA HA
...
DAMN IT, NO...!
STOP ...!
"IT'S YOUR FRIENDS WHO ARE DESTROYING YOU!"
"IT'S TIME YOU OPEN YOUR EYES."
B-DMP
B-DMP

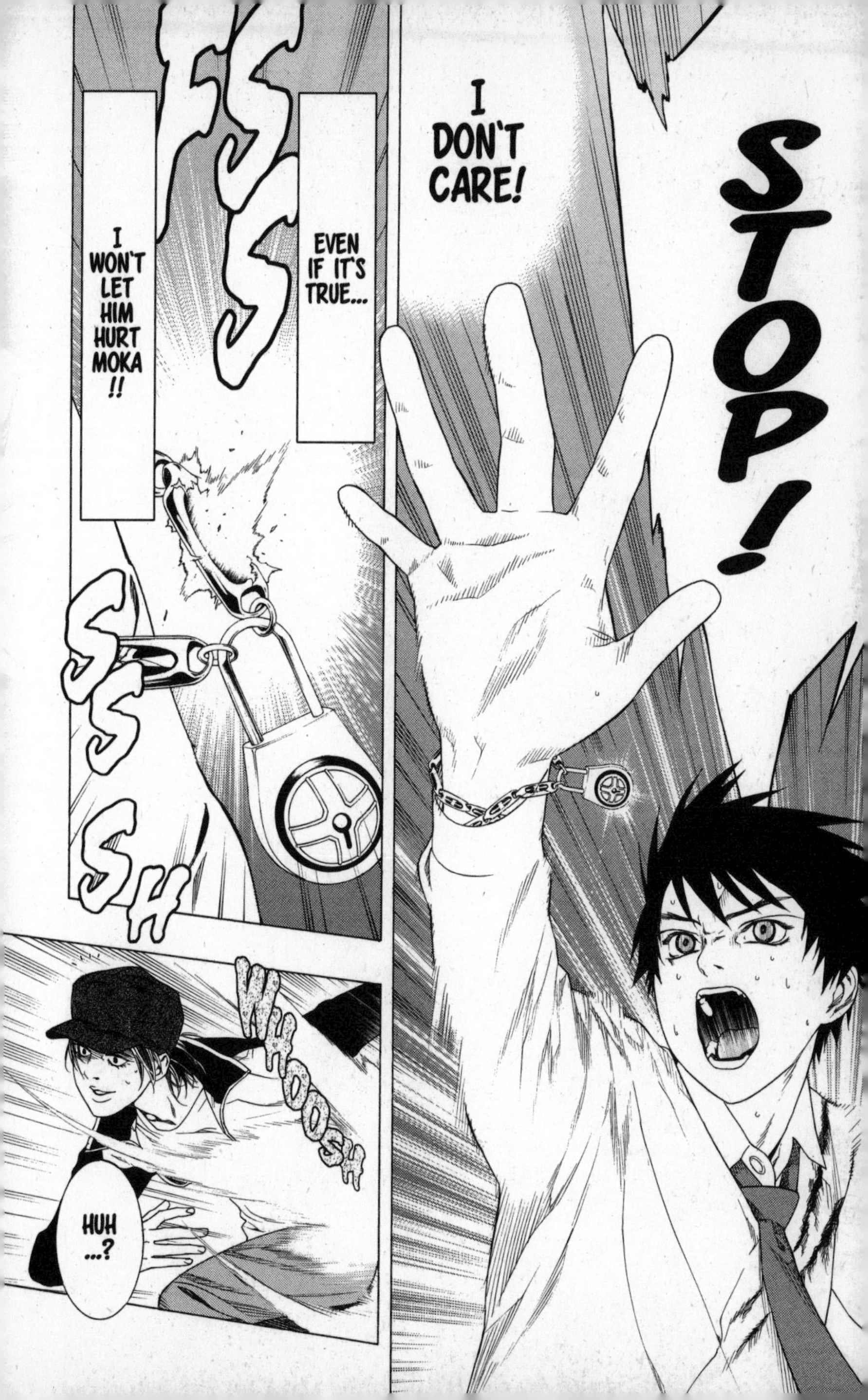
STOP!
I DON'T CARE!
EVEN IF IT'S TRUE...
I WON'T LET HIM HURT MOKA!!
FSS
SSSH
WHOOSH
HUH ...?

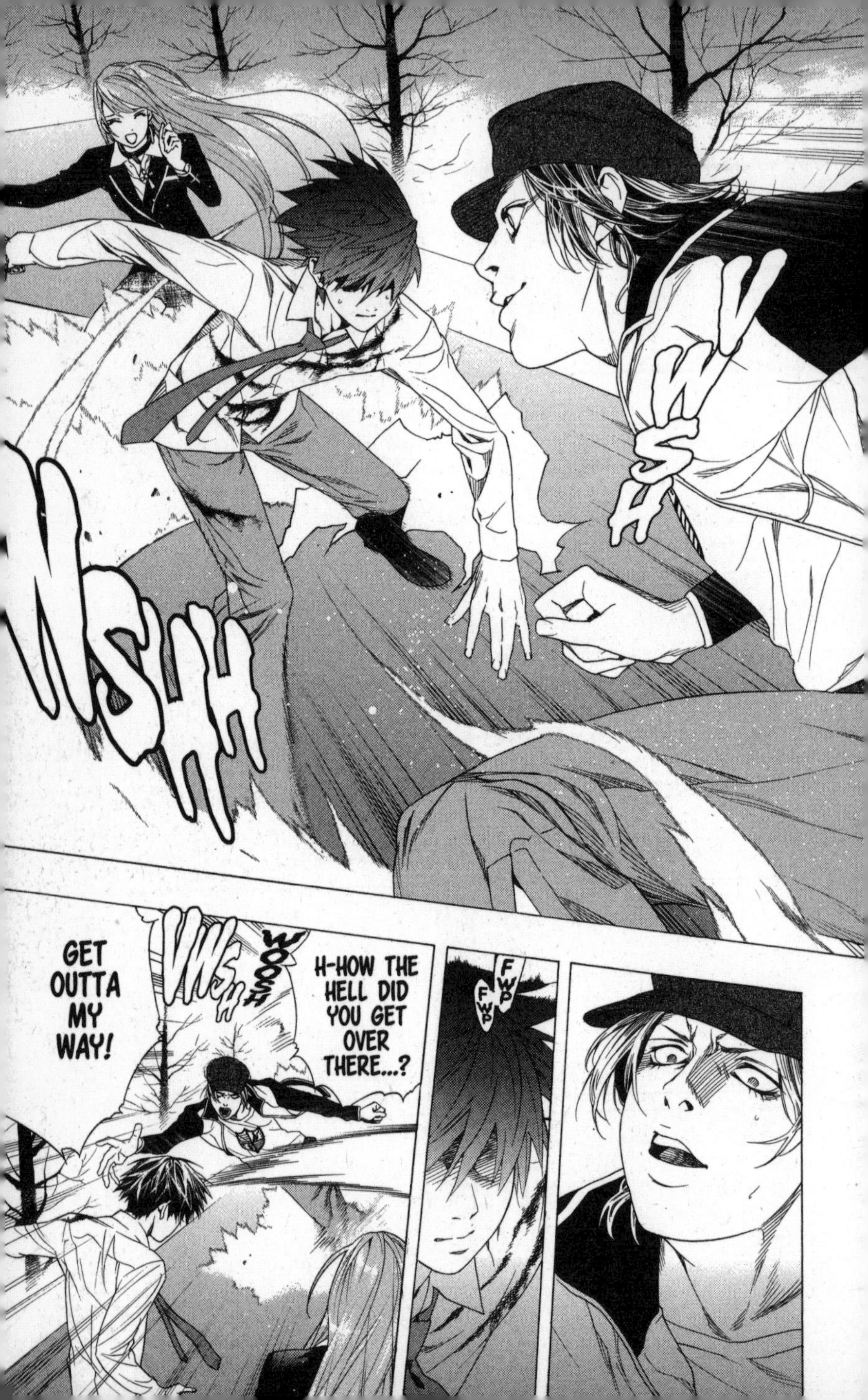

VWSH
WSHH
FWP
FWP
H-HOW THE HELL DID YOU GET OVER THERE...?
WOOSH
VWSH
GET OUTTA MY WAY!

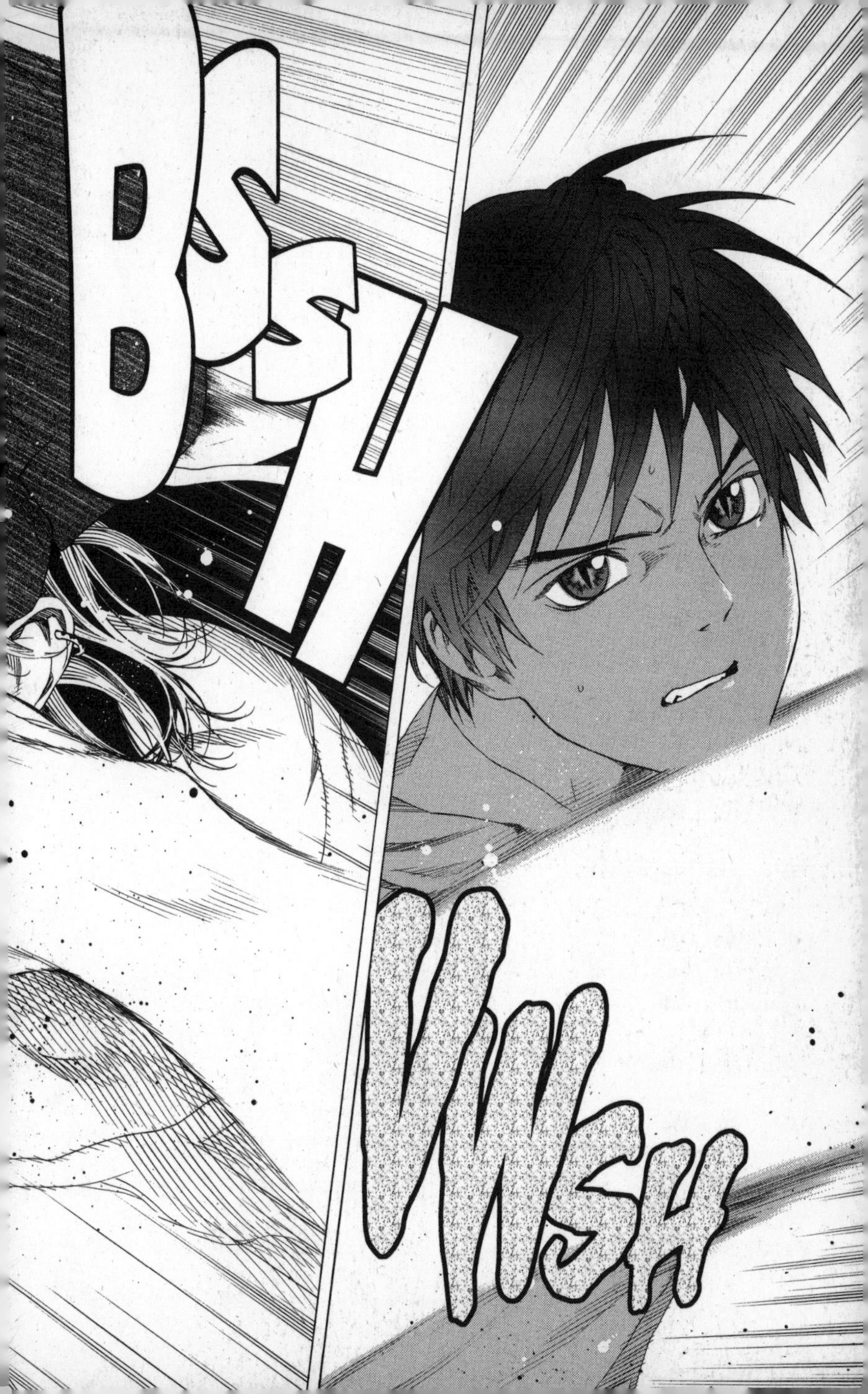
VWSH
BSSH

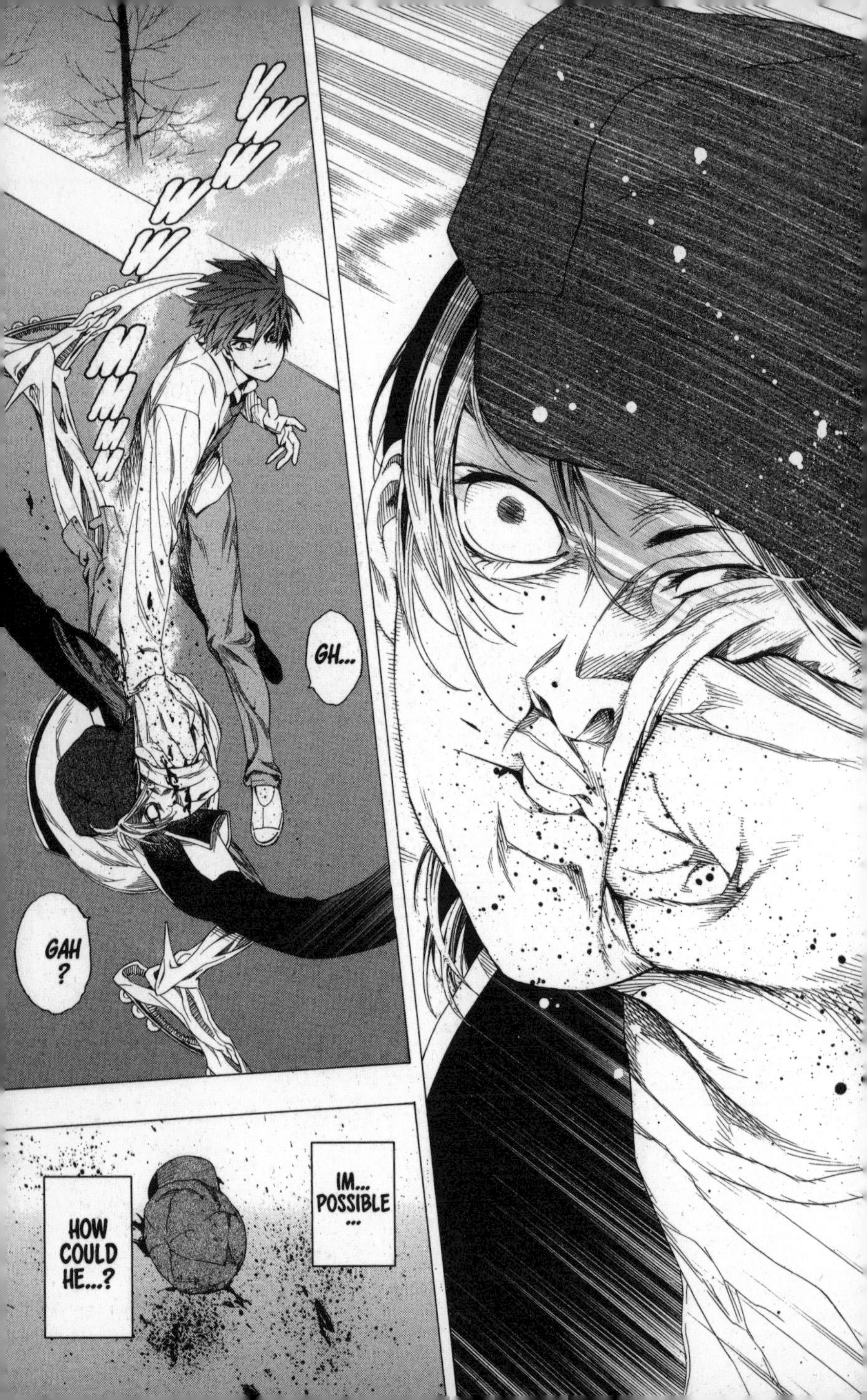
VWWWW
MMMM
GH...
GAH?
IM... POSSIBLE ...
HOW COULD HE...?

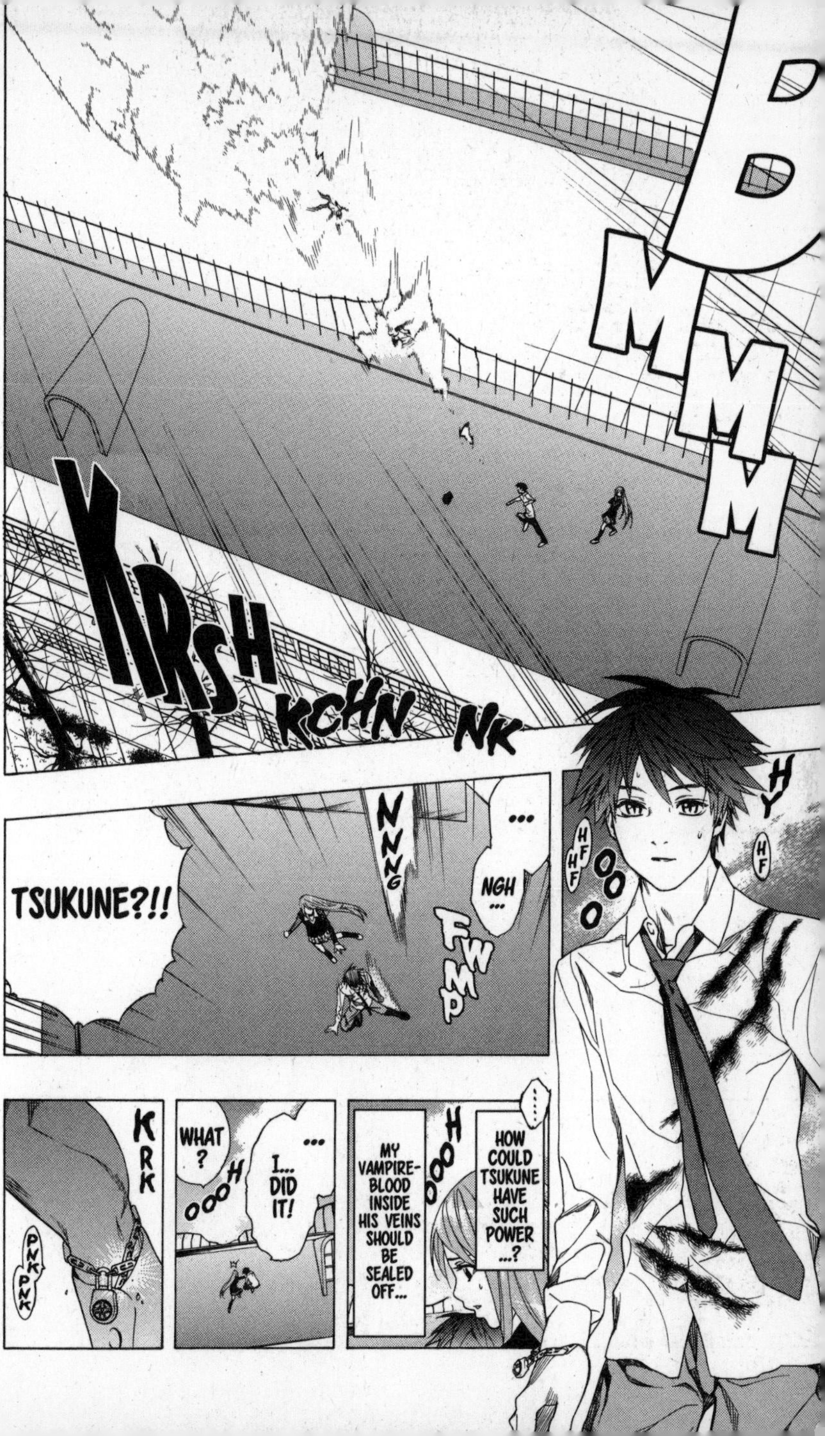
DMMMM
KRSH
KCHN
NK
HY
HF HF
HF HF
OOO
...
NGH ...
NNNG
FWMP
TSUKUNE?!!
......
HOW COULD TSUKUNE HAVE SUCH POWER ...?
HOOOO
MY VAMPIRE-BLOOD INSIDE HIS VEINS SHOULD BE SEALED OFF...
...
I... DID IT!
WHAT?
OOOH
KRK
PNK PNK

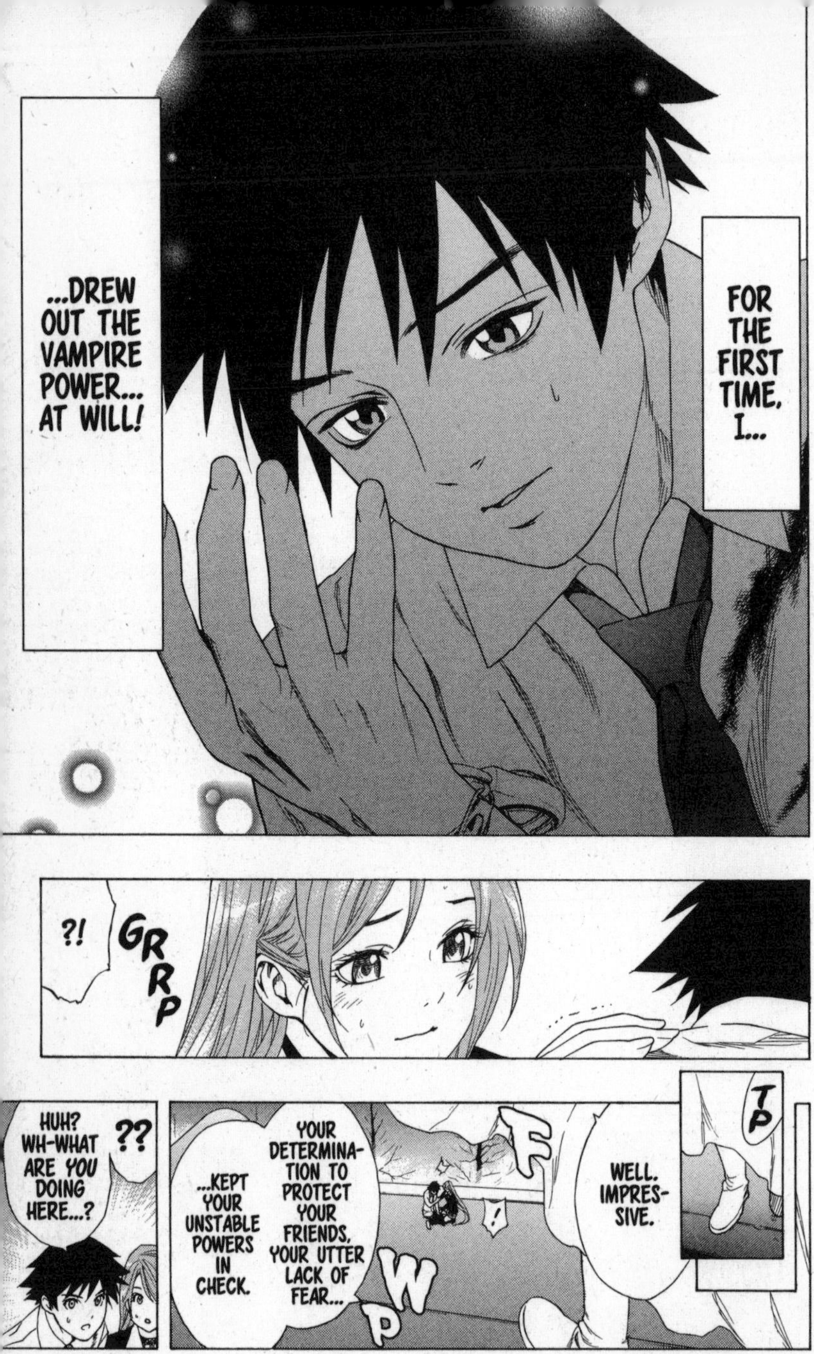
FOR THE FIRST TIME, I...
...DREW OUT THE VAMPIRE POWER... AT WILL!
GRRP
?!
TP
WELL. IMPRESSIVE.
F
YOUR DETERMINATION TO PROTECT YOUR FRIENDS, YOUR UTTER LACK OF FEAR...
...KEPT YOUR UNSTABLE POWERS IN CHECK.
!
WP
??
HUH? WH-WHAT ARE YOU DOING HERE...?

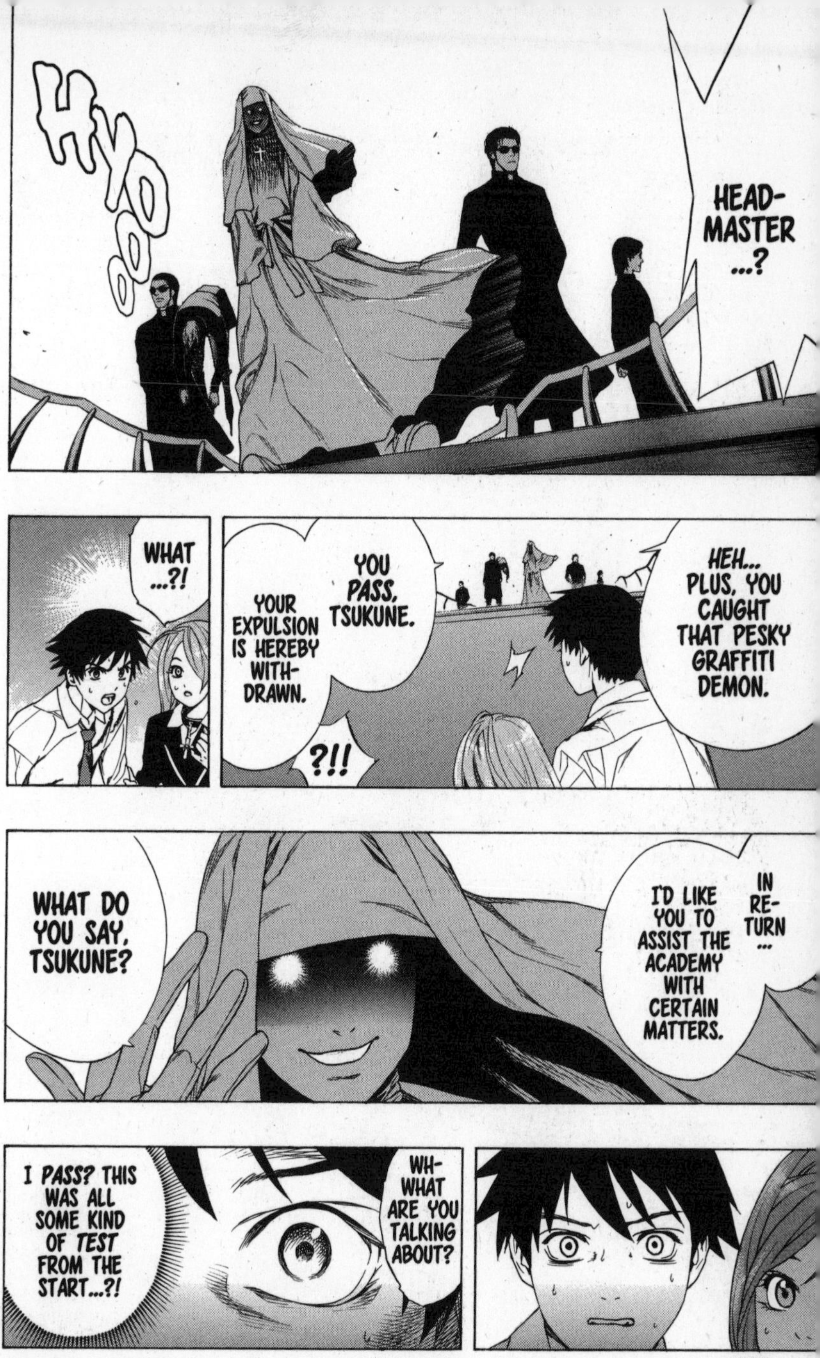
HEAD-MASTER ...?
HYOOOO
HEH... PLUS, YOU CAUGHT THAT PESKY GRAFFITI DEMON.
YOU *PASS*, TSUKUNE.
YOUR EXPULSION IS HEREBY WITH-DRAWN.
?!!
WHAT ...?!
IN RE-TURN ...
I'D LIKE YOU TO ASSIST THE ACADEMY WITH CERTAIN MATTERS.
WHAT DO YOU SAY, TSUKUNE?
WH-WHAT ARE YOU TALKING ABOUT?
I *PASS?* THIS WAS ALL SOME KIND OF *TEST* FROM THE START...?!

READ THIS WAY

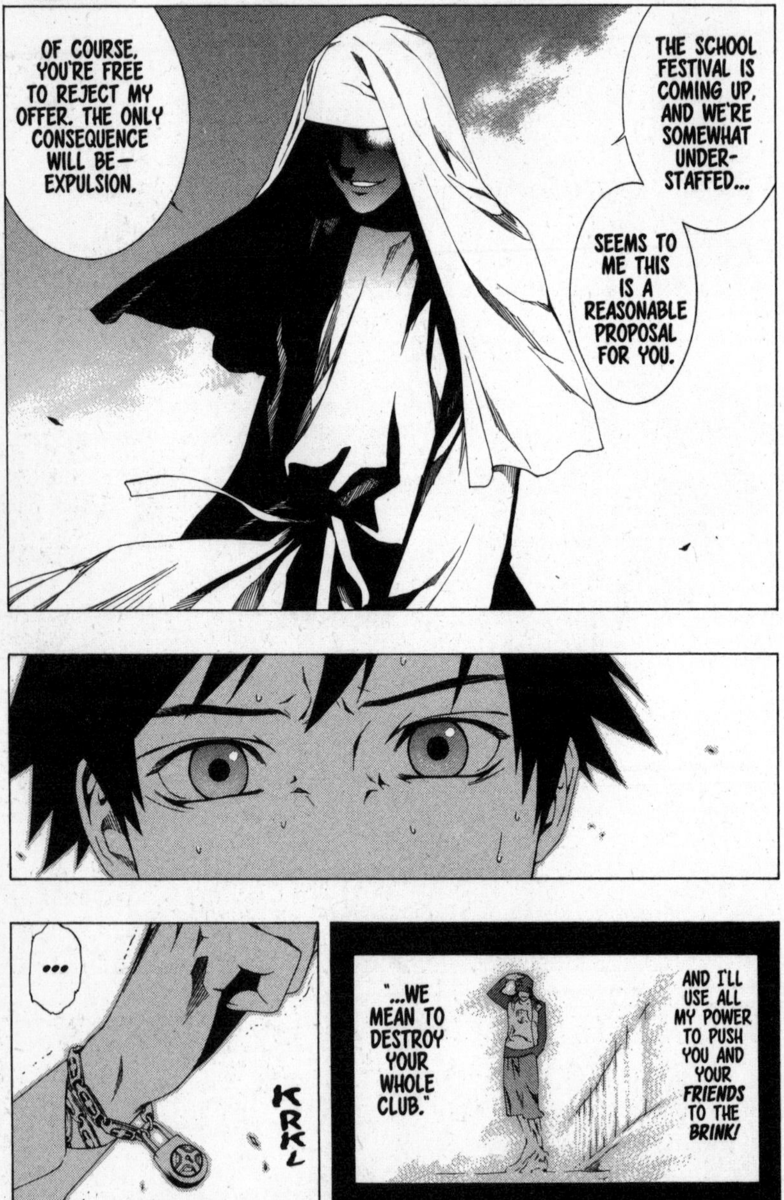
THE SCHOOL FESTIVAL IS COMING UP, AND WE'RE SOMEWHAT UNDER-STAFFED...
SEEMS TO ME THIS IS A REASONABLE PROPOSAL FOR YOU.
OF COURSE, YOU'RE FREE TO REJECT MY OFFER. THE ONLY CONSEQUENCE WILL BE—EXPULSION.
AND I'LL USE ALL MY POWER TO PUSH YOU AND YOUR *FRIENDS* TO THE *BRINK!*
"...WE MEAN TO DESTROY YOUR WHOLE CLUB."
...
KRKL

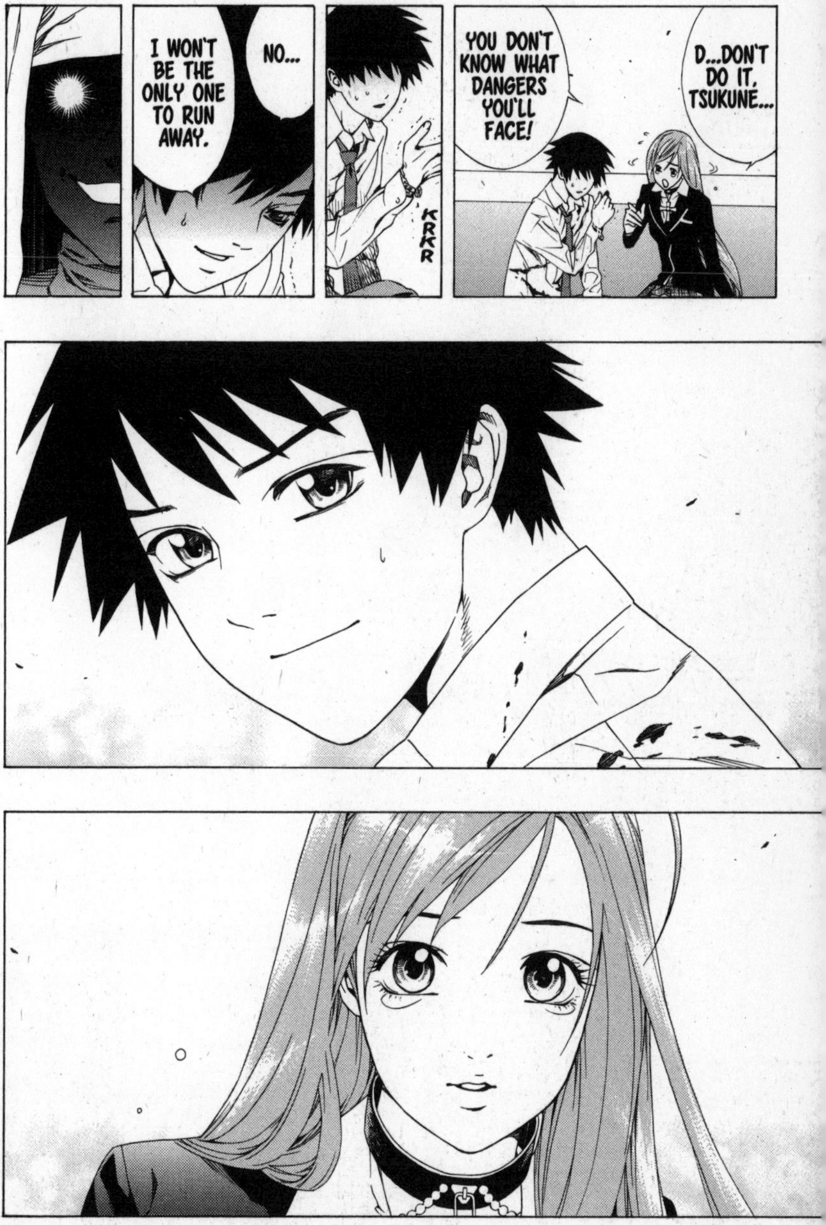
D...DON'T DO IT, TSUKUNE...
YOU DON'T KNOW WHAT DANGERS YOU'LL FACE!
KRKR
NO...
I WON'T BE THE ONLY ONE TO RUN AWAY.

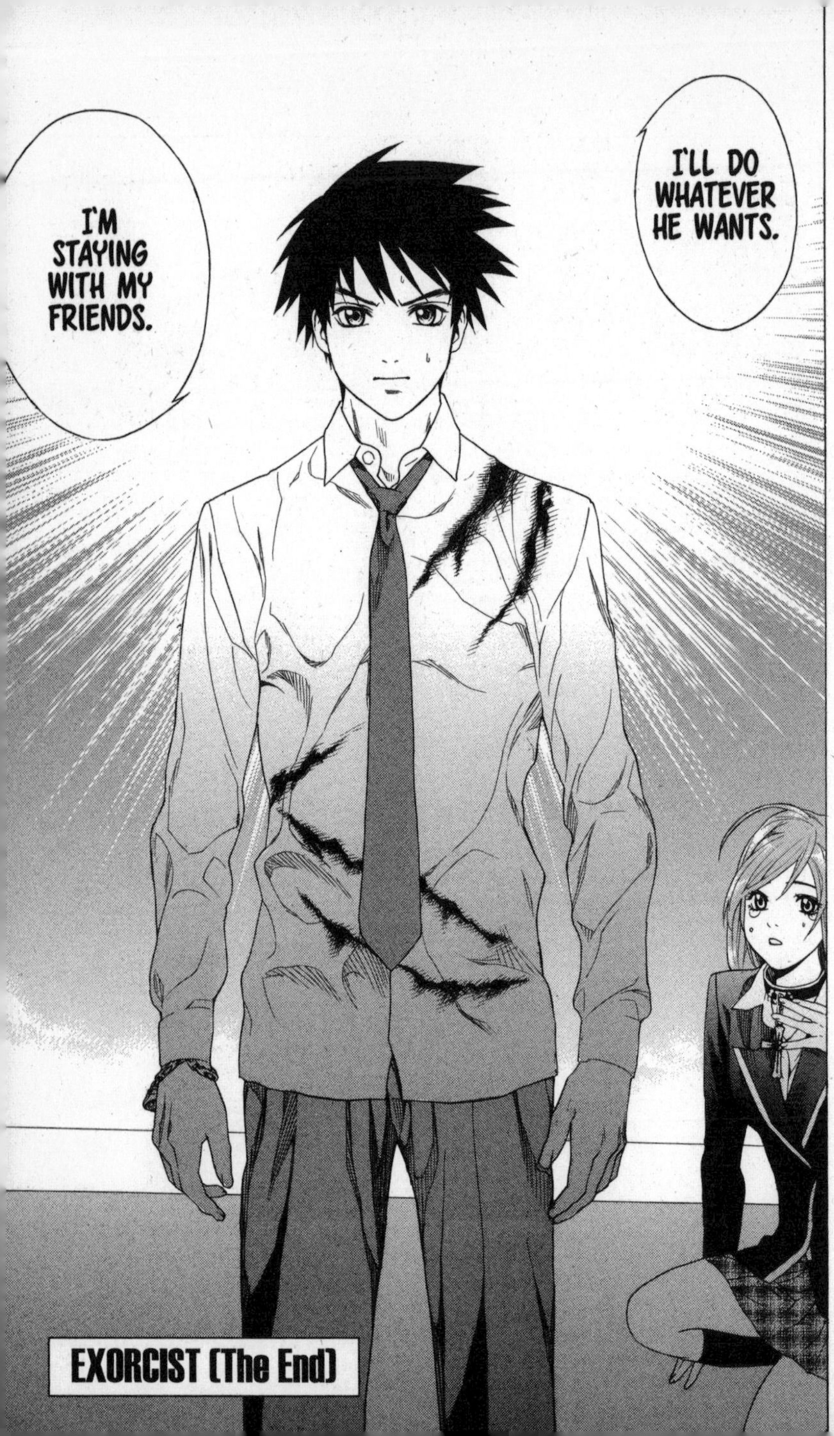
I'LL DO WHATEVER HE WANTS.
I'M STAYING WITH MY FRIENDS.
EXORCIST (The End)

# ROSARIO+VAMPIRE

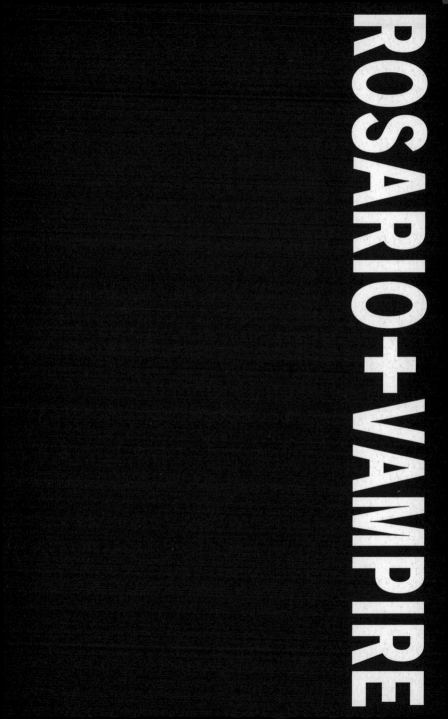

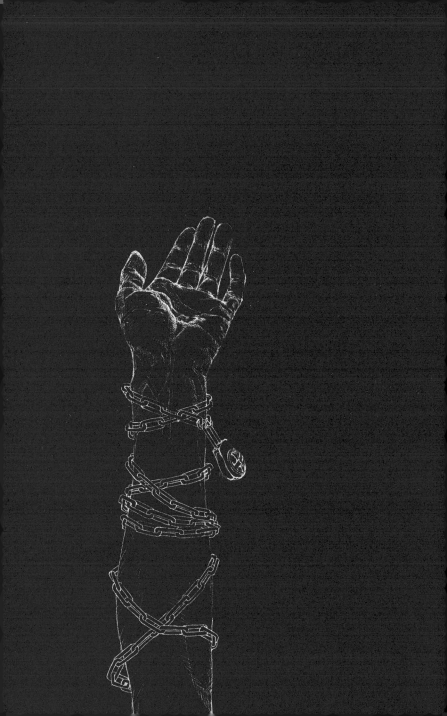

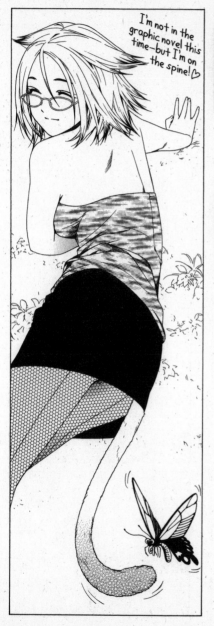

I'm not in the graphic novel this time—but I'm on the spine! ♡

# ROSARIO + VAMPIRE

## Meaningless End-of-Volume Theater

# VII

## • Default Setting? •

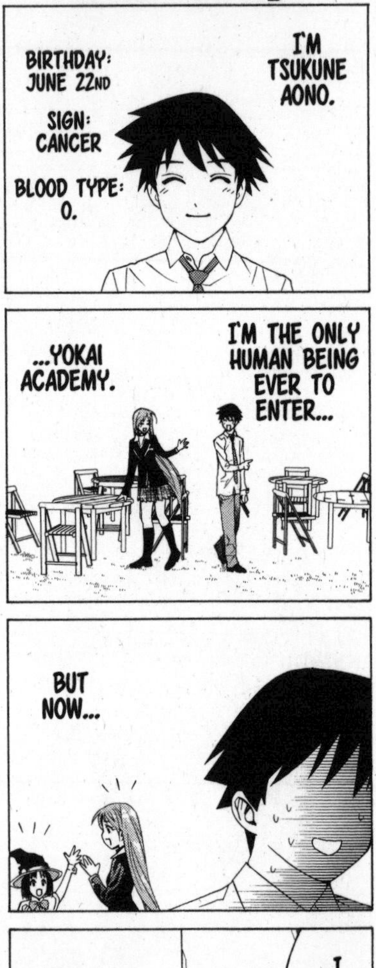
I'M TSUKUNE AONO.
BIRTHDAY: JUNE 22ND
SIGN: CANCER
BLOOD TYPE: O.
I'M THE ONLY HUMAN BEING EVER TO ENTER...
...YOKAI ACADEMY.
BUT NOW...
...I WANT TO SUCK BLOOD!
AM I STILL HUMAN?
HA
HA HA
HA

## • Looks Delicious?! •

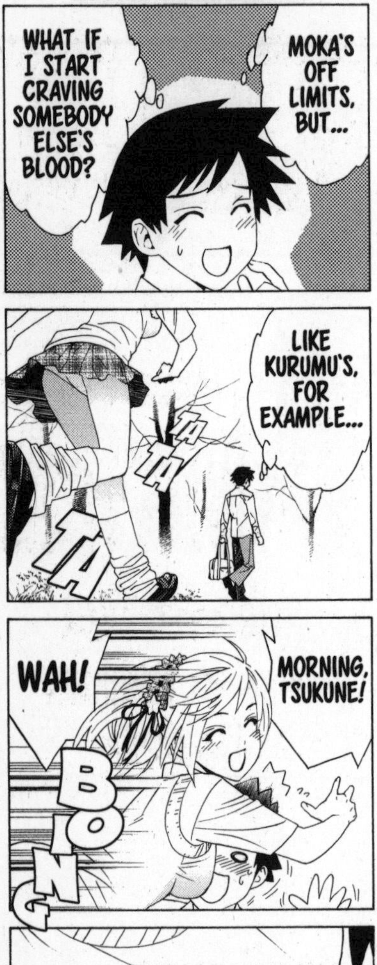
MOKA'S OFF LIMITS, BUT...
WHAT IF I START CRAVING SOMEBODY ELSE'S BLOOD?
LIKE KURUMU'S, FOR EXAMPLE...
TA
TA
TA
MORNING, TSUKUNE!
WAH!
BOING
GULP!

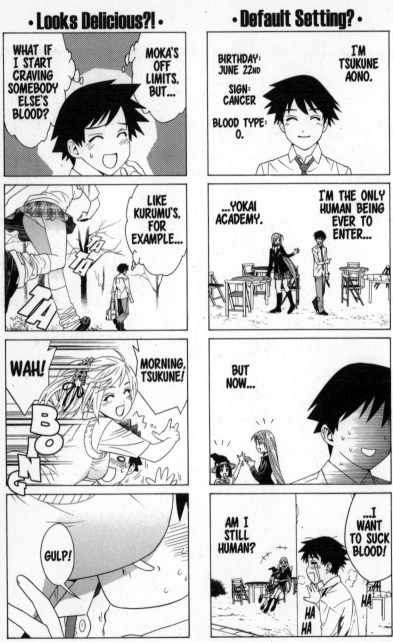

## • The Edge of Reason •

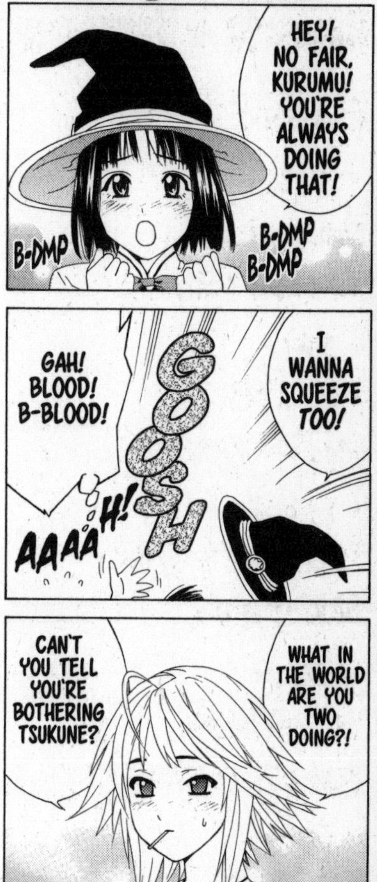
HEY! NO FAIR, KURUMU! YOU'RE ALWAYS DOING THAT!
B-DMP
B-DMP B-DMP
I WANNA SQUEEZE TOO!
GOOSH
GAH! BLOOD! B-BLOOD!
AAAAH!
WHAT IN THE WORLD ARE YOU TWO DOING?!
CAN'T YOU TELL YOU'RE BOTHERING TSUKUNE?
NO!
NO!
OOH! LOOKS LIKE FUN!
AIEE
Let me on this!
MREOW

## • I Get to Suck Blood, After All! ♡ •

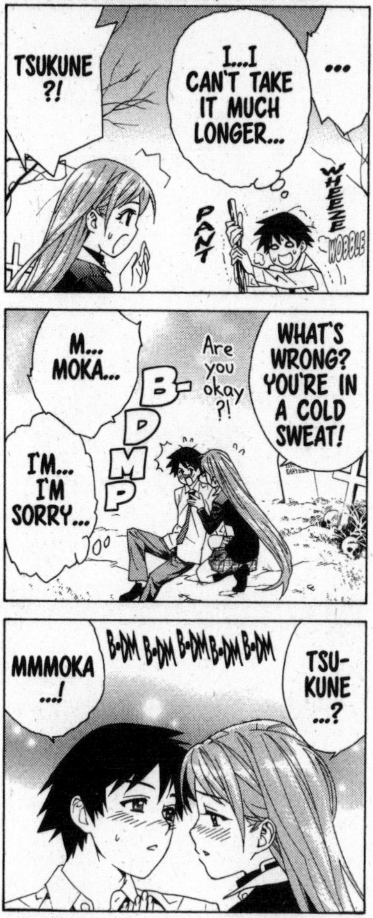
...
I...I CAN'T TAKE IT MUCH LONGER...
TSUKUNE ?!
WHEEZE
WOBBLE
PANT
WHAT'S WRONG? YOU'RE IN A COLD SWEAT!
Are you okay ?!
M... MOKA...
B-DMP
I'M... I'M SORRY...
TSU-KUNE ...?
B-DM B-DM B-DM B-DM B-DM
MMMOKA ...!
CHOMP
GAAAAAH

Please send questions and fan letters to ➡ Rosario+Vampire Fan Mail, VIZ Media, P.O. Box 77064, San Francisco, CA 94107

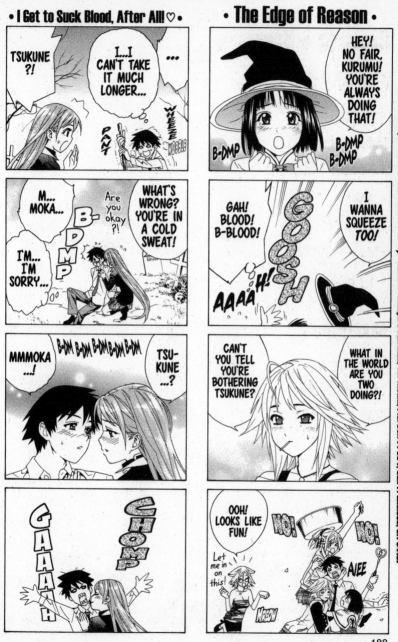

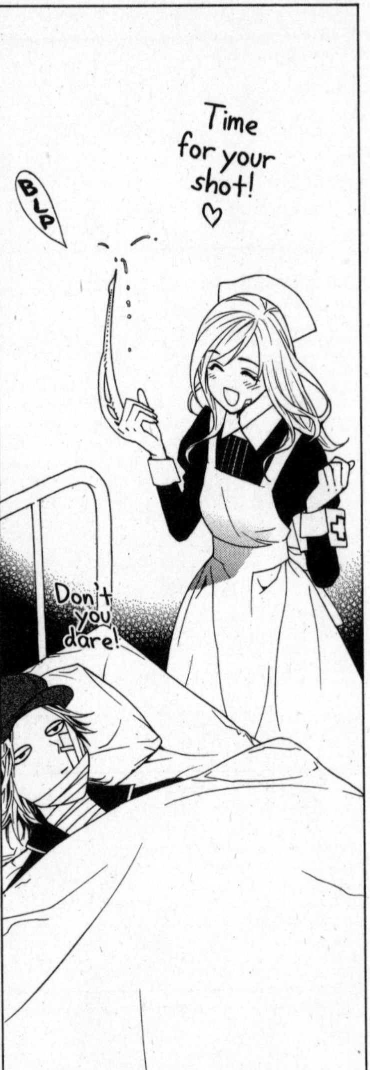
Time for your shot! ♡
BLP
Don't you dare!

# Rosario + Vampire

**Akihisa Ikeda**

• Staff •

Makoto Saito

Takafumi Ookubo

• Help •

Kenji Tashiro

Yuichiro Higuchi

• CG •

Takaharu Yoshizawa

Akihisa Ikeda

• Editing •

Satoshi Adachi

Tomonori Sumiya

• Comic •

Kenju Noro

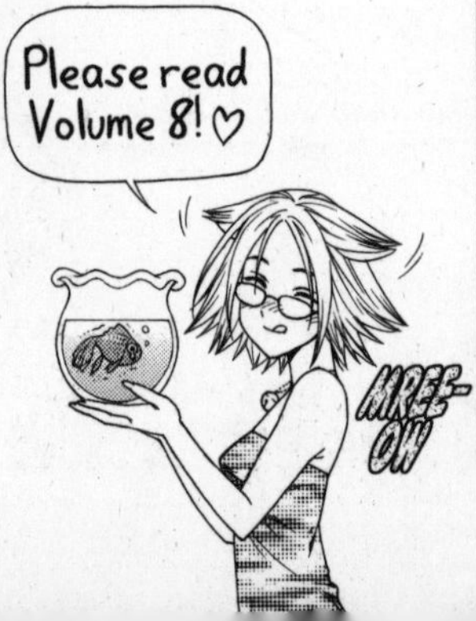
Please read Volume 8! ♡
HREE-OH

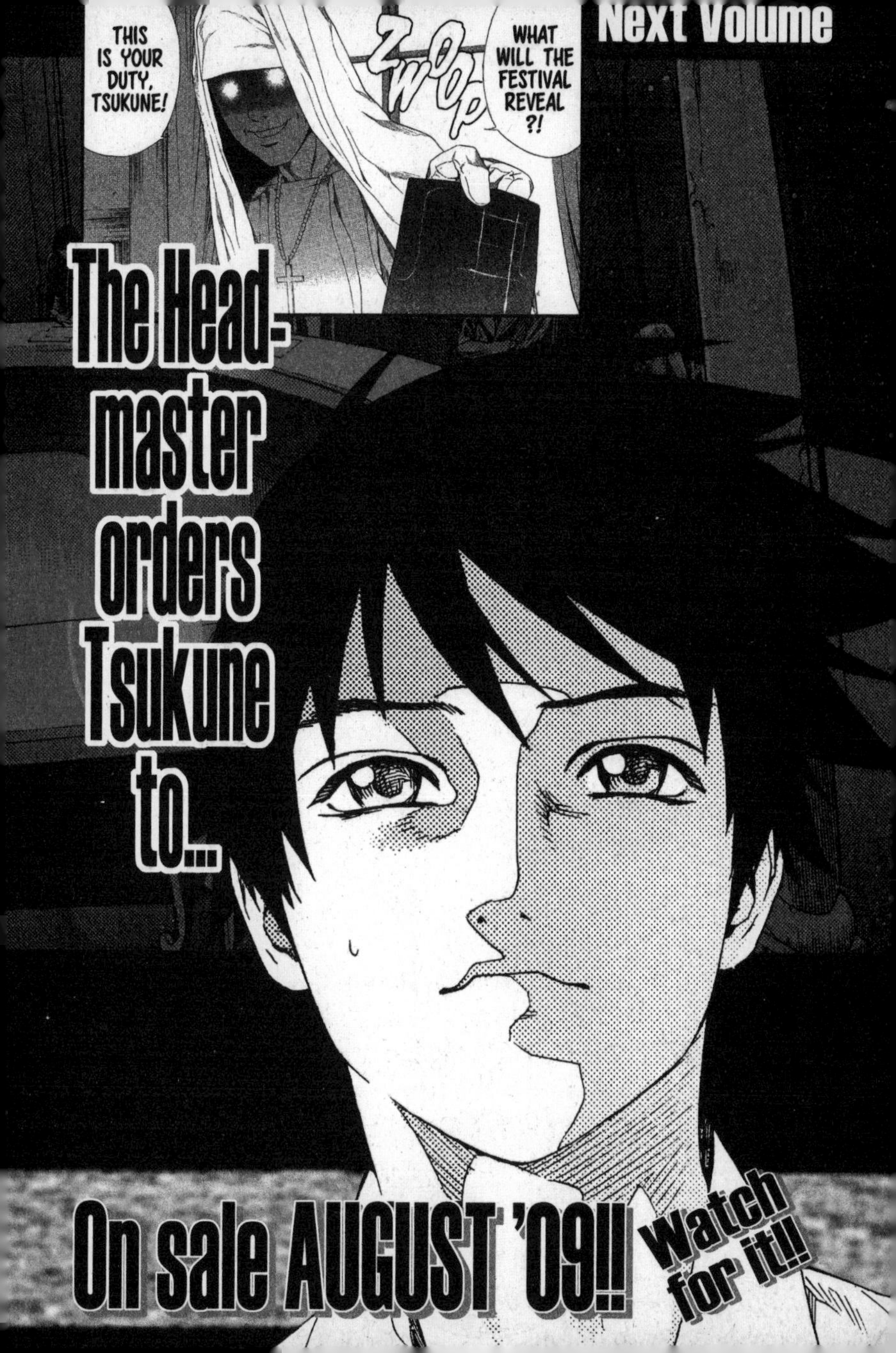
Next Volume
THIS IS YOUR DUTY, TSUKUNE!
ZWOOP
WHAT WILL THE FESTIVAL REVEAL ?!
The Head-master orders Tsukune to...
On sale AUGUST '09!!
Watch for it!!

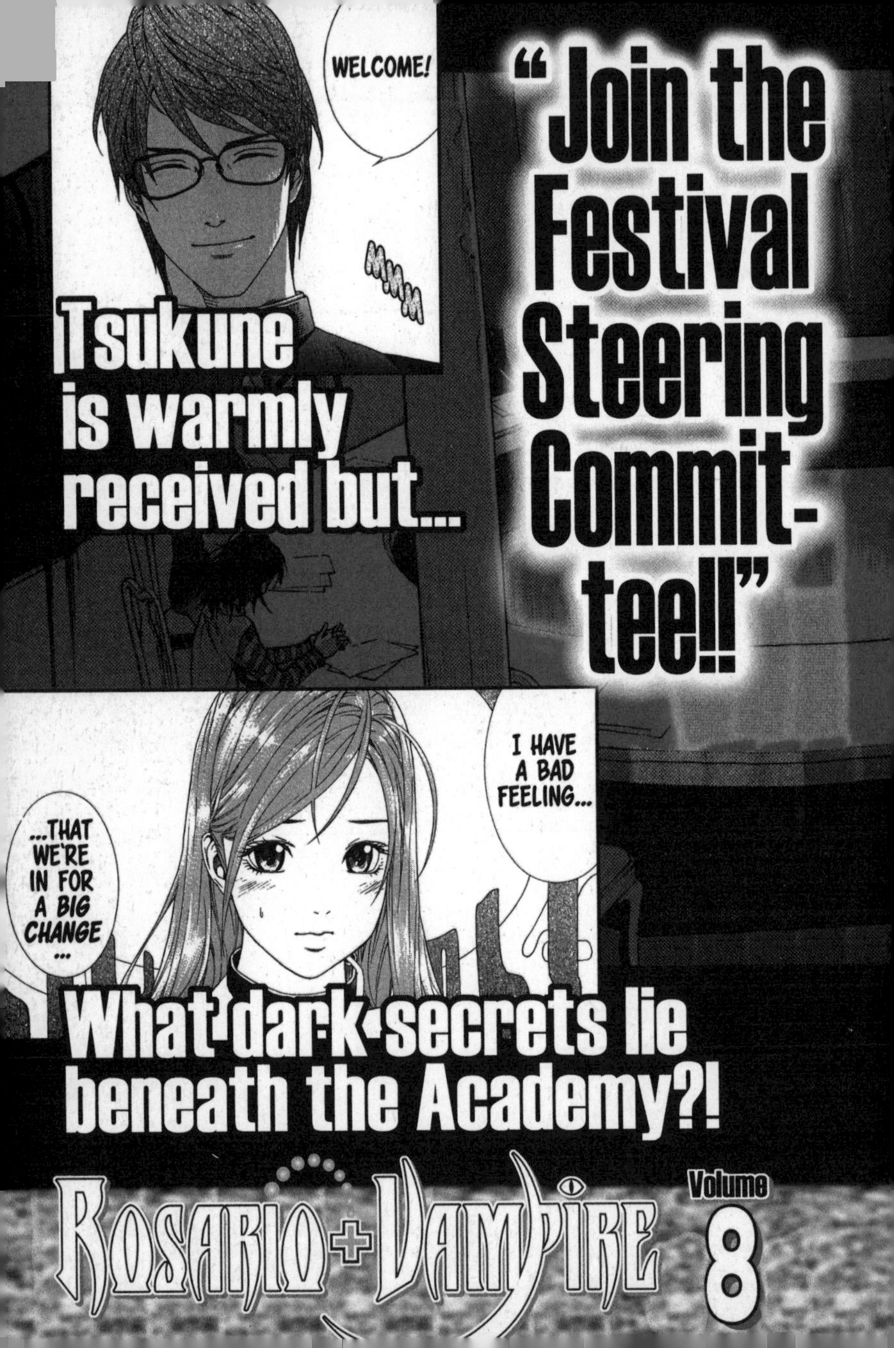
"Join the Festival Steering Commit-tee!!"
WELCOME!
MMM
Tsukune is warmly received but...
I HAVE A BAD FEELING...
...THAT WE'RE IN FOR A BIG CHANGE...
What dark secrets lie beneath the Academy?!
ROSARIO+VAMPIRE
Volume 8

# Crypt Sheet for Volume 8: Shikigami

QUIZ 8

**WHEN YOUR SCHOOL PRINCIPAL MAKES YOU PLAN A SCHOOL FESTIVAL WITH A CHARISMATIC LEADER OF THE STUDENT BODY WHO HAS HIS OWN PERSONAL SHIKIGAMI, YOU BETTER...**

a. not trust him as far as you can throw his one-eyed demon

b. follow his lead blindly

c. decorate the gym with colored toilet paper

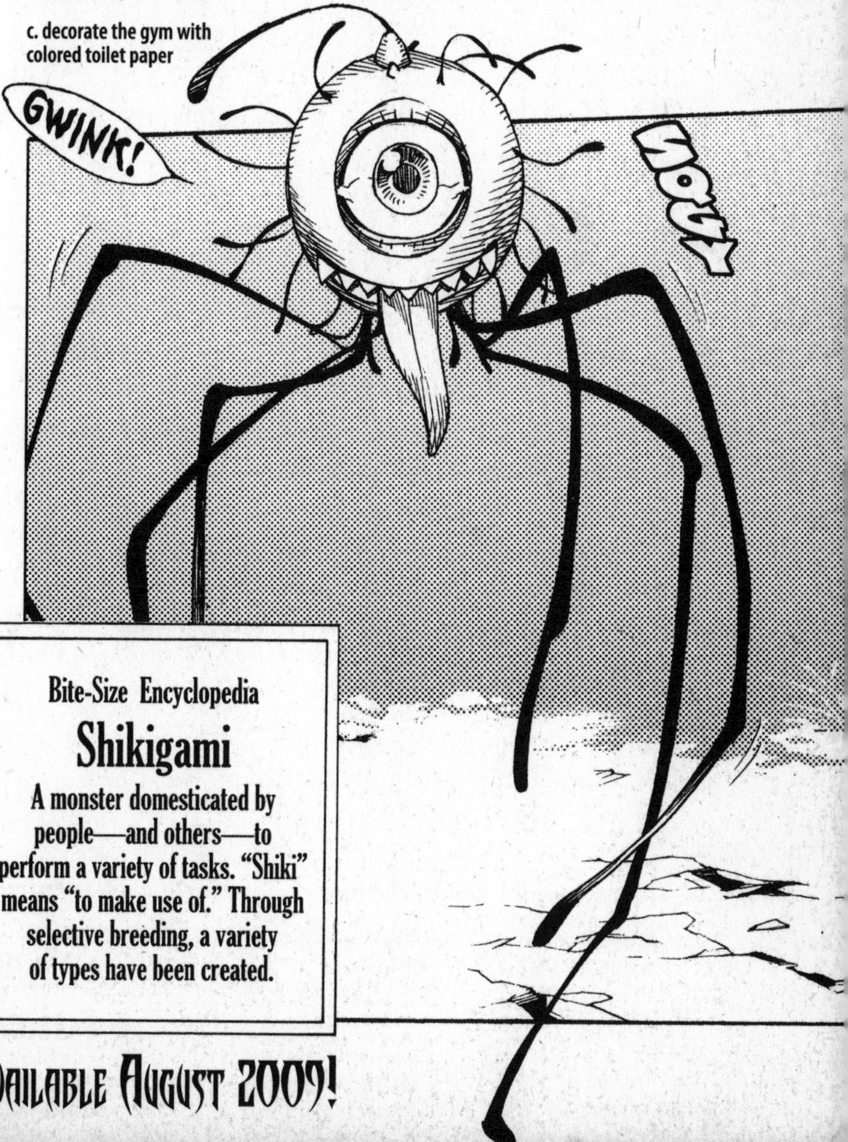
GWINK!

Bite-Size Encyclopedia

## Shikigami

**A monster domesticated by people—and others—to perform a variety of tasks. "Shiki" means "to make use of." Through selective breeding, a variety of types have been created.**

## Available August 2009!

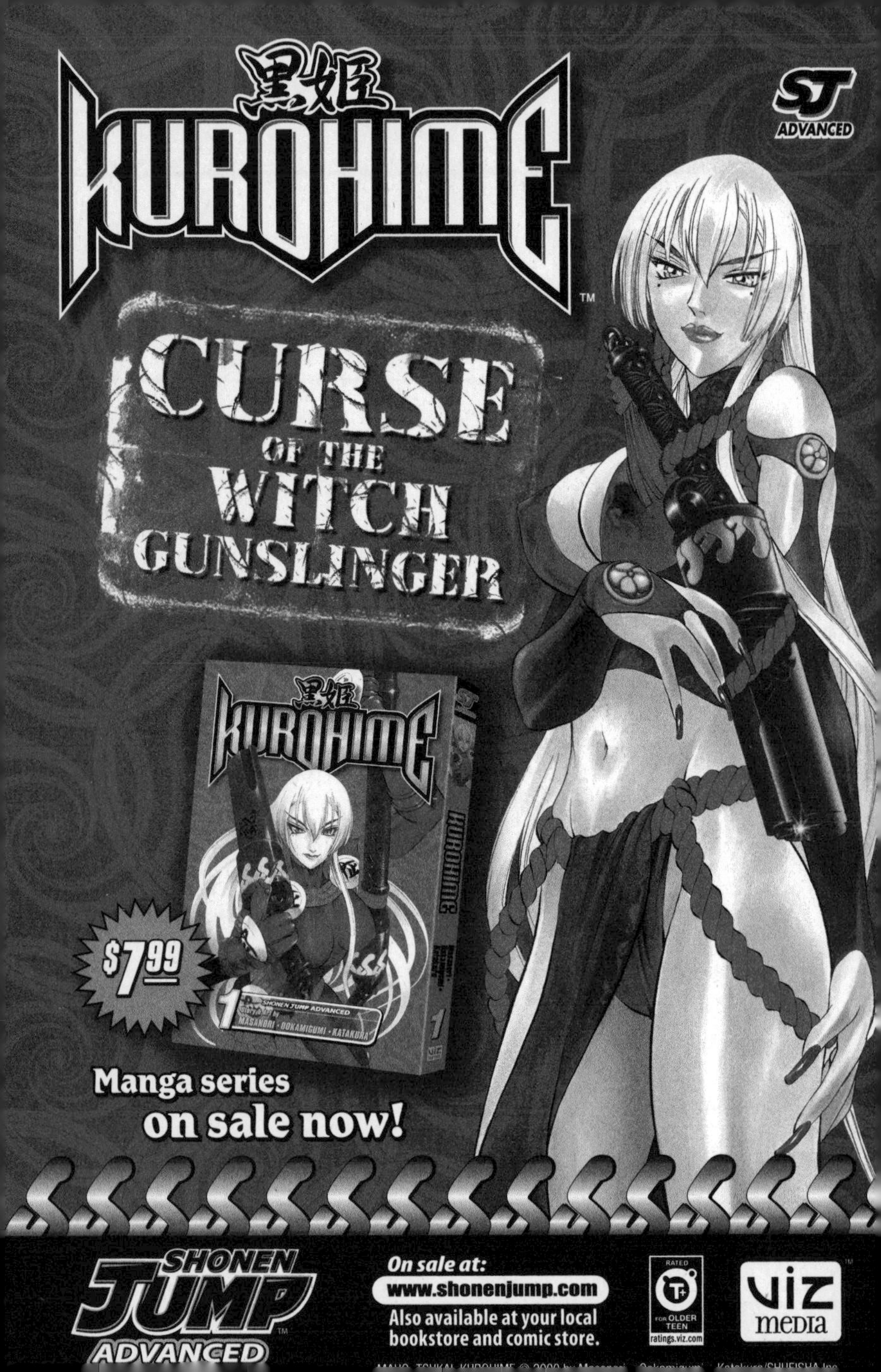

黒姫
KUROHIME™
SJ ADVANCED
CURSE OF THE WITCH GUNSLINGER
$7.99
Manga series on sale now!
SHONEN JUMP ADVANCED
On sale at:
www.shonenjump.com
Also available at your local bookstore and comic store.
RATED T+ FOR OLDER TEEN
ratings.viz.com
viz media

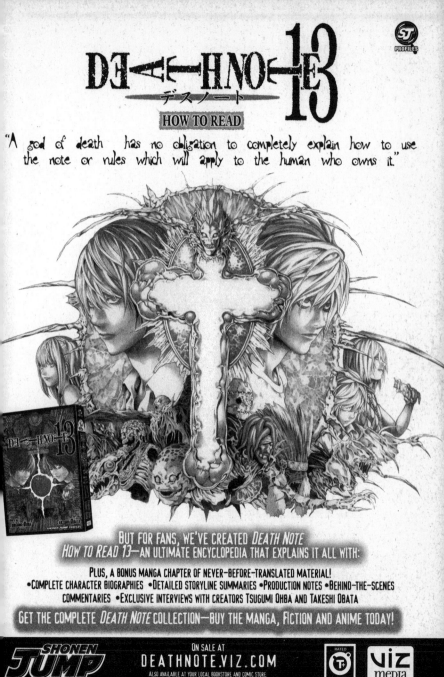

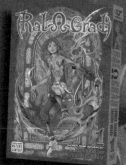
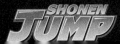

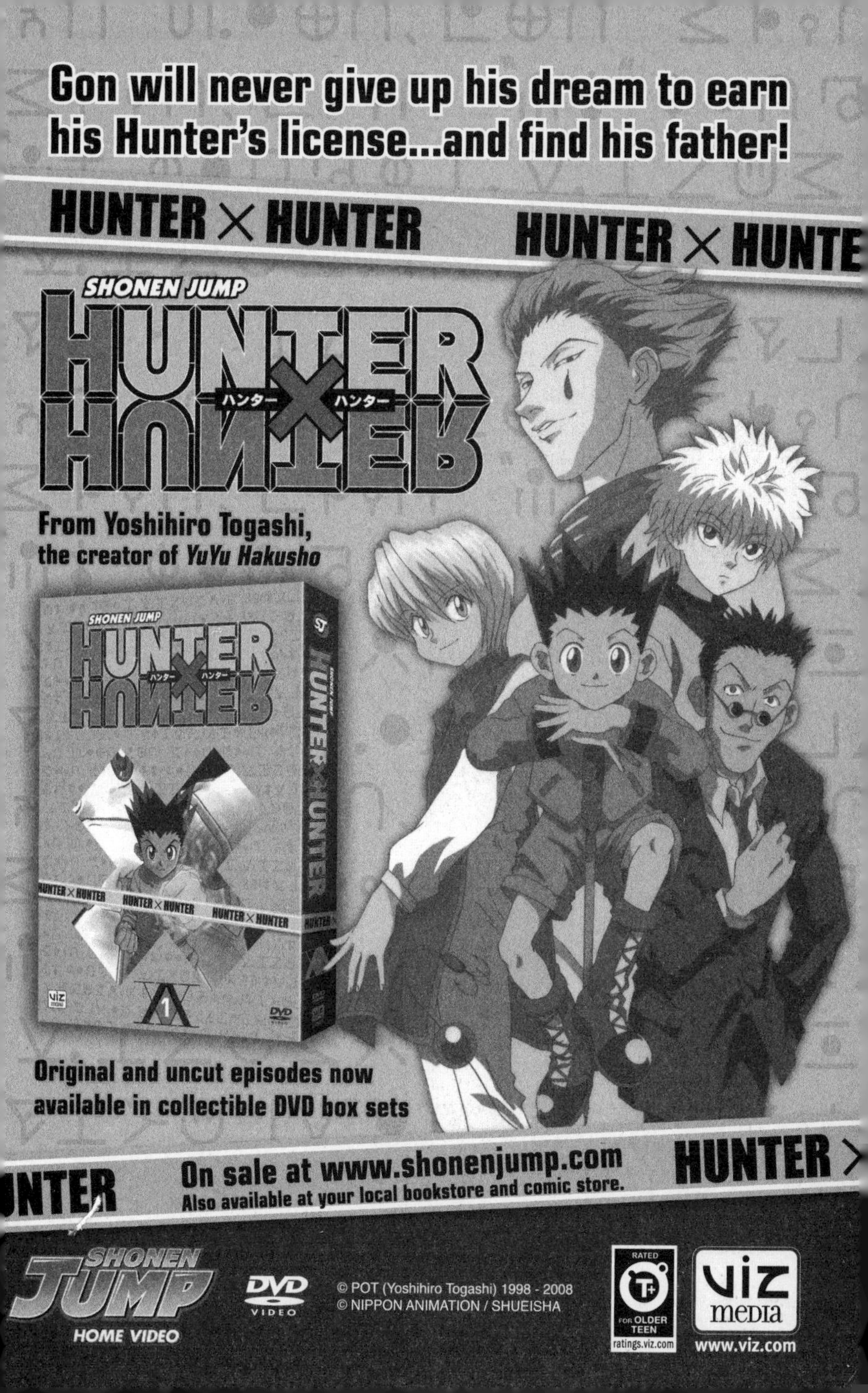

Gon will never give up his dream to earn his Hunter's license...and find his father!
HUNTER × HUNTER
HUNTER × HUNTE
SHONEN JUMP
HUNTER × HUNTER
ハンター ハンター
From Yoshihiro Togashi, the creator of *YuYu Hakusho*
SHONEN JUMP
HUNTER × HUNTER
Original and uncut episodes now available in collectible DVD box sets
NTER
On sale at www.shonenjump.com
Also available at your local bookstore and comic store.
HUNTER
SHONEN JUMP HOME VIDEO
DVD VIDEO
© POT (Yoshihiro Togashi) 1998 - 2008
© NIPPON ANIMATION / SHUEISHA
RATED T+ FOR OLDER TEEN ratings.viz.com
viz media
www.viz.com

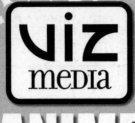
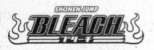 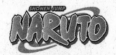 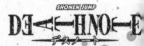

# Tell us what you think about SHONEN JUMP manga!

Our survey is now available online.
Go to: **www.SHONENJUMP.com/mangasurvey**

## Help us make our product offering better!

**THE REAL ACTION STARTS IN...**

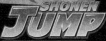

THE WORLD'S MOST POPULAR MANGA
www.shonenjump.com

ADVANCED

viz media

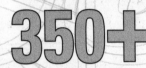
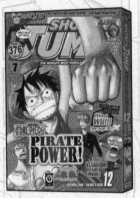
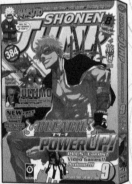
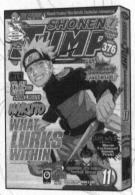

# SAVE 50% OFF
## THE COVER PRICE!

## IT'S LIKE GETTING 6 ISSUES
# FREE!

## OVER 350+ PAGES PER ISSUE

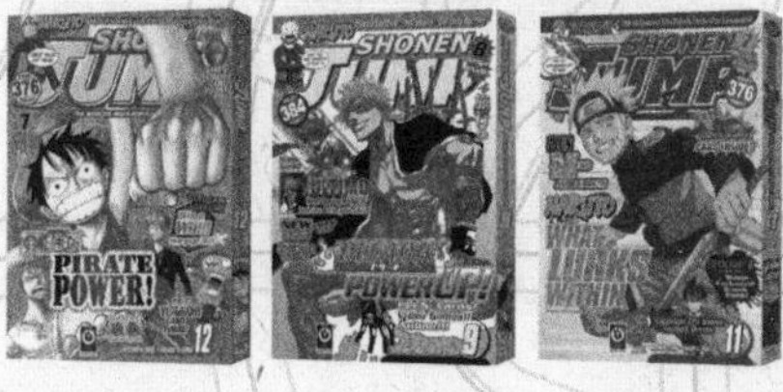

This monthly magazine contains 7 of the coolest manga available in the U.S., PLUS anime news, and info about video & card games, toys AND more!

❏ **I want 12 HUGE issues of SHONEN JUMP for only $29.95\*!**

**NAME**

**ADDRESS**

**CITY/STATE/ZIP**

**EMAIL ADDRESS**                                         **DATE OF BIRTH**

❏ YES, send me via email information, advertising, offers, and promotions related to VIZ Media, SHONEN JUMP, and/or their business partners.

❏ **CHECK ENCLOSED** (payable to SHONEN JUMP)   ❏ **BILL ME LATER**

**CREDIT CARD:** ❏ Visa ❏ Mastercard

**ACCOUNT NUMBER**                                          **EXP. DATE**

**SIGNATURE**

### CLIP&MAIL TO:
SHONEN JUMP Subscriptions Service Dept.
P.O. Box 515
Mount Morris, IL 61054-0515

**P9GNC1**

RATED
T
FOR TEEN
ratings.viz.com

VIZ
media
www.viz.com